THE
CLOCKS
OF
COLUMBUS

*The Literary Career of
James Thurber*

THE
CLOCKS
OF
COLUMBUS

The Literary Career of
James Thurber

—————

CHARLES S. HOLMES

Atheneum 1972 *New York*

To Marian

with

Gratitude and Love

Preface

I T I S H A R D F O R M E T O R E M E M B E R when I first became a Thurber fan, because I belong to the generation which grew up on Thurber, White, and *The New Yorker*. The magazine shaped our tastes in humor and in prose style, and for me the magazine was always Thurber. Thinking back, I suppose it was the famous cartoon showing a fencer slashing off the head of an opponent and calling out "Touché!" which first confirmed me as a Thurberphile. He has become so much a part of the imaginative world of so many people that Richard Armour, in his recent book, *Out of My Mind*, plays with the possibility that "thurber" might move into the language as a word in its own right, and in lower case. For example, there could be the adjective *thurb*, with the comparative *thurber* and the superlative *thurbest*. But of course, Armour adds, Thurber could never be merely comparative. He is always superlative.

I remember someone saying that you had to be from Ohio to appreciate Thurber. The statement is nonsense, of course, but there is something in it. You don't *have* to be from Ohio, but it helps. In fact, if you were born and bred in an Ohio town, you cannot escape Thurber. Reading *My Life and Hard Times* is just like going home, or at least that is the way it seems, so complete is the spell he casts over one's memory and imagination. But this is too narrow and proprietary a view: Thurber's Ohio is a country of the mind, and readers who have never been within three thousand miles of the Buckeye State feel that they belong there.

Peter Quennell, the English artist and critic, said that after he first saw Thurber's work he was astonished at the number of Thurber characters he encountered on the streets of London. The British embraced Thurber from the first, and some of them still find it hard to accept the fact that he is really American after all. It was a Viennese gallery which first included Thurber in an art show—an international exhibition of comic art in the early Thirties, to which Thurber was asked to contribute one of his *New Yorker* drawings, titled "Intelligent Woman." Someone had accidentally stepped on it, Thurber recalled, and the drawing bore the superimposed print of a large rubber heel.

He still has his Austrian following. On the train from Vienna to Innsbruck a few years ago, two Austrian lawyers spotted the Thurber book in my lap and talked so enthusiastically and so lengthily about him that I never did get around to finishing the lecture I was supposed to give at the university that evening. So Thurber is hard to escape, no matter where you live, because he is the sharpest, most uncomfortably honest, and funniest commentator on the situation of the middle-class man (and woman) who ever drew and wrote.

It is a pleasure to thank the many people who have helped me throughout the writing of this book. Helen Thurber not only spent long hours answering my questions about people and events, past and present, but she also went through the manuscript and corrected a number of factual errors. I am greatly indebted to her. Mr. Robert Thurber, James Thurber's brother, gave me many illuminating details about the family and wrote me invaluable letters about fact and fiction in *My Life and Hard Times*. Mr. Ralph McCombs, Dr. James Pollard, and Mr. John Fullen, who knew Thurber in Columbus, ransacked their memories and steered me to a variety of important sources of information about Thurber's early days. For Thurber's later career, Mr. and Mrs. J. G. Gude, Mr. and Mrs. Peter De Vries, and Mr. Bernard Bergman helped me so often and in so many different ways that this simple acknowledgment seems a poor way to repay them. I also wish to thank Mr. Morris Ernst, who talked to me at length about old times at *The New Yorker*.

Mr. Richard Ploch, in charge of Special Collections at the Ohio State University library at the time I was trying to find out what I could about Thurber's Columbus years, was unfailingly good-natured and helpful. I wish to express my special gratitude to another member of the Ohio State University community, Mr. Ronald Staub, an indefatigable researcher who was working on Thurber at that time, and who helped me out whenever I got stuck, which was often. My thanks are also due Mr. E. B. White, who kindly allowed me to look through his correspondence with Thurber, now in the Cornell University library, and to Professor George Healy and the staff of the Cornell library, and to Professor Scott Elledge of the department of English. The library staff of the Chicago *Tribune* made available to me the hard-to-get file of the Paris edition of the paper, and for this courtesy I am most grateful.

The colleagues and friends who took the time to read the manuscript in its early and late stages will get their reward in heaven. Professor Edwin Fussell, Professor Thomas Pinney, Dean Ray Frazer, and Professor Darcy O'Brien went far beyond the call of friendship and professional courtesy in the help they so generously gave me. Professor O'Brien ran his sharp editorial eye over the final draft and saved me from many a self-dug pitfall. And I must not forget to record my gratitude to Agnes Bracher, for the valuable suggestions she made when I was just beginning to write.

Finally, I wish to thank the American Council of Learned Societies and Pomona College for grants which made my research possible; Peggy Morrison and Mary Gammons for typing and good humor; and Tony Clark, of Atheneum Publishers, for editorial wisdom and personal support.

Contents

Illustrations

DRAWINGS

PHOTOGRAPHS
(following page 114)

THE
CLOCKS
OF
COLUMBUS

The Literary Career of
James Thurber

1

Columbus Boyhood

WHEN JAMES THURBER RETURNED to Columbus in 1953 to receive the Ohioana Sesquicentennial Medal, he thanked his hosts and said, "It is a great moment for an Ohio writer living far from home when he realizes that he has not been forgotten by the state he can't forget," and he added that his books "prove that I am never very far away from Ohio in my thoughts, and that the clocks that strike in my dreams are often the clocks of Columbus." [1]

He was not indulging in merely sentimental rhetoric. Although he lived more than half his life in the East and became one of the makers and shapers of *The New Yorker*, Columbus and the Thurber family pattern of old-fashioned domesticity and eccentric behavior were the primary forces in shaping his imagination. More than most writers, he depended upon his memory of personal experience for his artistic materials, and Columbus manners, Columbus mores, and Columbus values remained an essential part of his mind and personality. He returned time and again to the city of his birth, visiting his mother and his brothers, giving out interviews, making speeches, and reminiscing affectionately about people and events in the days gone by. "I have always waved banners and blown horns for

---

[1] "Thurber Response to His Award of the Ohioana Sesquicentennial Medal," October 24, 1953, in *Thurber on Humor* (a privately printed pamphlet for the Martha Kinney Cooper Ohioana Library Association, Columbus, Ohio, 1953), p. 9.

Good Old Columbus Town. . . . and such readers as I have collected
through the years are all aware of where I was born and brought up, and
they know that half of my books could not have been written if it had not
been for the city of my birth," he wrote in 1959.[2] On the other hand, it
is only one of the paradoxes of his complex character that he was a Columbus product who read Henry James and James Joyce, a parodist and humorist who appealed to a highbrow audience, a cosmopolitan equally at home
in London, Paris, Bermuda, and New York. He was a combination of
old-fashioned Middle Western values and intellectual culture, and it is the
tension between these forces which underlies much of the comedy and
some, at least, of the melancholy and nostalgia in his work.

The Columbus of Thurber's day was a city of some 180,000, the state
capital and seat of the university, a city of diversified business activity, the
center of a rich farming area, but still at heart a small town. Ohio State
was a land-grant university, emphasizing agriculture, engineering, and
other plain and practical activities. With its tree-shaded streets and comfortable two-story houses set back on pleasant lawns, Columbus spoke of
permanence, security, and the primacy of family virtues. Thurber recalled
that in his youth, "People liked to sit on the wide verandas on the hotter
Sundays, the men with their feet up on the balustrades, reading in the
sports pages about Corbett and Jeffries, Maud S and Star Pointer, Cy
Young and John McGraw. The women sat more decorously reading *The
Lady of Lyons* or *Lucille,* and the children, sprawled on the floor, eagerly
followed the comic adventures of the Katzenjammer Kids, Lulu and Leander, Happy Hooligan, Foxy Grandpa, Buster Brown, and Alphonse and
Gaston." [3] In Thurber's day it was (and it still is) conservative politically,
inordinately proud of the university football team, and rather indifferent
to intellectual and artistic activities. Its heroes were Mary Katherine Camp-
bell, the two-time Miss America contest winner, Hank Gowdy and Chic
Harley, of athletic fame, and Captain Eddie Rickenbacker.[4] Thurber once
described the Ohio of his youth as "a region steeped in the traditions of
Coxey's Army, the Anti-Saloon League, and William Howard Taft," [5] and
no better definition of Columbus's small-town orientation, plain Puritan
values and political conservatism could be made.

James Grover Thurber was born December 8, 1894, the second son of

[2] *Ohio State Journal,* February 14, 1959.
[3] "Letter from the States," *Bermudian,* July, 1950.
[4] "Jim Thurber Comes Here to Write Columbus Profiles," *Ohio State Journal,* November 5, 1938.
[5] "The Secret Life of James Thurber," *The Thurber Carnival* (New York: Harper and Brothers, 1945), p. 32.

Charles and Mary Agnes Fisher Thurber. The family group was close-knit and clan-minded in the old-fashioned way: "the adults around me consisted mainly of eleven maternal great-aunts, all Methodists, who were staunch believers in physic, mustard plasters and Scripture," he recalled.[6] The Fisher side of the family was prosperous and well-established, and the family history ran well back into the early history of Ohio. In *The Thurber Album* Thurber took special pleasure in recreating the characters and careers of his pioneering ancestors. There was his step-great-grandfather, Judge Stacy Taylor, for example, who came from Virginia to St. Mary's, Ohio, in 1826, traded with the Indians, practiced law, and lived to be eighty-seven. He wrote a remarkable autobiography, full of vivid details of life on the Ohio frontier. His son, Mahlon Taylor, who washed his hair in Old Dutch Cleanser and read every night until dawn, showed the book to Thurber. Thurber's favorite ancestor was his great-grandfather, Jake Fisher, the heroic blacksmith whose physical strength, high principles, and open nature made him an archetype of the larger-than-life characters who settled the country in the early days. Jake was so strong that he used to pick up the horses in his blacksmith shop and move them from one place to another. " 'It was easier to move 'em that way than to lead 'em, sometimes,' " Mahlon Taylor told Thurber.[7]

Grandfather Fisher was a successful wholesale grocer whose mild eccentricities made him something of a local figure. He had his teeth capped in gold, wore a black beard, and liked to walk down the street with a red rose between his teeth. He wanted to let people know who he was, and whenever he went into a hotel or restaurant, he always introduced himself with a flourish as "William M. Fisher of Columbus, Ohio." [8] He was never at ease with machinery, and his struggles with his electric automobile became part of the folklore of the East Side of Columbus. In his last years he managed to keep the world of Woodrow Wilson at bay by immersing himself in the memoirs of General Grant, his great hero. When Thurber came to invent a grandfather for *My Life and Hard Times*, he drew heavily upon his memory of Grandfather Fisher.

Grandmother Fisher was one of those strong women, warm-hearted, active and purposeful, for whom Thurber always reserved a special admiration. She was up at dawn every day, setting the routine of the house in motion, then going out on her numerous errands, visiting friends and relatives, and taking baskets of food to the needy. She and Grandfather

[6] "The Secret Life of James Thurber" *The Thurber Carnival*, p. 33.
[7] "Adam's Anvil," *The Thurber Album* (New York: Simon and Schuster, 1952), p. 33.
[8] "Man with a Rose," *The Thurber Album*, p. 37.

Fisher liked a houseful of people, and Thurber remembered the scores of relatives, "three generations of them," who visited the Fishers on Bryden Road: Dr. Beall, the homeopathic doctor who believed in the curative powers of kerosene taken internally, and whose favorite retort to any opinion advanced by others was "Tom-fool-er-y" and "Pop-py-cock"; his sister, Aunt Mary Van York, who smoked Star-plug chewing tobacco and delighted in telling Thurber and his brothers tales of Tarzan and Wild Bill Hickok; Aunt Fanny, plagued in her old age by recurring dreams in which she gave birth to Indian, Mexican, Chinese, and African twins; Aunt Melissa, "who knew the Bible by heart and was convinced that Man's day was done"; and Aunt Florence, who once tried to fix a broken cream separator on her farm near Sugar Grove and suddenly cried, " 'Why doesn't somebody take this goddam thing away from me?' " [9] The Jackson family reunions in Sugar Grove would often be attended by as many as a hundred people, and Grandmother Fisher "was the acknowledged head of the far-flung family on these occasions." [10]

Grandfather Fisher built the first residence on Bryden Road and, in retrospect, the spacious old house of his grandparents came for Thurber to stand for the serene and leisurely way of life which disappeared with World War I. There was an iron hitching post and a granite carriage block in front; the wide lawn set off the long, two-story house with its four porches; in the front hall there was "a monstrous oak bench whose high back supported an ornate mirror and whose seat could be lifted, revealing a gloomy chest jammed with gloves, overshoes, skates, ball bats, games, and whatnot." Above the bench was the lithograph of the Duke of Westminster's six prize hunting dogs which so impressed Thurber that he spent the rest of his life drawing them. In the parlor was an enormous portrait of James Grover, the Methodist minister (and first city librarian) after whom Thurber was named, sitting in a chair with a Bible on his lap.[11]

The Thurber side of the family was neither so numerous nor so distinguished as the Fishers, and more than one old Columbus resident has observed that it was a long time before the Fishers fully accepted the Thurbers as members of the clan. Thurber's father, Charles, was a mild-mannered likable man who never quite achieved the public success he hoped for. He grew up in Indianapolis, the only son of a widowed mother, and from the time he was in knee pants he sold papers and did odd jobs

[9] Thurber describes these relatives in "Time Exposure" and "Conversation Piece," in *The Thurber Album*.
[10] "Conversation Piece," *The Thurber Album*, p. 61.
[11] "Man with a Rose," *The Thurber Album*, pp. 39–41.

to help out. There were no relatives on either his father's side or his mother's to turn to. He had always wanted to be a lawyer, but there was never any time or money for law school. Instead, he served the Republican Party in a succession of minor appointive posts from the 1890's until his retirement in 1932. He was on the staff of two Ohio governors, he was state organizer for the Bull Moose Party in Ohio in 1912, and he was secretary to the mayor of Columbus from 1923 to 1931. He ran for public office two or three times, but was never elected. He was popular with his associates and enjoyed some small local reputation as a wit.[12] Thurber remembers him as a quixotic idealist, constantly hoping that each election would bring about a better world.[13]

There was a strain of melancholy in him which he passed on to his son: "he was sorrowfully aware . . . that most men, and all children, are continuously caught in one predicament or another." There were other parental legacies. Charles Thurber had a remarkable memory, and "could remember a speech or lecture almost as accurately as if he had taken it down in shorthand," and he was passionately addicted to the slogan and jingle contests sponsored by the newspapers of his time. James's own unusual memory and his fondness for word games showed the paternal influence, as did his total inability to handle mechanical contraptions of any kind. On one unforgettable occasion, Charles Thurber managed to lock himself into a rabbit hutch he was building for his sons, and James often referred to this episode as a significant part of his family inheritance.[14] His portrait of his father in *The Thurber Album* is warm and admiring ("He was easily the most honest man I have ever known"), but one can also see behind the figure of the kindly idealist the archetype of the ineffectual male who appears so often in James Thurber's work. The domestic society in which Thurber grew up was strongly matriarchal, and in contrast to the strong-minded females who dominated his recollections of his youth, the figure of his father is passive and indistinct.

His mother was a lively unconventional person, a natural clown and inveterate practical joker. As Mamie Fisher, she was "the livest wire of the old Rich Street and Mound Street schools." [15] She and a friend wrote the class paper, directed and played in most of the school theatricals, and

[12] Clippings from the *Ohio State Journal,* January 1, 1932, and the Columbus *Dispatch,* 1932 (no day or month noted), RTS (Thurber Collection).

[13] "Gentleman from Indiana," *The Thurber Album,* p. 118.

[14] *The Thurber Album,* p. 110; also "A Dozen Disciplines," *Let Your Mind Alone* (New York: Harper and Brothers, 1937), p. 28.

[15] Ruth White, "James Thurber: His Life in Columbus," Columbus *Dispatch,* March 10, 1940.

planned to run away from home and go on the stage. Unfortunately, Mamie's parents got wind of the project and immediately put an end to any such nonsense. The friend made his escape from Columbus, however, and enjoyed a successful career in the theater, most notably as Mme. Modjeska's leading man. Deprived of a larger audience, Mamie Fisher delighted in entertaining friends and even strangers with impromptu comic performances. "Mamie would grab up a shawl . . . a string of beads and begin to dramatize. She thought up all her own scripts, and with nothing to help her but her own keen wit and her own wild imagination, she would emote," recalls a family friend.[16] Her practical jokes were works of art and she kept in practice throughout her life. There was the time, for example, when Aunt Mary Van York came to visit. She was a strong-willed old lady, and she hated the two Thurber dogs, Judge and Sampson. Mrs. Thurber somehow cajoled Aunt Mary into agreeing to feed the dogs one evening. In preparation for the occasion, she had—with the help of six-year-old Jamie—filled the cellar with sixteen other dogs of the neighborhood. When Aunt Mary set down the plate and opened the cellar door, pandemonium broke loose. There was an explosion of snarling dogs and there was Aunt Mary's counter-attack with a broom. " 'Great God Almighty!' she screamed. 'It's a dog factory!' " When the last dog had been driven out and the house had been put back in order, Mr. Thurber said to his wife, " 'Well, Mame, I hope you're satisfied.' " [17]

Thurber's humor, the wildness of his imagination, and his dramatic flair are obvious legacies from his mother. In later years both mother and son were well aware of the connection. Speaking to an old friend about her own comic talent, Mrs. Thurber said, " 'It's all come out in Jamie, instead of me.' " [18] Thurber told Alistair Cooke that he never really made a conscious decision to become a humorous writer. "My mother made it for me. She was a born comedienne and her antics were pretty well known in Columbus in the eighty-nine years she lived. They're too elaborate to go into here, but a great many of the things I've written were either inspired by her or deal with her." [19] On another occasion, he said, "I owe practically everything to her, because she was one of the finest comic talents I think I've ever known." [20] In his mother's uninhibited style he saw the quality

[16] Ibid.
[17] "Lavender with a Difference," *The Thurber Album*, pp. 133–34.
[18] Ruth White, "James Thurber," March 10, 1940.
[19] "James Thurber in Conversation with Alistair Cooke," *Atlantic*, CXCVIII (August, 1956), 36–37.
[20] Interview with Henry Brandon, "The Tulle and Taffeta Rut," in Brandon, *As We Are* (Garden City: Doubleday and Company, 1961), p. 266.

of "confusion," that talent for comic anarchy which he celebrated over and over in his books.

Not everyone shared this admiration for Mame Thurber's talents. She was, like her son, a non-stop talker and show-off, and some of the neighbors found her trying. One old Columbus resident observed that she was "sadly afflicted with logomania." "I've known a lot of talkative women in my day," he went on, "but none to hold a candle to her as a compulsive talker from whom you would run. Jamie inherited that trait (perhaps more endearingly) and harnessed it to his typewriter." James did channel much of this energy into his writing, but there was still a good deal left over for talk, the wilder the better, and for charades, late-night songs, and one-man dramatic performances of all kinds.

Even in old age, Mame Thurber continued to entertain the world. After her son became famous, she was often interviewed, and she clearly enjoyed the opportunity to tell her stories and to play the role of the unconventional old party. She often visited her son in New York, and she set a fast pace, insisting on being taken to parties, shows, and nightclubs.[21] Thurber obviously enjoyed showing off his lively mother to his friends, and some of the best anecdotes about her come from them. Stephen Vincent Benét recalled the time, for example, when she staged an impromptu performance of Ophelia in Penn Station one night to embarrass a ticket agent who had doubted that she was James Thurber's mother.[22] Describing her comic style, a long-time friend noted that like her husband she had a remarkable memory and used it with great dramatic effect: she "kept in mind an incredible miscellany of birthday dates, telephone numbers, and details of family history, and she drew freely on all this to give her long, rambling anecdotes authenticity and authority," he said.

Thurber's mother was high-strung and erratic, and when the burdens of domestic responsibility became too much for her, the boys were sent off to stay with Aunt Margery Albright, in her little house on South Fifth Street.[23] Aunt Margery was not really an aunt. She was a widow who, with her daughter, took in boarders, did washing and ironing for the ladies of the neighborhood, and cultivated a wonderful herb garden. Thurber's brother William described Aunt Margery as "a truly remarkable woman." "She had a great influence on my father, and all three of his boys," he went

[21] Ruth White, "James Thurber," March 10, 1940; Thurber, "Lavender with a Difference," The Thurber Album, pp. 147–50.
[22] Stephen Vincent and Rosemary Benét, "Thurber: As Unmistakable as a Kangaroo," New York Herald Tribune Books, Sunday, December 29, 1940.
[23] Samuel Baker, "Thurber: The Columbus Years," unpublished Master's thesis, Ohio State University, 1962, p. 7.

on to say. "She was our nurse from early childhood, and left an indelible benign imprint on all of us. She particularly was associated with my brother James. He was molded to a great extent during his early childhood by her ministrations. She was an influence on his life, from childhood.[24] According to his brother Robert, James Thurber's first literary effort was a poem entitled "My Aunt Margery Albright's Garden at 185 South Fifth Street, Columbus, Ohio."

Aunt Margery was the embodiment of old-fashioned rural culture. Strong and self-reliant, she had only contempt for men and their shilly-shallying. She was particularly contemptuous of book-learning and the fancy ways of doctors, for she was a natural-born nurse, and knew all the herbs and all the ancient remedies of folk medicine. She knew that sour grass was good for dyspepsy and mint for naushy, and that slippery elm was good for all kinds of sore tishas. Aunt Margery was in attendance when Thurber was about to be born, and she delivered him when the doctor was late. When Thurber's father was seriously ill, it was Aunt Margery's no-nonsense nursing that brought him through. Her strange old house was an exciting place for a boy, "different from the dull formality of the ordinary home and in every difference enchanting." One of the boarders was Doc Marlowe, an old medicine-show con man, who brought with him the aura of the wild west. The impact of Aunt Margery's world on a boy's imagination is movingly described in *The Thurber Album*.[25] She was a type to which Thurber was always attracted—the country aunt or great-aunt who retained some of the salt and strength of the pioneering society in which she was born. Thurber's recollections of his boyhood are significantly full of such women.

The Thurber household was a happy and lively one. Mr. and Mrs. Thurber were sociable and company-loving people, the three boys were congenial, and there was the endless succession of interesting dogs, upon whom the family obviously conferred the status of full-fledged membership. An old friend of the family, reminiscing, said, "It was always fun at the Thurbers'—on the most ordinary day, something unusual would happen." [26] Although James on occasion would entertain the family with playlets or skits which he would act out in the living room,[27] his relatives remember him as quiet and studious, reading a good deal and staying out of many of the neighborhood games because of his eyesight. His inner life,

[24] William Thurber, letter to Ronald Staub, August 5, 1966.
[25] "Daguerreotype of a Lady," *The Thurber Album*.
[26] "Thurber Kin Gather at Final Rites," Columbus *Dispatch*, November 9, 1961.
[27] Baker, "Thurber," p. 18.

however, was hyper-active. He was always fascinated by words, and in his fantasy he constructed a "secret world of idiom" in which the commonplace was constantly being transformed into the strange and the wonderful. Sometimes, for example, the sleeping metaphors in everyday phrases would suddenly spring to life, and the businessman tied up at the office, the man who left town under a cloud, the old lady who was always up in the air, and the man who lost his head during a fire would take shape for him as literal realities. Such word games were an important part of what he later called "the secret surrealist landscapes" of his youthful imagination, the private world into which he escaped as often as possible.[28]

He could type before he was seven, and it was about this time that he began to draw. (In later years, Thurber liked to say that he took up drawing only as an emergency measure when he was editor of the Ohio State Sun-Dial, and all the artists had gone to war, but this is clearly a part of the legend which he delighted in weaving into the historical facts of his career.) The family considered William the artist, and a notebook of 1901 shows an interesting contrast between William's more correct and "promising" sketches, and Jamie's primitive but more expressive efforts.[29] One drawing in particular, picturing a Civil War scene, looks forward to Thurber's handling of crowds and movement in such later illustrations as those for "The Day the Dam Broke."

In 1901–02 the family moved temporarily to Falls Church, Virginia, while Mr. Thurber was working for a government commission, and it was there, in 1902, that young James suffered the painful injury which affected his entire life. Playing Indians with his brothers, he was accidentally shot in the eye by an arrow. The eye was not removed at once, and a severe infection set in which damaged the visual apparatus of the other eye as well. Finally, the blind eye was taken out, and, miraculously, the infection which threatened his remaining vision simply arrested itself. Some forty years later it flared up again, and this time it did not stop until it had blinded him completely. But for nearly forty years, Thurber had sight in one eye, however imperfect, and the doctors who treated him in 1940–41 could not understand it. By all the rules of medical science, he should have been blind all along, they told him.[30]

[28] "The Secret Life of James Thurber," The Thurber Carnival, pp. 33–34.

[29] "James Thurber in Conversation with Alistair Cooke," Atlantic, CXCVIII (August, 1956), 37.

[30] The accident and its aftermath are described in Baker, "Thurber," pp. 11–12; in Joel Sayre, "Priceless Gift of Laughter," Time, LVIII (July 9, 1951); in Brandon, "The Tulle and Taffeta Rut," As We Are pp. 278–79; and also in Thurber's letter to Elmer Davis, October 28, 1953, and his letter to Edmund Wilson, May 25, 1959.

The psychological impact of the injury was more significant than the physical. He was never a sissy or a mama's boy, and his schoolmates remember him throwing the 'baccy bag with his brothers and taking part in the to-and-from-school tussling and snowball throwing, although they also recall taking it easy with him because of his one eye and his glasses. Nevertheless, the accident tended to isolate him from the main interests and activities of most boys his age, and to turn him in upon himself.[31] He had to stay out of school for a year, and he was inevitably made to feel that he was physically inferior to others. Both his brothers were strong and active and good at sports, and James soon adopted the role of the observer, sitting on the sidelines, watching the others, studying the games, but not taking part himself. In compensation he cultivated his already crowded fantasy life, and developed his skills as a story-teller and comic mimic. Something of the intense competitiveness which marked his character throughout his life obviously derived from this childhood injury and his natural desire to make up for it.

The Columbus of Thurber's boyhood was not a lively place, even by the standards of 1905, but it had its diversions, and Thurber remembered them vividly and affectionately throughout his life. In Neil Park, there were the Columbus Senators. In the days before Chic Harley put Ohio State on the football map, Columbus was a baseball town. The Senators won the American Association pennant in 1905, 1906 and 1907, and Thurber recalls that "we 12-year-olds saved up our nickels to go to Neil Park." A game between Columbus and Toledo would bring a crowd so large that it overflowed onto the outfield grass, "and that has never happened since, and never will." [32] Like so many Midwestern boys, Thurber and his brothers shared in this passionate interest, and as grown men they delighted in challenging one another to name off the line-ups and the batting averages of the baseball teams of long ago. Thurber never lost his boyish enthusiasm for the world of sports. It appealed to the romantic side of his nature as a world of heightened significance in which authentic heroes performed feats of strength and skill beyond the capacity of ordinary men. And it obviously had a special glamor for the one-eyed boy who could never really enter it.

In later life, when he looked back on the world of his youth, the sports heroes were always at the center of the picture. In *The Thurber Album*, describing the unusual field where Frank James's Blind Asylum baseball teams held forth, Thurber ran over the list of Columbus athletic greats who

---

[31] Baker, "Thurber," pp. 11–12; Ruth White, "James Thurber," March 10, 1940; Ralph McCombs, letter to CSH, July 14, 1966.
[32] "Memoirs of a Fairly Old-Timer," Columbus *Dispatch*, October 28, 1945.

once played there: "The Avondale Avenue team came from the West Side, bringing with it, around 1908, a youngster of destiny, its captain and center fielder, Billy Southworth, who was later signed by the New York Giants. Hank Gowdy, hero of the 1914 World Series, must have played there, too . . . and old-timers distinctly remember Billy Purtell, who went to Chicago fifty years ago to play third base for the White Sox." And in the fall, when the field was turned over to football, "several famous football stars scrimmaged there as boys: Chic Harley, Ohio State's immortal halfback and three-time All-American; Allen Thurman, whose long, high, spiral punts helped the University of Virginia beat Yale, 10–0, in 1915; . . . and the celebrated Raymond (Fike) Eichenlaub, plunging fullback of the Notre Dame team of Rockne and Dorais, which dazzled and smashed Army in 1913." [33] Harley, of course, was special, not only for Thurber, but for all Columbus citizens alive in the second decade of the century. Thurber wrote about him often, in verse and prose. Reminiscing in his *PM* column in 1940, he said, "If you never saw Chic Harley run with a football, we obviously could not describe it for you. It wasn't like Grange or Harmon or anybody else. It was a kind of cross between music and cannon fire, and it brought your heart up under your ears." [34]

There were other entertainments and diversions. Columbus boasted three theaters in those early days, and the Thurber boys fed their imaginations on the popular melodramas of the time—the westerns, like *Custer's Last Fight*, *The Flaming Arrow*, *The Round Up*, and *Barbara Frietchie;* and the great mystery thriller *Sherlock Holmes*. Even more important were the nickel novels, which offered the readiest and easiest escape into the world of adventure and excitement. "The first nickel novel I read was called *Jed, the Trapper*. I bought it in 1905 at a little drugstore on the corner of Town and Sixth," said Thurber some forty years later, in one of those flashes of total recall that kept the past constantly alive in his mind. "*Jed* was a mild tale of wintry treachery, but it gave me a taste for the genre, and in a year or so I had a formidable collection—frowned upon by Aunts Lou, Hattie, and Melissa—of *The Liberty Boys of '76*, *Young Wild West*, *Fred Fearnot*, and *Old King Brady.*" [35] He read Owen Wister's classic, *The Virginian*, when he was "so young the gun duel on the lonely street at sundown made me sick to my stomach," and he never missed a W. S. Hart movie.[36] The western exercised a particular fascination for Thurber. His

[33] "The Tree on the Diamond," *The Thurber Album*, pp. 82–83.
[34] "If You Ask Me," *PM*, October 27, 1940.
[35] "Thix," *The Beast in Me* (New York: Harcourt, Brace, 1948), pp. 45–46.
[36] "Letter from the States," *Bermudian*, January, 1951.

earliest attempt at fiction was a story called "Horse Sandusky, Intrepid Scout," [37] and by the time he reached maturity, he considered himself an expert on the form. Not only was he an authority on the American western, he told his readers, he was probably "the first American research scholar to discover, collect, and annotate a series of dime novels written in French, published in Paris, and devoted to the exploits of Wild Bill Hickok and his friend Buffalo Bill, who whenever he was nonplussed, exclaimed, in English, 'Mercy me!' " [38]

At school, Thurber was a good student but so given to daydreaming that one of his teachers at the Sullivant school suggested to Mrs. Thurber that he might be deaf. Mrs. Thurber knew, however, that it was simply her son's way of shutting out the commonplace and giving free rein to the world of fantasy he preferred.[39] From the second through the sixth grades, he attended the Sullivant school, down in the central market district, in a tough neighborhood inhabited by working-class families. The impression made upon him by these early schooldays is suggested by the fact that years later he devoted two of his reminiscent pieces to Sullivant, and none at all to the Douglas School or to East High. Because of the accident which cost him his eye, Thurber was a year behind his age-group, but at Sullivant that was no cause for remark. The school had a legendary baseball team, made up for the most part of reluctant scholars who had never been able to master fractions and long division, some of whom had spent as long as seven or eight years in the fourth grade.[40] The oldest was twenty-two, but the toughest was a Negro center fielder named Floyd, who conceived a great admiration for Thurber's intellectual powers when Thurber pronounced "Duquesne" correctly during a history lesson, and appointed himself Thurber's protector. As a boy who always knew his lessons and who wore glasses in a school where fighting was a way of life, Thurber needed one.

Other Sullivant schoolmates were remarkable in other ways: there was Eva Prout, who dropped out of school after the eighth grade and went into vaudeville and then into the movies, and was the great love of Thurber's life for more than twelve years, and there was Ozni Cornwell, whose father used to ride a bicycle around the city, shouting through a megaphone, " 'Get ready! The world is coming to an end!' " It was at Sullivant that Thurber received his first encouragement as an artist. Miss Ballinger, the

[37] Benét, "Thurber."
[38] "Letter from the States," *Bermudian,* January, 1951.
[39] Ruth White, "James Thurber," March 10, 1940.
[40] "I Went to Sullivant," *The Middle-Aged Man on the Flying Trapeze* (New York: Harper and Brothers, 1935), p. 102.

fourth grade teacher, one day brought a white rabbit to class and asked the pupils to draw it. Detecting promise in Thurber's effort, she had him stay after class to try it again. "But with just the three of us there, Miss Ballinger, the rabbit and I, it was impossible for me to draw anything, with or without promise. Anyway, she was the first person in the world to tell me I could draw!" [41]

The Thurbers were, as one old friend recalls, "more often than not, fairly unprosperous," and the family did a good deal of moving as the tide of their fortunes ebbed and flowed. As a result, Thurber attended a number of different schools. He spent the seventh and eighth grades at the Douglas School, where he got good grades, but struck his teachers and some of his classmates as painfully shy. In the seventh grade he rated a "Good" in drawing, although Miss McElvaine, the eighth grade teacher, gave him only a "Fair." In language and composition he always received an "Excellent." Ruth Young White, an old friend, recalls that "he wasn't the . . . mischievous boy that you might think from reading My Life and Hard Times; in fact, he was quiet, studious and nervous." Others remember him as awkward and more than a little shabby in appearance. Miss McElvaine worried about him: "When I call on him to recite and he stands on his feet, his Adam's apple rolls around so wildly that he can hardly speak," she complained to Mrs. Thurber.[42] The talents which later made him famous were not yet apparent to everyone. One old classmate recalls that Thurber attracted far more attention with the macabre tricks he played with his glass eye than with his humor or his scholarship. On the other hand, the majority of the students at Douglas obviously considered Thurber something of a wit and writer, because they elected him class prophet when it was time to graduate to Junior High School.[43]

Thurber went to East High, the best of the Columbus high schools. Its faculty was intellectually stimulating, and many of the men and women there had advanced degrees and went on into college and university teaching. Students in those days chose either the Latin course, the German course (reflecting Columbus's ethnic make-up), or the Science course. Thurber took the Latin course, which emphasized the study and writing of English as well as the classics. He was a good student, and although he was well liked by his classmates, he was not a joiner or an activist. Some of his friends remember him as "scribbling all the time for his own amuse-

[41] "Thurber Looks Back," Columbus Dispatch Magazine, October 1, 1961.
[42] Ruth White, "James Thurber," March 10, 1940; also Ruth White, "Early Thurber," Life, VII (April 22, 1940).
[43] Ruth White, "James Thurber," March 10, 1940.

ment," and helping out with the school's dramatic productions, but he was never on the editorial board of the *X-Rays*, the high school literary magazine, nor is there any record of his having played a significant part in theatrical activities. His contributions to the *X-Rays* were limited to one short story, in May, 1913, and a column called "Sidelights," which he did after he had left East High and enrolled at Ohio State. The heroes in high school then, as now, were the athletes and the social lions, and Thurber was neither. He was, of course, a great sports buff. His brother Robert was captain of the baseball team, and Chic Harley, who played just about everything supremely well, was one of his friends.

During his last year at East, Thurber overcame some of his shyness and ran for class president. His opponent was the son of a prominent Columbus attorney, rather full of himself, and very sure that he would win. Robert Thurber recalls that James was stimulated to enter the race because he had been told that he had no chance. As it turned out, his quiet independence and his humor and intelligence impressed his schoolmates more than the social standing of his opponent, and he was elected. Years later he said that he still took enormous satisfaction in this high school victory.[44]

Not many samples of his high school writing survive, but two short stories, one a theme entitled "How Law and Order Came to Aramie," the other Thurber's first published story, "The Third Bullet," which appeared in the May, 1913, issue of the *X-Rays*, give some idea of the quality of his prose and the nature of his literary models at this stage of his development.[45] Both are fashioned out of the enduring clichés of the western form. In "How Law and Order Came to Aramie" there is the mild-mannered sheriff who wishes to substitute law for the rule of force, the loud-mouthed badman who accuses the sheriff of cowardice, and the inevitable confrontation in which the sheriff's cool composure cracks the nerve of the badman. "The Third Bullet" follows the same pattern. In the climactic gun-duel the villain's shots ricochet wildly off the desert rocks while the hero coolly holds his fire. Then with the villain at his mercy, he contemptuously spares his life: " 'Get up! Here be a man! if you know what such a thing is. Do you think I would stain my hands by shooting you? You aren't fit to die, you cur!' "

Both stories show the influence of O. Henry in their western settings and their efforts to provide the surprise ending regarded as obligatory by

---

[44] For this account of Thurber's years at East High I have drawn on Ruth White, "James Thurber"; on Baker, "Thurber"; on the Report for 1913 of the Superintendent of East High (in the Thurber Collection); as well as on letters to me from Robert Thurber and Ralph McCombs.
[45] Both are in the Thurber Collection.

young short story writers of that generation. All three Thurber boys were great readers of O. Henry, not only because of the effective blend of humor and melodrama in his work, but also because he was a part of Columbus history. He had written a number of his stories while he was serving time in the Ohio State Penitentiary, and there was a persistent rumor that he had given a great stack of manuscripts to the prison doctor, who had subsequently and mysteriously lost them. Years later, Thurber pursued the O. Henry legend, first in "The Talk of the Town," in *The New Yorker*, and then in *The Thurber Album*. Thurber's juvenile pieces are interesting only because they show the extent to which his imagination was shaped by the clichés of the popular adventure story. They contain few hints that their author would one day be regarded as a superb stylist and a genuine original.

There is, however, one remarkable exception. The class prophecy which he wrote for the eighth grade at Douglas School anticipates with uncanny accuracy the subject matter and the comic method of "The Secret Life of Walter Mitty." [46] In form, it is a fantasy in which Thurber imagines that at some date in the future, Harold Young, the most air-minded member of the class, has invented a wonderful airship called a "Seairoplane" in which he takes the class of 1909 on a tour of the United States and a trip to Mars. Jules Verne and the exploits of the local daredevils who tried out their makeshift aircraft at Driving Park on Sunday afternoons in Columbus were undoubtedly in Thurber's mind as he composed his fanciful narrative. The excitement of aviation was a national fever in Thurber's youth. "Everybody went out to Driving Park to see the first frail and fluttering biplanes soar in front of the grandstand, sometimes not more than 200 feet off the ground," he recalled in later years. "In every backyard in Ohio, men and boys were building airships." Columbus had its share of eccentric enthusiasts: Cromwell Dixon, "a youngster in short pants, slung a bicycle under a gas bag, geared it to a propeller, and not only went up in the crazy thing but came down safely, many times." [47] Thurber's great-uncle, Jake Fisher, built an airship in 1905 and put it on display in Indianola Park. "It was equipped with bells and whistles that raised a racket like Hallowe'en when it took to the air, but it made only one successful flight, drifting 3 miles and coming down in a cornfield north of town." [48]

Dreaming of improbable journeys and feats of daring, Thurber describes the wonderful trip of the Seairoplane. In the course of the voyage, he

[46] Ruth White's typescript of the prophecy is in the Thurber Collection.
[47] "Memoirs of a Fairly Old-Timer."
[48] "Conversation Piece," *The Thurber Album*, pp. 60–61.

characterizes the members of the class and their occupations in life. The craft takes off from "the celebrated field of Bull Run":

> The Seairoplane's course was directly upward and at first we experienced a sea-sick feeling, but soon became used to it. When night came on, earth was far below and hardly visible to us. In the morning of the next day, we consulted the hythenometer and found ourselves to be about 125 miles high.

> . . . At night Mars could be plainly seen and we stayed up until late to examine it. Crystal Fleming, the world renowned astronomer, told us all about the canals, mountains, etc., and gave her opinion as to whether Mars was inhabited or not, which was that there was strange people who largely resembled apes that inhabited the planet.
>
> Someone found out that Catharine Crawford was a playwriter, writing under the name of Helen McCafferty. . . . We had her read a play that she had just finished which was entitled "Who Threw Mush in Nellie's Eye." It was a very pathetic one and there were tears on almost everyone's face when she finished.

Most of the prophecy is pleasant fourteen-year-old nonsense of this kind, but the following sequence is full of interest:

> One day, as we were sailing easily along, Harold came rushing out of the engine room with disheveld hair and bulging eyes. We asked him what on earth was the matter. For answer he pointed to a piece of rope that had caught in a part of the machinery that was situated on the farthest end of a long beam which extended far over the side of the Seairoplane.
>
> Then he said, "Unless that rope is gotten out of the curobater we will all be killed."
>
> These awful words astounded us and we all became frightened. Suddenly amid all of our lamentations a cry from Harold was heard and we all looked up. What was our surprise to see James Thurber walking out on the beam.
>
> He reached the end safely and then extricated the rope, but when he turned to come back his foot caught and he pitched head foremost toward the deck. His unusual length saved him, for he landed safely on the Seairoplane. We were all very happy that the terrible crisis had been safely passed and afterwards learned that James was a tight rope walker with Barnsells and Ringbailey's circus.

Here, at the age of fourteen, Thurber reveals a dominant image of the fantasy life which was one of the richest sources of his mature art. The fact that it persisted almost unchanged from boyhood into manhood suggests something of the hold the material of Walter Mitty's dreams had on Thurber's imagination. What is particularly striking is that some of the most effective comic details of the later work go back to this juvenile sketch: the hythenometer and the rope caught in the curobater of Harold Young's Seairoplane are clearly the germs of the wonderful mock-technical language of "The Secret Life of Walter Mitty."

The inventive fantasy of the Eighth Grade Prophecy was an isolated flash of artistic promise; it was to be many years before Thurber wrote anything of comparable originality. Looking back on his youth, he confessed to an interviewer that his talent appeared late and developed slowly.[49] He was a late bloomer in every way—emotionally, intellectually, and artistically —and the dominant influence on his life until well into his college years was the family group. In his mother and father were the two opposing sides of his temperament—the fantasy side and the common-sense side—and two opposing models of personality, and he identified with both. The high-keyed, talented, theatrical mother was an obvious and often-acknowledged influence on his comic style as a writer and late-night-party entertainer; but the image of the quiet, kindly father, while less obvious, was no less important, and it appeared over and over in his work as the mild-mannered well-intentioned male threatened by the destructive forces of the world. The boyhood injury helped to confirm him as a dreamer and a loner, and undoubtedly fed his determination to succeed in the world. While he was still in his teens, he used to tell his brother Robert that "he was going to make the literary grade in time and that nothing was going to stop him." [50] When he came to write such fairy tales as *Many Moons*, *The White Deer*, and *The Thirteen Clocks*, he readily identified with the figure of the outsider—the jester, the third son, the wandering minstrel— who finally turns out to be the strongest and most talented of all.

[49] Letter to Frank Gibney, October 31, 1956.
[50] Letter from Robert Thurber to CSH, July 30, 1966.

2

University Days

I N THE FALL OF 1913 Thurber entered Ohio State University, which he attended on and off for the next five years, and which he left without graduating in June of 1918. It was a school of about 4000 students in those days, a land-grant school interested chiefly in vocational training (the Agricultural School was the dominant branch of the university) and suspicious of unfamiliar ideas and values.[1] It was solidly provincial in its outlook: nearly all the students and faculty were native Ohioans and tended to see life in Midwestern terms. "The Ohio Legislature was always glad to finance a new cow barn or horse building, but guffawed at the idea of a theater on the campus," Thurber observed in his portrait of Dean Denney in *The Thurber Album*, and he quoted with approval Denney's famous challenge on behalf of the humanities to the Philistine values of the university: "Millions for manure, but not one cent for literature." [2]

The student body as a whole was hostile to art and culture—it was worth your life, Thurber once observed, to be found with a copy of Shelley in your pocket; [3] and looking back at the university scene some thirty-five years later, he remarked that "perceptive and congenial young minds can

[1] Baker, "Thurber," p. 26; also Ronald Staub, "Summary of Thurber's Academic Career at Ohio State University, 1913–18," notes to CSH from Mr. Staub on his Ph.D. thesis in progress, Ohio State University, 1966.

[2] *The Thurber Album*, pp. 207–08.

[3] "Credos and Curios," Columbus *Dispatch*, October 28, 1923.

scarcely be said to have flourished like wild flowers in that time and region." [4] Ludwig Lewisohn, who taught German at Ohio State when
Thurber was an undergraduate, remembers the faces of the students as
pleasant, blank, and dull. "Not one . . . that betrays a troubled soul, a
yearning of the mind, the touch of any flame. . . . It is, as a matter of
fact, considered rather bad form among them to show any stirring of the
mind. It is considered 'high-brow,' queer, that is to say—different, personal,
and hence, by a subtle and quite mad implication, consoling to stupidity,
and emptiness—undemocratic." [5] Arthur M. Schlesinger, who was a student at Ohio State, and then an instructor in the History department, gives
a somewhat kindlier picture of the university, but he, too, remembers it
as intellectually unexciting. The library was barely adequate for undergraduate purposes, and although there were some good teachers, the faculty was
not noted for its research. President William Oxley Thompson set the tone:
he was a vigorous, kindly Presbyterian minister, a popular public speaker
and effective fund-raiser, but "in no sense an educational statesman." [6]
Still, the university boasted an unusually strong English department headed
by Joseph Villiers Denney, one of Thurber's lifetime heroes, and featuring
such notable teachers as Joseph Taylor, Louis Cooper, and Billy Graves.
And there was a small but lively group of students like Elliott Nugent,
Herman Miller, and Ralph McCombs who were actively interested in
writing and the theater.

Thurber's feelings about the university were always mixed. He was grateful for men like Denney and Taylor (in later years, he admitted to a special
fondness for "the species known as English Professor"),[7] and he felt many
of the usual alumni sentimentalities about the old school. He went back
to football games and attended reunions and kept a watchful eye on university traditions.[8] When in 1946 the administration wanted to change the
name of the Sun-Dial (the humor magazine which he had edited in 1918),
he wrote a letter of vehement protest to President Bevis.[9] In addition, one
of his closest friends, Herman Miller, was a member of the English department for many years, and through him Thurber remained in touch with
university personalities and politics. On the other hand, his moral and

[4] The Thurber Album, p. 171.

[5] Ludwig Lewisohn, Up Stream (New York: Boni and Liveright, 1922), pp. 155–56.

[6] Arthur M. Schlesinger, In Retrospect (New York: Harcourt, Brace and World, 1963),
pp. 22–23.

[7] Denney Hall Dedication Speech, Ohio State University Monthly, May, 1960.

[8] See, for example, "Never Again Will the Heart Leap So High," Columbus Dispatch
Sports Section, September 12, 1954; and Thurber's exchange of letters with S. B. Tracy
(Thurber Collection).

[9] Letter to President Bevis, April 24, 1946 (Thurber Collection).

intellectual judgment was outraged by the periodic interferences of ignorant trustees and spineless administrators with the free play of ideas on the
campus, and the general tone of his public remarks to and about the
university in later years was sharply critical.

On a visit to the campus in 1944 he spoke bitterly of the cultural
deficiencies of the university, particularly its failure to give adequate recognition to his favorite professor, Joseph Russell Taylor, "a really great man,
but few people realized it." He went on to say that he wouldn't be surprised
to hear that "the Legislature has banned the teaching of Shakespeare,
Shelley and Keats, because their love life was indecent." [10] In a letter of
1950 he described President Bevis's speech between halves of the Illinois
game as "straight out of Sinclair Lewis," and went on to say that the
university badly needed a new president. [11] The gag rule on visiting speakers
imposed by the trustees and administration in 1950 so outraged him that
it was nearly ten years before he could speak of the university with his old
affection. [12]

Thurber's first two years at Ohio State were not very successful. He felt
lost in his new environment and made few friends. He had a good academic
record his first year, but he hung back from other campus activities. [13] He
took European History, American History (under Arthur M. Schlesinger),
Latin, Psychology, English Composition ("Paragraph Writing"), Military
Science and Gym. It was in his Psychology course that he first realized that
he had an unusual memory. One day the instructor, Albert P. Weiss, read
the class several pages from a book and then asked the students to write
down what they could remember of it. Thurber remembered eighty-four
percent, and a week later he could recall fifty percent. He was inordinately
proud of his memory, and seldom passed up a chance to show it off. He
liked to describe himself as possessing "total recall": "I can remember
hundreds of telephone numbers, some of them going back as far as
1907. . . . I could visualize whole pages of a book after I'd read it," he
said in an interview of 1958. [14] Making due allowance for dramatic exaggeration, his memory *was* remarkable, and it was of central importance to him
as a writer. His best work came out of his recollections of his youth in
Columbus, and the literary punning and allusive brilliance of his later style

[10] Interview in *Sun-Dial*, January, 1944.

[11] Letter to H. S. Warwick, January 9, 1950 (Thurber Collection).

[12] James E. Pollard, "Thurber," *Ohio Authors and Their Books*, ed. William Coyle (Cleveland and New York: World Publishing Company, 1962), p. 636.

[13] Ruth White, "James Thurber," March 17, 1940; Baker, "Thurber," p. 26; Staub,
"Summary."

[14] Interview with Eddy Gilmore in London, reprinted as "Call Me Jim," Columbus *Dispatch*, August 3, 1958.

depended upon the fact that he seldom forgot anything he had heard or read.

As a freshman, Thurber was painfully shy and awkward, and his thick glasses, unkempt hair, and unfashionable clothes did not make him the kind of figure admired on college campuses in 1913. Elliott Nugent remembers him as a loner, "inclined to wander about the campus on cold winter days dressed in an old pair of pants, an old coat, no vest, no overcoat, and no hat." [15] He was tense and full of self-doubts. He worried about his ability to make good academically, to get into a fraternity, and to make the staff of the *Lantern* or the *Sun-Dial*. He and his best friend from East High, Ed Morris, were rushed by the Chi Phis, and Thurber was bitterly disappointed when Morris got in and he was left out.[16] As a result, says Nugent, "he spent his first year and a half at our great university feeling somewhat like an orphan child." He lived at home and took the streetcar back and forth to the campus. Almost nobody in the 4000-odd student body knew him.

Significantly his only extra-curricular writing during this period was a column of miscellaneous comment for the East High *X-Rays* in the spring of 1914. He obviously lacked the confidence to try to compete for attention at the university, while at East High he was still a well-known figure. The quality of the comment in "Sidelights" is ordinary, but the column is important because it shows Thurber carefully imitating the form and manner of Robert O. Ryder, the distinguished editor of the best paper in Columbus, the *Ohio State Journal*. "Ryder was the first influence on me as a humorist and it still lasts," he said in a letter of 1951. He called Ryder "one of the best American humorists," and went on to say that "I read all his paragraphs for many years and learned a lot from them." [17] When he came to explore his personal past in *The Thurber Album*, he included Ryder in the small company of those who had really influenced his life.

Ryder was one of the great masters of the art of "paragraphing"—the composition of a miscellany of brief humorous comments on local behavior and events as well as on the larger human scene. He wrote the editorial page of the *Ohio State Journal* from 1903 to 1929, and every day during that period he turned out his temperate, well-organized editorials on the first part of the page, and his sharply observed paragraphs on the second. The topics of the paragraphs ranged from the purity of the Columbus water

15 Elliott Nugent, "Notes on James Thurber, the Man, or Men," New York *Times* Theater Section, March 3, 1940.
16 Charme Seeds, "Jim Thurber," *Ohio State University Monthly*, April, 1930; also Robert Thurber, letter to CSH, July 30, 1966.
17 Letter to James E. Pollard, October 8, 1951 (Thurber Collection).

supply, the social distinction between green-dried-split-pea soup ("*de ri-gueur*, as we say in Ohio") and yellow-dried-split-pea soup ("hopelessly bourgeois"), to the problems of the car owner of 1916, and the behavior of politicians at home and abroad. As Thurber observed, Ryder's paragraphs were "a microcosm of the America of his time," and they were widely admired by newspapermen throughout the country.[18] The *Literary Digest* and the New York *World* reprinted hundreds of his paragraphs; it is significant that Harold Ross insisted on having a column of paragraphs when he started *The New Yorker.* Ryder's was a quiet comic art, perhaps a bit too genteel and kindly for mid-twentieth-century tastes, depending chiefly on justness of observation and neatness of phrase for its effect. For example:

> The eminent scientist who announced that 10 inches of snow make only one inch of water probably never wore guaranteed waterproof shoes.

> When the neighbor women can't find out anything definite against some attractive young matron of whom they don't quite approve, they say she has no background and seem fairly well satisfied.

> The line between youth and middle age is marked with a fair degree of accuracy by the time at which a man begins to want a winter top for his automobile.

> A woman is either hearing burglars or smelling something burning.[19]

Ryder's paragraphs have a casual, unstudied air, but he worked over them, in Thurber's phrase, "the way a poet slaves over a sonnet." The art of paragraphing, he once said, is to "make something that was ground out sound as if it were dashed off." [20] Even the arrangement of the paragraphs on the page was carefully planned—the longer paragraphs came first, then progressively shorter ones, and finally a series of one-liners, which gave a comic scatter-shot quality to the conclusion.

Thurber's first venture as a columnist, the "Sidelights" department of East High's the *X-Rays*, is a frank imitation of Ryder. He sent the older man a tear sheet every month and Ryder reprinted one item that winter.[21]

---

[18] *The Thurber Album*, p. 278, and letter to Pollard, February 9, 1952.
[19] *Ohio State Journal*, Monday, March 13, 1916; *The Thurber Album*, p. 282; *Ohio State Journal*, Tuesday, March 24, 1916.
[20] *The Thurber Album*, pp. 277–78.
[21] Letter to Pollard, February 9, 1952.

"Sidelights" is the work of a young and inexperienced writer, but it shows the salutary effect of following a good model. Most of the items deal with the rather special world of East High affairs, but some embrace larger areas of experience:

> Every freshman is confident that we, meaning the United States, could lick all Europe on the strength of Stuart's picture of Washington, and the midnight ride of Paul Revere, and with our adequate coast defenses, namely, the cannon in front of Memorial Hall, and the Star Spangled Banner, to back us up.[22]

> The acme of poise is to wear yellow gloves as if you weren't doing it because you bet on Johnson.[23]

This last, recalling the national excitement over the Jack Johnson–Jess Willard fight, is pure Ryder in its sensitivity to the manners of the day. What could be more embarrassing to a Columbus boy in 1914 than the thought of yellow gloves?

The April column shows Thurber exploring the comic possibilities of the rapid interplay of one-line gags with which Ryder often concluded his page.

> Whence I deduce, my dear Watson, that Troy fell because it was a one-horse town.

> Quick, Charles, the pulmotor!

> Next month: The Spoon: a stirring drama.

Puns and word-play of all sorts fascinated Thurber from the beginning, and the schoolboy punning of this passage is a cautious preview of the reckless word-play of his later style.

One of Ryder's most popular features was "The Young Lady Across the Way," a drawing (by Harry J. Westerman) with caption presenting the sayings of a pretty-but-dumb American girl. She is, as Thurber points out in his portrait of Ryder in *The Thurber Album*, the forerunner of F.P.A.'s Dulcinea and Kaufman and Connelly's Dulcy, and as such she is a significant figure in the American comic tradition. Ryder treats her gently, as the following example shows:

[22] "Sidelights," *X-Rays*, March, 1915.
[23] "Sidelights," *X-Rays*, April, 1915.

"De gustibus non disputandum est," we observed to the young lady across the way, and she said yes indeed we did and for her part, after more mature consideration, she did think it was a shame to leave it off the new gold coins.[24]

In the February "Sidelights," Thurber carefully follows Ryder's formula, basing his characterization on the young lady's verbal confusions:

We asked the Young Lady Across the Way if she used many theme tablets, and she said, my! she wouldn't think of taking a drug to stimulate her mind, even if she didn't get high grades on her themes.

Later, Thurber was to handle the subject of the American woman and her intellectual inadequacies with considerably more range and less tolerance, but it is interesting to note that the battle of the sexes was one of the themes in Ryder's work which he first chose to imitate.

Imitation of Ryder gave the youthful Thurber a subject and a point of view—the comic representation of the American scene, with special emphasis on the problems presented by women. It also gave him a sound model of style and a high standard of craftsmanship. High school exposure to Ryder did not, of course, suddenly transform him into a full-grown artist; he was slow and uncertain (as he himself said) in his development. But Ryder at least gave him a direction in which to grow, and it is significant that he continued to practice the art of the paragraph when he became editor of the Sun-Dial at Ohio State, when he did his "Credos and Curios" column on the Dispatch, and most notably when he did "The Talk of the Town" for The New Yorker.

His second year at the university was a low point in every way. Depressed by not having been invited to join a fraternity and agonizingly aware of his unprepossessing appearance and lack of money, he became more and more moody and withdrawn. Besides, the regimentation of the curriculum, with its requirements in science, physical education, and military drill, galled him, and after a while he simply quit going to classes. He had registered for a full program, but he completed none of his courses that year. He told no one at home of what he had done, and took the streetcar to the campus every day as usual. Once there, he spent his time at the Union and the library, "reading and brooding." [25] Strangely, neither his

---

[24] Robert O. Ryder and Harry Westerman, The Young Lady Across the Way (Columbus, 1908), p. 107.

[25] Earl Minderman, "We Knew Him When," Columbus Citizen, no day or month noted, 1934 (clipping in RTS); also Ruth White, "James Thurber," March 17, 1940; Staub, "Summary."

parents nor his brothers seem to have had any inkling that James was in trouble.[26] He had lived to himself for so many years, jealously guarding his inner life, that he and his family had simply fallen out of the habit of communicating, except on impersonal, everyday matters. A remark in a letter to his friend Elliott Nugent a few years later indicates to what an extent Thurber felt himself to be alone even in the bosom of his family: speaking of his efforts to write, he says, "Somehow I can't accomplish much here at home, since never have my folks understood me, altho' they have always sympathized and helped wonderfully." [27]

He came back to the university in the fall of 1915, and in the first semester he passed Elementary French, Survey of English Literature, and Advanced Composition, but experienced a memorable academic disaster in Botany I. He never did manage to satisfy the university requirement in biological science, and his misadventures in the strange land of science are one of the high points of his classic reminiscence piece "University Days." His dislike of physical education and military science was, if anything, more intense than it was the year before. Captain Converse, the commandant of the R.O.T.C. unit, was something of a martinet, and he took particular delight in ridiculing Thurber's efforts to master the intricacies of close-order drill. "You're the main trouble with this university," he once said. "Either you're a foot ahead or a foot behind the company." Thurber got even with the captain by mimicking him for the benefit of friends and family. The captain wore a black patch over one eye, and cut a rather striking figure; William Thurber recalls that James's imitation of the captain's mannerisms "was the source of many a good laugh at our house." [28] Years later, Thurber settled his final score with the captain by making him into the dim-witted and pompous General Littlefield of "University Days."

Because of his consistent absence from Military Drill, Thurber was not allowed to register for the second semester. He could have been reinstated by going to Captain Converse, but he could not bring himself to do it. So once again he was out of the university, and once again he kept the news from his family, and pretended to be attending classes as usual. At the end of three years he was still a beginning sophomore. But the year 1915–16 was not as unprofitable as Thurber's academic record might make it seem. In the Advanced Composition class, under Professor Beck, he met Elliott Nugent, and this personal encounter was to change his whole life

26 Robert Thurber letter to CSH, July 30, 1966.
27 To Nugent, March 25, 1920 (Thurber Collection).
28 William Thurber, "The Shadow of Fame," unpublished typescript of reminiscences sent to Ronald Staub by Mr. Thurber.

at the university.[29] Nugent was only a freshman (he was given special permission to take the Advanced Composition course), but he was socially sophisticated, handsome, popular, and reasonably athletic. His father was a famous performer-actor-playwright, and young Nugent had already had a career on the professional stage when he arrived at Ohio State. He had the poise and confidence that go with success, and before long he was known to almost everybody. "Elliott was a Big Man on Campus from the day he set foot on it, extrovert, worldly-wise, possessed of all the looks, style, and social grace of which Jamie had not a vestige," said an old friend. At Ohio State Thurber had so far only the taste of failure.

One day, as Nugent recalls it, Professor Beck read aloud a student theme entitled "My Literary Enthusiasms," which wittily described and parodied the popular dime novels of the day. Nugent was impressed by the piece, and complimented Thurber on it after class. This classroom meeting soon developed into friendship and mutual admiration. Nugent and his fraternity brother Jack Pierce were impressed with Thurber's "ability, wit and charm," [30] and when Thurber returned to the university in the fall of 1917, they became, in effect, his sponsors. Nugent got him to cut his hair and to dress more presentably, he encouraged him to try out for the *Lantern* and *Sun-Dial* staffs, and to join the dramatic society, The Strollers, and he and Pierce got him into their own fraternity, Phi Kappa Psi. Nugent gave Thurber friendship, confidence, and a new identity. Through Nugent Thurber found his first successful public role—that of court jester, whose irreverent wisecracks and dry ironic remarks made him a figure of consequence on the university scene. For the first time, he realized that his unconventional appearance and manner might be positive advantages rather than handicaps. With Nugent as his Svengali (as one classmate put it), Thurber at last had a role to play and an audience to play to.[31]

Thurber's last two years at the university were as different from his first three as could be. The withdrawn solitary figure who had spent the second half of 1915–16 brooding in the library was almost magically replaced by the busy journalist, campus humorist, and well-loved fraternity brother. He got himself reinstated in the fall of 1916 by ignoring the hated Captain Converse and going directly to President Thompson. "W.O.T. reinstated me on his own, without any letter from Converse," he told his friend James Pollard, in 1960; "The great Thompson said to me, 'Don't let the military

[29] Sayre, "Priceless Gift of Laughter"; Baker, "Thurber," pp. 30–32; Nugent, "Notes on James Thurber," and *Events Leading Up to the Comedy* (New York: Trident Press, 1965), p. 63; Staub, "Summary."
[30] Elliott Nugent, "Brother James Thurber," *Buckeye Phi Psi*, April, 1962.
[31] Ralph McCombs, letter to CSH, July 14, 1966.

get you by the neck.' " [32] Fired with academic zeal, he took a full course-load in the first semester—Introduction to American Literature, Nine-teenth-Century Poetry, Journalism, Political Science, and Principles of Economics. Two of these courses deserve mention: the Economics course, because it provided one of the most memorable anecdotes in "University Days"—the heroic effort of the professor to compose an examination easy enough for the simple-minded football star, Bolenciecwcz (whose real-life original was the peerless Chic Harley, according to Nugent), and the Nineteenth Century Poetry course, because it was probably Thurber's first meeting with Professor Joseph Russell Taylor, the man who more than anyone else shaped the young Thurber's literary tastes and ideals.

Taylor was one of the most popular lecturers at Ohio State, a witty and eloquent man who managed to awaken the interest of even the ignorant and Philistine students in the poetry of Housman or the characters of Henry James. His special field was the nineteenth century, and Thurber took the first half of the poetry course (Wordsworth, Shelley, Keats, and their contemporaries) in the fall of 1916, and the second half (Tennyson, Browning, Arnold, Swinburne, and Taylor's favorite, A. E. Housman) in the spring of 1918.[33] The impact of the course can be seen in the extent to which he quoted and parodied these poets in his own later writing. In 1917–18 he took Taylor's course in the novel (first semester, Richardson to Scott; second semester, Dickens to Meredith), and it was this course, above all, which he always looked on as the high point of his college career.

The encounter with Taylor was Thurber's first significant intellectual experience, and its impact lasted a lifetime. He particularly admired Taylor's freedom from dogmatism and academic convention. " 'I do not expect you to take notes in this class,' " he announced on opening day, and Thurber remembers that "forty out of the fifty young men and women present wrote that down in their brand-new notebooks with their brand-new fountain pens." " 'Don't quote me outside class,' " Taylor was fond of saying, " 'because my judgments are subject to change.' " He reversed his field on Conrad while Thurber was taking his course. Earlier he had dismissed Conrad as "merely a spinner of yarns"; later in the year he announced, " 'I have changed my mind about Conrad. He is Henry James in the waste places.' " [34]

For Thurber, Taylor was the embodiment of high intellectual and artistic standards and something which answered a deep need in his own youthful

[32] Letter to Pollard, June 28, 1960 (Thurber Collection).
[33] Staub, "Summary."
[34] *The Thurber Album*, pp. 167–69.

nature—the aesthetic view of life. Taylor was a minor poet, a painter (one of his protégés was George Bellows), a product of the genteel tradition, a devoted feminist, a seeker after beauty in the late Victorian fashion. Henry James was his great hero, the master of subtle psychology (particularly in his treatment of women) and of elegance and precision in style. *The Ambassadors* and Mme. de Vionnet he held up as absolute standards in their kinds, and he loved to quote James's idealizing comment on Mme. de Vionnet, "When she touches a thing, the ugliness, God knows how, goes out of it."

Listening to Taylor was a major experience for Thurber, introducing him to the world of serious literature, shaping his taste, and expanding his imaginative horizons. His portrait of Taylor in *The Thurber Album* is a memorable tribute to the quality of the man and his ideals. Thurber's most obvious legacy from Taylor is his lifelong admiration for Henry James: for him, as for the older man, James was the touchstone of literary excellence, and the figure of James looms larger in his work than that of any other writer. He admired James's craftsmanship, the orderly design of his stories, and the high polish of his prose, but his commitment went deeper than that. In a very real sense, James became a part of his imagination, and when he went to Europe for the first time, he saw it all as though he were a character in a Henry James novel.[35] His conception of the middle-aged American male owes more than a little to James's "poor sensitive gentlemen," and throughout his career he parodied, imitated, echoed and alluded to James's work. From "Something to Say" (1932), the wonderful parody of "The Coxon Fund," to the long appreciative critical essay "The Wings of Henry James," in 1961, James brought out the best in Thurber. In addition to James, there were Conrad, another of Thurber's lifelong enthusiasms, Meredith, and A. E. Housman, and in the twentieth century, there was Willa Cather—these were the major writers Thurber discovered under Taylor's direction, and they formed the basis of his literary taste. Outside the classroom he was reading Joseph Hergesheimer, whose romantic descriptive style, particularly in *Wild Oranges*, was an important early influence on his own writing.[36]

Taylor's influence on Thurber extended well beyond the discovery of particular writers. Many of Taylor's basic tastes and ideals, such as his preference for the polite, the civilized, and the genteel in art, his devotion

[35] Thurber's passion for James is a major theme in his letters to Nugent in 1918–20 (Thurber Collection).

[36] Letter to Frank Gibney, October 31, 1956; letter to E. B. White, April 15, 1956; Helen Thurber letter to CSH, July 6, 1966.

to "fitness and precision of speech," his insistence that "art is revision," and his belief that "nothing genuine need fear the test of laughter" became permanent parts of Thurber's mind. And in looking back at Taylor in the *Album* sketch, when he noted the curious mixture in the man of cosmopolitan aesthete and ineradicable Ohioan, he might well have been describing himself.

Taylor was a complex personality—magnificent in the classroom, he was frustrated in his ambitions to be a well-known writer and scholar. His poetic talent was too small to attract much attention, and he lacked the Ph.D. and the scholarly publications to get him the Eastern offer he yearned for throughout his career. He devoted years to a long and unpublished study of the Tristram legend, which a colleague rather unkindly described as "the autobiography of Joseph Russell Taylor," and to an also unpublished study of James, entitled "Taylor on James." After Taylor's death, Thurber read both essays and thought the Tristram piece "remarkable" and the James essay disappointing. "He could never get it down on paper," he said, summing up his memory of the man who had contributed so much to his own intellectual growth.[37]

In the second semester of 1916–17, Thurber enrolled in the famous short story course taught by William Lucius Graves. Graves was the most popular professor in the history of the university, "the friend of freshmen, the confidant of seniors, and the chum of alumni." [38] He liked to identify with the taste of his students, reassuring them that he, too, never missed an issue of the *Cosmopolitan*. At the same time, he liked to play the role of the dilettante and connoisseur of the arts, chiefly for the benefit of his colleagues and the Columbus matrons who invited him to dinner. Friendship with students and alumni was the center of his life. Aside from occasional verses, he did no professional writing whatever, but he contributed a weekly column to the *Lantern* and a monthly piece to the alumni magazine for over forty years—a total output of over two million words. His devotion to his fraternity was extravagant, even by the standards of those days. One brother estimated that he had visited the Beta house five thousand times between his graduation from Ohio State in 1893 and his death in 1943.

Thurber was too fastidious intellectually to be taken in by Graves's appeal to the popular audience. In the short story course, Graves's models were Fannie Hurst, Robert W. Chambers, Gouverneur Morris, Richard Harding Davis, and other popular writers of the day, and he forced the students to use ready-made plots in doing their stories. "There was the one

[37] Letter to James Fullington, March 18, 1952 (Thurber Collection).
[38] "BΘΙΙ," *The Thurber Album*, p. 186.

about a paralyzed woman who beseeches her daughter not to get married
and leave her, and the one about the cowardly condemned youth who goes
bravely to his death after his brother tells him that the real bullets have
been replaced by blanks," Thurber recalls in the *Album*. For an aspiring
writer looking for guidance and models, Graves's course was bound to be
a disappointment. Frustrated and bored, Thurber failed to hand in enough
papers and took a "deferred pass." He always resented the common assumption that Graves was the equal of a man like Taylor. In a letter to
his friend Professor James Fullington, he said of Taylor, "I got more out
of his classes than anybody else's," and of Graves he said, "I got very little
out of Billy's. . . . He had the only short story class, so I went to it." [39]

Thurber never took a course from Louis Cooper, the highly regarded
professor of modern literature at Ohio State ("I was not interested in Shaw
and Yeats then, but in Henry James and Housman, and hence Taylor was
the man for me" [40]), but in 1917–18 he did take both semesters of Joseph
Villiers Denney's Shakespeare course. Denney was one of the most remarkable men at Ohio State. When he died in 1935, the Columbus *Dispatch*
said, "Ohio State University is in large part the length and shadow of
Joseph Villiers Denney." [41] Throughout the twenty years when he was
Dean of the College of Arts and Sciences he fought energetically and
skillfully for the humanities and championed the cause of academic freedom at the university. When Thurber and Nugent wanted a strong and
humane faculty figure to stand up against the crude repressive force of the
trustees in their comedy *The Male Animal*, they modeled the character
of Dean Damon, the voice of sanity, on Dean Denney.[42]

Thurber's last year at Ohio State was full of rewards and satisfactions.
He had worked hard as a reporter for the *Lantern* and as a contributor to
the *Sun-Dial* in 1916–17, and now in 1917–18 he was editor-in-chief of
the magazine (with Nugent as his assistant) and he and Nugent were "issue
editors" of the paper. Thurber was in charge of the Wednesday issue of
the *Lantern*, and Nugent the Thursday, and they worked as a team, each
helping the other get out the paper. After the usual all-night sessions, they
would go to Marzetti's (in those days a favorite rendezvous for newspapermen) for coffee and sandwiches and conversation at dawn.[43] Nugent

[39] March 18, 1952.
[40] To Fullington, August 6, 1952.
[41] Quoted in *The Thurber Album*, p. 212.
[42] Nelson H. Budd, "Thurber-Nugent Comedy Will Open Tuesday in New York," Columbus *Citizen*, January (n.d.), 1940 (clipping in Robert Thurber Scrapbook); also James Thurber's letter to the Columbus *Dispatch*, Sunday, January 5, 1940, about *The Male Animal*.
[43] Nugent, *Events Leading Up to the Comedy*, pp. 65–66 and 70; also "Brother James
Thurber."

remembers Thurber as "surprisingly efficient" as an editor, but in retro-spect his competence should come as no surprise. Journalism was the career he had picked out for himself, and he took it seriously. Throughout his life he took a special pride in the fact that he could do just about everything involved in getting out a newspaper, with the exception of printing it.

Encouraged by Nugent and the friendship of his fraternity brothers, Thurber entered enthusiastically into the social life of the campus. He began to take out a number of girls, and one of them, Charme Seeds, reminiscing in the alumni magazine in 1930, remarked that "A considera-ble number of young ladies (who are now matrons) will remember that Jim Thurber was Ohio State's greatest romancer." [44] He and Nugent double-dated frequently, and on at least one occasion Thurber was able to borrow his grandfather's car, so that, as Nugent put it, "we showed some style." Nugent had got Thurber to join The Strollers, the college dramatic society, and he recalls that Thurber proved himself to be "a naturally good actor" from the start. They appeared together in a production of Arnold Bennett's one-act farce *A Question of Sex* in the spring of 1918,[45] and Nugent remembers playing the lead in a one-act spoof of psychoanalysis by Susan Glaspell,[46] which may have suggested a whole area of comic subject matter to Thurber. His first play, *Psychomania,* which he wrote and directed for The Strollers in 1923, was an exploration of the possibilities of the sub-ject,[47] and in *Is Sex Necessary?* (1929) and *Let Your Mind Alone* (1937) he handled it with comic mastery.

Nugent and Thurber also were members of a small student-faculty liter-ary society which called itself "La Boheme" and "met for dinner now and again in an appropriately arty-intellectual setting." [48] Inspired perhaps by this society and by Billy Graves's versification course, Thurber, Nugent, and Ralph McCombs amused themselves throughout the year by compos-ing scandalous triolets and rondeaus for the rather limited audience of the fraternity house. McCombs remembers that one of Thurber's efforts con-tained a stanza that went something like this:

> Never pinch a bulldog's balls
> Even if you're clever;
> Never pinch a bulldog's balls,
> He'll tear your ass from overalls.

[44] *Ohio State University Monthly,* April, 1930.
[45] "Strollers," *Makio* (Ohio State University Yearbook), 1918.
[46] Nugent, *Events Leading Up to the Comedy,* p. 70.
[47] "Strollers Christmas Plays," *Ohio State University Monthly,* January, 1923.
[48] Ralph McCombs letter to CSH, July 14, 1966; Nugent, "Brother James Thurber."

Once, testing out the literary expertise and alertness of the faculty censor
of the *Sun-Dial,* Thurber submitted under his own name this stanza from
a well-known Housman poem:

> Aye, lad, I lie easy,
> I lie as lads would choose;
> I cheer a dead man's sweetheart.
> Never ask me whose.

As Thurber remembers it, the stanza was "promptly and sternly rejected." [49]

The climax of Thurber's personal career at Ohio State was his election
to Sphinx, the senior honorary society. This distinction was generally reserved for men who were considered to be "leaders in campus activities,"
and Thurber's membership in a good fraternity, his reputation as a wit,
his editorship of both the newspaper and the magazine, his election to
Sigma Delta Chi, the honorary journalism fraternity, and his activity in
The Strollers constituted an impressive set of credentials. Nugent recalls
that on Link Day, when the graduating members of the society met on
the steps of University Hall to choose the new men from the junior class,
Thurber was nowhere in sight, although everyone was sure that he would
be elected. With characteristic diffidence he was lurking back of the shrub-
bery so that if he was not chosen he could make a quiet get-away. But his
name was called, and when he marched up to join the others, he was, as
Nugent says, a very different person from the shy unknown boy of two years
earlier: "He was now one of the 'Big Men in School.' " [50]

During his last two years of college, Thurber did a good deal of writing
for the *Lantern* and the *Sun-Dial,* almost all of it anonymous. In a nostalgic
moment some years later, he went through the November, 1917, issue of
the *Sun-Dial* and identified the authorship of many of the pieces. [51] About
half of them are his, and from this sample one can see the sort of thing
he was trying out as a university humorist. The *Sun-Dial* was typical of the
college humor magazines of the time, featuring cartoons, two-line jokes,
squibs about professors, light verse and miscellaneous satirical pieces.
Thurber tried his hand at every form within this prescribed framework—he
is editorialist, jokesmith, paragrapher, cartoonist, and poet, and it is obvious
that he relishes this chance to develop as many different skills as possible.
His literary manner ranges from bouncy undergraduate irreverence to the

[49] Letter to Pollard, June 28, 1960.
[50] Nugent, *Events Leading Up to the Comedy,* pp. 71–72.
[51] This copy is among Helen Thurber's papers.

Babbitt-like rhetoric of small-town boosterism which used to flourish in communities like Columbus two generations ago.

Many of Thurber's contributions to the *Sun-Dial* are mere formula stuff, but many show him trying out material and styles he was to use later. The November issue opens with an editorial salute to the football team which shows Thurber in the role of sports buff, booster, and Babbitt:

> ONE LAST CHEER. Long ere this greets the eye, the captains and the coaches have departed, and not only all is over but the shouting, but that is almost over too, due to hoarseness and general inability to give one more chirp for Ohio, the greatest old state and the greatest old football team in the west. . . . You got to hand it to the team . . . and you got to hand it to Coach Wilce. . . . Their names shine brightly carved in indelible ink on the granite pages of Ohio's pillars of marble!

This Babbitt style, a combination of journalistic bathos and Rotarian values, is especially strong in Thurber's "Credos and Curios" column in 1923; after he leaves Columbus in 1924 he seems to shed it, like an old skin.

Next is a page of paragraphs, adapting the manner and the form of Ryder's editorial page to the university scene. For example: "From observation we can say that nothing gets a tired business man so het up as to come home from work all fagged, get into his slippers and smoking jacket, pick up the evening paper, go over to his favorite chair,—and sit down on a ukelele." The staple of humor magazines like the *Sun-Dial*, of course, was a barrage of jokes of all kinds and descriptions. Few of them will add to Thurber's stature as a humorist, but some examples will help to illustrate the sort of thing he was practicing at Ohio State. He specialized in puns: "Lorraine—'Does he scintillate?' Lorry—'Till eight? He sins all night.' " A series of gloomy epigrams suggests something of the comic pessimism and economy of phrase characteristic of Thurber's later work: "Success is wind blowing over a burnt finger," "Friendship is a cigar made of iron," "Happiness is the coffee that conceals the castor oil," and so on.

Most of the drawings are by various members of the art staff, but one in the November issue is Thurber's, and it deserves a brief comment since it is one of Thurber's first published appearances as a cartoonist and because it is so different in style from the drawings which brought him fame on *The New Yorker*. Here, instead of the bold simplification and spontaneity of his later manner, is a careful, rather self-consciously arty representation of two figures seated in chairs before an old-fashioned fireplace and mantel-piece. The point of the drawing is a careful stylizing which makes the back of one chair look like a large human face and the human figures like pieces of interior decoration. Another Thurber drawing, in the December issue, carries this conception even farther, placing two figures in armchairs on an elaborately patterned rug, so that the figures are barely perceptible presences in the exotic overall design. Both drawings are elaborately shaded and cross-hatched, and have more than a little of art nouveau about them, suggesting that Thurber's cartoons were not as accidental, primitive, and "natural" as he liked to imply. Some of his drawings, however, do anticipate his later subject matter and style. In one, a cave woman is dragging a man by the hair, and the figures are represented in the highly simplified child-like fashion of his later work. Thurber was a much more sophisticated artist than he liked to admit (he had, after all, been drawing since he was seven years old), and these *Sun-Dial* sketches show him in the process of experimenting with different styles of representation.

In his verse, Thurber tried out a variety of modes, ranging from light verse to romantic love lyrics and on to rather obvious imitations of Henley and other popular literary models. "Reincarnation," for example, in the November, 1917, issue, blends an exotic setting and a swinging anapestic movement in the manner of popular nineteenth-century poetry:

> A million suns have shone
>   And a million moons have died
> Since I was a soldier with Cortez
>   And you were the Aztec bride.

Sometimes the imitation is more self-conscious. His hero-worshipping tribute to Columbus's own demi-god, the football player Chic Harley, owes
a good deal to the music of Poe's "The Raven":

> Out there, where madly smashing,
> Two teams are fiercely clashing,
> There comes a sudden dashing
> Blur of gray.
>
> Then a scarlet streak is flashing
> And the foemen's teeth are gnashing
> And the stands like waves are lashing,—
> Chic's away!

The most successful pieces in the November issue, however, are two
nonsense poems. In the first, "When the Linotyper Falls in Love," Thurber
plays with a formal device and a theme which he was to use with great
success in later years—the garbling of a famous quotation (a species of
parody) and the breakdown of sense into nonsense (a glimpse into the
potential chaos behind familiar appearances):

> Tell me not in mournful muxbuz
>   Life is but an excvt bewtrpfg
> For the soul of dzzftt that spblizt
>   And rubguppfg are not what they zboomwhoops.

In the second, "Poems of a Temperament," he draws on Lewis Carroll,
always one of his primary sources of comic inspiration, for the nice incongruity between the rambling, shaggy-dog anecdote told by the dim-witted
narrator and the implied order of the poetic form:

> Once upon a time,
> I forget now when
> I heard a father growl,
> Growl, "go, my son, and shoot me an owl—
> Shoot me an owl."
> And answered the son,—
> I forget just when,—

The son the father had,
Had, "Oh, my father, it's too bad,
Indeed too bad."
Just what he meant
I forget me now,
But I knew it once,
I forget it now—
No. By Jove, I have it sure,
   And four more lines to boot,—
He meant that in the neighborhood
   There were no owls to shoot.

There are no lost masterpieces in the *Sun-Dial*, but within the rather special limits of the form there are a number of interesting experiments: Thurber is trying to learn the art of paragraphing as practiced by Robert O. Ryder of the *Ohio State Journal*, he is sharpening his skills as imitator and parodist, trying out a number of different styles in prose, verse, and drawing, and he is discovering subjects and themes of potential comic value. Taken as a whole, the years at Ohio State were an important stage in Thurber's personal development. In many ways, the university atmosphere was stultifying, but men like Taylor and Denney were liberating forces, broadening his intellectual horizons and introducing him to a wider and more exciting world than that generally recognized by Columbus. Under their direction he discovered some of the great writers of the past and present, and began to establish the bases of his own literary taste and standards. In addition, the university gave him a chance to write—from his freshman course in paragraph writing to his editorship of the *Sun-Dial*. And finally, his friendship with Elliott Nugent emancipated him as a person, freeing him from the fears and self-doubts of 1913, and giving him the confidence and social poise he so desperately needed.

3

Paris: 1918–20

THURBER LEFT OHIO STATE in June of 1918. He did not graduate, since he was still minus a number of required credits; but he was restless and anxious to go with the rest of the boys his age. His one eye and flat feet kept him out of military service, and so he applied for a clerkship with the State Department. President William Oxley Thompson, by this time moderately well acquainted with Thurber and his problems, wrote a good letter of recommendation, noting that Thurber was "selected by the Sphinx Society . . . which selection may be taken as the student judgment as to his all around quality and standing as a student," and adding that "he has made a creditable record through the three years in the University." [1] In June, Thurber went to Washington for training as a code clerk, and in November of 1918 he was one of four candidates out of sixty chosen for duty at the embassy in Paris.[2]

During the summer he explored Washington in his spare time and wrote long letters to his family and friends from the Post restaurant, where he was in the habit of dropping in for coffee and a smoke late at night. Nugent was at home in Dover, Ohio, waiting for orders to report to the Great Lakes Naval Training Center, and the two began a close and intimate correspond-

---

[1] Letter of June 14, 1918, from President Thompson to the Honorable Breckenridge Long, Third Assistant Secretary of State, Washington, D.C. (Thurber Collection).
[2] Ruth White, "James Thurber," March 17, 1940.

ence which continued over the next four years. Thurber's letters are immensely revealing. They are long, detailed, confessional outpourings on life and love (especially on love) and books and dreams and all the things that one young man wants to confide to another. Their style is a mélange of the colloquial, the laboriously humorous, and the self-consciously literary. Writing to his best friend about things closest to his heart, he drops the mask of self-irony with which he generally faced the world, and shows just how romantic, sentimental, idealistic, and emotionally immature he really was at the age of twenty-four. The romantic strain in his nature was always significant, but in his professional work, particularly as he matured, he was able to view it with detachment and to capitalize on its comic possibilities; here, unburdening himself to Nugent, he shows it in all its adolescent innocence.

The main topics of the letters written during the summer of 1918 are his intense affection for Nugent and his romantic involvement with two girls at once. Something of Thurber's immaturity can be seen in the extravagance with which he sometimes addresses Nugent: asking for advice about his love life, he calls him, half kidding, half romanticizing, Don Juan, Lothario, Pythias, Romeo, Cyrano de Bergerac, berry-gatherer;[3] and later, thanking Nugent for a reassuring answer to a troubled letter, he says that he has given his heart to his friend, and that Nugent is a great white star in his firmament.[4]

But the full intensity of his adolescent romanticism is revealed in his long-continued account to Nugent of his love for Eva Prout and Minnette Fritts. The facts of the story make it clear that he was more in love with love than with either of the ladies involved. Eva Prout was the pretty girl with the beautiful contralto voice for whom he had conceived an intense schoolboy passion in the seventh grade. She had left town shortly thereafter, and had had a successful career in vaudeville, the movies, and musical comedy. She retired because of ill health at the age of twenty-five and settled down with her mother in Zanesville. Thurber had not seen her since her eighth-grade departure from Columbus, but over the years she had become for him the quintessence of romance, the dream girl, the beauty that is unattainable. She was the "sweetheart wraith" of the poem he wrote for one of his last issues of the *Sun-Dial* in 1918: [5]

> I held her in my arms,
> This one at present dear,

[3] Letter to Nugent, July 16, 1918 (Thurber Collection).
[4] Letter to Nugent, December 17, 1919 (Thurber Collection).
[5] Letter to Nugent, August 25, 1918 (Thurber Collection).

And there came from out the past
Your vision clear.

The human touch is strong
But close and warm as faith
Clings the memory of you,
My sweetheart wraith.

There had been a sporadic exchange of letters during Thurber's second year in college, but in 1918 he still had not seen her since schooldays. Describing her to Nugent, he fashions her out of the materials of his imagination: her beauty is the beauty of Helen of Troy and of the Helen in Poe's famous poem, and her voice is the voice of Keats's nightingale.[6] In another letter, like a Don Quixote creating his Dulcinea, he describes her as he imagines her to be: she will have rich, chestnut brown hair, and she will be dressed in blue, he says, confessing that he has always found the attractive power of pretty dark-brown-haired girls in trim Navy blue suits almost irresistible.[7]

His rhapsodic accounts of his feelings about Eva are sometimes accompanied by revealing self-appraisals. In one, he contrasts his schoolboy personality with his new-found college identity. When he was in grammar school and wearing short pants he was nothing but a grind and a teacher's pet, he says bitterly; now, his friend Gleeson McCarty has met Eva in Zanesville and given her an enthusiastic account of him as not a sissy but a regular fellow. His new sense of worth shows through at the end of the letter, where he tells Nugent that ten years ago he knew that Eva was the center of everything for him, and now that he is a big man in Sigma Delta Chi he is as sure of it as ever.[8]

At the same time that he was breathing new life into his dream of Eva, he was becoming more and more involved with the actual in the person of Minnette Fritts, an attractive, intelligent, and popular Columbus girl whom he had taken to the 1917 Phi Psi Christmas dance. Nugent had warned him not to get serious, since she liked to play the field, but a chance meeting in June led to a series of dates, moonlight drives along the Scioto, and all the stage properties of romance, complete with what Thurber ruefully described as his dampness of temperament and imbalance. The result, somewhat to his surprise, was an exchange of pledges, and after his departure for Washington, a steady stream of love letters. He supposed they

[6] Letter to Nugent, July 16, 1918 (Thurber Collection).
[7] Letter to Nugent, October 15, 1918 (Thurber Collection).
[8] Letter to Nugent, August 25, 1918 (Thurber Collection).

were engaged, he wrote Nugent in July, 1918, obviously a bit taken aback at the intensity of the response he had aroused and at the speed with which events had moved.[9] A few weeks later, however, he has convinced himself that he is in love with both Minnette and Eva, and is clearly fascinated by his dilemma. He loves Minnette's cleverness and spirit; she represents the ideal of woman as friend and companion. Eva, on the other hand, stands for passion, impossible dreams, and Shelleyan visions.[10] Over the next two years, until this particular dream of romance was finally corrected by contact with reality, he saw the two girls in terms of these opposing principles—Minnette, the girl of reason (and later, of Henry James); Eva, the heroine in the movies, the girl of dream and romance.[11]

The letters to Nugent show, as nothing else could, how little of the world Thurber knew just before he went to Europe in 1918, how adolescent his inner life still was, how dependent it was on models derived from his reading. Like most boys of his region and generation, his emotional life was shaped by the forms and language of late Victorian sentimentalism, particularly the cult of Ideality. It was not until *Is Sex Necessary?* (1929) that he was able to view these stereotypes as comic and to destroy them through mockery.

Thurber was originally appointed to the American legation at Berne, but at the last minute his assignment was changed, because of the flu epidemic in Switzerland, and in November of 1918 he was posted to the embassy in Paris. He sailed on the troopship *Orizaba*, which took twelve days to zigzag across the Atlantic. When they landed at Saint Nazaire, on a cold grey morning, the first things Thurber saw—fresh from Columbus, with his head full of Henry James—were a detachment of German prisoners being marched along, "without expression in their eyes, like men coming from no past and moving toward no future," and "a young pink-cheeked French army officer" dismounting from his bicycle and entering a brothel.[12]

Thurber arrived in Paris without any baggage. The *Orizaba*, not being organized to handle civilian effects, had managed to lose both his trunk and suitcase. The suitcase arrived in April, and the trunk several months later, everything in it thoroughly impregnated with melted Hershey bars. With one year of Ohio State French to guide him, Thurber had to equip himself with a new wardrobe. His comic-opera efforts to get a suit at "a

[9] Letter to Nugent, July 16, 1918 (Thurber Collection).
[10] Letter to Nugent, September 15, 1918 (Thurber Collection).
[11] Letter to Nugent, March 25, 1920 (Thurber Collection).
[12] "The First Time I Saw Paris," *Alarms and Diversions* (New York: Harper & Brothers, 1957), p. 7.

shop deceptively called 'Jack, American Tailor,' " and his failure to find a hat are the subjects of two of his best sketches in "Credos and Curios," the weekly column he did for the Columbus *Dispatch* in 1923.[13]

His embassy duty, as he recalled it years later, was not arduous, consisting of coding and decoding messages like this: TEMEC JKRM THGB BJPL ERWO IKYWE. The codes were simple affairs, "dating back to the time when Hamilton Fish was Secretary of State, under President Grant, and they were intended to save words and cut telegraph costs, not to fool anybody." [14] There were moments which taxed the resources of the staff, however, like the message which included the baffling phrase "Pause City." It was not until Thurber, his imagination already responsive to the challenge of word games, suggested that they try "paucity" that the dispatch yielded up its meaning.[15]

Describing the experience twenty-five years later, in "Exhibit X," Thurber saw his very presence in Paris as an example of the unreliability of the State Department code and the infinite possibilities of verbal confusion. On arrival in Paris, he found himself one of fifteen newly arrived code clerks assigned to Colonel House at the Hotel Crillon, the headquarters of the American Peace Delegation. Colonel House, it turned out, did not want even one code clerk, let alone fifteen, and the whole group was put to work at the embassy. Thurber's theory was that Colonel House had cabled Washington requesting twelve or fifteen code books, not code clerks. "The cipher groups for 'books' and 'clerks' must have been nearly identical, say 'DOGEC' and 'DOGED,' and hence a setup for the telegraphic garble. Thus, if my theory is right, the single letter 'D' sent me to Paris, when I had originally been slated for Berne." [16]

He was in Paris from November of 1918 until March of 1920. This first encounter with a city and a country which were to mean much to him in later years made a profound impression on the young Midwesterner fresh from Professor Taylor's English novel course. His letters to Nugent are full of enthusiastic responses to the romance and excitement of the Parisian scene, but he captured it best thirty-five years after the event, in "The First Time I Saw Paris," one of his finest memory pieces. In his mature imagination, Paris was the "City of Light and of occasional Darkness, sometimes in the winter rain seeming wrought of monolithic stones, and then, in the days of its wondrous and special pearly light, appearing to float in

[13] "Credos and Curios," May 27, 1923, and June 3, 1923; also "The First Time I Saw Paris," *Alarms and Diversions*, p. 8.
[14] "Exhibit X," *The Beast in Me*, p. 60.
[15] Ruth White, "James Thurber," March 17, 1940.
[16] "Exhibit X," *The Beast in Me*, p. 62.

mid-air like a mirage city in the Empire of the Imagination. . . ." [17]

He approached it dreaming of "the tranquil, almost somnolent city of Henry James's turn-of-the-century novels," but what he found was a city given over to a compulsive gaiety. "Her heart was warm and gay all right, but there was hysteria in its beat," he recalled. "Girls snatched overseas caps and tunic buttons from American soldiers, paying for them in hugs and kisses, and even warmer coin." [18] The Folies Bergères and the Casino de Paris were unofficial headquarters for the uninhibited Americans. Doughboy French was the new language—" '*Restez ici* a minute,' " a soldier would say to his girl, " '*Je* returny *après cet* guy partirs.' " Every night there was a brawl in which the Americans fought the Australians, the management of the cafés, the gendarmes, or each other. Thurber obviously relished the disorder and excitement, the carnival atmosphere of Paris during those Peace Conference days. It "would have delighted Hadrian, Playboy of the Roman Empire, who enjoyed colorful spectacles brought together from the corners of the world," he said.

The strangeness and incongruity of the American presence in the French setting fascinated Thurber. The area around the Avenue d'Iéna and the Rue de Chaillot was the American quarter—the chancellery of the embassy, where Thurber worked with his code books, was at 5, Rue de Chaillot; on the Place des Etats-Unis was the house where Woodrow Wilson stayed, and a statue of Washington and Lafayette shaking hands, and the monument to the Americans who died in the Lafayette Escadrille, the Foreign Legion, and the American Field Service. American Navy Headquarters were near by, and "United States Marines used to play catch and knock out flies in the Place d'Iéna to the amazement of the French populace ('c'est bizarre, ça!'). You could hear 'How Ya Gonna Keep 'Em Down on the Farm?' and 'Mademoiselle from Armentières' and 'Smiles.' Soldiers and sailors, secretaries of the Embassy, stenographers and code clerks made the district as American as Pennsylvania Avenue." [19]

Thurber threw himself wholeheartedly into the exploration of the city and the varieties of experience it offered. He sat at the cafés with the soldiers and the French girls (in one essay he speaks of pursuing his "sociological studies" on the terrace of the Café de la Paix with a French girl who had learned her English from reading Shakespeare), he wandered the boulevards, and he ate at the famous restaurants. He wrote Nugent that

[17] "The First Time I Saw Paris," *Alarms and Diversions*, p. 15.
[18] Ibid., p. 7.
[19] "An Afternoon in Paris," *My World and Welcome to It* (New York: Harcourt, Brace, 1942), p. 250.

he had already been to Voisin's and to the Café de la Paix and the Café de Paris, and that he intended to continue his exploration of the food and wine of France as soon as he accumulated a few more francs.[20] Guidebook in hand, he visited the great monuments. "Notre Dame always lures," he said, and summing up his impressions in a letter to his brother Robert, he concluded that "Paris is easily the most wonderful city in all the world." [21] He explored the villages and countryside around Paris, and he visited the battlefields. The trips to the battlefields were not so much touristic excursions as they were acts of piety. He and another embassy clerk spent days exploring the devastated fields of Soissons and Verdun, and near Soissons they visited the American Marine Cemetery. Thurber sent a snapshot of it home. "It was quiet and sunshiny when we were there, and a hundred birds were singing. I cannot forget nor describe that place," he wrote to his family.[22]

Thurber saw Paris as not only a wider and more varied human scene than that offered by Columbus, but also as the essence of romance, history, and aesthetic values. His letters to Nugent overflow with excited responses to the picturesque charm of the city. From his little balcony he can look through a line of sycamores and watch the colorful traffic on the Seine, only half a block away. There is glamor in the idea that like the poets and art students in the novels of Edith Wharton, he is living in a pension in Paris, but the realities of pension life are somewhat different from the idea, he confesses. Dark old stairways and high windows have a certain charm, but after four months it is hard to find the charm in carrots three times a week and a total absence of running water.[23]

Nevertheless, he is more like one of James's provincial Americans abroad than anything else, thirstily drinking in the beauty of the present scene and the romance of the past. He bought a copy of the New York edition of *The Ambassadors* for five dollars, and read and re-read the book while he was there in Strether country. He wrote to Nugent that James had become his greatest literary enthusiasm, and that James's art, his ideas, and his values had affected him profoundly.[24] In the spring of 1919 he was dating Charme Seeds, a former Ohio State girl now in the Red Cross, and he described their evenings together in terms of Jamesian romance: they had tea and cakes in the attractive garden of her hotel in the Latin Quarter, and a duck dinner at the Tour d'Argent, where, he reminds Nugent,

[20] Letter to Nugent, March 20, 1919 (Thurber Collection).
[21] Letter to Robert Thurber, May 31, 1919 (Thurber Collection).
[22] Letter to Robert Thurber, April 9, 1919 (Thurber Collection).
[23] Letter to Nugent, March 20, 1919 (Thurber Collection).
[24] Letter to Nugent, April 4, 1920 (Thurber Collection).

Strether and Mme. de Vionnet dined together.[25] And when he toured Normandy in September of 1919, he saw it through the eyes of one of James's passionate pilgrims to the Old World. The pervasiveness of the sense of the past excited him: everything in Normandy is old and rich in history, he wrote Nugent; there are old country houses, old castles, old abbeys, old cathedrals, and even Roman ruins. At the famous church of St. Ouen the beautiful galleries, the stained glass, the play of candlelight, and the figures of the old women kneeling at prayer seemed an incarnation of the romance of the medieval past.[26]

Thurber's identification with the Jamesian character and experience went deeper than a simple response to the charm of the Old World culture, however. Like Strether, his favorite Jamesian protagonist, he felt the pull of both worlds. In a letter to Nugent of March, 1919, the aesthetic lure of Paris is countered by the plain wholesome virtues of Columbus. He acknowledges that Paris is wonderful, fabulous, the center of art, literature, culture, everything to excite the mind and the imagination. But it is (as Henry James feared) too worldly and sophisticated, too pagan in its values. Parisian morals are unthinkable for Americans, he says. All his Midwestern prudery comes out in a tribute to American sexual purity: the American soldier has been brought up to respect and worship the clean American girl, and the temptations of Paris have not kindled any base passions in American breasts, he asserts with more than a little defensiveness. He follows this with a passage full of the stereotypes of nineteenth-century nationalism which so many Americans took abroad with them in that more innocent time: the contrast between our soldiers in Paris and the soldiers of other countries makes you love America, he says, because Americans are more youthful, open, high-spirited, happy, and vigorous than the people of any other country.[27]

At this moment, in the spring of 1919, he is sure that he wants to come home. Writing to his brother Robert, he says, "I think I have seen enough of Paris. . . . there are more things to go back for than to stay for. My heart is in Ohio." [28] And to Nugent he writes that he wants to go back to Ohio State and take some courses—particularly Cooper's drama course —and to make some decisions about his future.[29] But in June of 1919 he has changed his mind. He will stay in Paris as long as he can, he says, and he confesses to Nugent that the spell of the city will be hard to break. It

[25] Letter to Nugent, June 11, 1919 (Thurber Collection).
[26] Letter to Nugent, September 24, 1919 (Thurber Collection).
[27] Letter to Nugent, March 20, 1919 (Thurber Collection).
[28] Letter to Robert Thurber, April 9, 1919 (Thurber Collection).
[29] Letter to Nugent, March 20, 1919 (Thurber Collection).

is every bit as irresistible as dear old Henry James said it was. The summer concerts in the Tuileries, with the orchestra playing selections from *Madame Butterfly* and *Thaïs*, while the moon spreads its soft light over the formidable presence of the Louvre, are the quintessence of romance. But at the same time he hears the call of Columbus and the voice of conscience. He must go back and get started on a career, he says, something difficult to think about while one is in Paris.[30]

Throughout these letters of 1919 to Nugent, Thurber sees the conflict between the two worlds in strictly Jamesian terms—Europe represents romance, beauty, the larger life (including immorality); Columbus stands for reality, duty, moral soundness. One of the problems of living abroad is that it upsets one's old certainties. By September, Thurber is sure that he wants to stay, but he is aware of the ambiguities of his situation. Life in Paris is great, he says, but it is also confusing. Specifically, he is experiencing a disturbing loss of self-confidence. In part, this was a consequence of the general reassessment of values which Paris forced upon him, but it had chiefly to do with his doubts about his future career. Nugent had written that he was working on a play, and this news prompted Thurber to think about his own talent as a writer. He too has been trying to put together some ideas for a play, but he confides—with remarkable prescience—his fear that his range will not extend beyond the limits of the short sketch. The realization that it is one thing to write for the Ohio State *Sun-Dial* and quite another to put that talent to the test in the world at large requires a kind of realistic self-examination hardly possible in the setting of Paris, he says.[31]

Generally speaking, the letters to Nugent show Thurber's aesthetic side and reveal more of his inner life; his letters to his family show his Columbus side, and have more to do with sports, popular songs, and Columbus friends than with the meaning of his European experience. The difference between the two ways in which he looked at things is neatly pointed up in his account to his brother Robert of the same date with Charme Seeds he described in his letter to Nugent. Here, no references to Henry James, no overtones of cosmopolitanism dress up his breezily colloquial account. Charme was "one of the most popular girls in the whole daggone campus in her day, and is yet for all of that," he says. "So I grabbed the afternoon off and we buzzed out to her place, a Red Cross hotel in the Latin Quarter, and there we had tea in a very pretty garden, and cakes and marmalade and a long talk about the people at State and things back on the old campus

[30] Letter to Nugent, June 11, 1919 (Thurber Collection).
[31] Letter to Nugent, September 24, 1919 (Thurber Collection).

in general. She certainly is a dandy girl to know, and I am glad that she presented herself." [32]

His brother Robert, who had the historian's instinct for the significant detail, supplied him with long, detailed accounts of family and community life, newspaper clippings, theater programs, lists of popular songs, and so on. Thurber's delight in what he called "Robert's Weekly Journal and Log Book of Ohio" is obvious: "The past three days have been quite crowded with joy, for your very wonderful letter-newspaper-history-dissertation-drama and comedy arrived," he begins one letter, and goes on to report that he has bought a French mandolin and can now "tear off 'D.T.S. Ball' and 'Smiles' perfectly with regular jazz time." [33]

His letter to his brothers Robert and William describing the Interallied Games in June, 1919, shows how strong the tastes, prejudices, attitudes and values of his Columbus background really were. The letter is full of the Thurber family passion for sport. The games are "the biggest thing going on at the present time" and Thurber promises to see as many events as he can, so that on his return home he can stand cross-examination "by the former captain of the EHS baseball team." He indulges in a little purple prose—rare in his letters home—as he describes the colorful effect of the flags of many nations playing over Pershing Stadium: the "silk new flags of all the allied nations whip the air into a scrambled rainbow effect. . . . So that the stadium is like a huge kettle into which some Giantess of a witch with a savages [sic] appetite for bright colors, had dumped twenty different kinds of material and fifty different dyes, stirred them up in the middle and then tossed them with a big stick around the field, onto the flag staffs, into the stands 'n' everywhere." This is the splashy romantic sort of style he admired in Hergesheimer and which he affected on occasion until he began to write for *The New Yorker*. His Midwestern provincialism shows itself in his smug report that "in all five heats of the 200 meter dash, the only English speaking runners entered in each event took the first places every time. . . . The Anglo-Saxon stuff gets there." Americans are just naturally better at everything, even at making whoopee: "Whenever there is anything to celebrate here . . . the Americans always do the most and the loudest and the fastest and the peppiest stunts of all the rest put together." Sounding like a character out of Sinclair Lewis, he concludes that "Of all the nations of the earth, the Yanks easily lead in the matter of pep and enthusiasm, endurance and gogettem stuff." [34]

[32] Letter to Robert Thurber, May 31, 1919 (Thurber Collection).
[33] Letter to Robert Thurber, April 9, 1919 (Thurber Collection).
[34] Letter to Robert and William Thurber, June 25, 1919 (Thurber Collection).

In the winter of 1919–20 the various American missions abroad were cutting down on staff, packing up their papers, and getting ready to come home. Thurber was released in February of 1920, and he went back to Columbus, uncertain whether to go back to school or look for a job. Some of his friends from Ohio State tried to get him to join them in the advertising business in Detroit, but he refused to give up his literary ambitions. Shortly after his return he wrote Nugent that although he had no specific plans as yet, he was determined to make his way as a writer. It was that or nothing, he said, and he intended to strike hard, to keep at it, and to try for the big things, however long it might take him. He recognizes that he has no guarantee of success or even of talent, but he says that he feels an inner confidence which he is sure will grow as he grows and develops.[35] It is a prophetic statement, and it shows that at some deeper level than that of the conscious mind, Thurber knew himself and his potentialities better than he realized. He *did* have the necessary determination, he *did* develop slowly and surely, and it was his long-accrued self-confidence which enabled him to survive the shock of blindness and to continue his career as a writer in spite of his handicap.

Nevertheless, the spring of 1920 was an uncertain time for Thurber, made all the more so by the fact that Nugent's prospects looked so bright—he already had a comedy under option to a New York producer, and he was obviously on the threshold of getting some good parts as an actor. Thurber, on the other hand, was beset by self-doubts, and his letters to Nugent during this period show him taking stock of himself, assessing the value of his recent experience, and trying to look ahead to the future. Running through these letters is a frank concern over his own temperament. Writing from Paris in September of 1919, he had confessed that throughout his life he had been subject to spells of melancholy and depression, dark moments in which it was hard to summon up the will to keep going.[36] Back in Columbus, he refers somewhat guardedly to having had a bad time of it with his nerves in Paris, and he describes himself as just pulling out of a period of mental and physical near-wreck.[37] So acute was his fear of this dark side of his temperament that he told Nugent that he had decided not to have any children, because they might inherit the nervous instability which ran in the Thurber family.[38] Nevertheless, he is sure that he has grown and matured since leaving the university in June

[35] Letter to Nugent, March 25, 1920 (Thurber Collection).
[36] Letter to Nugent, September 24, 1919 (Thurber Collection).
[37] Letter to Nugent, March 25, 1920 (Thurber Collection).
[38] Letter to Nugent, April 4, 1920 (Thurber Collection).

of 1918. He is more of a man than the erratic, dreaming Jamie of college days ever was, he says, and in spite of occasional relapses, he is confident that he is at last on the road to balance and sanity.[39]

Like so many Americans of his generation, he had his first sexual relationship in Paris. He wrote Nugent that he had a picture of Ninette, a wonderful dancer, and memories of Remonde of Provins, the pretty French girls with whom he had taken his first steps aside. He had no regrets, he said, but he obviously saw himself as having escaped from a dangerous period of dissipation. He described it to Nugent as a whirl which whirled so fast that he had to get home to save himself. He recalls a scene in Ninette's Montmartre apartment, in which she warns him that at the rate he is going he will last about two weeks, and he, lighting his Pall Mall and offering his glass for some more Porto, replies with elegant world-weariness that on the contrary, he will last all of ten days. Here, in spite of his misgivings about the pace of his life in Paris, Thurber clearly enjoys playing the unaccustomed role of man of the world.[40]

Eva Prout, however, was still the incarnation of romance for him, the girl of his dreams. Soon after he returned from France he visited her in Zanesville and came away even surer than before. He wrote to Nugent that she had depth, poise, cleverness, and stability, and that, incredibly, she preferred him to a good-looking Beta who wore the D.S.C. Sounding something like a twentieth-century Cyrano, he added that it was his letters, the expression of his inner self, which moved the lady to choose him over the handsome war hero.[41] But less than two weeks later, after Eva and her family had visited the Thurbers in Columbus, he came to think that Eva was not the girl of his dreams after all, and that he had been in love with an image so ideal that no one could live up to it. Face to face with the actual girl, he found her not quite so beautiful as he remembered, her voice not so thrilling, her personality sweet and comfortable rather than glamorous.[42] In 1918, he admits to Nugent, all he wanted was moonlight and honeysuckle, but now he is looking for a wider basis for a relationship—and having some difficulty finding it. As a matter of fact, his eye is on a couple of other girls at the moment: he has just met a girl at Wurlitzer's Victrola store whose image may stay in his mind for a day or two, and he has run into Marion Poppen (on whom he has had a silent crush for years) looking attractive in a tight bodice decorated with a spray of sweet peas. The

[39] Letter to Nugent, March 25, 1920 (Thurber Collection).
[40] Letter to Nugent, April 4, 1920 (Thurber Collection).
[41] Letter to Nugent, March 25, 1920 (Thurber Collection).
[42] Letter to Nugent, April 4, 1920 (Thurber Collection).

memory of his love for Eva never left him, however, and in the first short story he published in *The New Yorker*, "Menaces in May" (1928), he wrote about Eva and himself, investing the story with the romantic yearning and the sense of loss which were the essence of his feelings about her.

That same spring he gave up his dream of love with Minnette Fritts, who had in the meantime got married and moved to Chicago. Their romance was only the ephemeral product of May dances, college days, and June nights, he wrote to Nugent; their real relationship, he says, was an intellectual communion, a sympathy of interest best exemplified in the novels of Henry James. He has seen her on one of her visits to Columbus, and he describes their friendship in the language of the Master: when he and Minnette are together, it is like walking into one of James's cool old churches or into the neatly ordered gardens of his fine communions; their friendship has the fineness of art and the serenity of peace; she counts him her Great Friend, and he counts her his; their understanding of one another is a thing of fine proportion, and when he leaves her it is with horizons raised and doors opened. To sum it up, it is just the thing James would have Maria Gostrey call "wonderful." [43]

Thurber's commitment to James at this stage of his life is so complete that he looks at everything through Jamesian eyes—even himself. Telling Nugent the story of his involvement with Eva, he insists on the Jamesian quality of this relationship as well, and casts himself in the role of one of James's "poor sensitive gentlemen." James was a connoisseur of the special case, he says; what happens to the central characters in such stories as "The Jolly Corner," "The Friend of the Friends," "The Altar of the Dead," and "The Beast in the Jungle" could happen to only one person in a million. To the average reader, these Jamesian characters are too frail, too attenuated, to be believable, he says, but he finds them perfect images of himself, both in the uniqueness of their experience and in their quality of thought. Unfortunately, the Jamesian fineness is paid for by a special liability to pain and heartbreak; therefore, he says, he is both proud and miserable to be a follower after what he calls the great god James.[44] Here, Thurber is obviously seeing himself in terms of social timidity, inner sensitiveness, and a special code of values, and finding encouraging models in James.

One can see Thurber growing up in the letters to Nugent of 1918–20. The Parisian experience is a kind of watershed, marking his first encounter with life away from home, Columbus, and the U.S.A. It enlarged his

[43] Letter to Nugent, March 25, 1920 (Thurber Collection).
[44] Letter to Nugent, April 4, 1920 (Thurber Collection).

imaginative horizons, developed his taste in music, and gave him his first experience with sex. He lasted a little more than a year in the gayest city in the world, he confided to Nugent, and it is an illuminating comment on the mores of fifty years ago that it never occurred to Thurber to question the fact of their virginity until the war came along and threw them into strange and unsettling environments. Perhaps the best index of the emancipating effect upon Thurber of his year and a half abroad is his remark to Nugent that he is planning an article on France versus America which no American magazine would print, because his bias is about sixty-seven to thirty-three in favor of France.[45]

[45] Letter to Nugent, April 4, 1920 (Thurber Collection).

4

Newspaperman: Columbus

I N THE SPRING OF 1920, Thurber got a job as a reporter on the Columbus *Dispatch*, the afternoon paper, for twenty-five dollars a week.[1] His apprenticeship was an exacting one. Norman Kuehner, the city editor of the *Dispatch*, was a demanding taskmaster, hard on all new recruits, and especially hard on college graduates. He was a newspaperman of the *Front Page* school—he cultivated a hardboiled exterior (Thurber says that he had "the aggressive air of a man who would snap 'Buy a watch!' if you asked him what time it was"),[2] and his practiced baiting of the reporters reduced more than one of the female staff to tears, and once goaded a rewrite man to a pitch of homicidal fury. He was aggressively anti-intellectual ("If he ever read a book after becoming city editor he never mentioned it"),[3] and he used to call Thurber "Phi Beta Kappa" until Thurber told him that he hadn't graduated. They got on better after that.[4]

Kuehner's conception of newspapering was shaped by his background as a police reporter: above all, he loved stories of crime, fire, and accident, and he insisted that news stories follow the tight formulas and use the time-honored clichés of journalistic tradition. " 'Write a flowery introduc-

[1] Minderman, "We Knew Him When."
[2] *The Thurber Album*, p. 214.
[3] Ibid., p. 228.
[4] Interview with Robert Vincent, "Thurber Still Dreams of Reportorial Days," Columbus *Dispatch*, November 13, 1959.

tion in the first paragraph,' he told one cub reporter. 'In the second paragraph, tell who, when, where, what, and how. Then, in as few paragraphs as possible, relate the most important details. Write an equally flourishing conclusion. Spend the next five minutes finding the sharpest pair of shears in the office, and cut off the first and last paragraphs. You'll have a helluva good news story.' " [5] He detested literary flourishes even in feature stories, and once when a man turned in a rather flamboyant article, he yelled, " 'This story is in *bloom!*' "

His technique with new reporters was first to ignore them, and then to give them the dullest and most trivial or the virtually impossible assignments. If they survived, they were ready to settle down to the business of getting the news for a city paper. Thurber moved out of the apprentice ranks when he brought back a photograph of a boy who had drowned. The top police reporter had been thrown out by the grief-stricken parents, but Thurber went to the high school principal and got a photograph which would enlarge nicely. Kuehner was pleased, in his grumpy way, and the next day, Thurber found himself given a permanent assignment as City Hall reporter.[6]

It was recognition of a sort—he had passed the tribal ordeal—but the affairs of City Hall failed to stir his imagination. The wrangles of the city council over the streetcar franchise and the gas rate, and the "Who, Where, When, What, Why and How" formula insisted on by Kuehner made him restless and impatient. He was careless about statistics, and once he did a story in which he magnified the municipal debt by six million dollars. Kuehner put a notice on the bulletin board that Thurber would no longer be allowed to deal with sums running into more than five figures.[7] Ruth White, a colleague on the *Dispatch*, remembers Thurber as "sublimely unhappy" in his reportorial role.[8] Nelson Budd, another newspaper friend, reinforces this picture, adding that Thurber was really "too humane, too creative, too big to be a good reporter in the strictest sense."

His best stories, according to Budd, were the impromptu parodies of newspaper accounts of council meetings, fires, and interviews with local citizens with which he used to entertain his fellow reporters at Marzetti's restaurant. Thurber and John McNulty were the central figures in a group of reporters from the three Columbus papers (the *Journal*, the *Citizen*, and the *Dispatch*) which used to gather regularly at Marzetti's to talk shop and

[5] *The Thurber Album*, p. 226.
[6] Ibid., pp. 218–20.
[7] *The Years with Ross* (Boston: Atlantic–Little, Brown, 1959), p. 68.
[8] "James Thurber," March 17, 1940.

entertain one another.[9] Some years later Thurber and McNulty were to make Tim Costello's in New York into a similar gathering place for the writing fraternity. Budd recalls that in these sessions Thurber was able to exercise the gifts of caricature and satire so consistently frustrated by his job as City Hall reporter.

Practical jokes offered another outlet for Thurber's imaginative energy. After the old City Hall burned down (during a council meeting on the local gas rate which Thurber was covering for the *Dispatch*), several city offices were temporarily set up on the second floor of the Public Library building. Bert Killiam, the secretary of the Civil Service Commission, played in a local band and kept his tuba at the office. Leroy Rose, assistant City Clerk, often said, in Thurber's hearing, that what he missed most in their quarters over the library was the brassy clangor of the old fire gong in the City Hall. The possibilities appealed to Thurber's imagination, and on several occasions, he sneaked into Killiam's office and blew a couple of resounding notes on the tuba. The impact on the readers in the library below was all that could be hoped for. After several such episodes, official pressure was brought upon Killiam to store his tuba elsewhere.[10]

At the same time, Thurber was developing his talent for imaginative revelry. When Donald Ogden Stewart, an old Columbus boy, returned to town, already a success as a literary humorist, Thurber was assigned to interview him. These were prohibition days, and Thurber brought with him a gallon jug of something evolved from a secret recipe of a maternal aunt. Stewart's memory of the occasion is understandably cloudy, but he notes that this was possibly one of the few interviews in the history of journalism "which included the repeated singing of 'Down by the Old Mill Stream.'" "Then as always," Stewart remarked recently, "Thurber could remember the exact words of every song." [11] This was a talent which Thurber cultivated as time went on: he was an inveterate late-night-party singer, and he took pride in his repertory of old songs and his ability to remember verse as well as chorus of such standards as "Moonlight Bay" and "Bye, Bye, Blackbird."

As time went on, Thurber managed to break out of the confinement of the City Hall beat. He did his share of human-interest stories, and he wrote to Nugent of his effort to get from a heavy-breasted sorrowing widow with nine children the dreary story of their lives, and he spoke resignedly

[9] Nelson H. Budd, "Personal Reminiscences of James Thurber," *Ohio State University Monthly*, January, 1962, p. 12.

[10] Bob Kanode, "Columbus Still Home to Thurber," Columbus *Dispatch*, June 15, 1950.

[11] Donald Ogden Stewart, "Death of a Unicorn," *New Statesman*, November 10, 1961 (clipping in RTS).

of the difficulty of catering to the tastes of pathos-hungry readers.[12] More to his taste, he contributed brief items to the "observation" column on the editorial page, reviewed occasional movies and plays for H. E. Cherrington, the drama editor, and did feature stories on such notable events as the opening of the James Theater and the dedication of Ohio Stadium. Most important, in 1923, he and the artist Ray Evans were given a half page in the Sunday magazine section to do with as they liked.[13] But these were only crumbs. He wanted to try his hand at fiction and the theater, and besides, he was never really happy with the *Dispatch* as a paper.

The pay was low and the atmosphere unsympathetic. "The *Dispatch* fired lots of people and didn't do much to hold the others. After four years I was still getting $40, the same amount that Milt Caniff was getting after five years. . . . Sayre worked for many months for $10 a week," he recalled with some bitterness in a letter of 1952.[14] Like most newspapermen, he moonlighted to stretch his income—he was Columbus correspondent for the *Christian Science Monitor* (a congenial association, since the *Monitor* liked stories about the literary and academic worlds) and press agent for the Majestic Theater and for Indianola Park. He resented the Philistine standards of Kuehner and Heinie Reiker, the managing editor ("who rewrote and ruined two or three humorous feature stories I did on the *Dispatch*"), and the timid political conservatism of Arthur Johnson, the editor. Thurber lost his Sunday half page when some irate readers from Urbana, Ohio, complained about an item in Cherrington's column, which appeared just above Thurber's. Robert Wolfe, the owner of the paper, ordered the entire page canceled, and neither Johnson nor Reiker made any effort to protect their writers.[15] More important, Thurber never forgave Johnson for "murdering" his feature story on the big open-air meeting of the Ku Klux Klan in 1922. It was "the best news story I ever wrote," he said, still angry after thirty years, but Johnson, afraid to take a stand on the touchy issue of the Klan, cut it down to "a single, cautious, emasculated paragraph." The rival *Ohio State Journal*, under the talented leadership of Robert O. Ryder, printed a "colorful and accurate story of the meeting." [16] He would have been happier on the *Journal*, where Ryder encouraged young reporters and backed them up on controversial issues. In a letter to his friend Dr. James Pollard, Thurber recalled that Joel Sayre

[12] Letter to Nugent, April 4, 1922 (Thurber Collection).
[13] Ruth White, "James Thurber," March 17, 1940; Baker, "Thurber,"p. 49.
[14] Letter to James E. Pollard, February 9, 1952 (Thurber Collection).
[15] Letter to Pollard, February 9, 1952 (Thurber Collection).
[16] Letters to Pollard, February 5 and February 9, 1952; letter to James Fullington, January 31, 1952 (Thurber Collection); *The Thurber Album*, pp. 314-15.

once did a front-page feature story on the Hallowe'en celebration in downtown Columbus for the *Journal:* "It was an impressionistic piece that Ryder liked . . . but Arthur Johnson would have killed it, and Kuehner snarled, 'This goddam story is—modernistic.' " "Ryder was the editor for me," he concluded, "as he was for Joe [Sayre] and McNulty. . . ." [17] He made several efforts to get on the *Journal* as drama critic, but when he was finally offered the job, the pay was not good enough, and he had to turn it down.

Thurber's feelings about his newspaper days in Columbus were obviously mixed. At the time, he was frustrated and half-resentful, but he was also excited by the challenge of learning his new trade. There was also the pleasure of becoming a member of a lively company of reporters which included such talented people as John McNulty and Joel Sayre, who were his friends and later became important contributors to *The New Yorker.* In later years he tended to look back at the whole experience nostalgically, but the traumatic impact of early exposure to Kuehner remained a permanent part of his memory. In his portrait of Kuehner in *The Thurber Album* he wrote that the anxiety dreams of many Columbus newspapermen still centered in the city room of the old *Dispatch.*

> In one of my own recurring dreams, I am pounding away at a story I can't handle, because my notes are illegible and the type bars make no marks at all on the gray copy paper. The hands of the clock on the east wall of the city room, facing the reporters' desks, are frozen at a quarter after one, fifteen minutes past deadline, and there is a large, amorphous figure just over my right shoulder, standing there gloomily, saying nothing—the ghost of Norman Kuehner.[18]

Thurber kept up his university connections, and soon after his return from France he was active once more in the affairs of the dramatic club, The Strollers, and of the newly formed men's musical show organization, The Scarlet Mask Club. Scarlet Mask modeled itself on the Princeton Triangle, Hasty Pudding, and Mask and Wig clubs, and its shows featured football-player chorus lines, satiric books, and catchy tunes. Thurber saw *'Tain't So,* the first production of the club, in the spring of 1920. It was written by his friend Ralph McCombs, and Thurber found it "very good." He was excited by the possibilities of the organization, and he wrote Nugent about some ideas for future productions, one of which, *The Call,* was to be a Henry James–like piece about mental telepathy, a subject which

[17] Letter to Pollard, January 26, 1952 (Thurber Collection).
[18] *The Thurber Album,* p. 238.

fascinated Thurber throughout his life.[19] Nothing came of the idea, but when McCombs left Columbus later in the year, Thurber became, in the words of one old acquaintance, "playwright-in-ordinary to the club." Over the next four years he wrote (sometimes in collaboration with others) and directed or helped direct five Scarlet Mask productions.[20] Many years later, Thurber credited his experience with the Scarlet Mask shows for his part in the success of *The Male Animal.* When Nugent expressed surprise at his gift for writing playable dialogue, Thurber said, "What he didn't know was that I wrote and directed the annual musical shows for the Scarlet Mask . . . from 1921 to 1924. I acted in them, too. We went on tour with the shows, and as a different member of the all-male cast was drunk every night, I had to jump in as general understudy." [21]

Unfortunately, the books of these old shows have disappeared, but the programs, the music sheets, and the reviews in the local papers give one a pretty good idea of what they were like. Clearly, no masterworks of the musical theater have been lost, but most of them had a lively undergraduate irreverence which local audiences found attractive. *Oh, My! Omar,* staged in the winter of 1920–21, had to do with a reincarnation machine which brings Omar Khayam into a 1921 houseparty attended by such characters as Mary Elton, "a girl of today," Betty Brown, "a little old-fashioned," Professor Jameson, "who knows his Persia," Mrs. Dodson, "who is opposed to parties," and Jazzbo and Jasmine, the Negro servants. Thurber and Hayward Anderson did the book, Richard E. Fidler the music, and Jackson the costumes and sets. Audiences were especially delighted with the Oriental dancing numbers and the songs, among which were "Gypsy Love," "Orientale," "Dream Time," and "Daddy Don't You Love Your Babe No More?"

Many Moons, in the 1921–22 season, received even higher praise. "The book unquestionably sets a high mark for the club, being the work of James Thurber, ex-'19, and easily the cleverest yet written for this undergraduate men's musical organization," said the *Ohio State University Monthly.*[22]

[19] Letter to Nugent, April 4, 1920 (Thurber Collection).
[20] *Oh, My! Omar* (with Hayward Anderson, 1921); *Many Moons* (with W. W. Havens, William Haid, R. E. Fidler and others, 1922); *A Twin Fix* (with Hayward Anderson, 1923); *The Cat and the Riddle,* 1924; *Tell Me Not,* 1925. Thurber also wrote *Nightingale* for the club in 1924, but it is not clear whether or not it was ever produced; there is a typescript of the libretto in the Library of Congress. Morsberger lists Thurber as the author of *Amorocco,* the club's 1926 production, but it is doubtful that he had anything to do with it. Bowden does not list it.
[21] Interview of January 14, 1940 (with whom and where, I cannot say; I have lost my note on this).
[22] February, 1922, p. 19.

The plot dealt with the efforts of the ruler of Polonia to solve his problems through instituting a program of "Jazzing-up Government," with "chorus-girls as ministers and the application of syncopation to affairs of state." Thurber was delighted with the success of the show, and he wrote to Nugent proudly that Billy Graves and others thought it the best Scarlet Mask play yet.[23]

A Twin Fix followed in 1922–23, and received the usual local praise. The program book included a paragraph on Thurber and his accomplishments, along with a photograph showing him neatly dressed, wearing a stiff collar and glasses, and looking rather clerkish. The Cat and the Riddle, in 1924, burlesqued the popular mystery plays—Seven Keys to Baldpate, The Cat and the Canary, The Thirteenth Chair, and so on—and Herman Miller, reviewing it for the Ohio State Lantern, called it the best that Scarlet Mask had ever done. "It is a good book lifted above the level of parody into Thurberlesque by such pixie-pranks of the imagination as the amazing lantern scene, which reads like a page from 'Alice in Wonderland,' " he wrote, in what is probably the first critical comment on the essential quality of Thurber's comic imagination. "Mr. Thurber has proved again his sure dramatic sense and the adeptness of his easy-going pen in the writing of witty dialogue," he added.[24] The musical numbers included "Jazzy Dance of Dixieland," "Creepy Blues," and "It's the Cat," for which Thurber wrote the lyrics. His last Scarlet Mask show was Tell Me Not, in the winter of 1924–25. Prefiguring The Male Animal in a way, the story takes place in the home of a Midwestern college professor, and has to do with the explosive effect of a visit by a French countess into the professor's quiet household. In this, as in most of the Scarlet Mask productions, Thurber also directed the principals.

He was also writing, directing, and acting in plays with The Strollers. For the Christmas program of 1922 he wrote a one-act satire on psychoanalysis called Psychomania which so impressed the reviewer for the Dispatch that he said it deserved a hearing on the professional stage.[25] Here, as in many of these university productions, Thurber is anticipating techniques and areas of subject matter which were to become important in his later work—The Cat and the Riddle is another early example of his fascination with parody, and Psychomania is a preview of his treatment of popular psychology in Is Sex Necessary? and Let Your Mind Alone. Also on the Christmas program were Lord Dunsany's A Night at an Inn, with Thurber

[23] Letter to Nugent, April 4, 1922 (Thurber Collection).
[24] February 5, 1924.
[25] According to the Ohio State University Monthly, January, 1923, p. 11.

and Herman Miller in the starring roles, and a fantasy by Kenneth Sawyer Goodman and Ben Hecht called *The Wonder Hat,* directed by Thurber's new wife, Althea.

Thurber first met Althea Adams at a Strollers Club rehearsal in 1921. Her mother was a member of the Home Economics department at the university and her father was a retired army officer. She was handsome, statuesque, poised and self-confident. She was one of the beauty queens of the campus (in 1922 she was selected a "Rosebud") and she belonged to one of the best sororities, but she was also a person of strong intellectual and artistic interests.[26] In many ways she was the embodiment of F. Scott Fitzgerald's version of the American young man's dream of success and romance—she represented beauty, intelligence, and social position. The only thing she lacked was money. Thurber was ready to fall: in both Eva and Minnette, something had been missing, but in Althea, the two halves of his dream of love, the romantic attraction and the intellectual companionship, seemed to be joined in a single person. Going out with her was a triumph, a form of public recognition that he was a person of consequence. Writing to Nugent about a banquet they had attended together, he devoted more space to reporting what other people said about Althea than to his own feelings about her. Seeing her through other people's eyes (at least in part), he declared enthusiastically that she was more beautiful than starlight on fresh snow, and that she was wonderfully intelligent besides.[27] After an intense courtship, they were married in 1922 and set up housekeeping in an apartment near the university.

In the eyes of some of their friends it was an odd marriage: Althea the campus beauty and Thurber the unkempt newspaperman did not seem to go together. One Columbus acquaintance suggested that in Althea Thurber thought he saw a girl out of Henry James, and that it was Thurber's artistic potential, rather than his everyday personality, which attracted her to him. On another level, marriage to Althea was for Thurber a way of belonging, of becoming a part of the world of attractive and popular people from which he had been excluded until he met Elliott Nugent. Paradoxically, Althea saw in Thurber a way out of Columbus and its limited possibilities. She wanted a more exciting society and a larger life than that offered by the well-brushed young lawyers and businessmen she might have married. In many ways, she *was* a Henry James girl, but she was closer to Kate Croy than to Mme. de Vionnet. Thurber soon must have discovered that there was a difference between a Henry James girl in a book and one

[26] Ruth White, "James Thurber," March 17, 1940; Baker, "Thurber," p. 52; Ralph McCombs, letter to CSH, July 14, 1966.
[27] Letter to Nugent, April 4, 1922 (Thurber Collection).

in the flesh. Althea was not only intelligent and imaginative; she was also strong-minded and ambitious for her husband. She encouraged and helped him, but she pushed him faster than at first he wanted to go. She was also highly competitive and accustomed to occupying the center of the stage. Since stage center was a psychological necessity for Thurber, there was a conflict of egos from the start. For all his admiration of her looks and intelligence, he was intimidated by her, and he became increasingly resentful. Before long, the marriage began to show signs of strain, and in 1934 it ended in divorce.

It was while they were rehearsing for the 1922 Strollers Christmas production that Thurber and Herman Miller became friends.[28] They had known one another during college days, but it was not until they played in *A Night at an Inn* that they began to really appreciate one another. The friendship deepened over the years, and Thurber dedicated *The Thurber Album* to the memory of Miller, whom he called "my oldest and closest friend." Miller was a dynamic, witty, entertaining person, talented as a writer and actor, somewhat sloppy in appearance and inclined to be skeptical of rules and conventions. He and Thurber soon found that they saw things in the same way and stimulated one another as comic observers of the local scene. Miller joined the faculty of the university soon after graduating, and taught in the English and Speech departments from 1920 to 1940, when he resigned to devote his full time to play-writing. His academic credentials were minimal, but some of his colleagues recall that as a conversationalist he was without peer, and that his exchanges with Dean Denney at the faculty club were memorable displays of wit and invention.[29] His real talents lay in these improvised exchanges and in appreciation of the work of others, rather than in his own writing, but Thurber kept encouraging him to write and offered him helpful criticism throughout the years. After Miller's death in 1949, Thurber spoke of his "Henry James awareness," and later, thinking of vanished friends, he said that he missed Miller and Harold Ross and John Mosher (of the early *New Yorker* staff) most of all.[30]

In addition to his work for the *Dispatch* and his theatrical activities, Thurber was full of literary plans. He wrote Nugent in April of 1922 that he was going to settle down to free-lance fiction writing. He wanted to do some stories which would convey the true flavor of American life, he said, and he added that he was toying with a story about college life, featuring

[28] Herman Miller, "Jim Thurber's Life History Sketched," Columbus *Citizen*, December 1, 1940.

[29] Dr. James E. Pollard and Mr. John Fullen to CSH, October, 1966.

[30] Letter to Dorothy Miller, 1957; also "Letter from the States," *Bermudian*, July, 1950.

a mooncalf sort of hero. It would be a parody, written with all the appearance of intense earnestness.[31] Columbus and the everyday life of the Midwest was much on his mind as a literary subject. He had grown up in the tradition of Howells-like realism represented by Ryder's sharp comments on the domestic scene, and now there were the more spectacular examples of *Winesburg, Ohio* and *Main Street.* Writing to Nugent in September of 1922, he said that he had an idea for a play which he hoped to try out on The Strollers the following spring. It would be an honest attempt to represent middle-class family life in Columbus, a city, he added, as typical of America as any city in the country.

He was also thinking about an autobiographical novel set in a Middle Western town which would draw upon his own experiences at the university, in Paris, and in the newspaper world.[32] In 1925, when he went to France to try his hand at fiction, he wrote several chapters of a novel rather similar in conception to his idea for a play, but he abandoned it and never took it up again. Perhaps it was no coincidence that at the time he was churning with ideas for plays and stories about Columbus he had just read Ludwig Lewisohn's *Upstream*, which included a perceptive and hostile picture of Columbus and Ohio State. Lewisohn's picture of the city and the university was cruel but truthful, he wrote Nugent; it was exaggerated here and there, but for the most part it was exactly right, he said, calling it one of the most remarkable commentaries on American life ever written.[33]

During these years of apprenticeship, Thurber's literary reach usually exceeded his grasp. Nothing much came of the plans he confided to Nugent, but he kept on turning out short stories in his spare time, piling up rejection slips from the *American Mercury* and other magazines. He sold his first story, "Josephine Has Her Day," to the Kansas City *Star* Sunday Magazine in March of 1923.[34] It is about a young couple and their little mongrel dog, and while it is the work of an inexperienced writer, it is interesting as his first handling of a subject which he was to make uniquely his own. Thurber's devotion to dogs was one of the enduring passions of his life. He was fond of saying in later years that the world would be better off if it were run by the French poodle rather than by Man. What he saw in dogs generally was a range of qualities he admired in life—courage, loyalty, love, dignity, gentleness, and humor—only simpler, less mixed with

[31] Letter to Nugent, April 4, 1922 (Thurber Collection).
[32] Letter to Nugent, September (no day), 1922.
[33] Ibid.
[34] Letter to Frank Gibney, October 31, 1956; also "Foreword, with Figures," *Thurber's Dogs* (New York: Simon & Schuster, 1955), p. xi.

weaknesses and failings than is the case with humans. When he wrote about dogs he usually managed to stay this side of sentimentality, partly because he saw each dog as an individual, with his own oddities and eccentricities, and partly because he saw the relationship between dogs and humans as inevitably comic. The plot of "Josephine Has Her Day" is a bit strained and improbable, but the details are observed with that blend of sympathy and humor which is one of the marks of his best fiction. Here, for example, Josephine's owner cures her of the hiccups:

> At length Dick knocked the ashes from his pipe determinedly, got out of the car and lifted Josephine down after him. He set her in the road. Then he suddenly leaped at her and barked.
>
> The puppy plunged down into the ditch by the roadside, her ears flatly inside out in abject terror. Dick hurried after her and retrieved a very wet and very muddy Josephine.
>
> "Have you lost your mind?" exclaimed his wife. But Dickinson held up Josephine and examined her carefully. There were no more hiccups.
>
> "By golly," he said, "these home remedies are the goods."

Thurber's most significant writing during his years on the *Dispatch*, however, was his Sunday half-page column, "Credos and Curios," which he did in collaboration with the artist Ray Evans from February 18 to December 9, 1923. It was his professional debut as a writer of humor. The format of "Credos and Curios" owes a good deal to Franklin P. Adams, Don Marquis, and the others who made the newspaper column of forty years ago a vehicle of wit and literate entertainment. These men were sharp observers of the American scene, and in their hands the column became a highly personal miscellany of comment on books and fashions and the oddities of contemporary behavior. "Credos and Curios" follows the formula of Adams's "The Conning Tower," mixing prose and verse, the general and the personal, the light and the serious. A typical issue would contain a column of literary discussion ("The Book End"), or a folksy comment on current manners and mores ("Dad Dialogs"), a brief essay or anecdote, a parody of some sort, poems, a substantial ballast of miscellaneous paragraphs in the manner of Robert O. Ryder, humorous squibs based on silly public remarks, bad writing, or typographical errors, and at least one cartoon (and usually more) by Evans.

"Credos and Curios" is a big step forward in Thurber's development. It is clearly the work of a young writer in the process of finding himself, but in such pieces as "The Menace of the Mystery" or the anecdote about his father's efforts to rid the house of an intruding bat, he shows a quality of comic imagination and a command of style which anticipate his best work. At one time Thurber considered including some of these early columns in a retrospective collection, but he decided against it. "I am reading them with alarm, disbelief, and some small pleasure here and there," he said in a letter. "It was practice and spade-work by a man of 28 who sometimes sounds 19, praises 'clean love' and such books as 'Faint Perfume' and 'If Winter Comes' and practically any play or movie I ever saw, and attacks Cabell, Joyce, Hecht, and Sherwood Anderson." [35]

Most of "Credos and Curios" is "practice and spade-work," to be sure, but one may guess that it was the revelation of his youthful mind and values as much as the apprentice quality of the writing which caused Thurber to reject it so completely. It is full of the tastes and attitudes of the young man from Columbus whose horizons were limited by Midwestern Puritanism on the one hand and the aesthetic tastes of the Genteel Tradition on the other. But this same young man had read Henry James and lived in Paris and wanted to be a writer. It is the unresolved conflict between the provincial values of Columbus and the cosmopolitan values represented by Europe and the literary life which is the center of interest in "Credos and Curios" and which gives this early column a special importance in understanding Thurber.

To speak for Columbus and American middle-class values generally, Thurber invented the character of Dad, whose common-sense values and plain-man idiom regularly assess various forms of affection and folly. Dad is a conservative, measuring contemporary behavior against that of the good old days; he is a comfortable pipe-smoking practical man who prefers his newspaper to books; he is skeptical of whatever cannot be explained "in terms which a credit manager or a councilman could understand."

Dad's common sense is an especially effective weapon against cultural pretension and artiness.

> "Fritz Kreisler has a brilliant technique," said Dad's daughter. "I think that's because he plays foreign pieces," said Dad. "I understand there ain't any at all in 'Suwanee River' for instance. It had to be a tune you can't carry. If there's a de or a couple of las in a song, it more than likely has a lot of technique. Now if it was Suwanee de la Riviera, you could put technique into it, you see. But fortunately it isn't." [36]

[35] Letter to Gibney, October 31, 1956.
[36] "Credos and Curios," Columbus *Dispatch*, March 4, 1923.

The theater is corrupted by the concept—"It's . . . a kind of grand attempt to make table legs look poetic or something," says Dad. "So instead of Othello choking his wife to death he does a dance with a batik scarf whilst a green light plays over the stage."

Dad's language is the perfect expression of his simplistic view of things. It is plain, colloquial, sometimes ungrammatical, but always full of life. It is the language of a culture suspicious of book-learning, but appreciative of good sense and humor. Its effect is generally reductive, redefining the complex, the pretentious or the fancy in terms of the simple, the familiar and ordinary. Dad's language is most effective when it is turned on some form of popular nonsense, as in his attack on the sentimental evasions of tabloid journalism in reporting a crime of passion:

> "The story gets into the papers and is called a 'Romance.' They try to show that 'Love' rises supreme to 'Convention.' The only convention love is actually supreme to is a political convention. The rest have got the drop on it and it's got to behave or end in jail."

Thurber's ear for the vocabulary and the rhythms of Midwestern speech is impressive in this early work. In later years, he would commit himself more and more to dialogue as his primary method (although he would not often return to Dad's folksy idiom), and it is interesting to see him here experimenting with the possibilities of dramatic speech. In the character of Dad, Thurber is trying out a comic point of view and a style long established in the American tradition. The role of the plain man questioning the values of intellectual culture had exercised a strong appeal to American humorists from Seba Smith to Will Rogers, and so the character and language of Dad were—to an extent—ready made. But it was a convention in which Thurber felt at home. Dad, with his simple certainties and his conservatism, represented a way of life and a set of values to which a part of Thurber was deeply committed throughout his life.

The last "Dad Dialog" appeared in the April 15 issue. On April 22, a new department, "The Book End," appeared for the first time, and three weeks later it was moved to a featured left-hand position on the page, where it remained for the rest of the life of the column. In the "Book End" department, Thurber assumes a very different character and set of values from those of Dad; here, he is the arbiter of taste and the defender of literature, art and culture in a Philistine community. In fact, the emphasis of "Credos and Curios" as a whole becomes more and more literary in its last six months. It is full of arguments about modern literature, and it features parodies and imitations and literary jokes and allusions. An occasional feature is the large portrait-sketch of an important literary figure by Evans, with a brief accompanying comment by Thurber. There are portraits of Henry James, Aubrey Beardsley, A. E. Housman, Somerset Maugham, Carl Sandburg and Stacy Aumonier.

From his position as challenger of Columbus values, it is not surprising that he looked upon Mencken and Nathan as champions in the good fight. Their aim, "to dethrone certain false gods of the nation in the interest of art, literature and culture," as he described it, was one to which he himself (at times) aspired, and he spoke admiringly of their attacks on "the Methodist church, the Elks, the Rotary Club, the Klux, the American Legion, luncheon clubs, Owen Davis, Stuart P. Sherman, the courts, God and everything else." He was impressed by the union of buffoonery and seriousness in their work, and noted that their writings showed "the keenest and most comprehensive insight into America . . . that may be found anywhere." His view of their cultural significance is expressed in his defiant statement, ". . . if you do not consider them two of the world's greatest humorists, you are a Babbitt." [37]

When the new student literary magazine, the *Candle*, ran into financial trouble, Thurber devoted the better part of three columns to the cause of culture at Ohio State. The magazine was really too good "to last at the O.S.U. college for football players, Boost Ohioers and stock judging teams." As might be expected, no one was supporting it. "Out of the 8000 students, not more than 150 actually know or care about lyrics or short stories or the novel," he complained. Here, as upon other occasions in the short life of "Credos and Curios," Thurber identifies himself with the aesthetes against the Philistine mass. "These sensitive persons reflect, after all, the lasting . . . vitalities . . . of the land," he wrote in a column on the reading tastes of undergraduates. "The rest are the supernumeraries shouting and murmuring in the off stage regions of Main Street and Zenith and Winesburg."

On the other hand, there was too much Columbus in Thurber for him to repudiate football, Boosterism and Dad's comfortable middle-class tastes. After passing judgment on Ohio State's low preference for football over literature, he quickly reassures the reader that he is as enthusiastic a football fan as anyone ("we give place to no man in our ardor for the game as it is played at Ohio State"), and that what he is pleading for is a balance of interests, a society catholic enough to produce people who like *A Shropshire Lad* as well as Nick Altrock.[38]

[37] "Credos and Curios," Columbus *Dispatch*, August 12, 1923.
[38] "Credos and Curios," Columbus *Dispatch*, October 28, 1923.

The new realism was one of the liveliest literary issues of the day, and Thurber devoted a number of columns to it. He praises Zona Gale's *Faint Perfume* for its "note of idealistic love," which he rather grandiloquently describes as "a fresh rose among the sordid sex stuff that prevails in present day novels, the novels of Hecht and Lawrence and Joyce and Anderson." [39] He expands the point in the following issue in a long, rambling and rather sophomoric effort to prove that the younger generation is "clean" and "incurably romantic," and that "the modern sex era in literature" is the creation of older men like "Hecht and Cabell and Lawrence and Joyce." These are the men responsible for "the preponderance in present day fiction of the introspective, psychopathic probing into . . . physical . . . and mental reactions." The young university writers like Fitzgerald, Dos Passos and Stephen Vincent Benét are full of the "romantic fire," and even the sex irregularities in their work "become radiant with a wistful charm of a delicate idealism." [40]

Thurber's youth and inexperience, his adolescent Puritanism, and his sentimental-romantic taste are painfully obvious here, although it should be noted that his coolness toward Lawrence and Joyce in 1923 foreshadows his disapproval of the "sick" and "morbid" themes of playwrights and novelists in the 1950's. Thurber himself recognized a number of the confusions and overstatements in his essay, and in a later discussion he sharply qualified his repudiation of realism, asserting that it was "the lastingest thing in literature," and that what he really wanted was "realism without dirt." [41]

At times his position is close to that of another Columbus newspaperman and critic, William Dean Howells. Updating Howells's famous theory that the American novel should deal with the smiling aspects of life, since these were the more American, Thurber contended that American writers should not follow the example of Joyce, Lawrence, and other Europeans, since Americans are "cleaner, fresher, less complicated and less 'complexed' " than foreigners. "Pollyannaism grew up in this country because of these facts," he asserts. But at other times, he sees life in very different terms. Noting that "America is filled with sects, orders and societies consecrated . . . to the . . . misapprehension that the whole point and purpose in existing is to exist always in a genial, comfortable . . . or hopeful mood," he points out that in fact "life is mainly depressing and anyone with any sense at all knows it." The great accomplishments always come from those

[39] "Credos and Curios," Columbus *Dispatch*, June 3, 1923.
[40] "Credos and Curios," Columbus *Dispatch*, June 10, 1923.
[41] "Credos and Curios," Columbus *Dispatch*, July 15, 1923.

who have suffered, like Hamlet, Shelley, and Abraham Lincoln. "There is a majesty in melancholy," he says, sounding a little like Melville's Ishmael, and the Ella Wheeler Wilcoxes and Mary Baker Eddys and the Pollyannas are simply "stupid." [42]

Thurber sums up his youthful literary opinions in "A Conversation on Cabell," a dialogue which owes something to the spirit and rhetoric of Mencken: "I like Hergesheimer and Willa Cather and Edith Wharton and Henry James. All my affections run to their sort of thing. . . . One thing further, too: I hate symbolism. Cabell's books are reported to be soggy with it. . . . Whenever I suspect that a character in a play I have been led to believe is an English lord is in reality the Decadence of the British Upper Classes . . . I grope under the seat for my hat. When I find such stuff in a novel I give it to my barber." [43]

The most interesting piece of literary criticism in "Credos and Curios" is "The Comic Urge," a discussion of the American comic strip as a significant art form.[44] Thurber liked best those that dealt with the domestic American scene. Clare Briggs and Cliff Sterrett, his two special favorites, "project American life with much more incisiveness, realism and cleverness than the average American play," he said. Briggs's "Days of Real Sport" and "When a Feller Needs a Friend" rival Booth Tarkington's studies of adolescence, and Sterrett's "Polly and Her Pals," for all its farcical elements, "hits off a note of authentic family life." He also praises Sidney Smith, whose "The Gumps" creates situations and characterizations full of the true "spirit of Babbittry," although he objects to Smith's "predilection for a continuous stream of cheap vaudeville witticisms" and his grotesque drawings.

Significantly, his favorite aside from these "masters of the family fetich and foible" was Walter Hoban, whose "Jerry on the Job" was "remarkable for a peculiar sort of fantasy, a rare quality in American artists of any medium." Hoban's strips deal with the everyday scene—Jerry the office boy encountering various harassed adults—but the dialogue usually builds to a climax of illogic or mental idiosyncrasy of the kind that Thurber always relished. Thurber also liked the fantasy in "Krazy Kat," and Fontaine Fox's "Toonerville Trolley." When he went to New York to stay, he had a whole trunkful of his favorite comic strips with him. There is no doubt that Thurber's treatment of family life in *My Life and Hard Times*, for example, owes something to the combination of farcical slam-bang, sharp observa-

[42] "Credos and Curios," Columbus *Dispatch*, September 23, 1923.
[43] "Credos and Curios," Columbus *Dispatch*, July 8, 1923.
[44] "Credos and Curios," Columbus *Dispatch*, May 20, 1923.

tion of the domestic scene, and excursions into the realm of fantasy he found in his favorite comic strips.

In "Credos and Curios" Thurber is constantly experimenting with the forms he was to master in later years, particularly the paragraph, the literary parody, and the anecdote of personal misadventure. There is a good deal of verse and verse-parody in "Credos and Curios" as there was in the *Sun-Dial.* There are poems and parts of poems by Wordsworth, Shelley, Browning, Henley, Arthur Symons, Housman, Alice Meynell, Edna St. Vincent Millay, and others, and there are parodies and imitations of Whittier, Browning, Housman, Lewis Carroll, Sandburg and Vachel Lindsay. One of Thurber's best imitations is the mock-ballad "The Captain's Dominoes." The refrain was suggested, says Thurber, by an episode in Conrad's *The Nigger of the Narcissus* in which the Swede, Wamibo, who speaks only this one line in the whole story, cries out during the rescue of Jim Wait, "Hoo! Hoo! Strook 'im!" On this mysterious line, Thurber constructs a haunting tale of an old sea-captain whose obsession with the game of dominoes finally destroys him.

> The ship rolled over upon her side
> And her seams ripped long and her seams ripped wide,
> And she shipped an ocean of bilge beside,
> Hoo, strook 'im, mateys, strook 'im!

Thurber was fond of mystery stories and he often parodied them, most notably in such later pieces as "The Macbeth Murder Mystery" and "The White Rabbit Caper." One of the most successful ventures in "Credos and Curios" is "The Cases of Blue Ploermell," an elaborate twelve-part spoof of the Conan Doyle tradition of the detective story. When Thurber went through his old columns in the 1950's, thinking that he might find some pieces suitable for inclusion in a new collection of his work, the Blue Ploermell series was one of the few things that pleased him. It is full of uninhibited slapstick and youthful high spirits.

Blue Ploermell, "the famous psycho-scientific detective," is obviously modeled on Sherlock Holmes and other eccentric gentlemen detectives. He has the requisite peculiarities—"his attractively crossed eyes," and his fondness for animal crackers, which gives him an air of absent-mindedness. Ploermell has an equally eccentric Chinese servant, Gong Low, who speaks a barely intelligible brand of pidgin and takes pleasure in playing tricks on his master. As in the Sherlock Holmes stories, visitors with difficult problems come to the great detective for help, and during these interviews the detective shows off his powers of observation and deduction. "I shall startle you with such a series of deductions as has not occurred since Conan Doyle gave up Sherlock Holmes and went in for spiritualism and fairies," says Ploermell to a new client.

"Now," continued the famous sleuth, fixing his cross-eyes on the man's right shoulder and left ear, "you are a married man with one or two small children."

"How did you guess that?" asked the man, with surprise.

"Your watch chain has been repaired several times showing that your children play with it," said Blue, "and you have a black and blue mark near one eye where the watch has struck you."

"I am a bachelor," said the man. "Fathers never let their children play with their watches, anyway. They always set the children upon the watches of their bachelor friends who come to call. Put that in your book, if you are writing one."

"I'm not writing a book," said Blue Ploermell.

"Fine," said the visitor.[45]

Among the forms which Thurber used most inventively as a mature writer were the essay and the anecdote of personal experience, and in "Credos and Curios" he tried his hand at both. The essays deal lightly and briefly with a variety of topics: the impossibility of communicating with Parisian cab drivers, who simply take you where they want to go, anyway, the trials of buying a hat in Paris, the corruption of American speech by unlovely contractions like " 'smatter?" and "gunna," the romantic appeal of the long dress, and so on. One, on the difference between the popular image of the newspaper columnist and the reality, shows Thurber moving toward a character-type, that of the nervous inadequate middle-aged man, which was soon to become one of his major comic resources. Most people, their heads full of romantic tales about newspaper life—Gertrude Atherton's *Black Oxen* and Robert Chambers's *Eris*, for example—look upon the columnist as having "the grace of a Lord Beaconsfield, the social amenities of a Pepys, the over-coffee repartee of a Voltaire and the parlor tricks of a Richard Harding Davis." The truth, says Thurber, is far otherwise:

The gentlemen who get out a daily column, or a weekly one, are, in truth, wearers of shiny pants, owners of touseled hair, losers of buttons from coats, carriers of umbrellas, with a tendency to spot their ties, neglect their shoes and ride up near the motorman so as

[45] "Credos and Curios," Columbus *Dispatch*, March 18, 1923.

not to be seen. They are notorious evaders of drawing rooms and tea parties. They haven't got a thing to wear, and they look funny in it.[46]

The anecdotes of personal experience in "Credos and Curios" show Thurber making his first trial of the literary personality which turned out to suit him best—himself. He had tried the anonymous, institutional personality of the editorial or columnist's "we," and he had tried the special homespun personality and vocabulary of Dad. Now, in a number of comic anecdotes involving the little crises and frustrations of everyday life, he is James Thurber, victim or closely involved spectator. The anecdotes deal with such experiences as waiting in the doctor's office, trying to get the telephone connected (an early treatment of one of Thurber's richest themes, the plight of the individual dealing with a large impersonal organization like the phone company), trying to ride a horse (Thurber will stick to dogs), and watching father try to drive a bat out of the house one summer night.

The episode involving father and the bat is a preliminary study for the anecdotes of domestic misadventure which make up *My Life and Hard Times*. Father's performance is described as though it were a memorable moment in the history of bat-hunting, a demanding sport with its own special rules and techniques. "It was one of the closest games we have ever witnessed, with every now and then father in the lead, and every now and again the bat ahead." The entrance of the bat is described with a nice attention to onomatopoetic values: "It was shortly after 1 o'clock in the morning when the bat slipped through the ropes, whushed into the hallway, flacked through the door and took to flut-flutting against the living-room walls." Thurber and his two brothers attack it with books ("the accepted weapons in a four-handed game"), and father, awakened by the uproar, and "thinking that a new armistice had been signed or a water pipe had burst," appears at the head of the stairs.

When he grasps the situation, he picks up a broom and, "clad in a directoire nightgown," joins the fray. " 'Leave this bat to me,' " he says and swings the broom, knocking "a brass candlestick, a copper pin tray and a sheaf of letters off the mantel." One of the observers cries out, " 'Bat's round!' "

The bat now apparently disappeared, only to switch back into the room from an unexpected angle, forcing father into a clinch with

[46] "Credos and Curios," Columbus *Dispatch*, September 16, 1923.

a chair. The bat whirled and flapped widely down the fairway. Father rose and let him have it. But the bat didn't want it. He dodged. And besides, a broom, unless properly swung, will curve. It did; garnering a student lamp, six magazines and an ash tray. "Bat's round!" cried the judges.

Father sinks exhausted into a chair, while the bat swoops "lightly here and there, like a peppy young lightweight showing off before the crowd as he is introduced while the veteran champion watches in dismay." Finally, after father has smashed the living-room chandelier in another swipe with the broom, one of the boys stuns the creature and they put it in a shoebox. " 'Here, let me have it!' " cries father, and throws the box out of the window, not noticing that there is a screen in it. The box bounces back and out flies the bat. "Father fell helplessly across the broom and the judges solemnly raised the bat's right wing in token of triumph." [47]

In this episode, Thurber is obviously exploring what was to become his own very special material and manner—the world of domestic chaos and uproar, drawn from the everyday life of his own family in Columbus, Ohio. The mock-heroic manner is handled without strain or forcing, and the language is (with trifling exceptions) natural and expressive. In this, as in the little essay on the glamorous image of the columnist, Thurber is clearly coming into his own as an artist.

Nevertheless, the overall impression of "Credos and Curios" is of immaturity and uncertainty. At this stage in his career he was not sure whether he belonged to Dad and Columbus or to the world of Henry James. The romantic vein in him was strong: he loved the novels of Joseph Hergesheimer and poems like Henley's "Samarcand," full of exotic names and dream-stuff; oftentimes, experimenting with the manner of Henry James, he saw life as primarily an aesthetic matter. At the same time, he was a parodist, a satirist, a football fan and a regular fellow. In the next few years he was to purge himself of his sentimental romanticism and to find his real subject in the comic interplay between romantic impulse and the world of everyday.

[47] "Credos and Curios," Columbus *Dispatch*, May 13, 1923.

5

Newspaperman:
Paris and New York

THE LOSS OF HIS COLUMN in December of 1923 was a discouraging blow and Thurber became more than ever disenchanted with life on the *Dispatch*. Althea was ambitious for him and kept pressing him to leave Columbus and seek his literary fortune in the greater world of New York.[1] Thurber was reluctant at first, but finally, in the summer of 1924, he quit his forty-dollar-a-week job, and he and Althea took a cottage in the Adirondacks, where he settled down to writing short stories and working on the book for a musical which he hoped to sell to a Broadway producer. A news item in the *Dispatch* noted that his collaborator was to be Frank Bannister, the song writer, author of "Say It with a Uke." [2] The musical was called "Nightingale," and a look at Thurber's libretto (which survives in the Library of Congress) [3] makes it clear why it never reached the stage. It is low on comic invention and almost devoid of entertaining dialogue. Even with a lively musical score—and there is no record of what happened to the projected collaboration with Frank Bannister—it is doubtful that "Nightingale" could have made it.[4]

[1] Ruth White, "James Thurber," March 17, 1940; also Thurber's letter to E. B. White, December 22, 1952 (EBWP).
[2] "Summer Views of Things and News," undated clipping in Helen Thurber's possession; also Thurber's letter to White, March 1, 1954 (EBWP).
[3] Stapled typescript, Class D 69000, dated October 2, 1924.
[4] Thurber tells how the manuscript was lost on the subway in his letter of March 1, 1954, to White (EBWP).

"Nightingale" got as far as the copyright office of the Library of Congress, but that was its farthest flight. Thurber had no better luck with his short stories that summer. After three months of trying, he had a pile of rejection slips and a friendly note of refusal from the *Saturday Evening Post*.[5] His sole publication was an item he sent to Heywood Broun, who ran it in his column, "It Seems to Me," in the New York *World*.[6] It is a strained effort in the vein of the nineteenth-century tall tale about nature's abundance, and it shows little promise that the author would one day become an outstanding humorist. Discouraged, he and Althea came back to Columbus in the fall, only to find that his old job on the *Dispatch* was no longer available. For the next several months he worked as a free-lance publicity agent for such institutions as a local movie house, Olentangy Park, the Elks Circus, and the Cleveland Symphony.[7]

In May of 1925, having saved $200, the Thurbers packed up and followed the trail of so many other ambitious young American writers of the 1920's to France. They rented a farmhouse in the little village of Granville, in Normandy, and Thurber started on a novel about his Columbus boyhood days. The central character was his old friend Herman Miller, by then the drama director at Ohio State. He did five chapters that summer, and when he showed them to his wife she said that they were terrible.[8] He agreed, and since they were running out of money, Thurber got a job in September on the Paris edition of the Chicago *Tribune* at $12 a week. He liked to recall the way he got it: a sports writer named Egan took him to the desk of Dave Darrah, the city editor, and Darrah said sourly, " 'I got thirty men ahead of you who want jobs. . . . What are you, by the way, a poet, a painter, or a novelist?' " " 'I'm a newspaperman,' " Thurber told him, and was hired on the spot.[9]

In Paris he was a rewrite man on the night desk with Elliott Paul, Eugene Jolas ("who pounded a typewriter so hard he usually used one up every three weeks"), and William L. Shirer. He was proud of the fact that he was one of the few trained newsmen on the paper at that time. As a graduate of Norman Kuehner's hard school, he knew how to write headlines and almost always set up the two-column fourteen-point Cheltenham feature headlines.[10] Writing for the Paris edition of the Chicago *Tribune* required

[5] Letter to Frank Gibney, October 31, 1956.
[6] Undated clipping in Helen Thurber's possession.
[7] Ruth White, "James Thurber," March 17, 1940; also Thurber's letter to Gibney, October 31, 1956.
[8] Minderman, "We Knew Him When."
[9] *The Years with Ross*, p. 30; also letter to Gibney, October 31, 1956.
[10] Letter to Hudson Hawley, July 27, 1954.

adaptability and, above all, a talent for improvisation. The paper got only fifty words of cable a night, and the city editor would take sentences out of the cable and pass them around to Shirer, Paul, and Thurber, saying "Write a column on that." One night, he handed Thurber a sentence reading, "Christy Mathewson died tonight at Saranac." [11] The paper had no morgue in Paris, and so Thurber had to do the whole thing relying on his memory and imagination. Fortunately, his knowledge of baseball history was encyclopedic, and he turned out a full-column obituary, full of facts, dates, and anecdotes about the personal character as well as the prowess of the great pitcher.[12] He had to improvise a little more in a feature on Byrd's flight to the North Pole, a subject about which he knew nothing. Years later he could recall one phrase from his Byrd story—"with the ice of the North Pole clinging on their wings."

On the other hand, he was ludicrously out of his depth on one of his assignments, which was to cover the international financial situation. He had to have Shirer look up the word "moratorium" in his French-English dictionary, he recalled; they both had thought it had something to do with memorial statements. A typical assignment was a series of articles on Poland, including the history of the zloty. The series was obligatory, because Poland was an advertising customer of the paper. Thurber got most of his material by cribbing from articles in *Le Figaro* and other influential Parisian papers. Reminiscing about it later, he confessed that he probably knew less about finance than anybody else in the world.[13]

Life was informal on the Paris editions of American newspapers in those days, and there was a tradition of practical joking which Thurber found immediately congenial. When things were slow, he would make up parody news features, just as he had for the group at Marzetti's in Columbus, and one of these—involving fifteen or twenty international figures in a totally mythical tale of burglary, rape, gambling, and gun-fighting—got down the chute and was set up in type, complete with headline, by a linotyper who knew no English. Darrah, the city editor, nearly had a heart attack, recalled Thurber, since according to the estimate of one reporter, the paper would have had to pay eight billion dollars in libel suits if the story had ever appeared. Some of the old hands still dream about that libel suit, said Thurber many years later. He did manage to sneak in a number of phony filler items, however: one, under a Washington dateline, purported to quote

[11] "Old Newspaperman Recalls Some Troubles He's Seen," Fire Island *News*, June 18, 1954; also letter from Helen Thurber to CSH, August 2, 1965.
[12] "Death Takes 'Big Six' Mathewson at Saranac Lake," Chicago *Tribune*, Paris edition, Friday, October 9, 1925 (archives of Chicago *Tribune*).
[13] Letter to Hawley, July 27, 1954.

President Coolidge as saying at a convention of the Protestant Churches of America that a man who does not pray is not a praying man.[14]

Working on the night desk, Thurber was free during the daytime to renew his acquaintance with the endlessly fascinating city of Paris and the delightfully unpredictable ways of the French. This second exposure to French life provided him with the material for a number of feature articles which he wrote for magazines and Sunday supplements back home. Most of these deal with the tribulations of the American traveler abroad and the contrast between American and European ways of doing things; others are more conventional journalistic features on interesting personalities, oddities of history, and so on. About half of these articles were written in the summer and fall of 1925, and about half in early 1926, when the Thurbers had moved down to Nice. Among them were "Playships of the World," a feature on the U.S. cruiser *Pittsburgh*, "The Fate of Joan's White Armor," on Albert Bigelow Paine's search for the armor of Joan of Arc (New York *Herald Tribune* Magazine, July 4, 1926), and "The Evolution of an Ambassador: How Myron T. Herrick Won His Laurels as the Foremost American Dignitary in Europe" (Kansas City *Star* Magazine, October 4, 1925). Herrick was from Columbus, and Thurber did two more pieces on him in the next few years. His romantic feelings about Paris and his skill as an interviewer come through in an attractive human-interest piece on Leon Barthelemy, who had been President Wilson's barber in the Peace Conference days ("Wilson's Paris Barber," New York *World*, Sunday, September 20, 1925).

The most interesting of the free-lance pieces Thurber did in 1925–26 are those in which he exercised his talent as a social observer, contrasting the French way of doing things with the American. He had experimented with the subject in his pieces on the Paris taxi driver (one of his favorite subjects) and the vagaries of French tailoring in "Credos and Curios"; now, with fresh material at hand, he was to do more with it. " 'Tip, Tip, Hurray'—The Battle Cry of Greedom" (Kansas City *Star* Magazine, August 23, 1925) sketches in rather broad strokes two of the stereotypes of the International Subject—the greedy French porter or taxi driver and the loud-talking, big-spending American tourist. Spoiled by the ostentatious extravagance of the Americans, French porters demand outrageously large tips and make life impossible for the "poor student or teacher trying to make his $300 go as far as possible"—a group with whose problems Thurber readily identifies. On the dock at Cherbourg, says Thurber, he

14 Ibid.

gave what he knew was too much to the man who carried two suitcases for him:

> I handed him the 10 francs, expecting a grateful *"merci bien,"* and maybe even a touch of the finger to the forelock and a scrape of the foot. But no. He flew into a temperamental rage. He gesticulated wildly, and began to argue in the injured tone of one who has been enormously abused. . . . Many Americans arriving or leaving Cherbourg, he said, think nothing of handing out 20 to 25 francs in tips, maybe even more. It was the custom, he insisted. I was transgressing a precedent, and, what is more, an American precedent. His tone hinted that I was unpatriotic and probably, if the truth were known, traitorous in the bargain.

The portrait of the American tourist is done with even more hostility. The French image of the American as a loudmouth who rushes about "fraternizing genially with servants, handing them large gratuities and proclaiming constantly, " *'J'ai beaucoup d'argent!'* " is not greatly exaggerated, says Thurber. The " *'beaucoup d'argent'* " men are at their worst when they embark for home. Throwing their last French money at the dockside porters, they cry, " 'Take the darn stuff, it won't be any more good to me! Here you are, boy, buy yourself a café on me!' " All this to the accompaniment of "ribald shouts, hearty slaps on the back, happy thoughts of getting back to the land of the percolaters and doughnuts—and a careless barrage of French money cast among the porters."

"Quick, the Other Side!" (*Detroit Athletic Club News,* November, 1925) is a high-spirited treatment of the strange and confusing ways of the French railroads, and "Balm for Those Who Didn't Go Abroad" (New York *Herald Tribune* Magazine, December 6, 1925) reassures stay-at-homes by describing the classic frustrations of the guided tour through historic monuments. A more original piece is "A Sock on the Jaw—French Style" (*Harper's Magazine,* February, 1926), for which Thurber received $90— his largest check so far. It came in the nick of time, since his *Tribune* salary of $12 a week was grotesquely inadequate to the cost of living. He and Althea were always having to borrow money, and they were in debt to their hotel. The check from *Harper's* made them wildly rich, Thurber recalled, and gave him more financial pleasure than anything else he ever earned.[15]

The essay is a study of comparative manners focusing on the contrast between French and American behavior in argument, and it is full of the

[15] Letter to E. B. White, December 22, 1952 (EBWP).

freshly observed detail which characterizes Thurber's mature work. In America, the fist-fight is an institution: "no schoolboy's youthful mettle can be properly tempered without recourse to it; it is an honorable tradition at West Point; it is part of the bulwark of American civilization." In France, it is the verbal exchange preceding the fight which is of greatest interest. What Thurber enjoys most about the French style is the way in which the dispute moves from the commonplace fact to the philosophical implication and back again. A taxi driver grazes the hub of a wagon, and after an initial exchange of insults, the argument escalates to a debate about government policy in which all the bystanders join, and then veers sharply back "to the grazed hub and the pro-German proclivities of the chauffeur and the fact that the teamster's children will grow up to be acrobats." Thurber concludes with the observation that one reason why the French never resort to fisticuffs is that "an ill-timed right swing" would be regarded as interfering with one of the most jealously guarded of all French perquisites—"the right of free community debate."

Thurber had plenty of opportunity to observe the oddities of French street arguments at first hand. In a letter to Hudson Hawley, in 1954, he recalled that when he worked for the Paris *Tribune* he was the only man who hadn't grown a beard. The taxi drivers always mistook the newspapermen for Germans, and there was a big fight one night when several taxi drivers started bumping the bearded journalists around. Since fists were not acceptable weapons in a French brawl, Thurber said, everyone folded his arms and butted everyone else.[16]

In December, Thurber went down to Nice as co-editor of the *Tribune*'s Riviera edition. B. J. Kospoth was the editor, and Lamar Middleton, Nathan Zatkin, and René Lavaillant were among the staffers. The Riviera edition was even more casual and impromptu than the Paris edition: Thurber recalls that he wrote a good deal of the copy and most of the headlines; his wife was society editor, and he and the other staff members made up wonderful social notes for her when she ran short, all about fictitious visiting diplomats, generals, royalty, and millionaires.[17] His experience as editor of the Ohio State *Lantern* came in handy his first night on the job, when they found themselves far short of copy at two o'clock in the morning. Since the Riviera *Tribune* was exactly the size of the *Lantern*, Thurber knew how to get out of this sort of crisis—"I had all the stuff reset in 10-point—came out exactly right." [18]

[16] Letter to Hawley, August 20, 1954.
[17] "Memoirs of a Drudge," *The Thurber Carnival*, p. 19.
[18] Letter to Frank Gibney, October 31, 1956.

Looking back on his days as editor of the Ohio State *Lantern* and the Riviera edition of the *Tribune*, Thurber remarked that editing such papers was like "playing a crosseyed left-handed woman tennis player. You never know where anything is coming from, and everything takes a queer bounce." [19] In Nice, Frank Harris used to drop in nearly every night and reminisce about Wilde, Shaw, Hardy, Whitman, and other great figures of the literary world. He was so diverting that often they did not get the paper out until dawn. About once a week the printers would go on strike, protesting the American demand for consistency in typesetting. After a good deal of shouting and gesticulating, everyone would adjourn to the bar next door, where a truce would soon be agreed upon.[20]

Nice was the kind of place that appealed to Thurber—polyglot, uninhibited, and—if such a word can be applied to a town—irresponsible. Everything that happened in Nice had a touch of carnival about it. Some years later he paid tribute to it in an essay titled "La Grande Ville de Plaisir," and what he remembered with keenest relish was that it was one of those places, like Columbus, Ohio, where almost anything was likely to happen. Confidence men flourished, traffic policemen were being continually knocked down by motorists, and the *bagarre* was a way of life. "*Bagarre* means 'violent disorder, uproar, crush, squabble, scuffle, fray,' " he noted, relishing each separate kind of disturbance listed by his dictionary, and then went on to summarize the account in the Nice *Eclaireur* of an incredibly mixed-up disorder which began with the attempt of three or four people to close the Institute of Actinology (the whys and wherefores not given in the report), and which quickly involved a beating with brass knuckles, an attempted shooting, and " 'a crowd of three hundred people . . . shouting and gesticulating.' " [21] What Thurber liked about the whole affair was the confusion and the illogic of both the episode itself and the casual treatment of it by the *Eclaireur*. It summed up the spirit of Nice for him—violent, unpredictable, bizarre.

A good deal of the work on the Riviera *Tribune* involved interviewing visiting notables, and Thurber interviewed Isadora Duncan (a painful experience, in which he had to get her to comment on the reported suicide of her former husband), Rudolph Valentino, who seemed "indestructibly healthy," and the elusive financier Harry Sinclair, who never once looked Thurber in the eye throughout their conversation. His most interesting assignment, however, was the Helen Wills–Suzanne Lenglen tennis match,

[19] "Old Newspaperman Recalls Some Troubles He's Seen."
[20] "Memoirs of a Drudge," *The Thurber Carnival*, pp. 19–20.
[21] "La Grande Ville de Plaisir," *My World and Welcome to It*, p. 265.

in Cannes. This was the event of the 1925–26 season in France, and because of its international character and the sharply contrasting personalities and playing style of the contestants, it became one of those athletic meetings which take on a significance far beyond their meaning in the world of sport. "It was the tennis battle of the century in sport's golden age," wrote Allison Danzig recently,[22] and it was attended by kings and princes, lords and ladies, and as many of the international sporting and social set as could squeeze themselves into the Carlton Tennis Club. The rooftops of adjoining houses were lined with spectators, and the more adventurous climbed the eucalyptus trees which bordered the club.

Thurber's front-page story of the match, which Mlle. Lenglen won, 6–3, 8–6, casts the whole encounter into the shape of a Henry James novel. Helen Wills is the young, inexperienced American girl ("little poker face . . . not yet out of her teens") who has only her courage and gallantry, while Suzanne Lenglen is the mature, accomplished European woman ("the greatest woman tennis player in the world since the time Helen was fondling dolls"). For Thurber, the match is the conflict between innocence and experience, moral character and technical virtuosity, America and Europe. Helen Wills's fine showing is described as though it were the initiation of the American innocent into the complex world of Europe: "Helen Wills met a baptism of fire which was strange and new to her, she encountered a variety and a brilliance of technique that she had never encountered before."

The sentimentality with which Thurber viewed the whole match—and his weakness for the rather musky poetic prose of Hergesheimer—is most obvious in the impressionistic paragraphs describing the scene on the courts when it was all over:

> A rush of people struggling around a livid woman in pink colored silk, a sudden rioting of flowers from somewhere, a bright glittering of silver in the sun . . . The crowd that watched from the stands was a little stupefied. It had all been too swift and dazzling. . . . And then a girl in white walked silently away from the colorful, frenzied throne they were building around the woman in pink silk. The crowd that watched from the stands could comprehend it now. The silent girl in white detaching herself from the mad maelstrom was a note of familiar sanity. Helen Wills had been defeated and was going home.
>
> She went home quietly, directly, without looking around, as she

22 "Sports of the Times," New York *Times*, August 7, 1960.

always does when a match is ended. The only color that relieved the whiteness of her face and of her dress, a whiteness so pathetically odd against that silver and red and pink colored scene, was a bright flush on her cheeks.

. . . to the crowd that watched from the stands, it was a sort of red badge of courage. . . .[23]

John R. Tunis, the sports writer, later said that Thurber's account "betrayed no knowledge whatever of tennis, but a considerable grasp of women." [24] The extent to which Thurber's Jamesian spectacles distorted his view of the actual can be seen in the difference between his sentimental account and Allison Danzig's retrospective column on the great match in the New York *Times*, August 7, 1960. Danzig, like Tunis, one of America's most expert tennis reporters, revisited the Carlton Tennis Club in 1960, and talked with Tom Burke, the professional, who was there in 1926. Burke makes it clear that although Helen Wills was younger and less experienced than Suzanne Lenglen, it was Lenglen who was nervous, and Wills who was calmly confident. "She missed shots she never did ordinarily," said Burke of Lenglen. "When she finally won at 8–6 she was on the verge of collapse. If she had lost the set she would have been finished."

Thurber says nothing of the contrast in styles between the two, because it did not fit into the stereotype which shaped his view of the occasion. In point of fact, Helen Wills was a strong, aggressive player, a slugger, while Suzanne Lenglen was a placement artist, the epitome of elegance and grace. "She looked more like a dancer," recalled Burke. Thurber simply could not see his Henry James heroine as a confident, hard-hitting performer who wore her opponents down psychologically as much as physically.

The months abroad in 1925–26 were valuable experience for Thurber—he learned that he was probably not a novelist, he became a part of that free-floating circle of American newspapermen working abroad (an education in itself), he renewed and extended his acquaintance with France, and he kept his hand in as a writer of humorous sketches in the tradition of Benchley and his followers. The contrast between the sharp comic observation of the sketch he sold to *Harper's*, "A Sock on the Jaw—French Style" and the sentimentality and over-writing of the account

[23] "Wills Goes Down Fighting," Chicago *Tribune*, Riviera edition, February 17, 1926 (Thurber Collection). The Riviera edition apparently lasted only a short time. The files are lost; even the Chicago *Tribune* has no record of ever having put out such a paper. The copy in the Thurber Collection is thus very rare.
[24] "Old Newspaperman Recalls Some Troubles He's Seen."

of the Wills–Lenglen match shows, however, that in 1926 Thurber was still unsure of where he was going, and that he was still looking for a style and manner of his own.

France had been instructive and entertaining, but he was anxious to get established as a writer in the States. Althea wanted to stay on a little longer, and so Thurber came back alone in June of 1926. When he landed, he had $10 in his pocket. He borrowed enough money from a girl he had met in Nice to last him until July, rented a $5-a-week room on West 13th Street, and started to write short pieces which he sent off hopefully to *The New Yorker*.[25] He had first heard of the magazine in the fall of 1925 in Paris, when the Paris *Herald* ran a first-page story on a piece by Ellin Mackay in *The New Yorker* called "Why We Go to Cabarets." Since Miss Mackay was the socially prominent daughter of the millionaire head of Postal Telegraph, and her essay took an irreverent view of Park Avenue society, the whole thing was news, and the struggling little magazine got its first international notice.[26] When Thurber got back to New York, in June, he took some of his manuscripts to Brandt and Brandt, the literary agents, and asked them whether they thought he had any chance of being published.[27] They suggested that he try *The New Yorker*—not really much of a compliment, since the future of the magazine in the summer of 1926 was anything but promising. He was eating in doughnut shops, scrounging anchovies at cocktail parties ("not good for breakfast"),[28] and his pieces came back with discouraging rapidity and regularity. One piece, about a six-day bicycle racer named Alfred Goullet, did not, however, and Thurber called at the *New Yorker* office one day in June hoping for good news.

John Mosher, the literary editor of the magazine (and later Thurber's good friend), met him in the reception room, as Thurber tells it in *The Years with Ross*, "looking like a professor of English literature who has not approved of the writing of anybody since Sir Thomas Browne. He returned my manuscript saying that it had got under something, and apologizing for the tardy rejection. 'You see,' he said, 'I regard Madison Square Garden as one of the blots on our culture.' " [29]

His money gone and his prospects zero, he was still determined to make the grade as a writer. He turned down a good offer from the New York

[25] Interview with Maurice Dolbier, "A Sunday Afternoon with Mr. Thurber," New York *Herald Tribune* Book Review, November 3, 1957.

[26] *The Years with Ross*, pp. 30–31.

[27] Interview with Robert Van Gelder, *New York Times Book Review*, May 12, 1940, reprinted in Van Gelder, *Writers and Writing* (New York: Charles Scribner's Sons, 1946), p. 52.

[28] *The Years with Ross*, pp. 32–33.

[29] Ibid., p. 34.

Evening Post in July, and accepted the invitation of Clare Victor Dwiggins, the cartoonist, to spend the summer with him and his family at Green Lake, New York. Thurber had met and interviewed Dwiggins in Nice. At Green Lake, Thurber turned out a 30,000-word parody of four current best sellers called *Why We Behave Like Microbe Hunters.* The targets of the parody were a strange mixture—Paul de Kruif's enormously successful *Microbe Hunters,* George Amos Dorsey's *Why We Behave Like Human Beings,* one of the popular psychology books which inundated the 1920's, Milt Gross's *Nize Baby,* and Anita Loos's *Gentlemen Prefer Blondes.*[30]

In September, Dwiggins loaned Thurber $100 to get to New York and find an apartment. Althea had returned from France, and the couple set up housekeeping in a basement apartment on Horatio Street, near the Ninth Avenue El. Thurber peddled his manuscript from publisher to publisher, but without any luck. The closest he came was an encouraging letter from a man at Henry Holt, but the sales department turned the book down. In the meantime, he got a $40-a-week job as a general-assignment reporter for the *Evening Post,* where some of his colleagues were Nunnally Johnson, Laura Z. Hobson, and Russel Crouse (later to be on *The New Yorker*). Thurber was not really much interested in reporting, and when the big stories broke—fires, wrecks, jail-breaks and other such catastrophes—and all the telephones in the office would begin ringing, he would put on his hat and go home. "There was a standing order not to send me to Brooklyn," he recalled. This was the result of the time the city editor, a dedicated man who wanted today's news in today's paper, sent Thurber to an address in Brooklyn to cover a theater fire.

> I rode subway trains, elevated trains and street cars. I kept getting back to Chambers St. They sent me out at 1:30. At 4 o'clock I got out at Chambers St. the last time and got into a taxicab.
>
> On the way over to Brooklyn I stopped off for a minute and bought a Post, and the story about the fire was all over the front page. So I told the cab driver to turn around and take me home.[31]

Thurber liked to tell this story, describing the look on the city editor's face as he repeated, "A four alarm fire, and this fellow just can't find it!" [32] After that, he was assigned to write overnight features. "I used to make

[30] Letter to Gibney, October 31, 1956; also *The Years with Ross,* p. 35.

[31] Interview with Joseph Mitchell, New York *World-Telegram,* undated clipping in RTS, but obviously early in 1935 (Thurber Collection). Thurber also recalls his days on the *Evening Post* in "Memoirs of a Drudge," *The Thurber Carnival,* pp. 22–23.

[32] Robert M. Coates, "James Thurber," *Authors Guild Bulletin,* December, 1961 (Thurber Collection).

them all up," he told an interviewer, with obvious exaggeration.

It was the managing editor of the *Evening Post* who decided that in order to give the news stories in the paper greater impact, all leads should consist of one word. This was the kind of challenge Thurber preferred to chasing fires. He opened his next story this way: "Dead." The second paragraph went on to say, "That was what the man was the police found in an areaway last night." The editor grumbled a bit, but continued to insist on the one-word leads. One night he sent Thurber out to cover a sexy play which was attracting a good deal of notoriety. Thurber's one-word lead was a word no paper would print. The second paragraph went on, "That was the word flung across the footlights yesterday." The managing editor knew when he had met his match. " 'All right. All right,' " he said. " 'Thurber and everybody else are starting to kid the hell out of it, so we'll go back to leads that make sense.' " [33]

In his nearly six months with the *Evening Post*, Thurber did a number of special features. He got the first interview ever granted to the press by Thomas A. Edison. He prepared a questionnaire and sent it in ahead of time, and the great man then received him and gave him the answers.[34] On another assignment, he met Mrs. Harry Houdini, the widow of the great magician. They talked of books and book collecting, and Thurber so charmed the lady that she gave him seventy-five volumes from her late husband's library, ranging from a seventeenth-century Latin book on magic to *The Harrison Log Cabin Song Book of 1840 revised for the Campaign of 1888 with Numerous New Songs to Patriotic Airs*. He got a five-dollar bonus for a feature on the Houdini books, and another for a story on an epidemic of trench mouth. He also did a three-part survey of the city water system, and he wrote home about this with justifiable pride in his Columbus-learned skill as a reporter: "The New York water supply system being the greatest in the world is an interesting thing to study up and my city hall training in Columbus helped me to know how to go about the thing." [35]

His emotional ties with Columbus and the family circle remained close, as they did throughout his life. One letter of this period opens with the salutation, "Dear Father, Mother, Brother and Airedale." Another, to his brother Robert, mourns the death of two old family dogs, Muggs (the

[33] Interview with Eddy Gilmore, "Call Me Jim," datelined London, and reprinted in the Columbus *Dispatch*, August 3, 1958.
[34] Minderman, "We Knew Him When"; also interview with Earl Wilson, Columbus *Dispatch*, June 14, 1959.
[35] Letter to "Dear Father, Mother, Brother and Airedale," February 6, 1927 (Thurber Collection).

original of "The Dog That Bit People") and Rex (the wonderful bull terrier memorialized in "Snapshot of Rex"). "I still feel bad about Rex and often dream of him," Thurber wrote, and he went on to discuss the whole mystery of mortality and the nature of the after-life. "I have always expected to find Rex in the company of some such guy as, say, Frank Luke or Raoul Lufbery and maybe Muggs will have Christy Mathewson with whom to scamper across the porphyry and chrysoprase fields." [36]

While working on the *Evening Post*, Thurber was still doggedly turning out light verse and prose in the hope of making a connection somewhere. He was just about ready to give up and go home in September, when Franklin P. Adams accepted and printed in "The Conning Tower" a burlesque treatment of the Hero and Leander story as it might have been reported if the modern tabloids had covered it. It begins:

I

LOVE PACT IS BARED
AS LEANDER DROWNS!   Daily Tab, Sept. 15

SWIMMER MISSING IN
HELLESPONT CROSSING!   Daily Glass, Sept. 15

The story develops in a series of provocative assertions:

IV

"HE SWAM TO SEE MAMA
EVERY NIGHT," PENS HERO   Daily Tab, Sept. 18

TURK SWIMMER SAYS LEA
NEVER CROSSED HELLES   Daily Glass, Sept. 18

And ends on an appropriate note of grotesquery:

XV

CRIPPLED GRANDMA SETS
NEW HEL DEATH SWIM MARK Daily Tab, Sept. 29

WOMAN, 87, EASILY BEATS
HERO'S "RECORD" MARK   Daily Glass, Sept. 29

[36] "Dear Robert," undated letter of 1927 or 1928 (Thurber Collection).

The piece appeared in F.P.A.'s New York World column of September 28, 1926 (not in December, as Thurber has it in The Years with Ross), over the signature, "Jamie Machree." [37] Thurber was so bucked up by this recognition that he decided to stay on and keep trying. Finally, after his wife had convinced him that he was being too meticulous and taking too long on the pieces he was sending to The New Yorker, he set the alarm clock to ring in forty-five minutes, and, burlesquing the current craze for channel swimming, flagpole sitting, and the like, wrote a brief anecdote about a man who sets the world's record for going around in a revolving door.[38] The New Yorker bought it—after having rejected twenty previous contributions—and the Thurbers spent the money on a Scotty named Jeannie, who later became the occasion for Thurber's first and only real fight with Harold Ross.

Thurber's story of the man in the revolving door is only a brief anecdote, but it has a sharper satiric edge than most of the things he had done before. His chief comic subject had been—and continued to be—the problems of everyday life—waiting in the doctor's office, getting the telephone installed, and so on—but here, the subject is the values of society as a whole. A little man has had a fight with his wife, and now he is grimly going round and round in the revolving door of a large department store. A crowd gathers and disrupts traffic. A policeman is sent for, but he fails to stop the little man. A psychiatrist tries next, but his luck is no better. A richly dressed gentleman pushes his way through and says, " 'I'll give him $45,000 if he can go for another two hours. I'm a big chewing gum magnate from the West.' " Bets are laid. The crowd grows to such proportions that firemen are called out. The little man finally makes it, and is taken to the Presidential suite of a nearby hotel. By midnight he has received more than $100,000 in offers from vaudeville and the movies.

The whole anecdote is a striking anticipation of Thurber's later mastery of the fable form as an instrument of social criticism. The title of the piece, "An American Romance," points up the irony of the tale as an American success story in which a silly or meaningless act is rewarded on a fairy-tale-like scale, and as a love story, in which the fatuousness of the little man's only comment, " 'I did it for the wife and children,' " suggests the emptiness and unreality of the slogans which dominate popular culture. Once having sold "An American Romance," Thurber found it easy to place other things with The New Yorker. He had two poems in the February 26, 1926, issue, neither of them remarkable, but his foot was in the door.

[37] The Years with Ross, p. 35.
[38] Ibid., p. 36.

In February, 1927, Thurber first met E. B. White, who was shortly to become his office-mate at *The New Yorker* and one of his closest friends. The Thurbers had met White's sister on the *Leviathan* in 1925, and White had heard about Thurber's talent as a writer from Russell Lord, who had gone to both Cornell and Ohio State, had worked on *The New Yorker*, and knew both White and Thurber.[39] White made an appointment for Thurber with Harold Ross, and took Thurber in to introduce him. Although White and Thurber had met only a few minutes before, Ross was under the impression that they were old friends, and so he hired Thurber at seventy dollars a week. In a typically impulsive gesture, he telephoned Thurber later in the day and raised it to ninety, and by the time the weekly paycheck arrived, it was for a hundred. "I couldn't take advantage of a newspaperman," said Ross.[40]

This splendid gesture was not so much an expression of confidence in Thurber's promise as a writer as it was Ross's hope that he had found the managing editor who would bring perfect order and efficiency to the operation of the magazine. Ross was a perfectionist and dreamer, and one of the dreams he pursued most obsessively was the dream of perfect order and system at the office. The dream of order protected him, more or less, from his neurotic certainty that everything was about to collapse: "Nobody ever tells me anything," he used to complain, and when things got too much for him, he would roar, "God, how I pity me!" At the heart of the dream was the idea of a central executive post manned by a master of efficiency, "effortlessly controlling and coordinating editorial personnel, contributors, office boys, cranks and other visitors, manuscripts, proofs, cartoons, captions, covers, fiction, poetry, and facts, and bringing forth each Thursday a magazine at once funny, journalistically sound, and flawless." [41] This super-managing editor's role was generally referred to by the staff as "the Jesus," and by Ross as "the Hub." In the early days of the magazine, nearly every new man was tried out at this position, whether he knew it or not. It was weeks before Thurber found out that he was the new Jesus. Every week a secretary brought him a set of papers to sign, and it was not until he asked her what they were that he realized that he was the managing editor and that the slips of paper were the payroll.[42]

Thurber wanted to write, but his duties during his first few months with the magazine were almost entirely editorial and administrative. "Writers

[39] Ibid., p. 38.
[40] Ibid., p. 9; also letter to Gibney, October 31, 1956.
[41] *The Years with Ross*, pp. 7–8.
[42] Interview with Robert Van Gelder, in *Writers and Writing*, pp. 52–53.

are a dime a dozen, Thurber," Ross told him when they first met. "What
I want is an editor. I can't find editors. Nobody grows up. Do you know
English?" [43] This last was one of Ross's obsessions: he worried over minus-
cule points of grammar and usage as though the world depended on the
principle of correctness. In his search for administrative order, Ross was
constantly moving people from one office to another, knocking out walls
and putting up new partitions. "There must have been a dozen Through
the Looking Glass conferences with him about those damned walls,"
Thurber remarked in *The Years with Ross*. Well aware of his own lack of
talent for this sort of thing, Thurber began drinking martinis at lunch to
fortify himself against these sessions. Ross's devotion to the magazine was
fanatical and during Thurber's first two months the two of them worked
seven days a week, often late into the night, without a day off. The pace
was frantic and the editorial work was dull—reading copy for the sports
departments, men's and women's fashions, and new housing—and Thurber
began to lose weight.

Hoping to get himself demoted to a writing job, he began to make
deliberate mistakes and to let things slide. Ross, however, was determined
to view him as a man of high executive ability. Once he brought Thurber
a letter from a men's store complaining that it was not getting fair treatment in the "As to Men" department. "What are you going to do about
that?" he asked. "The hell with it," said Thurber, and swept it off the desk
onto the floor. "That's direct action, anyway," said Ross, and he later
remarked to White, " 'Thurber has honesty . . . admits his mistakes, never
passes the buck. Only editor with common sense I've ever had.' " [44] Even
when in the midst of one of their executive conferences a secretary brought
in a heavy typescript bound in imitation leather and titled "Mistakes Made
by J. Thurber as Managing Editor," Ross's confidence was unshaken.
Instead of firing Thurber, he wanted to fire the critical staff member who
had compiled the report.

By the end of the summer Thurber had had all he could take. "I finally
told Ross . . . that I was losing weight, my grip, and possibly my mind,
and had to have a rest." Ross told him to take a couple of weeks off, and
Thurber, Althea, and Jeannie, the Scotty, went to Columbus. Jeannie got
lost just before they were to return. With the help of newspaper ads and
the Columbus police they found her, but Thurber was two days late getting
back to the office. Ross called him in. " 'I understand you've overstayed

[43] *The Years with Ross*, p. 5.
[44] *The Years with Ross*, p. 14; also Dale Kramer, *Ross and The New Yorker* (New York:
Doubleday, 1952), chapter x, *passim*.

your vacation to look for a dog,' he growled. 'Seems to me that was the act of a sis.' " "Sis" was too much for Thurber, and his always volatile temper exploded. He tells the story in *The Years with Ross:*

> The scene that followed was brief, loud, and incoherent. I told him what to do with his goddam magazine, that I was through, and that he couldn't call me a sis while sitting down, since it was a fighting word. I offered to fight him then and there . . . and suggested that he call in one of his friends to help him. Ross hated scenes, physical violence or the threat of it, temper and the unruly.
>
> "Who would you suggest I call in?" he demanded, the thunder clearing from his brow.
>
> "Alexander Woollcott!" I yelled, and he began laughing.

They ended up at Tony's for a couple of drinks and dinner, and that night marked the beginning of a close and unbroken friendship.[45]

Not long afterward, Ross came into Thurber's office and said, " 'You've been writing. . . . I don't know how in hell you found time to write. I admit I didn't want you to. I could hit a dozen writers from here with this ash tray. They're undependable, no system, no self-discipline. Dorothy Parker says you're a writer, and so does Baird Leonard. . . . All right then, if you're a writer, write! Maybe you've got something to say.' " [46] Thurber had won his demotion.

[45] *The Years with Ross*, pp. 15–16; also letter to Gibney, October 31, 1956.
[46] *The Years with Ross*, pp. 16–17.

6

The New Yorker: *Early Days*

JOINING THE NEW YORKER in March of 1927 was the turning point in Thurber's career, and perhaps in that of the magazine as well. He was thirty-two years old (older than most of the *New Yorker* staffers), a frustrated writer and wandering journalist who had not yet found himself or a place where he could do what he wanted to do. The magazine was in the process of developing from a doubtful experiment into an established reality, and Thurber brought to it the versatility and the kind of comic talent it was looking for. *The New Yorker* gave him the chance he needed to practice his craft as a humorist, and more important, it brought him into close association with two men who had a considerable influence on the shaping of his style at this critical moment in his development––Harold Ross and E. B. White.

In 1927 the magazine was moving into the black financially, and its special formula of original cartoons, superior reporting, and a miscellany of light essays and stories was beginning to take shape. E. B. White's "Notes and Comment" led off the magazine, and set the tone of intelligent observation and civilized prose which has been its hallmark ever since. "The Talk of the Town" (at that time done by Russel Crouse) followed, with its verbal snapshots of the New York scene; such soon-to-be-famous features as "A Reporter at Large" (chiefly the work of Morris Markey, who was to become one of Thurber's close friends), "The Wayward Press" (in

those days done by Robert Benchley), and the profiles of interesting contemporary people were beginning to establish themselves; and, perhaps the
most original feature of all, the remarkable cartoons by such artists as Helen
Hokinson, Peter Arno, Otto Soglow, and Garrett Price were giving the
struggling new magazine a special luster.[1]

The first two years of *The New Yorker* had been shaky, and few of Harold
Ross's friends had given it much chance to survive. It first appeared on
February 22, 1925, an unimpressive little magazine of thirty-six pages and
very little advertising. The best thing about it was Rea Irvin's cover,
showing the top-hatted nineteenth-century dandy inspecting a butterfly
through a monocle.[2] The public response was apathetic. Circulation
dropped from an opening issue of 15,000 copies to a low of 2700 in August,
and the magazine was losing $5000 a week. As Thurber put it in *The Years
with Ross*, "*The New Yorker* was the outstanding flop of 1925, a year of
notable successes in literature, music, and entertainment." Ross was driven
to extraordinary measures to keep the magazine afloat. On one occasion,
he tried to get new money by entering a poker game with some of the high
rollers of the Thanatopsis Literary and Inside Straight Club, a little circle
within the Algonquin circle, and managed to lose $29,000.[3] He was saved
at the last moment when Raoul Fleischmann, the original angel of *The
New Yorker*, and Hawley Truax, who managed its business affairs for many
years, went out and raised enough money to give the magazine a fresh start.
Ross's rates were very low at first, and he sometimes had to pay his writers
in stock rather than cash. The slenderness of the magazine's resources in
the early days is neatly summed up in the anecdote in which Ross, meeting
Dorothy Parker somewhere, asked her why she hadn't been in the office
the day before to do a piece she had promised him, and she is reported
to have replied, "Because someone was using the pencil." [4]

Harold Ross himself seemed to have few of the qualifications for launch-
ing a magazine designed to appeal to a well-to-do New York audience. He
had grown up in Colorado and Washington and had quit school early to
follow the life of an itinerant newspaperman. He got his first newspaper
job (on the Salt Lake City *Tribune*) when he was fourteen. In the early
years of World War I he knocked around from city to city and from paper
to paper, developing the fierce independence and the hardboiled pragma-
tism of the old-time reporter. During the war, he was on the editorial staff

[1] The early history of *The New Yorker* is well described in Dale Kramer's *Ross and The
New Yorker* and in Thurber's *The Years with Ross*.
[2] Kramer, *Ross and The New Yorker*, p. 63ff.
[3] Ibid., p. 71.
[4] *The Years with Ross*, p. 22.

of the *Stars and Stripes* in Paris, where two of his colleagues were Captain Franklin P. Adams and Corporal Alexander Woollcott. After the war, he held a variety of editorial jobs, one on the *American Legion Magazine* and another (his last before starting *The New Yorker*) on *Judge*, the old family humor magazine.

Ross was self-educated, and his intellectual and aesthetic tastes were simple. Herbert Spencer was his philosopher, and the only writers he really liked were the manly ones, like Conrad, Twain, and O. Henry.[5] He knew nothing of modern fiction and never did get anything out of music, painting, or poetry. (He once instructed an assistant, "Never leave me alone with poets.") In experience, character, and manner he was the Western type: physically he was rawboned, his face was craggy, his hair stiff and unruly; his manner was casual and informal (meeting Sherwood Anderson for the first time, he said, "Hi, Anderson," and launched into a lecture on English usage, one of his favorite subjects).[6]

Yet for some obscure reason, this ex-newspaperman from Salt Lake City was determined to put out a magazine which would appeal to a wealthy and sophisticated New York audience. His experience with *Judge* had convinced him that the old two-line He-She joke had had its day, and that no humor magazine could survive the attempt to reach a national middle-class family audience. His new magazine would be aggressively parochial. In the "Prospectus" which he drew up to attract backers, he announced that it would be "a reflection of metropolitan life." It would not be "edited for the old lady in Dubuque," he added, somewhat gratuitously. Its tone would be marked by "gaiety, wit and satire," and it expected to be "distinguished for its illustrations."[7] This last turned out to be Ross's most accurate prediction, since he was lucky enough to get Rea Irvin to act as art director from the very beginning.

In spite of its low rates and uncertain future, *The New Yorker* attracted outstanding contributors from the beginning, precisely because it was new, open to experiment, not yet committed to a formula, and because Ross made it clear that he was looking for excellence. Early issues of the magazine carried pieces by Ernest Hemingway (a parody of Frank Harris's *My Life and Loves*), John O'Hara (a satiric look at the world of Ivy League alumni), and Elmer Rice (a series of reminiscent essays on his New York childhood), and its cartoons were making it the center of American comic art. By 1929 there was a solid ballast of expensive advertisements, and there

[5] Kramer, *Ross and The New Yorker*, p. 14.
[6] *The Years with Ross*, p. 78.
[7] Kramer, *Ross and The New Yorker*, p. 62.

was little doubt that *The New Yorker* stood alone as the magazine for the upper-middle-brow, upper-middle-income audience.[8]

Ross had his limitations and eccentricities, but he was a great editor. He was a perfectionist with a special passion for clarity and accuracy. He had "an almost intuitive perception of what was wrong with something," Thurber recalled, and his marginal comments and opinion sheets were classics of meticulous editing—badgering, questioning, prodding, suggesting, until, as Thurber put it, you knew your story and yourself better than you had before.[9] His famous questions, "Who he?," "What mean?," and such notations as "unclear" and "cliché" show his dedication to the ideals of precision and accuracy in style. He surrounded himself with dictionaries, especially Fowler's *Modern English Usage* and the *Oxford English Dictionary*, which he read, says Thurber, "the way other men read fiction." [10] Sometimes his obsession with detail led him into ludicrous blind alleys. Coming across an allusion in a piece by S. J. Perelman to "the woman taken in adultery," he queried, " 'What woman? Hasn't been previously mentioned.' " [11]

In the weekly art conferences where the cartoons and covers were discussed and selected, he showed the same concern for clarity and accuracy. One story has it that when a cartoon was submitted showing two elephants looking at their baby, with the caption, "It's about time to tell Junior the facts of life," Ross asked, " 'Which elephant is talking?' " On another occasion, when a drawing of a Model T delivery truck driving along a dusty country road was up for discussion, Ross turned to his assistant and said, " 'Take this down, Miss Terry. . . . Better dust.' " [12] The famous checking department of *The New Yorker* was simply an extension of Ross's passion for accuracy. His great dream was to get out a magazine free from all taint of error, and he used to say that despite the telephone company's careful checking, it had never yet got out a directory with fewer than three mistakes.[13]

The ordeal of submitting copy to Ross's demanding examination was a valuable experience for Thurber, and he acknowledged the debt time and again. Looking back at the nature of Ross's influence from the vantage point of 1955, he told George Plimpton and Max Steele that while Ross was not the man to develop a writer, his passion for clarity was a healthy

[8] Ibid., chapter xii, *passim.*
[9] *The Years with Ross,* p. 80.
[10] Ibid., p. 82.
[11] Ibid., p. 262.
[12] Ibid., p. 48.
[13] Ibid., p. 29.

influence on all those who wrote for the magazine. "He was a purist and a perfectionist and it had a tremendous effect on all of us: it kept us from getting sloppy," he said.[14] His admiration was not uncritical, however, and in later years he became increasingly uneasy about Ross's fussy precisionism, worrying in particular about its possibly damaging effects on writers with highly original styles like John McNulty. Ross's addiction to the comma as the key to clarity was always a source of contention, and he was capable of insisting that the phrase "the red, white, and blue" be punctuated in this way, while Thurber countered that it was better without any commas at all. Once, when he had had all he could take, Thurber sent Ross a stanza from Wordsworth's "She Dwelt Among the Untrodden Ways" punctuated according to Ross:

> She lived, alone, and few could know
> When Lucy ceased to be,
> But, she is in her grave, and, oh,
> The difference, to me.[15]

Ross never set down his ideals of style in any systematic fashion, but implicit in all his editing was a demand for accurate reporting, stylistic clarity, and a casual, offhand manner. He set great store by the casual style as the proper trademark of the magazine as a whole. Hence the title of his departments—"Notes and Comment," "Profile," "A Reporter at Large," and so on. He liked to refer to the short pieces of fiction and humor featured by the magazine as "casuals." [16] He wanted to avoid anything labored, studied, or arty, and much of his admiration for White and Thurber was based on the easy informality of their prose.

One of the chief reasons for Ross's astonishing success as an editor was his ability to surround himself with talent. Among those on the *New Yorker* staff in the late Twenties and early Thirties were Dorothy Parker, Robert Benchley, Russel Crouse, Alexander Woollcott, Frank Sullivan, St. Clair McKelway, Ogden Nash, Clifton Fadiman, Clarence Day, and Robert M. Coates; and the list of those who were frequent contributors would include S. J. Perelman, Marc Connelly, Ring Lardner, Sally Benson, John O'Hara, Kay Boyle, John Collier, and Morris Bishop.

Certain people were particularly important in the shaping of the maga-

[14] Interview with George Plimpton and Max Steele in *Writers at Work*, ed. Malcolm Cowley (New York: Viking Press, 1959), p. 95. Originally in *The Paris Review*, X (Fall, 1955), 33–49.
[15] *The Years with Ross*, p. 267.
[16] Ibid., p. 13.

zine in the early days. In addition to White and Thurber, there were Katharine Angell, Ralph Ingersoll, and Wolcott Gibbs. Katharine Angell (later Mrs. E. B. White) was the literary editor. She joined the magazine six months after it started, and Ross depended on her in all matters involving taste and culture. A staffer of those days said, "She had a sure, cold sense of what was good, what was bad, what was in poor taste. She balanced Ross." [17] Ingersoll was with the magazine from 1925 until 1930, when he quit to become an editor of *Fortune.* Thurber recalls that it was he who created the formula for "The Talk of the Town" and who took care of the hundreds of managerial details necessary to keep the department going. "Without his help and direction . . . I could never have got 'Talk of the Town' off the ground," he said. [18]

Wolcott Gibbs was one of the three men Ross considered indispensable—the other two were, of course, White and Thurber. "If you and White and Gibbs ever left this magazine, I would leave too," Ross once told Thurber. [19] Gibbs joined the magazine in 1927, just a few months after Thurber did, and like White and Thurber, he brought to it a remarkably versatile talent. He substituted for White on "Notes and Comment," he did some of *The New Yorker's* most famous profiles (those on Henry Luce and Alexander Woollcott are masterpieces of witty malice), he wrote short stories and superb parodies ("Death in the Rumble Seat" is surely one of the best of Hemingway parodies), and he conducted the theater and occasionally the movie reviews, where his wittily expressed disapproval of practically everything made him the delight and despair of readers across the land. " 'Maybe he doesn't like anything,' " Ross once said to Thurber when they were discussing an article in *Harper's* complaining about Gibbs's crotchets as a reviewer, " 'but he can do everything.' "

In addition to his other talents, he was, in Thurber's words, "the best copy editor *The New Yorker* ever had." In 1935 or 1936 he sent Ross a memo entitled "Theory and Practice of Editing New Yorker Articles," a distillation of the ideals of style which guided the magazine for many years. Thurber reprinted it in *The Years with Ross.* The emphasis in the memo is on a clean, functional, informal style, and it was just these standards which Thurber encountered when he first joined the magazine, at a time in his career when he was ready to give up journalese and find a voice of his own. Association with Ross and the early *New Yorker* writers was undoubtedly important in shaping Thurber's style, but with one notable

[17] Kramer, *Ross and The New Yorker,* p. 140.
[18] *The Years with Ross,* p. 121.
[19] Ibid., p. 135.

exception, the influence was one of generally shared assumptions about writing rather than of the clearly demonstrable effect of one man on another. The exception was E. B. White, whose influence on his artistic development Thurber often and generously acknowledged.

White had been on the magazine less than a year when Thurber joined the staff. He was a graduate of Cornell, where he had edited the university paper, and he had tried his hand at newspapering in Seattle, where he found that feature-writing suited him better than conventional reporting. He came to New York in 1923, hoping to make his way as a writer, and went to work for an advertising agency. His literary models were the great columnists of the day—Don Marquis, F. P. A., and Heywood Broun—and he spent his spare time writing verse and short prose sketches. He began to sell to *The New Yorker* in 1925, and late in 1926 Katharine Angell hired him at a salary of $30 a week.[20]

He was a sharp observer of the human and natural scene, and he liked to wander the streets of New York or to sit in Grand Central Station, watching the people. He was shy and reflective by nature, and he had always wanted to be a poet. The world he liked best was the rural village world of barns and horses and fields and trees. He carried a copy of *Walden* with him wherever he went. He had a natural easy prose style which could report the surface as well as suggest expansions of meaning, and this is probably what Marc Connelly meant when he said appreciatively of White that he "brought the steel and music to the magazine."[21] His versatility was exactly what Ross needed in the early days, and he made *The New Yorker* famous for two of its departments—the "newsbreaks," those typographical garbles which unintentionally enliven the columns of many a newspaper, and the "Notes and Comment" page which opened the magazine.

The newsbreaks show White's talent as a professional humorist. They are, in general, unexpected explosions of the absurd in the midst of the commonplace, and his sure taste in selecting the best of these, and his comic inventiveness in creating the categories under which they were to appear—"Raised Eyebrows Department," "Neatest Trick of the Week," and "How's That Again?"—raised a standard feature of the humor magazine (both *Punch* and *Judge* collected newsbreaks) to the level of comic art.

Thurber's favorite among the thousands selected by White was this:

[20] Thurber, "E.B.W.," *Saturday Review*, October 15, 1938, pp. 8–9; also Kramer, *Ross and The New Yorker*, pp. 141ff.
[21] Kramer, *Ross and The New Yorker*, p. 141.

The Departure of Clara Adams
[From the Burbank (Cal.) Post]
Among the first to enter was Mrs. Clara Adams of Tannersville, Pa.,
lone woman passenger. Slowly her nose was turned around to face
in a southwesterly direction, and away from the hangar doors. Then,
like some strange beast, she crawled along the grass.[22]

But it was the White of "Notes and Comment" that Thurber had in
mind when he said that he "learned about writing from Andy White." In
this weekly page of deceptively simple paragraphs and essays, White exercised his remarkable talent as observer and critic of the contemporary scene
as well as poet and amateur philosopher. His manner was casual, offhand,
and lightly ironic. His effects were always underplayed. What he did best
was to take one of the small facts of everyday life and give it a sudden
surprising extension of meaning. A good example of his material and
method is the little essay "Accomplishment," which appeared in "Notes
and Comment" April 20, 1929. It is a defense of jaywalking as one of the
last possible expressions of individualism in an over-organized society.
White develops the theme in a series of mock-heroic comparisons which
invest the unthinking behavior of twentieth-century pedestrians with surprising significance.

> We are a people of dangerous intent, and courage. The superannu-
> ated messenger, bundle under arm, faces death with a balance, a
> rhythm, a sense of time and motion that would make an American
> Indian walking the forests seem clumsy. Every citizen is capable of
> making crossings where the slightest error of judgment or faulty
> timing would crush him out. And for all his artistry, there is a fine
> simplicity in his performance, a lack of ostentation. He survives
> because he is fit. This is our security, our protection against invasion
> by the Visigoths. Strong men may come down, but they will never
> be able to cross our vehicular boundaries; hiding behind a phalanx
> of Checker cabs we will meet the enemy and they will be ours.

Thurber and White shared a closet-sized office for several years and
found themselves in sympathy from the beginning. White was shy at first,
and when Thurber suggested that they go out to lunch together one day,
White demurred, saying, "I always eat alone." [23] Soon, however, they were
lunching together, drinking together, going to the fights at Madison Square

[22] *The Years with Ross*, p. 94.
[23] Kramer, *Ross and The New Yorker*, p. 154.

Garden and to ball games together, and establishing a personal and creative rapport which was to last until the end of Thurber's life. After 1937, when White moved to Maine, where he stayed until 1943, they saw less of each other, but they sustained their friendship in a warm and lively correspondence which continued until the late 1950's. Their letters are full of domestic anecdotes, private jokes, and news of friends, as well as exchanges of opinion on public affairs, discussions of current literary projects, and mutual encouragement and appreciation. In their relationship, White was the older brother. Thurber always felt that it was White who had really discovered his talent; his first book was done in collaboration with White, it was White who insisted that *The New Yorker* use his drawings, and it was White's introduction to *The Owl in the Attic* which launched Thurber as a literary personality. When Thurber needed literary advice or help, it was White he turned to, as he did in 1943 with *Many Moons* and in 1950 with *The Thirteen Clocks*. Writing for the *Saturday Review of Literature* in 1938, Thurber called White "the most valuable person on the magazine," and spoke of his "silver and crystal sentences which had a ring like the ring of no one else's sentences in the world." [24]

Thurber acknowledged few influences on his work. Among living authors he usually named only two—Robert O. Ryder and White. Ross and Gibbs were influences, to be sure, but in their editorial capacities rather than as creative examples. The influence of White was direct and personal. In a 1956 letter he pays tribute to White and gives a curious account of the state of his own writing at the time he joined *The New Yorker:*

> I can see by "Credos and Curios" that I matured slowly. Until I learned discipline in writing from studying Andy White's stuff, I was a careless, nervous, headlong writer, trailing the phrases and rhythms of Henry James, Hergesheimer, Henley, and my favorite English literature teacher at Ohio State, Joe Taylor.
>
> I would use "in fine," "as who should say," and the like. . . . The precision and clarity of White's writing helped me a lot, slowed me down from the dog-trot of newspaper tempo and made me realize a writer turns on his mind, not a faucet. I rewrite most things five to ten or more times. [25]

Thurber's debt to White was very real, but nowhere in his early *New Yorker* pieces is there badness of the kind he accuses himself of here. The charge applies to the self-indulgence of the Chicago *Tribune* Riviera edition

[24] "E.B.W.,"*Saturday Review,* XVIII (October 15, 1938), 8–9.
[25] Letter to Frank Gibney, October 31, 1956.

feature story of the Wills-Lenglen tennis match, written early in 1926, but he had purged himself of this sort of thing before he began to write for *The New Yorker* in 1927. His generous statements of indebtedness (made many years after the fact) should not be taken too literally, but as affectionate hyperboles, speaking the truth, but overstating it for dramatic effect. What they really mean is that Thurber felt himself to be at a turning point when he joined *The New Yorker,* and that White stood out as a model of the kind of style he was developing on his own. White gave Thurber confidence in what he was already trying to do, and confirmed him in the direction he wanted to go. Specifically, he demonstrated to Thurber the artistic values of simplicity and understatement.

White's stylistic ideals are admirably set forth in his 1959 revision of Strunk's *The Elements of Style.*[26] Strunk had been White's teacher at Cornell, and his book so impressed White with its pith and good sense about writing that some thirty years later he took the trouble to revise and add a chapter of his own, "An Approach to Style." The basic position of the whole book is set forth in these sentences from White's chapter:

> The beginner should approach style warily, realizing that it is himself he is approaching, no other; and he should begin by turning resolutely away from all devices that are popularly believed to indicate style—all mannerisms, tricks, adornments. The approach to style is by way of plainness, simplicity, orderliness, sincerity.

These were the qualities which characterized White's own writing. His essays and humorous anecdotes were almost always low-keyed, avoiding farcical and grotesque effects, and staying close to the level of everyday life.

It is just this simplicity of treatment, this willingness to let the material speak for itself without much apparent manipulation, which was one of the lessons White could teach Thurber, and which helped Thurber find his own easy, natural, casual style. Of course it should be pointed out that the reason Thurber could learn from White was that the two men were extraordinarily alike to begin with—their relish of the ironies of existence, their taste in literary clowning, their view of modern man and his environment were essentially the same. In the summer of 1928, Thurber contributed frequently to White's "Notes and Comment" page, and it would be a fine-tuned ear indeed that could distinguish the Thurber items from the White. For example, there is this, in the June 23, 1928, issue:

[26] William Strunk, Jr., and E. B. White, *The Elements of Style* (New York: Macmillan, 1959).

A little train we sometimes take, to a country place we know, becomes a very friendly train when it gets north of where the twenty-minute commuters depart. Only a few passengers remain, and mostly these are old friends of the conductor, a wise and a kindly man. He inquires after their children, listens to them tell how their gardens are coming on, and has a wealth of sound advice on many things. He knows what to do for poison ivy and for cinders in the eye and for drooping spirits. Recently he admonished us on the evils of reading newspapers, and particularly risking the eyesight upon them in a fading light, and pointed out, as a far better thing to study, the first fireflies of the season lighting up in the fields. By comparison with psychoanalysts we have known, our genial conductor seems to us to bring considerably more repose to the soul.

and this, from the June 30, 1928, issue:

Some organization is trying to save the wild flowers. We see its pleading signs on all the trains we take. "A plucked flower fades quickly, a flower in the field is a joy forever." We gather that the iris and the dogwood and the wild rose are departing from the countryside under the onslaught of the holiday-makers. Our heart is with the crusade but our hope is not high after what we saw the other day. A gang of flower bandits got on our train at a station which marks the line where the noises of the city fade and you can hear the crickets and the frogs. The arms of each were heavy. It was a rowdy crowd, and before the train reached 125th Street the men were fencing with blossoms and some of the women were slapping each other playfully with blue flags. There is, however, a little hope. More poison ivy is about this year than for a long time.

The first is Thurber's, the second is White.

During Thurber's first two years on the magazine, Ross refused to pay him extra for his contributions to the literary department, on the grounds that not getting paid for writing would make him concentrate better on his editorial duties.[27] But Thurber turned out a steady stream of short pieces notwithstanding, and finally Ross relented and began to pay him the regular rates. Most of this work between 1927 and 1929 is best described by that over-used term, "transitional." He stayed within the established patterns of American literary humor with which he had been experimenting since college days—the paragraph, the anecdote of personal experience (usually dealing with the trivial misadventures of everyday life),

[27] Letter to Harvey Breit, November 25, 1949.

the comic essay (a flexible form adaptable to a great range of subjects and modes), the parody, and light verse. Looming up behind most of these forms was the inescapable figure of Robert Benchley.

In a review of a posthumous collection of Benchley's work, Thurber called him "the humorists' humorist." [28] This was not mere conventional praise of a departed colleague, for it was Benchley, more than anyone else, who gave definitive shape to the forms and subject matter of American literary humor in the 1920's and early '30's. Like Stephen Leacock, to whom he always acknowledged his debt, he saw the great comic subject of modern life as the predicament of the ordinary man confronted by a complex technological-business society which he neither understands nor approves, and by a host of minor domestic problems which he can never quite handle. Benchley's protagonist is usually the well-meaning bumbler, either as harassed father and husband or as slightly stuffy businessman, politician, or scientist. Thurber took over this figure and reshaped it to express his own temperament and personality, making it into a darker, more neurotic and complex character than Benchley's.

Benchley's art is essentially the art of parody, whether his subject is the style and form of a novelist or the language and values of popular culture. His literary parodies are humor and criticism of a high order. Who can ever feel quite the same about Dreiser after reading "Compiling an American Tragedy"? Thurber's own favorite was the parody of Galsworthy called "The Blue Sleeve Garter," and he once said in a letter, "I would rather have Benchley's 'The Blue Sleeve Garter' and Cyril Connolly's parody of Huxley than all the junk written between Washington Irving and the end of the Civil War." [29] More than once he said that he would rather have Benchley's praise than anyone else's, and he summed up his view of Benchley as a force felt by a whole generation of writers of humor in his review of *Chips Off the Old Benchley*, in 1949:

> Benchley got off to a fast start ahead of all of us on the New Yorker, and our problem was the avoidance of imitation. He had written about practically everything, and his comic devices were easy to fall into. White once showed me something he'd written and asked anxiously, "Did Benchley say that?" In a 1933 preface I said that we were all afraid that whatever we had engaged on had probably been done better by Robert Benchley in 1924.[30]

[28] "The Incomparable Mr. Benchley," *New York Times Book Review*, September 18, 1949.
[29] Letter to James Fullington, August 6, 1952 (Thurber Collection).
[30] *New York Times Book Review*, September 18, 1949.

Thurber's talent took its own shape, and his mature work is very different from Benchley's, but the lines it followed during its early development were the lines laid down by Benchley.

One of the first pieces Thurber sold to the magazine, an ironic fable entitled "News of the Day" (April 2, 1927), recalls Benchley's satiric treatment of popular sentimental attitudes. It is more flippant and superficial than Thurber's later fables, but one can see in this early piece the preparations for such classic reversals of popular folklore as "The Little Girl and the Wolf," with its moral, "It is not so easy to fool little girls nowadays as it used to be." The brief anecdote tells the sad tale of little Marjorie Morrison, aged eleven, whose father has gone to Canada with a stenographer who subsequently murdered him, and whose mother has just killed her lover by choking him with an oil mop. A kindly adult world shields her from the ugly facts, but one day little Marjorie disappears and everyone is sure that she has learned the truth and killed herself.

> And then along about five P.M. the next day little Marjorie came back to her aunt's house in the Bronx.
>
> "My precious!" cried her happy aunt, "where has Aunty's precious been?"
>
> "I'm booked solid for twenty-six weeks in vaudeville at five grand a month," said little Marjorie.

He followed the Benchley model in several anecdotes of personal misadventure, like "Camera vs St. Bernard" (June 7, 1928), dealing with the tribulations of the American tourist trying to get a camera repaired in Paris, and he did a number of parodies as well. Most of them are best forgotten, but one, a parody of Hemingway entitled "A Visit from Saint Nicholas" (December 24, 1927), gives promise of better things to come. It is a re-telling of " 'Twas the Night Before Christmas" in the Hemingway manner, and the comic incongruity between subject and style is effectively developed.

> I went to the chimney and looked up. I saw him get into his sleigh. He whistled at his team and the team flew away. The team flew as lightly as thistledown. The driver called out, "Merry Christmas and good night." I went back to bed.
>
> "What was it?" asked Mamma. "Saint Nicholas?" She smiled.
> "Yeah," I said.
> She sighed and turned in the bed.
> "I saw him," I said.

"Sure."

"I did see him."

"Sure you saw him." She turned farther toward the wall.

In addition to the Benchley-style anecdotes and parodies, Thurber did a number of short stories and a rather unsuccessful profile of Myron T. Herrick in his first two years on the magazine. The profile was a new form, original with *The New Yorker,* and it was just in the process of development when Thurber tried his first one. The traditional journalistic biographical piece was almost always a success story with strong moralistic and inspirational overtones, but the *New Yorker* writers, after some early backing and filling, worked out the detached, ironic, somewhat skeptical view of the subject which has since become a trademark of the magazine.[31]

He had already written a feature story on Herrick for the Kansas City *Star* Magazine in 1925, and the difference between the two pieces suggests the kind of influence *The New Yorker* had on Thurber as a writer. "The Evolution of an Ambassador" is a conventional journalistic feature article, praising the good work, personal charm and democratic instincts of an admirable American abroad. To the French, he will always be a hero for his famous response to those who urged him to leave Paris for a safer place in 1914: "There are times when a dead ambassador is of greater service than a live one." "Master of Ceremonies," Thurber's profile of Herrick in *The New Yorker* (July 21, 1928), takes a rather ironic view of Herrick's success story, balancing the record of his achievements against the implication that his position owed more to his nice smile and his cultivation of the right people than to his intellectual or political talents. The profile emphasizes Herrick's magnetism and his talent for the theatrical, citing as an example the famous quotation about the dead ambassador. This time, Thurber wickedly adds a detail absent from his earlier account: "Embassy men smile when you ask them if Herrick really said that. But the French will doubtless carve it some day on a monument to him."

Many of these early *New Yorker* pieces show Thurber staking out his own territory, assimilating the examples of Benchley and White, but shaping them to his own artistic purposes. "The Thin Red Leash" (August 13, 1927) is his version of the anecdote of humiliating experience, and he handles it in the way of White rather than in the way of Benchley. Benchley almost always employed the persona of the bumbler or the victim, and his anecdotes were usually heightened and stylized for strong comic effect. Thurber did many pieces in the Benchley manner throughout his

[31] Kramer, *Ross and The New Yorker,* p. 245.

career, but his own way was to draw more directly on autobiographical experience, to appear as himself, more or less, rather than to use a persona, to manipulate the material as little as possible, letting it assume a natural form, following White here, but unlike White, to treat it more fictionally than essayistically; that is to say, to treat it as a specific dramatic occasion rather than to generalize upon it.

"The Thin Red Leash" has to do with Thurber's embarrassment in walking a little Scotty down in a tough neighborhood of the Village.

> It takes courage for a tall thin man to lead a tiny Scotch terrier pup on a smart red leash in our neighborhood, that region bounded roughly (and how!) by Hudson and West Streets, where the Village takes off its Windsor tie and dons its stevedore corduroys. Here men are guys and all dogs are part bull. Here "cute" apartments stand quivering like pioneers on the prairie edge.

The Thurbers were living in a small apartment on Horatio Street near Ninth Avenue in 1927, the dog is obviously Jeannie, and the experience is clearly autobiographical. The local toughs stare and ask rude questions (" 'What d' y' say me an' you and the dog go somewheres and have tea?' "); Thurber dies a thousand deaths. There are characteristic touches of fantasy in the presentation of Thurber's state of mind—the men of the local gang seem to him gigantic physical specimens, one obviously a man "who blows through truck exhaust-whistles to test them," another a smokestack wrecker, still another "an artisan who lifts locomotives from track to track when the turntables are out of order"—but for the most part, the anecdote stays close to the pattern of everyday probability. The conflict is resolved when the locomotive lifter turns out to be an admirer of the breed, and Thurber and his dog are at last accepted.

In "I Burn My Bridge Behind Me" (December 1, 1928) and "The Psyching of Mr. Rogers" (April 27, 1929) Thurber explores one of his most original subjects—the humorous treatment of psychological distress. "The Psyching of Mr. Rogers" deals with a timid man whose self-consciousness about taking a straw hat to the cleaners turns into a classic neurosis. "I Burn My Bridge" is the interior monologue of a man who has just been defeated and humiliated in a bridge game, and whose mind is surging with fantasies of revenge and triumph. The subject is typically Benchley—the blow to the ego of having been shown up as inept on some social occasion—but Thurber's treatment gives it an extra psychological dimension. The speaker's fantasies are paranoid, and he is obviously in danger of losing control of himself at any moment.

I'd love to play him and that woman, just the three of us, somehow, under bright lights, as in a fight ring, with a crowd watching. Play him off his feet. Think fast, major! Think fast! Whammy! Play on that! Whammy! Play on that! Whammy! Play on *that!*. . . Too bad, major, didn't count on *that* baby, did you?

Thurber's most ambitious early experiment, however, did not quite come off. "Menaces in May" (May 26, 1928), as Helen Thurber says in her introduction to *Credos and Curios,* was his first *New Yorker* story to depart from the comic casual formula. It is a very uneven piece, sentimental in part, and ironic in part, and so it lacks real unity, but it is nonetheless significant as an effort to treat another of his favorite subjects—the romantic personality—in "serious" terms. Like "One Is a Wanderer" and "The Evening's at Seven," written a few years later, it is closely autobiographical.

The opening scene sets the mood of romantic nostalgia developed more fully in the two later stories. Three people are in a New York hotel room late on a rainy spring night—the protagonist ("the man"), Julia, the girl he was in love with eighteen years ago, and her husband, Joe, now running to fat and thinning hair. The phonograph plays Gene Austin's "What a day was yes-ter-day for yes-ter-day gave me you-u-u." The man is racked with frustrated longings. Julia and her husband are in vaudeville; the man "had been shy, 'smart at his lessons,' one doesn't win Julias that way." (The autobiographical origins of the cast of characters are striking: Julia is Eva Prout, the dream-girl of Thurber's boyhood and adolescence, who went on to have a successful career as a vaudeville performer; "the man" is of course Thurber, who described himself in almost exactly the same way in a letter to Nugent back in 1918—"teacher's pet—grind—nothing. . . .")

On the way home, his emotions in a turmoil, the city's ugliness and random violence assail him: the noise of ashcans being rolled around, the curses of a young man being beaten up by two policemen, the angry ramblings of a drunk, disappointed in love, the memory of a Cuban who killed himself in the subway after a holdup. He finds himself frightened, and when a panhandler accosts him and he gives the man a handful of coins, he berates himself for being a coward. In a moment of self-mockery, he thinks of romantic heroes like Lord Jim and Cyrano and how they faced their deaths.

Back in his apartment, he looks at a bronze candelabrum his wife had brought back from France. She is away on a visit, and he thinks of her taste and her beauty, and of the good times they had together on the Riviera. "What a finely wrought thing they had made of life," he muses, seeing himself in Jamesian terms. But the chaos and violence of the city expose the inadequacy of the aesthetic illusion.

In the story, the self-mocking protagonist measures himself against two forms of the ideal—the romantic hero, here and elsewhere symbolized by Conrad's Lord Jim, and the aesthete, always for Thurber best represented by Henry James—and finds disappointment and humiliation in the contrast. But the humiliation is not very well dramatized, and Thurber is not sure whether it is a comic or a serious experience. The gap between the ideal and the actual was one of Thurber's great subjects, but he had to see it as comic to get the best out of it. Treated straight, as it is here, it yielded only pathos and sentimentality. Thurber himself was well aware of the story's shortcomings, and in a letter to Herman Miller in 1935, he said that he did not include it in *The Middle-Aged Man on the Flying Trapeze* because it seemed to him "a little sugary and fuzzy."

"Menaces in May" shows that Thurber was not yet ready to handle the romantic experience seriously, and it points to an even larger fact: that his imagination was unshakably comic. When he trusted it, it brought him wonderful insights into human thought and behavior, but as soon as he tried to see things seriously or straight, he saw them less interestingly and originally. His true perception of romance was that it always turned into the ludicrous, and in a 1931 letter to Miller he suggested that there ought to be "a fine novel" about a romantic idealist whose "noble dedications in one chapter are seen with their hair in their eyes" in the next. His later romantic stories, "One Is a Wanderer" and "The Evening's at Seven," are technically accomplished, but they look rather conventional and derivative when set beside "The Secret Life of Walter Mitty."

Thurber worked hard to develop his skills in the humorous essay and the fictional sketch, but between 1927 and 1935, when Russell Maloney took over, he did most of his writing for "The Talk of the Town." [32] They were eight years of wandering the city and writing about its places and people. "I wrote about a million words for Talk in my time," he once recalled.[33] Ross attached particular importance to this department and to White's "Notes and Comment" page which preceded it, because it was here that the tone of informal conversation which was his ideal for the magazine as a whole was to be established. In the early days there were weekly "Talk" conferences, attended by Katharine Angell, White, Ingersoll, and Thurber, during which Ross worried over the style and content

[32] Thurber devotes a chapter in *The Years with Ross* to his work on the "The Talk of the Town."
[33] Letter to Frank Gibney, October 31, 1956.

of the department with the full force of his neurotic perfectionism. "Talk" was a group enterprise, depending on the reportorial energies and imaginations of a number of different people. Ralph Ingersoll and Bernard A. Bergman were the chief idea men for the department in Thurber's day, and Charles H. Cooke (the original "our Mr. Stanley") was the best reporter. Thurber was the rewrite man. He did his own legwork on a few items each week, but his chief job was reworking facts and anecdotes submitted by others.

Ross was always hard to please, and at first he was convinced that Thurber had worked too long on newspapers to do "Talk" properly.[34] " 'He can't write Talk the way I want it. He'll always write journalese,' " he said, and for three months he rewrote nearly every one of Thurber's contributions, filling them up with favorite expressions of his own like "and such," which he thought would give them a casual, offhand air. Thurber's "The studio walls are hung with oils and water colors, with here and there a gouache and silverpoint" became "The studio walls are hung with oils and watercolors, and such." [35] It was not until the issue of December 2, 1927, after what Thurber called "three months of slavery" that Ross accepted and praised a piece by Thurber, and this only after forcing him to rewrite it six times. " 'Now you got it,' he said. 'Write it the way you would talk to a dinner companion.' " The piece in question, "A Friend of Jimmy's," was a brief character sketch of a man named William Seeman, a friend of Mayor Walker's and president of the White Rose salmon cannery. It is an undistinguished sketch, but Thurber remembered it as a second turning point in his relationship with Ross.[36]

Even so, the early days were full of conflict between editor and rewrite man. Ross's revisions were sometimes heavy-handed or finicky, and more than once he spoiled a good anecdote. On occasion, when things were at an impasse, Thurber would rewrite Ross's revisions and fake his "R" of approval on the sheet. Gradually the tension relaxed, as Ross came to realize that Thurber was exactly what the department needed. "Talk" was to be an entertaining miscellany of anecdotes about interesting people and events on the New York scene. It needed an easy informal style, blending the reportorial and the essayistic, and a strict economy of means. This is exactly what Thurber had to offer. His mastery of the art of paragraphing, which he had learned from the peerless Robert O. Ryder of the *Ohio State Journal,* was the ideal apprenticeship for "The Talk of the Town." As Robert

[34] *The Years with Ross,* p. 39.
[35] Ibid., p. 102.
[36] Ibid., p. 40.

M. Coates, his old friend and colleague on the magazine, once observed, " 'Talk' was just made for him, as he was made for it, and it is no more than simple fact to say he 'made' the department . . . into its present image." [37]

Thurber's "Talk" pieces are much more impressive than the casuals he did during his first two or three years with the magazine. He is clearly more at home in the sharply limited world of the paragraph or brief anecdote than in the short story or the humorous essay. Almost from the beginning, the "Talk" pieces show an ease and flexibility and control of tone not yet mastered in his other work. Although "The Talk of the Town" was un-signed, Thurber collected some twenty-eight of the pieces he had done between 1928 and 1935 under the general title "Time Exposures" in *The Beast in Me*. He selected only those for which he had done the legwork as well as the writing, and for which he would thus take full responsibility. Taken together, this group of short pieces gives a compact picture of the range and variety of Thurber's performance in this highly specialized de-partment of *The New Yorker* as well as the growth and development of his style over a period of eight years.

The first item in "Time Exposures," a piece on the new Reptile Hall at the Museum of Natural History, is dated February 18, 1928, only a few months after he was assigned to "Talk," and yet it already has the easy style, the informal reportage, and the low-keyed comic comment which made the department one of the most widely admired journalistic features in America. The opening sentences set the tone:

> The New Reptile Hall was officially opened a few days ago in the Museum of Natural History and we visited it amidst a group of youngsters who kept crying "Good night!" and their mothers who kept murmuring "Mercy!" The place is like that.

The exhibits are described with an eye on the little unexpected incongrui-ties which make life diverting.

> In one case reposes the world's largest frog and although right next door is a tiny reptile whose sex life and fighting skill are described minutely, the sign by the world's largest frog frankly says, "Nothing is known of its habits," thus giving us an example of the oddities of scientific research to ponder about. . . .

The character assumed by the writer (the editorial "we" which is still the persona of the department) is that of a wanderer of the city, a solitary

[37] "James Thurber," *Authors Guild Bulletin*, December, 1961.

observer who is interested in out-of-the way matters like the old cemeteries in New York, the haunts of O. Henry, now almost forgotten, as well as more up-to-date matters like the exotic new Childs restaurant under the Paramount Theater, and the landing of a damaged Zeppelin at Lakehurst, New Jersey. His manner is casual and informal, his treatment of his subject deliberately unsystematic and impressionistic. His area is generally the overlooked, the significant piece of trivia.

The account of the Zeppelin landing, titled "Hot Dog" (October 27, 1928), shows Thurber extending the range of the typical "Talk" piece, moving beyond the area of the amusing oddities to be found in the city to a moral judgment of human behavior. The four-paragraph piece describes the sensation-hungry crowd and the hot-dog men and the novelty sellers who come to see the wounded ship try to land.

> A tall colored man, who wore a silk hat and sold peanuts, also dispensed jollity like merchandise. We gathered that he followed disaster around the country because the prospect of disaster whets the appetites of people. On this occasion the prospect was an overdue airship with a hole in one of its stabilizers. The hawkers jollied the crowds. "Well-l-l, a loaf of bread and a pound of meat and all the mustard you can eat."

The method of the piece is objective and reportorial, but the details are selected to convey a picture of mindless thrill-seeking, callousness, and vulgarity.

"The Talk of the Town" was Thurber's first unqualified success. It was in doing this weekly stint of informal reporting and commentary that he found the style he had been looking for—casual, economical, flexible. Looking back on Thurber's many accomplishments, Robert M. Coates said, "I think . . . that in some ways he was proudest of all his exploits in the old 'Talk' days, when after briefly studying some anecdote or other small item that had been sent in to us he would put it down beside his typewriter in the jammed-up little office we happily shared and proceed to rewrite it equally swiftly, giving it just the right turn of phrasing that added point and pungence—or when, seizing on a 'visit' suggestion, he would put on his hat and, demon reporter–like, go out to get the material for a piece on some landmark or other in our ever-beguiling city and come back and write it in time for our Thursday deadline." [38]

The late Twenties and early Thirties were the high-water mark of

[38] Ibid.

"Talk." After a while, the weekly conferences were abandoned, and Ross's interest shifted to other departments. Thurber himself wearied of the routine after eight years, and quit in 1935. Thereafter it was handled by a succession of able writers, but in Ross's view, it was never the same after Thurber dropped out. Writing to Thurber in 1946, Ross lamented the decline of his favorite department: "Give me you, Shawn, and Cooke and I'll get out a Talk department," he said. "It's up to God to send some young talent around this place, and He's been neglecting the job. That's the trouble." [39]

Looking back on his experience, Thurber described the "Talk" formula and the *New Yorker* form and style generally in a long letter to John McNulty written in the late Thirties. McNulty had joined the magazine in 1937, and during his first year or two he despaired of ever getting the hang of doing pieces for "The Talk of the Town" and "Notes and Comment." Thurber was by this time an acknowledged master of the *New Yorker* forms, and he could look at the magazine with some objectivity. His letter is primarily an effort to help and encourage his friend, but it is also a remarkable piece of informal literary criticism. He is sympathetic with McNulty's frustration, because he went through the same ordeal himself: "Ross ran my stuff through his typewriter for months, threw it away by carloads, often rewrote the things so I didn't find a phrase of mine left. I would try to imitate his rewrites of my rewrites, keeping in mind what he always said 'limber it up, make it easy and off-hand, like table-talk.' What came out often sounded like the table talk of bindle stiffs." Listening to Ross's advice will probably be more confusing than helpful, he says. "He's likely to fill you up with too many ideas and maxims and instructions!"

> He could rattle off "Don't build it up, make it limber, we don't have to know too much, we want goddam it like table talk, interesting stuff, full of facts, to hell with the facts, we don't have to be experts, let yourself go, thousand interesting things in the city, for Christ's sake, etc. etc." I got bewildered. I finally figured what he wanted, in a way: "A man we know was telling us the other day about gaskets. Seems they are little funny kind of what's-its-names. Fellow named Pritch or Feep invents them, or imports them, or something of the sort. Otto H. Kahn has ninety-two and a Mrs. Bert Geefle of the Savoy Plaza seven. Nobody else has any, except Madame Curie who was presented with four thousand by the city of Nantes for telling

[39] *The Years with Ross*, p. 110.

the city what time it was one night when it called Meridian 1212 and got her by mistake."

Writing for "Talk" is chiefly a matter of learning the formula, and the formula is one of style. White "was the first guy to write perfect Talk pieces," and "everybody has in a sense imitated him." "It is a formula, all right," Thurber concedes, although it is not as tight as the sonnet. Everyone writing for "Talk" or "Comment" has to follow it—"John Steinbeck, Walt Whitman, Evelyn Waugh, and Shakespeare would all have to get the knack of it, if they got any stories printed."

Thurber then points out, reassuringly, that "Talk" and "Comment" are not typical of the magazine as a whole; in the other departments, the writer can write as he pleases. "People sometimes speak of a New Yorker style," he says, "but they are either thinking of Talk or of the form and shape of the casuals; what makes them look alike is their length and form. Where nothing runs much over 2 or 3 thousand words—as in casuals—there is bound to be a similarity of form." There is a subtle danger in this sameness of form, he confesses. Years of writing casuals have probably shaped his imagination for life, he says. "I find most of my stories, after I have typed them, run to 6 and a half or seven pages. I haven't tried for that. My brain has unconsciously formed that kind of mould for them. In a way this is bad, because everything I start—play, two-volume novel, or what-not, finally rounds itself out into 6 or 7 pages—seems complete, too." He goes on to define the casual. It is a form of its own, "neither essay nor short story, but a little of each. . . . Slighter than the short story, stronger than the essay." Ross always said that he would never use a short story, says Thurber. "I think he vaguely means by a short story something with more than four characters and at least three changes of scene." Sally Benson writes the purest casuals, in Thurber's opinion. "You never confuse her stuff with a real short story." Robert M. Coates, on the other hand, "has ingeniously managed to get short stories into the casual form."

The trademark of the *New Yorker* casual is the inconclusive ending. "We have invented, or perfected, something that is neither a happy ending nor an unhappy ending. It might be called the trailing off." Thurber is obviously a bit puzzled by this phenomenon, and he reaches out to baseball and ballet for analogies. "We seem to find a high merit in leaving men on bases," he says. "It's the ballet finish; rather than the third act tag or the black out. More people are left standing and looking in ballets and New Yorker casuals than in any other known art forms."

After having described the *New Yorker* form, Thurber warns McNulty not to try too hard to imitate it. "I don't care what the fashion in casuals is, nor should you," he says. "I read very few of them. It is easy to get New Yorker glut, casual fag. Don't read the magazine too consistently. If you read it from cover to cover it's like eating a two pound box of candy." It is bad to read it so much that "its little tricks of form and style keep running through your head." Finishing the letter the next morning, he adds a few maxims ("Don't let the magazine new-yorker you, mcnulty the magazine") and words of encouragement ("There's nothing more you have to learn from the New Yorker—the rest is what it's got to learn from you").[40]

---

[40] Undated letter, probably of the late 1930's.

7

The First Two Books

THE PUBLICATION OF *Is Sex Necessary?* in 1929 brought Thurber and White their first national recognition and their first taste of the financial rewards of popular authorship. The critics praised the book enthusiastically (Will Cuppy called it "a minor classic"),[1] and it became a best-seller, going through twenty-two printings in its first year.[2] It has continued to sell: partly because of its provocative title it is still in print in a variety of editions, and it has been translated into half a dozen foreign languages.

It is not surprising that Thurber and White should have made their first venture into the book form a joint enterprise. Each man was at the stage in his career where he wanted to do something bigger than the *New Yorker* casual, and each man found in the other a congenial and creatively stimulating friend and colleague. The wave of sex-and-psychology books which were the latest phenomenon of the publishing world struck both of them as a prime subject for parody, and in the spring of 1929 they began to work on it. They planned the book together, and then, instead of collaborating on the writing throughout, they divided it up, each man writing his own chapters. Thurber did the Preface, chapters 1 ("The Nature of the Ameri-

[1] New York *Herald Tribune* Book Review, December 8, 1929.
[2] Edwin T. Bowden, *James Thurber: A Bibliography* (Columbus, Ohio: Ohio State University Press, 1968), pp. 8–9.

can Male"), 3 ("A Discussion of Feminine Types"), 5 ("The Lilies-and-Bluebirds Delusion"), 7 ("Claustrophobia, or What Every Young Wife Should Know"), the Glossary, and the illustrations, which took him one evening. White did the Foreword, chapters 2 ("How to Tell Love from Passion"), 4 ("The Sexual Revolution"), 6 ("What Should Children Tell Their Parents?"), 8 ("Frigidity in Men"), "Answers to Hard Questions," and the concluding "Note on the Drawings in This Book." [3]

Three years before, Thurber had unsuccessfully peddled the manuscript of his parody of current best-sellers, *Why We Behave Like Microbe Hunters*, from publisher to publisher; now, in collaboration with White, he made the best-seller lists himself. The success of the book lies in the fact that it offers the reader more than parody, or at least parody of such a high order as almost to transcend the limitations of the form. It not only mocks the literature of popular psychoanalysis, it also offers a wonderfully comic view of courtship and marriage in the modern world. Like so much of the art of the Twenties, its satiric energy is directed against the Victorian cult of Ideality, but at the same time it sees the absurdities in the search for emancipation through Freud. It looks at sex as neither romantic mystery nor scientific problem, but as embarrassment, trap, predicament, or battleground. And finally, the whole performance is given a startling new dimension in Thurber's unconventional drawings.

As parody, the book takes hold of the pretentiousness of the popular psychology writers—the pseudo-philosophy, the glib social history, the labored classifications, the indigestible terminology, the pedantic citation of authorities—and transforms all this bad writing and muddy thinking into delightful absurdity. The special language of psychoanalysis provides some good moments: describing a particular stage in the development of the man-woman relationship, White observes, "Her essential Narcissism (pleasure of looking in a mirror) was met by his Begonia-ism (concept of the potted plant)." Absurd case-histories, like that of George Smith, "who had freed his libido without difficulty from familial objects, and was eager to marry," but who became obsessed by the challenge of the pigs-in-clover puzzle game and suffered a "physico-psychic breakdown," and passages of mock history, imitating the fondness of the psychologists for facile generalization, are the basic elements of parody in the book.

But it is in the style that the spirit of mockery is at its liveliest. Both Thurber and White practice the art of comic deflation, juxtaposing the poetic and the colloquial, the romantic and the realistic in constantly

[3] Norris W. Yates, *The American Humorist: Conscience of the Twentieth Century* (Ames, Iowa: Iowa State University Press, 1964), pp. 384–85.

Family portrait, 1915: back, *William, James, and Mrs. Thurber;* front, *Robert and Mr. Thurber*

At East High, 1913

In the playbill for the Scarlet Mask Club's
A Twin Fix, *1923*

To:— Katharine Angell, god
bless her, who brought this
on herself.
H. W. Ross

Harold Ross in the early days of The New Yorker, *c. 1928*

Robert Benchley, c. 1935

E. B. White, 1940's

At the Columbus opening of the film version of The Male Animal, *1942:* left to right, *William, Robert, Mrs. Thurber, James, and Helen*

Author at work, 1943

At the drawing board, 1950

With E. B. White at Rosemary
Thurber's wedding, 1953

"I'm not mild and gentle. . . . ," 1960

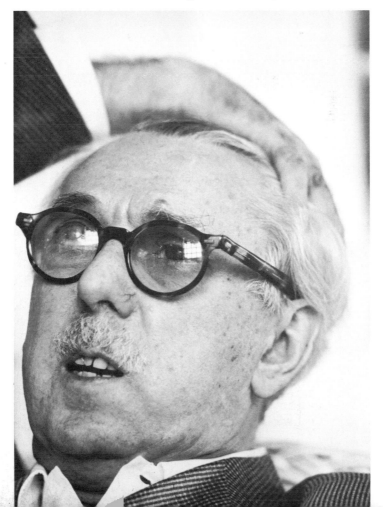

Mild and gentle, 1960

incongruous patterns. Here is Thurber's account of the origin of man's desire to worship woman:

> Right then and there Man conceived the notion that Woman was so closely associated, so inextricably entwined with the wonders and terrors of the world, that she had no fear of them. She was in quiet league with the forces of life. She was an integral part of the stars and the moon, she was one with the trees and the iris in the bog. He fell down on his knees, the pitiable idiot, and grasped her about the waist.

Here is White, describing the problem of the young man who finds himself objectively assessing the experience while kissing a girl (" 'Say, this is pretty nice, now,' " he says to himself): "Instead of his soul being full of the ecstasy which is traditionally associated with love's expression, his soul is just fiddling around." This abrupt deflation of the high through an unexpected collision with the low is the major comic device of the book as a whole. Thurber is perhaps most effective with it in his drawings, which in their rude simplification of the human figure and their fanciful creatures have a devastatingly reductive effect. Two examples should suffice: on the facing page of the preface two guinea pig–like rodents stand nose to nose, in obvious parody of the subject of a book entitled *Is Sex Necessary?* Thurber's mock-historical discussion of man's idealization of woman is illustrated by a drawing of a dumpy and unappetizing nude woman on all fours entitled "Early Woman." A figure less likely to elicit worship would be hard to imagine.

The special target of most of the chapters in *Is Sex Necessary?* is the Victorian sentimentality about womanhood, sex, and marriage. "It got so that in speaking of birth and other natural phenomena, women seemed often to be discussing something else, such as the Sistine Madonna or the aurora borealis," says Thurber in the opening chapter. One young bride, suffering from "The Lilies-and-Bluebirds Delusion," believed that she would have a baby when her husband brought bluebirds into a room filled with lilies. On the wedding night the husband is taken aback to find their hotel suite filled with lilies-of-the-valley. He asks her who has died. She asks him if he has brought the bluebirds. They are immediately at cross-purposes.

> "Now, dear," said her husband more reasonably, "let's try to get this thing straightened out. What are you talking about, anyway?"
> "Sex—if you want to know!" she blurted out, and swooned.

Throughout this chapter one can see Thurber repudiating the attitudes which dominated the Midwest of his youth. He himself was a romantic by nature, a sentimentalist, emotionally immature even in his mid-twenties. The extravagance and unreality of his language and attitudes in the letters to Nugent describing his love for Eva Prout is striking evidence of the extent to which the stereotypes of nineteenth-century woman-worship shaped his emotional life. Here, at the age of thirty-four, those stereotypes were still lively enough in his memory (and in the memories of millions of other Americans of his generation) to be worth attacking.

In chapter 7, "Claustrophobia," Thurber moves into the area which he always felt was the richest in comic possibilities—the domestic American scene. His special view of it was as a stage on which the tragedy of the trivial was constantly being enacted. Marriage is seen as a trap, and the American man as a victim driven by its demands beyond the borders of sanity. A woman's desire to potter about the house and build a safe, secure world out of domestic routine is likely to give a man "a strange 'boxed-in' feeling." "He will strive to get out of the house, and his wife should allow him to go."

White's contributions are virtually indistinguishable from Thurber's. The parody of the topics and the jargon of the sexology books, the passages of mock-history, the deflation of the romantic by juxtaposing it to the commonplace—all these basic methods and materials are the interchangeable properties of both writers. If there is a noticeable difference, it is that White is more likely to be discursive, while Thurber is generally more dramatic, casting the material into the form of a scene, with character, action, and dialogue.[4] But even this distinction applies only about half the time.

Stylistically, White has more variety, subtlety, and range than Thurber. One can see why Thurber took him as his model. Here is a typical White sentence, in which the wit consists in the odd conjunction of occasions: trying to distinguish love from passion, says White, is a disturbing question. "Usually it arises at some inopportune moment: at the start of a letter, in the middle of an embrace, at the end of a day in the country." Or there is this comment on Thurber's drawings, where the wit lies in taking a sleeping metaphor literally: "All I . . . can do is to hint at the uncanny faithfulness with which he has caught—caught and thrown to the floor—the daily severity of life's mystery. . . ."

The drawings, which add so much to the comic values of the book, are

---

4 Kramer, *Ross and The New Yorker,* pp. 204–05.

Thurber's professional debut as an artist. He had, of course, been drawing all his life—since 1901, he told Alistair Cooke, but except for the sketches he did when he was editor of the Ohio State *Sun-Dial* (all the artists were away at war, he liked to say, and there was nobody else to do them), these are his first published work. As a schoolboy he had covered the flyleaves and margins of Caesar's Commentaries with men and animals, and at the university he enlivened his copy of the Manual of Arms with Mutt and Jeff cartoons.[5] During his newspaper days at Columbus he began to draw his famous dogs on the memo pads of busy executives as a practical joke. He told the story of how it all began to Alistair Cooke:

> Let me take you back to Columbus, Ohio, in the early 1920's. I was out of school then and working as a reporter, and one of my friends was a high-powered real-estate man of that vintage and he had two or three telephones on his desk, and every time I dropped in to see him he also had three or four memo pads and the phones were all ringing. "Pardon me, Jim," he'd say. "Yes, Harry, yeh, I'll get that down," and he'd write it down. "And another thing, Harry, about that Johnson deal—just a second. . . ."

One time the executive left the room for three minutes, and Thurber drew a dog on each page of the memo pads.

> When he came back again, he said, "Sorry, Jim," and sat down and the phones began their old routine and he said, "Hey, Bill. Yes, yes, I'm sorry. What was that—eighty-three five? Just a minute, just a minute, Bill," and he began tearing off dogs. "Hold it, will you?" And there was a dog on each page. Finally he had brains enough to write the number down on the dog. That's how the dog began.[6]

Some years later, Thurber added to the legend: the peculiar configuration of his dogs, with their large heads and very short legs, was the result of accident, he said. When he started to fill up his friend's memo pad, he had intended to draw bloodhounds, he said, but the pad was too small to accommodate a true bloodhound's proportions, and so he had to compromise on the legs.[7]

Drawing was a superior form of doodling, a nervous release, an aid to cerebration, or possibly a joke for Thurber, but he never thought of his

[5] Letter to Herman Miller, undated, but probably 1935–36 (Thurber Collection).
[6] "James Thurber in Conversation with Alistair Cooke," *Atlantic*, CXCVIII (August, 1956), 37–38.
[7] "How to Name a Dog," *The Beast in Me* , p. 41.

sketches as having any artistic value until White became interested in them. Thurber was in the habit of drawing on yellow copy paper while he was thinking about something he was writing. At the end of the day, the wastebaskets and the floor would be covered with his absent-minded creations. One day in the spring of 1929, as the now-familiar story goes, White inked one in—a sketch of a seal on a rock looking at two distant dots and saying, "Hm, explorers"—and sent it in to the weekly art meeting at *The New Yorker*. Rea Irvin, the art director, thought it was a gag, and drew a seal's head on the same paper and sent it back with the note, " 'This is the way a seal's whiskers go.' " White sent it back the next week with the note, " 'This is the way a Thurber seal's whiskers go,' " but the drawing was rejected, as were the next fifteen Thurber submitted. It was not until 1930 that he was able to sell his drawings to the magazine (the "Pet Department" series marked his first appearance as a *New Yorker* artist), and for nearly two years White had to ink in the lines for him. After this, Thurber got up the courage to draw straightway in ink.[8]

It took Ross some years to convince himself that Thurber's drawings really amounted to anything. He found it hard to swallow that the British took Thurber seriously as a comic draughtsman, and in the early days he liked to say, " 'Thurber's drawings are a fad of the English, a passing fancy.' " [9] When Thurber had dinner with George Grosz, the famous German artist, in 1931, he told Ross that Grosz had said that he wanted to meet the American artist whose work began where that of other cartoonists left off. Ross asked, " 'Did he?' " and Thurber answered, " 'He meant me.' " " 'Hogwash,' " said Ross. A few years later, when a disgruntled cartoonist complained, " 'Why do you reject drawings of mine and print stuff by that fifth-rate artist Thurber?,' " Ross corrected him: " 'Third-rate,' " he said. Later on, he became an unabashed admirer of Thurber's art, and near the end of his life, he wrote Thurber proudly that *The New Yorker* had published three hundred and seven of his captioned drawings.[10]

When White suggested that Thurber illustrate *Is Sex Necessary?* Thurber dashed off thirty or forty drawings in one night, and took them down to the publisher's the next day. White laid them all out on the floor, and after a stunned silence, one of the Harper editors asked hesitantly, " 'I gather these are a rough idea of the kind of illustrations you want some artist to do?' " White answered firmly, " 'These are the drawings that go with the book.' " After the book became a success—a success due in no

[8] Undated letter to Herman Miller (Thurber Collection).
[9] *The Years with Ross*, p. 64.
[10] Ibid., p. 66.

small part to the drawings—Ross came grumbling into Thurber's office and asked about the rejected seal drawing. " 'Something created in his own office, something he had had first shot at, had been printed by a publisher, a species of freak with whom Ross never ceased to do battle.' " Thurber told him he had thrown it away. " 'Well, don't throw things away just because I reject them!' he yelled. 'Do it over again.' " [11] Later on, when Thurber's drawings had become one of *The New Yorker*'s most prized features, Ross denied that he had ever rejected the seal cartoon, and he and Thurber argued about it for years.

The illustrations are closely keyed to the text of *Is Sex Necessary?* and show men and women in various baffling situations, as well as a series of fanciful creatures, whose relationship to the problems of sex is somewhat more indirect. In "A Note on the Drawings," White defines the underlying themes of Thurber's art with uncanny accuracy. They are "the melancholy of sex" and "the implausibility of animals." "Implausible" is exactly the right word for Thurber's creatures. They look like a child's imagining of what the world of fish and animals might be like. Uninhibited by the requirements of realism or accurate observation, they take their own shapes and assume their own personalities, and their relation to the text is generally one of comic contrast or parallelism, as in the case of the nose-to-nose rodents.

White's description of the men and women in Thurber's drawings is especially significant. He notes that in almost every instance "the man . . . is badly frightened or even hurt."

> These "Thurber men" have come to be recognized as a distinct type in the world of art; they are frustrated, fugitive beings; at times they seem vaguely striving to get out of something without being seen (a room, a situation, a state of mind), at other times they are merely perplexed and too humble, or weak, to move. The *women*, you will notice, are quite different: temperamentally they are much better adjusted to their surroundings than are the men, and mentally they are much less capable of making themselves uncomfortable.

The "Note" is a kind of landmark, since it is the first critical definition of Thurber's subject matter and his special angle of vision. Here, as in his Introduction to *The Owl in the Attic*, White is introducing his friend to the public, and trying—in his offhand way—to say what kind of humorist he is.

[11] Ibid., p. 58.

The drawings are in a variety of styles. Thurber had obviously not yet settled on the character-types and settings which in a few years were to become the trademark of his cartoons, nor had he yet found a single and consistent technique. Some of the drawings come directly out of his Ohio State style—more realistic in intention and more detailed in representation. Some of the same props turn up, like the large chair, back to audience, which is featured in several of his *Sun-Dial* cartoons. Here, in the chapter on Claustrophobia, a husband is peering furtively around it. There are also a number of drawings in the *Life-Judge* manner—flappers, or couples kissing in the park—where there is an obvious effort to represent an attractive young woman dressed in the fashion of the day (as opposed to the shapeless and dowdy women who dominate his later work). Both of these styles—which Thurber soon gave up—are amateur and primitive in the pejorative sense, because he is trying for a realism or conventional style of representation which is simply beyond his reach. The best drawings in *Is Sex Necessary?* show Thurber experimenting with the drastic simplification which soon became the essence of his comic draughtsmanship.

In subject matter, the drawings can be divided into two groups. About half of them deal with the everyday domestic scene—a disconsolate suitor in the kitchen while his girl makes fudge (Diversion Subterfuge), a baseball player taking a good cut, a wife trying to explain to her husband about the guest towels. The other large group of drawings deals with the world of fantasy and the unconscious. Most of the figures in these drawings are symbolic representations of psychic states or conflicts. Most striking are the "Unconscious Drawings," in which picture and caption work together in a fine parody of the concepts and the language of psychoanalytic interpretation. Here the figures are large and dream-like, vaguely reminiscent of the figures in late nineteenth-century symbolic statuary. They wear no clothes, but they do not look nude. In "Unconscious Drawing, 3," a girl lies on her stomach, resting her chin on her clasped hands. Her features are sketched in, and she is obviously daydreaming. Standing on her forearm is a tiny, crudely drawn male figure, striking a rather pugnacious attitude. The caption says, "This is the work of Grace McFadden, aged eleven, of Bucyrus, Ohio . . . and was drawn on the day the Principal, K. L. Mooney, of the Paulding County Concentration Grade Schools, was married. Here the Pleasure-principle and the Wish Motive are both overshadowed by the Bridegroom Fallacy."

Is Sex Necessary? is a notable advance in Thurber's development as a humorist. It is his first significant treatment of his great subject, the battle of the sexes. His style is sharper and more controlled (thanks in part to his association with White), his comic invention is surer, and his insight into the ways of men and women is more illuminating than it was in his early *New Yorker* pieces. And, most important of all, it represents his debut as a comic draughtsman.

The Owl in the Attic (1931) is a collection of Thurber's *New Yorker* pieces done between 1928 and 1930. It is divided into three sections—the Mr. and Mrs. Monroe stories, "The Pet Department," and the "Ladies and Gentlemen's Guide to Modern English Usage"—which show off his versatility as fiction writer, draughtsman, and parodist. It is in this collection that Thurber reaches artistic maturity and independence. His talent was slow to develop, but once he found his true home on *The New Yorker* it flowered quickly.

E. B. White introduces the book with a mock biography describing Thurber and his background as though he were a character in a Conrad novel:

> I saw Thurber first in the summer of 1919. It was a steaming forenoon, when even the hot streets of Raritonga seemed deserted. The little packet-boat *Numidia* had slipped into the harbor during the night, to discharge copra, and when I saw a skiff being lowered I walked down toward the beach. The skiff had hardly grounded when Thurber stepped ashore, carrying a volume of Henry James and leading a honey bear by a small chain. As it happened, I was not to meet him again until years later, for my schooner left the island that afternoon to coast lazily eastward on the trade wind; but somehow his name kept bobbing up in the port gossip of those seas. . . .

The parody of the Conradian character and setting is delightful in its own right, but beneath the fooling White is making an important point about Thurber's imagination, which from the beginning was filled with romantic images and ideals. White's portrait of Thurber as romantic dreamer and victim of neurotic apprehensions ("in constant dread of something falling on his head from buildings" and "trailing a thin melancholy") could be taken as the beginning of the Thurber legend, a blend of biography and fiction in which Thurber came to look more and more like a character in one of his own stories.

White goes on to identify some of the main features of Thurber's work—his drawing ("This talent for drawing simple objects with an unsharpened pencil he decided to leave undeveloped, on the advice of friends"), his interest in grammar and usage (his articles on the subject "have worked their way . . . into the curricula of many Eastern universities as models of English prose and imperfect communication"), his interest in small animals (in particular, "the curious irrelevancies of man and beast"), and most significant of all, his concern with the relation between the sexes ("Above the still cool lake of marriage he saw rising the thin mist of Man's disparity with Woman. In his drawings one finds not only the simple themes of love and misunderstanding, but also the rarer and tenderer insupportabilities"). A better description of Thurber's literary personality and the subject matter of his work could hardly be imagined.

The eight Mr. and Mrs. Monroe stories are Thurber's first really definitive dramatization of marriage as a state of perpetual uneasiness. The discords here are minor and the tone is good-humoredly ironic, in contrast to many of the later stories, where the tensions are seen as destructive and the tone is bitter. Mr. Monroe is the archetypal Thurber husband—a romantic dreamer, given to heroic and amorous fantasies, while in fact he is timid, bewildered, and totally unable to cope with the demands of everyday life. Mrs. Monroe is small, bright, and supremely competent—except for the opening story, in which she arrives tipsy at a tea party, and causes her husband acute embarrassment.

The basic plot of most of the stories brings Mr. Monroe's fantasies about himself into conflict with some humiliating actuality—overpoweringly physical men like furniture movers, being left alone in a country house on a winter night, the practical difficulties involved in starting up a love affair. Mrs. Monroe is there either to set things right or to comment on the situation from the vantage point of her superior wisdom. Her manner to her husband is that of a mother to a retarded child. This picture of the American household may owe something to Thurber's early devotion to the comic strips. He was a lifelong admirer of such cartoonists as Clare Briggs, Cliff Sterrett, and Sidney Smith, whose specialty was the humorous treatment of the domestic scene, and the great stereotype within which they all worked invariably cast the husband in the role of weak protagonist and the wife as strong antagonist.

However, Thurber had no need to look into the popular arts for his picture of married life. His own observation and experience furnished him with quite enough material. In the household of his parents the pattern of well-meaning but ineffectual father and dominant mother was present in its purest form, although the overt conflict between husband and wife was muted. Thurber discovered all he needed to know about marital conflict in his own first marriage. The Mr. and Mrs. Monroe series, like most of Thurber's writing, is closely autobiographical. "Any novel by and of me, however, would be so flagrantly historical as to be embarrassing. The Monroe stories were transcripts, one or two of them varying less than an inch from the actual happenings," he confessed in a letter to Herman Miller.[12] Which one or two, it is impossible to say, but almost all of them have the ring of truth remembered. The central detail in "The 'Wooing' of Mr. Monroe" is a transformation of a real-life episode of 1931 in which Thurber was unable to turn off the hot water tap in the bathroom and filled the entire apartment with steam just before the guests were to arrive for a party in honor of Paul Nash. A few are based upon episodes referred to in Thurber's other writings. The efforts of the Monroes to find the freight terminal to which their new French poodle was delivered from Chicago in "The Monroes Find a Terminal" anticipates closely Thurber's account of the arrival of their prize-winning dog, Medve, in "Memorial" (*PM,* October 17, 1940, reprinted in *Thurber's Dogs,* 1955).

The Monroe stories are best read *in toto,* as a series of anecdotes characterizing Mr. and Mrs. Monroe and playing variations on the central theme of married life as a sequence of small discords, but two or three are more fully done than the others, and can stand as examples of the rest. In "The Imperturbable Spirit" Mr. Monroe indulges in heroic fantasies about himself. He likes grand philosophic conceptions and big words like "imperturbable," which give one a feeling of security and power. He is reading a book on "God, ethics, morals, humanism, and so on," full of words like "eschatological," and "teleology," and begins to feel that he is the master of his fate.

This euphoric self-image collides with reality when he goes to the dock to meet his wife on her return from Europe, and discovers that in her baggage are twelve illegal bottles of Benedictine. He panics. The porters on the pier suddenly seem to be guards, he sees himself in court, the helpless victim of a merciless district attorney, the grand philosophic concepts and big words no longer have any value. The irony of his situation is underscored by the ending. Safely back in their apartment, the danger passed, Mr. Monroe reads aloud from his book about God, ethics, and imperturbability. "He read in a deep impressive voice, and slowly, for there was a lot his wife wouldn't grasp at once."

"Mr. Monroe and the Moving Men" is the most devastating of the sketches showing Mr. Monroe's inadequacy in the face of the practical demands of everyday life. His wife has gone away and he is left to cope with the movers. He imagines himself ordering them around in a masterful

[12] Letter to Herman Miller, September 27, 1931 (Thurber Collection).

way (" 'See here, my man,' he heard himself saying, coldly, *I'm* in charge here—get that!' "), but in fact, he is totally unable to remember his wife's careful instructions about which things are to go to the summer place in Connecticut and which are to go into storage. When the movers come—"huge, sweating, rough fellows"—his indecision and nervousness provoke their amused contempt. At first they call him "chief" and "mister," but as the afternoon wears on, they begin to call him "buddy," "pardner," and finally, "sonny." The whole episode is a small epic of humiliation and inadequacy, and defines Mr. Monroe as a classic example of the "little man" created by Leacock and Benchley and developed and given greater inwardness by Thurber.

The gap between Mr. Monroe's romantic temperament and the real world is most effectively portrayed in "The Middle Years," a story particularly interesting because it is Thurber's first use of Henry James as a source of comedy. Mr. Monroe's unsuccessful effort to embark on a love affair is set against a background of Jamesian character and experience. James's stories of "poor sensitive gentlemen" who timidly miss out on life provide a set of ironic parallels and contrasts which enlarge both the comedy and pathos of Mr. Monroe's situation. The opening paragraph—a good example of Thurber's growing command of style—is full of Jamesian echoes, particularly from the beginning of "The Beast in the Jungle."

> When, as John Monroe was helping the lovely lady on with her coat, she leaned ever so slightly—and unnecessarily—backwards, he was conscious of a quick, warm glow. He was even more conscious of a vague perplexity, the reason for which—or one of the reasons, anyway—finally came washing up to him on the stream of memory. This had all happened before, almost precisely as now, but with another girl, and years before.

Mrs. Monroe is out of town for a week and the lady's husband is in Bermuda. The stage is set for a romantic adventure, but Mr. Monroe finds himself curiously reluctant. He decides that instead of calling the lady right after breakfast, he will drop in on her about midnight. He imagines her "reading, stretched out, filmily, on a divan." To prepare himself for the adventure ("the word 'ordeal' just grazed his consciousness"), he takes down a copy of *The Golden Bowl*. "He would begin the communion on a . . . 'wonderful' plane," he thinks to himself, sounding like any number of middle-aged Jamesian gentlemen, and he has a bad moment when it occurs to him that the lady might have something more in mind than Henry James provided. After three minutes with *The Golden Bowl* he begins to fall asleep. He decides to take a nap, and sets the alarm clock. As he undresses, he catches an unflattering glimpse of himself in the long mirror ("a tall thin man looks like an ass in socks and garters. The thought depressed him terribly"). The conclusion is as inevitable as that of "The Beast in the Jungle"—when the alarm rings at quarter of one, he snaps it off and rolls over and goes back to sleep.

In the Monroe stories Thurber takes full possession of his basic subject— the American marriage—and in Mr. and Mrs. Monroe he creates the archetypes of his American male and female—the ineffective dreamer and the coolly competent realist. His prose is crisp and spare. No signs of his too susceptible reading of James and Hergesheimer remain. The liveliness of his dialogue shows his command of the dramatic encounter, and his comic invention supplies an abundance of fresh and original details. His most impressive step forward, however, is his use of literary reference and allusion as a way of setting up comic parallels and contrasts to the predicaments of the people he writes about. In his later work, the baroque profusion of quotation, allusion, and parodic devices becomes an end in itself, but here, in "The Middle Years," the Jamesian background is evoked just enough to enhance the comedy of Mr. Monroe's situation.

The Monroe stories show Thurber committed to the basic comic pattern of *Is Sex Necessary?*—the ironic conflict between the romantic dream and the cold actuality. His imagination turned instinctively to parody. In a letter to his old friend Herman Miller, in 1931, he spoke half-regretfully of his inability to write a serious novel. "It would slowly begin to kid itself," he said, "and God knows what it would turn out to be like." [13] As E. B. White put it in his Introduction to *The Owl in the Attic*, "It is always apparent to Thurber that at the very moment one's heart is caught in an embrace, one's foot may be caught in a piano stool."

It is precisely in this situation that Thurber saw himself, and he returned to it again and again in his fiction. Writing to Herman Miller about the Monroe stories, Thurber speaks ruefully of his own romantic temperament and his habit of ending up with his hair in his eyes. He alludes to "that awful day" at Ohio State University when what was to have been a memorable tryst with Minnette Fritts in the old chemistry building did not quite come off. This embarrassing experience suggests to him the plot for a novel "with all the impressive periods of a Henry James 'Beast in the Jungle' about a charming fellow, a sensitive gentleman, whose great good fortune it is to enjoy a number of encounters with lovely ladies but who, at the

[13] Ibid.

most exquisite moments—those moments, rare and far apart and ineffable which mean everything in life—is suddenly assailed by a horrible necessity to pee, and not only to pee, but to pee again and again." The setting of the final chapter would be a university building:

> The sensitive gentleman, waiting there, with the dying of a pretty day, for the Loveliest Encounter of All, has arrived in time so that he may run in and out of The Great Good Place as often as need be. . . . A friend is with him who eventually, as the lady fails to arrive, has to go. The gentleman is now left alone and it gradually is proved to him, that instead of abating, his cursed necessity is increasing, so that when at last the porter locks up the men's room for the day, he is forced to leave by a side door just as he beholds the lady of his tallest dreams coming down the Long Walk. There is nothing in James more haunting than that ending.[14]

The letter to Miller, like the Monroe story "The Middle Years," shows an interesting development in his attitude toward James. As a disciple of Joseph Russell Taylor at Ohio State, Thurber had embraced James as the quintessence of romance and the aesthetic way of life. James was important to him in a very personal way, opening up a whole new set of possibilities and standing for values seldom honored in Columbus, Ohio. Now, a little more than ten years later, with the confidence born of personal and artistic maturity, he can see James and the aesthetic view of life as materials for comedy. He never repudiated his position as "a James man" (except for a time or two near the end of his life when he admitted to a cooling off in his admiration), but throughout his career he delighted in exploiting the comic incongruity between life as James would have us see it and life as it most often really is.

The balance of *The Owl in the Attic* is taken up by "The Pet Department" and "Ladies' and Gentlemen's Guide to Modern English Usage." In these pieces, Thurber turns once again to parody, and the freshness and originality of his subject and treatment (who would think of the pet department of the New York *Evening Post* and Fowler's *Dictionary of Modern English Usage* as likely targets?) is one index of the growth of his skill and confidence.

"The Pet Department" is one of Thurber's most original conceptions. The drawings are not subordinated to the text nor the text to the drawings, but the two modes of expression interplay in a surprising fashion to create

[14] Ibid.

a strange and surreal world where things occur and relate to one another as they do in dreams. Years later, in "A New Natural History," he was to carry the method even farther, inventing a whole new kind of reality out of the punning interplay between visual and verbal elements. Thurber's imagination always moved between two poles—the realistic representation of "the domestic American scene" (Ryder would be the model here), and the world of nonsense, dream, and fantasy (Lewis Carroll would preside over this). "The Pet Department" is Thurber's first notable exploration of the world of fantasy, a world which he evoked with particular success in his drawings, and so it is an important milestone in his development. Animals always appealed to Thurber's fanciful side, and in *Is Sex Necessary?* he had drawn some strange-looking creatures—a lion whose shape and expression owe more to heraldry than to nature, a gallery of odd-looking fish, and at the end of chapter 1, something that looks like a cross between a wild pig and a fish with legs.

The drawings in "The Pet Department" create a dream-like world of improbable creatures—the fish with ears, the stuffed cockatoo (eyes closed) resting on "an iron dingbat," the gull which looks "like a rabbit backing up," the cast-iron lawn dog (a favorite image in Thurber, undoubtedly a boyhood memory of the big old houses along Broad Street in Columbus), the moose which is in fact a horse with antlers strapped to its head. More familiar creatures are shown in improbable postures and settings—the horse peering through the curtains into the drawing room, the polar bear in front of the hearth (the whole bear, not simply the skin), the dog on his back in a trance, and so on.

In the best of "The Pet Department," the surreal effect is a consequence not of the drawings alone, nor of the text, but of the expressive interaction of the two. Take the stuffed cockatoo, for example: the drawing resists rational interpretation—the bird sits, eyes shut, on an unidentifiable object. The question, associating the bird and its perch with the detritus which used to clutter up the attics of old houses, haunts the imagination:

Q. My wife found this owl in the attic among a lot of ormolu clocks and old crystal chandeliers. We can't tell whether it's stuffed or only dead. It is sitting on a strange and almost indescribable sort of iron dingbat.

The answer only compounds the mystery of the origin, function, and meaning of the piece. It remains improbable, inexplicable, hallucinatory.

Stuffed Cockatoo

A. What your wife found is a museum piece—a stuffed cockatoo. It looks to me like a rather botchy example of taxidermy. This is the first stuffed bird I have ever seen with its eyes shut, but whoever had it stuffed probably wanted it stuffed that way. I couldn't say what the thing it is sitting on is supposed to represent. It looks broken.

The "Ladies' and Gentlemen's Guide to Modern English Usage" is a lively parody of one of Thurber's favorite books, Fowler's *Dictionary of Modern English Usage.* Throughout his life Thurber was fascinated by the whole subject of language, both by the rules which made it an instrument of precision and sharpness, and by the possibilities of the strange and unexpected meanings locked in the connotations of words and word-sounds. He had the precisionist's passion for the fine points of grammar and good usage, and in his later years he made a personal cause out of the defense of the language against the forces of mass culture which were conspiring to vulgarize it and blunt its fine edge.

The "Ladies' and Gentlemen's Guide" takes hold of Fowler's very British upper-class view of usage as essentially a matter of social relationships, a branch of manners, the sign of a gentleman's education, and distorts it into delightful absurdity. The opening discussion of the vexing problem of *who* and *whom* is typical of Thurber's method. In Fowler's best manner, the whole thing is referred to the standard of good taste, but the example cited is subversively preposterous: "Take the common expression, 'Whom are you, anyways?' That is of course, strictly speaking, correct—and yet how formal, how stilted! The usage to be preferred in ordinary speech and writing is 'Who are you, anyways?' 'Whom' should be used in the nominative case only when a note of dignity or austerity is desired." Ultimately, the "Guide" asserts, whether to use *who* or *whom* depends upon one's sense of the social requirements of the situation. "The word 'whom' is too austere to use in connection with a lowly worker, like a street-cleaner, and its use in this form is known as False Admiration or Pathetic Fallacy."

This discussion of the pitfalls awaiting the unwary user of *which* shows Thurber's skill as an imitator of styles. Citing examples of the mind-numbing complications which *which*-users get into, he pays passing tribute to one of his stylistic heroes, Henry James, as a man who could get out of almost anything, but his special admiration in this case is reserved for Ernest Hemingway and his Draconian simplification of prose style.

> In his youth he was trapped in a which-clause one time and barely escaped with his mind. He was going along on solid ground until he got into this: "It was the one thing of which, being very much afraid—for whom has not been warned to fear such things—he . . ." Being a young and powerfully built man, Hemingway was able to fight his way back to where he had started, and begin again. This time he skirted the treacherous morass in this way: "He was afraid of one thing. This was the one thing. He had been warned to fear such things." Today Hemingway is alive and well, and many happy writers are following along the trail he blazed.

The "Guide" follows up with this advice: "It is well to remember that one 'which' leads to two and that two 'whiches' multiply like rabbits." The discussion ends with a picture of a long-eared bouncy creature labeled "American Rabbit, or 'Which,'" and the admonition, "Never monkey with 'which.' Nothing except getting tangled up in a typewriter ribbon is worse."

8

The Seal in the Bedroom

T HE SEAL IN THE BEDROOM (1932) and *My Life and Hard Times* (1933) are the twin peaks of Thurber's early career. *Is Sex Necessary?* and *The Owl in the Attic* showed him in the process of mapping out the area of his comic materials—the battle of the sexes, parody, and the visual fantasy of "The Pet Department." Here, in these books of 1932 and 1933, he takes full possession of the imaginative territory he was to occupy for the next ten years. Not until his failing sight and the traumatic impact of the Atomic Era began to change his view of life was there any significant change in either his subject matter or style.

The Seal in the Bedroom has a special significance as a milestone, since it was his first collection of drawings, and it established him as a comic artist of major importance. Thurber always deprecated his drawings and tended to resent the fact that he was more widely known as a cartoonist than he was as a writer. Writing was his life's work, while drawing was for him simply a casual recreation. In an interview with Los Angeles art critic Arthur Millier in 1939, he complained that although he slaved over his prose, rewriting every piece from three to ten times, and had published six volumes already, people still said when his name was mentioned, " 'Thurber, the bird who draws?' " "I'm not an artist, I'm a painstaking writer who doodles for relaxation," he said.[1] He liked to point out that he

[1] Interview with Arthur Millier, Los Angeles *Times* Sunday Magazine, July 2, 1939.

had never taken longer than three minutes on a single drawing in his life, and that he did all the drawings for *Is Sex Necessary?* in a single evening.[2] When Harold Ross commiserated with him about having to give up drawing on account of his blindness, he wrote, "If I couldn't write, I couldn't breathe . . . but giving up drawing is only a little worse than giving up tossing cards in a hat." [3]

Nevertheless, his cartoons in *The New Yorker* reached out to a larger and more varied audience than his writing ever did. He was immediately taken up by serious art critics, who recognized the drastic simplification of style in Thurber as similar to the method of artists like Klee, Matisse, Picasso, and some of the surrealists. So, as a matter of fact, did ordinary gallery-goers: once, at a Picasso exhibition at the Museum of Modern Art, a man paused before "Ladies by the Sea" and cried to his companion, "It's Thurber!" [4] In 1933 Smith College exhibited drawings by Thurber and George Grosz, and in 1934 the Valentine Gallery in New York put on a one-man show which was widely reviewed. The Museum of Modern Art included one of his drawings in its ambitious Fantastic Art–Dada–Surrealism show in 1936.[5] At the same time, people with little or no interest in the trends of twentieth-century art delighted in the touch of fantasy in Thurber's representations of the predicaments of everyday life. In Europe, where the language barrier limits the number of people familiar with his writing, he has been well known as a comic artist since the early 1930's. A drawing called "Intelligent Woman," a hasty sketch which bore the mark of a rubber heel where someone had stepped on it, was exhibited in Vienna at a show of the comic art of all nations.[6]

The subject matter of *The Seal in the Bedroom* is the subject matter of Thurber's stories and sketches translated into visual terms. The largest group pictures the battle of the sexes; another represents the world of fantasy, dream, and neurosis; still another deals with animals, particularly dogs.

The women in Thurber's cartoons are pictured with undisguised hostility. They are large, shapeless, dowdy, sexless. Their hair is straight and sparse, their noses are long, and their chins recede. Young and old, their faces express disapproval, determination, and sometimes a kind of manic

<hr>

[2] Interview with Henry Brandon, "The Tulle and Taffeta Rut," *As We Are*, p. 263; also interview with Alistair Cooke, *Atlantic*, CXCVIII (August, 1956), 38.

[3] *The Years with Ross*, p. 66.

[4] Reported in the *New York Times Magazine*, December 17, 1939 (RTS).

[5] *Time* reviewed the Valentine Gallery show December 31, 1934; its review of *Men, Women and Dogs*, November 15, 1943, refers to Thurber's drawings in the Fantastic Art show at the Museum of Modern Art.

[6] Letter to Herman Miller, undated, but probably 1935–36.

glee. They appear in a variety of roles, few of which contribute to man's comfort or peace of mind. The classic image of Woman in Thurber's world is probably that of the physically overpowering female bearing down on or intimidating the male. In one scene, a large, grim-looking woman is playing croquet with her two little boys. She is taking a full swing at the ball, like a golfer, and as Thurber draws her, she is the embodiment of aggressive force. The boys stand in the background, and one of them is saying to the other, "Mama always gets sore and spoils the game for everybody." The same frighteningly physical type appears in another mood in an ice-skating scene: here, she is a huge Maenad, hat flying off, hair and eyes wild, crying "Stop me!" as she careens out of control across the ice, about to collide with a small male skater, who looks up at her with the expression of blank apprehension with which most Thurber men look at life.

"*Stop me!*"

A subtler kind of threat is posed by woman in her role of seductress. This is a secondary role for Thurber's women, but it is one which his men must cope with. The best-known of these little scenes of sexual aggression is the one in which a man and two women are having a drink at a table, and the woman across from the man, her eyes cast down demurely, has put her foot on his. The man is looking up, an expression of surprise and mild dismay on his face; the wife, a large, bossy-looking person sitting between the other two, is looking at her husband and saying, "Well, what's come over *you* suddenly?" (In *The Years with Ross,* Thurber recalled that "a charming editrix" inked in the foot of the designing lady to make sure that no one missed the point. "Everybody took liberties with my drawings," he observed.[7]) In a few of these episodes, the woman appears as stylish or sexually attractive. In one, a dark buxom siren sits on a sofa, legs boldly crossed, surrounded by admiring men. Two grumpy, homely, straight-haired women sit in the background, and one says to the other, "What kind of a woman is it, I ask you, that goes gallivanting around in a foreign automobile?" The young lady in "A penny for your thoughts, Mr. Griscom" may be real or may be a fantasy-object, but she is very obviously nude and—for a Thurber female—attractive.

But there are not many sirens or enchantresses amongst Thurber's women. Most of them are middle-aged middle-class housewives, and they are generally pictured in an indoor, conflict-ridden setting. Sometimes they are shrewish and comically unreasonable, as in the scene showing a sourly unkempt husband sitting on the bed in his underwear, a drink in his hand and socks and shoes in disarray all over the floor; his wife, arms akimbo, is saying angrily, "Why don't you get dressed, then, and go to pieces like a man?" Occasionally they are represented as symbolic forces: in "Ad Astra," a huge female figure looms over a mountain landscape, pointing with outstretched arm to three stars over the peak, while a small child-like male figure looks doubtfully at the steep way up. Woman's capacity to inspire and drive man onward and upward is always a source of apprehension in Thurber's world. The male's fear of the female as the embodiment of conscience is the subject of "The Furies," where four fat and dumpy females point accusing fingers at an uneasy-looking male in formal evening dress.

Thurber's men are essentially victims. They all have the baffled look of people who have somehow got themselves into situations they would like to get out of. In a letter to Herman Miller, Thurber once described the men in his drawings as "given to bewilderment, vacillation, uncertainty, and downright fear." [8] They are clearly inferior to the women they encounter—they are often smaller physically, and they are almost always weaker psychologically. Their blank, faintly surprised expressions underline their passive role. Caught by her husband with her lover ("I'm helping Mr. Gorley with his novel, darling"), the woman is strong and brightly smiling.

[7] *The Years with Ross,* p. 58.
[8] Undated letter to Miller.

Both men have the numb look of people to whom too many things have happened. There is a pathos in the faces of most of Thurber's men, and the kind of innocence he associates with animals. The kinship between the male human and the animal is given a wonderfully fanciful touch in the cartoon showing a man happily dancing with a very large dog, while the wife, disapproval in every line of her figure, says, "Will you be good enough to dance this outside?"

Thurber's view of the relation between the sexes is most fully expressed in "The Race of Life," a parable in pictures showing the life story of a man, his wife, and their child. Thurber's tale is a parody of the traditional metaphor picturing life as a journey: the characters are unclothed, to emphasize their archetypal significance, and the setting is the universal out-of-doors, with its changing weather, its wild animals, its deserts, rivers, and mountains. The opening panel sets the key for the whole. Starting out on their journey, the wife leads the way, confident and smiling; the man follows, his physical manner lethargic, and his facial expression sheep-like; the little boy, as determined as his mother, brings up the rear holding aloft a banner reading "Excelsior." At the end of their difficult journey the little boy leads the way up a dangerous cliff. Ahead are some silly-looking pearly gates and in the sky some improbable angels. The wife points with excited encouragement to this glorious prospect, but the husband has by this time sunk to his knees under a rain cloud and seems likely to stay there.

"The Race of Life" is a twentieth-century version of *The Pilgrim's Progress,* and much of its comic effect derives from its parody of the form and the values of the whole tradition of symbolic narratives in which man's life is represented as a spiritual journey. The optimistic overtones of religious quest and fulfillment in this classic tale are replaced in Thurber's version by a highly Freudian view of life in which man has lost his heroic stature and is clearly incapable of reaching the shining goal. The end of the story for man as Thurber tells it is not new life, new strength, or new achievement; it is failure and despair. For woman, of course, it is a different matter. As Thurber's little fable makes clear, the real problem for man is not the dangers along the way—the bone-strewn deserts or the bogey-men—but woman herself. Her perfect competence and superiority have robbed him of his former role as leader and protector, and now he can only see himself as ineffectual, pathetic, and ridiculous.

Most of the drawings in *The Seal in the Bedroom* have a touch of that strange, dream-like quality which was always to be one of the hallmarks of Thurber's imagination. Neurosis, hallucination, the whole area of the irrational were subjects which held a particular fascination for him throughout his career. Many of his drawings haunt the imagination because they confront us directly with images which seem to have popped up from the unconscious or to have been recalled from dreams. His most famous cartoon, "All right, have it your way—you heard a seal bark" shows a man and a woman in bed, and looming up behind the headboard, a pleasant-looking seal. The woman is querulous and impatient at her husband's nonsense, and the man is silently exasperated because she won't believe him. The scene has that mixture of the familiar and the strange which is the essence of dreams, and like dream-images, it resists logical explanation.

The experience offered is similar to that in many of the bizarre scenes in "The Pet Department." Dorothy Parker singled out this enigmatic quality as the primary characteristic of Thurber's drawings in her Introduction to *The Seal in the Bedroom*. Thurber, she wrote, "deals solely in culminations. . . . You may figure out for yourself, and good luck to you, what under heaven could have gone before, that his sombre citizens find themselves in such remarkable situations. It is yours to ponder how penguins get into drawing rooms and seals into bedchambers, for Mr. Thurber will only show them to you some little time after they have arrived there. . . . He gives you a glimpse of the startling present and lets you go construct the astounding past."

In speaking of his drawings, Thurber often implied that they were as much mysteries to him as to his readers. Most of them were spontaneous, unplanned, accidental, he said. He liked to describe himself as a "Pre-Intentionalist": he would simply start drawing and let one thing suggest another until a figure or a scene of some sort emerged. After that, he would think up a caption. If he worked in the other direction, he told Henry Brandon, "a stiffness was likely to get into the figures . . . and then the fact that I was not a draftsman—never took a lesson—can't really draw—came out." [9] In an essay, "The Lady on the Bookcase," [10] he divided his drawings into three main categories: those which had their origin in the Unconscious (and he refers to the possibility of Jungian interpretations of these), those which were the result of Accident (and he makes a tongue-in-cheek reference here to Freud and the theory of the Purely Accidental versus the theory of Haphazard Determination), and those which were Intentional or Thought Up. In Thurber's view, all his best drawings were products of the Unconscious or of Accident.

The classic case is the famous seal in the bedroom. After the success of *Is Sex Necessary?* Ross asked Thurber to redraw the cartoon of the seal

[9] Brandon, "The Tulle and Taffeta Rut," *As We Are*, p. 263.
[10] Collected in *The Beast in Me*, pp. 66–75.

and the explorers he had submitted in 1929, and about two years later Thurber gave it a try. He got the seal started all right, but the rock began to look more like the head of a bed. So he followed out this new development and put a man and a woman in the bed, and then gave the woman her immortal line to speak. This happy accident turned out to be one of Thurber's most successful cartoons.[11] When it appeared in *The New Yorker*, Robert Benchley sent Thurber a telegram saying, "Thank you for the funniest drawing caption ever to appear in any magazine." This was high praise indeed, since there was no one, Thurber observed, whose good opinion any American humorist or cartoonist would rather have had. When Ross saw Benchley's telegram, he capitulated—as he had done once before in agreeing that Thurber was really a writer and not an editor—and accepted him as an established *New Yorker* artist.

"All right, have it your way—you heard a seal bark"

The same fortuitous process was responsible for what is probably Thurber's second most famous drawing, the lady on the bookcase, which appeared in *Men, Women and Dogs* in 1943. The scene shows a woman crouched on all fours on top of a bookcase, and a man is saying to a visitor,

[11] Thurber told this story often: in interviews with Arthur Millier, in 1939, with Henry Brandon, in 1958, on the BBC program "Frankly Speaking," later in 1958, and he wrote it up in *The Years with Ross*, pp. 54–58.

"That's my first wife up there, and this is the *present* Mrs. Harris." Thurber had intended to draw a woman crouched at the head of the stairs, but as he told Henry Brandon, "Having no skill in draftsmanship, I lost perspective and the stairs turned instantly into a bookcase, or what looked like a bookcase if you made transverse lines—so I made it into a bookcase—and there was this naked lady on top of a bookcase. A great many of the drawings came out accidentally like that—a great many. And it was a great deal of fun not to know what you were going to end up with." [12]

Ross, who valued clarity and explicitness above all, and who lived in constant fear that the clever people who contributed to his magazine were going to put something over on him, was instantly suspicious when he saw the lady on the bookcase. He telephoned Thurber to ask, " 'Is the woman on the bookcase alive, or stuffed, or just dead?' " Thurber said that he would have to think it over and call Ross back. When he did call, he offered an explanation calculated to deepen the mystery and increase Ross's uneasiness. " 'She has to be alive,' I told him. 'My doctor says a dead woman couldn't support herself on all fours, and my taxidermist says you can't stuff a woman.' He thought about it for a few seconds and then roared into the phone, 'Then, goddam it, what's she doing naked in the house of her former husband and his second wife?' I told him he had me there, and that I wasn't responsible for the behavior of the people I drew. . . . 'Thurber's crazy,' Ross told someone later, but it wasn't the first time he had so diagnosed my condition." [13]

The drawings which spring from the Unconscious (or "Stream of Nervousness," as Thurber called it in "The Lady on the Bookcase") are those dealing with neurosis, hallucination, and other psychic disturbances. Some mix dream elements and reality so that we are never quite sure which is which, as with the seal in the bedroom. The series of scenes captioned "A penny for your thoughts, Mr. Griscom (Gardiner, Jaffe, Speaks, Garber, Coates)," each one showing a man and woman talking, and an attractive and usually nude young woman standing invitationally behind the older woman, is a good example: is the bold young woman really there or is she a projection of Mr. Griscom-Gardiner-Jaffe-Speaks-Garber-Coates's fantasy? Some drawings are "Unconscious" in the sense that their meaning is obscure, like the images in dreams. Often the dream-like quality is the effect of the cryptic captions, which offer a fragment of conversation suspended in mid-air, so that the logic of the scene is always just out of reach. In one scene a woman gazes reflectively into space and says to the

[12] Brandon, "The Tulle and Taffeta Rut," *As We Are*, p. 264.
[13] *The Years with Ross*, p. 60.

man, "I told the analyst everything except my experience with Mr. Rines-
foos."

There are four drawings in *The Seal in the Bedroom* which project a
fantasy-world free from neurotic tension and conflict. They show a fabulous
imaginary garden filled with large flowers and exotic creatures, and in their
implications they are closer to fairy tale than to Freud. They are much more
sophisticated in technique than Thurber's more familiar drawings: everything is carefully stylized and worked into an overall decorative pattern.
The flowers have long attenuated stems and delightfully artificial blooms,
and they tower gracefully over animals and men. The animals look like
children's toys and the man and the woman who appear in two of the scenes
have the same child-imagined quality as the animals, except that they lack
their charm. The most striking of these drawings—and the most uncharac-
teristically Thurberian—shows two elegant lions resting in a wispy forest
of flowers. The mystery and grace of these creatures suggests the figures
in medieval manuscript illuminations. In fact, the fanciful subject matter,
the crowded details, and the combination of naiveté and sophistication in
style which characterize these four drawings make one think of medieval
art or of the twentieth-century example of Klee.

They are obviously images of innocence, presenting an ideal land existing

somewhere just beyond the real. One of them is captioned "End of Paved Road," and shows two small and hesitant people entering a scene dominated by enormous flowers and a variety of creatures—a fox, a dog, a snake, a bird, a bumblebee—all living in harmony in a world that cannot be reached by car. Another shows a bird and a snake framed by flowers. In the center is a large cornucopia-like plant overflowing with some sort of natural bounty.

Thurber's most touching symbols of innocence, of course, are his dogs, and it is in *The Seal in the Bedroom* that the famous Thurber dog first appears. Thurber had done dogs in "The Pet Department," but the sweet-faced, lop-eared basset-like hound, all gentleness and seriousness, which Thurber added to the animal kingdom makes his debut in this collection. The real-life model for the Thurber dog was the lithograph of the Duke of Westminster's hunting dogs which hung in Grandfather Fisher's hall. These dogs, with their "strong muzzles, long ears, and melancholy eyes . . . were to remain permanently in my memory for fond, if perhaps imprecise, reference later on, when I began to draw," he wrote in *The Thurber Album*.[14] Thurber drew dogs as a form of doodling, as he often said, but his creation of these sad and gentle creatures was obviously something more

The Bloodhound and the Bug

14 *The Thurber Album*, p. 40.

than a gesture of nervous release. In a world filled with conflict and guilt, the dog, with his simple needs and unquestioning loyalties, represents a wholeness and a harmony with the outer world and the world of self which man has tragically lost. Thurber's dogs are his contact with peace and innocence.

In *The Seal in the Bedroom* the cast of characters, the situations, the settings, and the handling of line which gave Thurber's drawings their individual stamp are all present. Most of them were done in 1932, especially for the book, and there is a notable advance in confidence and skill over the drawings in *Is Sex Necessary?* and *The Owl in the Attic.* Thurber always disparaged the notion that there had been any development in his drawing technique (he told Alistair Cooke that he thought his drawings were about what they were in 1901, and on another occasion he said that the only change he could find, in comparing early and late drawings, was "a certain tightening of my lack of technique . . . the inevitable and impure result of constant practice"),[15] but in fact the figures in *The Seal in the Bedroom* are more individualized and more expressively handled than those in *Is Sex Necessary?* The earlier drawings tend to be abstract and disembodied, sparse in background and simpler in design and movement.[16] The drawings in this later collection, by contrast, are dynamic and full of significant detail. A number represent figures in motion or crowd scenes, like parties, city streets, bars and restaurants, and the handling of line and composition in many of these is both economical and evocative. He liked the grace and motion of the world of sports, and in the six panels titled "Tennis" he shows a determined player waiting for service, executing a drop shot, making a forehand smash, and so on. The drawings boldly ignore anatomy and proportion, but the overall effect is dramatic and full of the sense of forceful movement.

Thurber took pleasure in the fact that his primitive style puzzled and alarmed many people. One reviewer, his tongue obviously in his cheek, suggested that he might have been influenced by what he had seen in Egyptian tombs or abandoned telephone booths.[17] Reminiscing to Alistair Cooke, Thurber said, "Some people thought my drawings were done under water; others that they were done by moonlight. But mothers thought that I was a little child or that my drawings were done by my granddaughter."

[15] "Author's Memoir," *The Seal in the Bedroom* (new edition; New York: Harper & Brothers, 1950).
[16] Robert E. Morsberger makes this point in his *James Thurber* (New York: Twayne Publishers, 1964), pp. 162–63.
[17] Lisle Bell, review of *The Seal in the Bedroom*, New York *Herald Tribune*, December 4, 1932.

Earlier, he told of the time a state trooper, investigating a crime in West Cornwall, saw Thurber drawings in several people's houses, and asked, "How old is the little boy who did these drawings?" and was told, "Forty-nine, going on fifty." [18]

After *The Seal in the Bedroom*, Thurber's drawings, unlike his prose, changed very little in either subject matter or style. In *Men, Women and Dogs* (1943), the last significant collection of his *New Yorker* cartoons, the women are still large, dowdy, and overpowering, the men timid and baffled, and the dogs serene, gentle, and innocent. The backgrounds are perhaps done with a little more fullness, particularly the depressing old-fashioned domestic settings, and the men, as Dorothy Parker pointed out,[19] may be more consistently middle-aged and ineffectual-looking, but the characters in Thurber's world and their central predicament—the battle of the sexes —are essentially the same from start to finish.

There are, however, a wealth of entertaining variations on familiar themes in *Men, Women and Dogs*. The hostility of woman is shown in a wonderfully incongruous setting in "Look Out, Harry!" where in a game of mixed doubles an unattractive woman stands behind her partner, racket raised, obviously to deal him a blow, while the man's male counterpart across the net shouts his warning. Woman takes out her aggression on Dog as well as Man: in one scene, a dowdy, angry-looking woman glares at a large, abashed dog, and says, "For Heaven's sake, why don't you go outdoors and trace something?" Several scenes show man fighting back. In one uncaptioned drawing, a woman stands in a meadow under a large tree, calling someone, bad temper in every line of her face; up on the top of the tree a man reclines quietly, a wicked look in his eye. He obviously has no intention of replying. A more overt representation is "The War Between Men and Women," with its scenes of combat, like "The Fight in the Grocery" and "Capture of Three Physics Professors"; its moments of individual heroism, like "Mrs. Pritchard's Leap"; and its climax in "Gettysburg," "Retreat," and "Surrender," in which the general of the women acknowledges defeat by handing over a baseball bat to the general of the men.

Dream and fantasy continue to be primary subjects (and primary sources) of Thurber's drawings. One of his most striking dream-images or hallucinations is the big tree-shaded Midwestern house, the back of which dissolves into the face of a woman turned to stare disapprovingly at a very small

[18] "Letter from the States," *Bermudian*, October, 1951.
[19] "Preface," *Men, Women and Dogs* (New York: Harcourt, Brace and Company, 1943).

Home

startled man standing in front. Thurber classified this drawing as one of those which came spontaneously from the Unconscious, "while the artist was thinking of something else," as opposed to those which were conceived or planned beforehand. Somewhere between this dream-world and the world of reality is the scene in which a woman, arms akimbo, faces a large, benign hippopotamus-like animal at whose feet are a hat, a pipe, and a shoe, and demands, "What have you done with Dr. Millmoss?" Like the famous lady on the bookcase and other fantasy-drawings, this scene developed accidentally: Thurber drew the hippopotamus to please his little daughter, and then, he said, "Something about the creature's expression when he was completed convinced me that he had recently eaten a man. I added the hat and pipe and Mrs. Millmoss and the caption followed easily enough." [20]

The relation between caption and drawing in the creative process varied from time to time, in Thurber's experience. Although he obviously preferred the drawings which came of their own accord and then suggested captions afterward, a few of his most famous came into being in exactly the opposite way. One of the most popular cartoons in *New Yorker* history

[20] "The Lady on the Bookcase," *The Beast in Me*, pp. 72–73.

was the scene in which a fencer slices off the head of his opponent and cries out "Touché!" The idea was submitted to *The New Yorker* by Carl Rose as a natural Thurber subject, and Thurber rendered Rose's conception with beautiful simplicity and energy of line. He liked to improve on the story of how he came to use Rose's idea, however, and as he tells it in "The Lady on the Bookcase," Rose submitted a drawing with the caption. The *New Yorker* editors liked the idea, but felt that his rendition was too gory, and asked Thurber to work on it, since his people were so obviously creatures of fantasy rather than real life. As Thurber said of the drawing: "No one who looks at 'Touché!' believes that the man whose head is in the air is really dead. His opponent will hand it back with profuse apologies, and the discommoded fencer will replace it on his shoulders and say, 'No harm done, forget it.' " [21]

Although the imaginative effect of Thurber's cartoons is primarily the result of the creative interplay between drawing and caption, many are chiefly what might be called illustrated captions, where the comedy lies almost entirely in the oddity, the illogic, or the fatuousness of what one of the characters is saying, and the drawing is of secondary interest. A good example is the domestic scene—wife, husband, two children, dog—in which the woman says to the dispirited man, "Well, I'm disenchanted, too. We're *all* disenchanted." [22] The remark occurred to Thurber first; then he did the drawing. Over the years he refined and developed the special art of the caption and made out of it a wonderfully expressive form. Throughout the 1930's and the early 1940's he wrote hundreds of these one-line comic histories, and the variety and originality of his output is impressive. Any sample of his best-known captions would have to include, "It's a naive domestic Burgundy without any breeding, but I think you'll be amused by its presumption" (which lacks the quality of strangeness characteristic of most of Thurber's captions, but which for its satirical accuracy is a classic); the perfect interplay of the commonplace and the bizarre in "I wouldn't rent this room to everybody, Mr. Spencer. This is where my husband lost his mind"; and the pure zaniness of "I thought you'd enjoy Miss Perrish, darling. She has a constant ringing in *her* ears, too"; "She has the true Emily Dickinson spirit except that she gets fed up occasionally"; and the unforgettable "Well, if I called the wrong number, why did you answer the phone?"

[21] Ibid., p. 74. Carl Rose tells a slightly different story in the Boston *Morning Globe*, November (?) 1961.
[22] "The Lady on the Bookcase," *The Beast in Me*, pp. 74–75.

At the other extreme, Thurber always did a large number of uncaptioned drawings, where line and movement make their own statement without the aid of words. In these there is a wider range of subject and even of method than in the drawing-and-caption form. Some make a harsher satiric statement than usual, as in the scene showing a sidewalk crowded with hurrying pedestrians, each intent on the business of the day and oblivious to the fact that just behind the iron fence bordering the sidewalk is a graveyard equally crowded with headstones. The title is "Destinations." In a totally different vein, there are the lively impressions of Paris Thurber did in 1937–38, and which Helen Thurber published for the first time in *Thurber and Company.* Thurber did these—as he did so many of his drawings—for his own amusement and the diversion of his friends. He dashed off hundreds of drawings at parties and in restaurants, using table-cloths, napkins, menus and whatever else was handy, and he gave them away with reckless prodigality. As he so often ruefully observed, there were probably more of his drawings in the hands of friends and acquaintances than there were in his own files. "I have yet to meet anybody I have ever known, even casually, who hasn't got at least one of my drawings," he remarked to Herman Miller.[23] Writing to Patricia Stone, in 1948, he said, "My best stuff is in pencil on yellow paper and it has never been published, but at least thirty people . . . own from forty to fifty done with pencil while cockeyed." [24]

Some of Thurber's most attractive drawings are the "spots"—those quick untitled sketches of people and animals used to decorate and enliven a blank portion of a page in *The New Yorker* or in a book. There are boxers, fencers, skiers, musicians, and drinkers, as well as quieter and more reflective figures, like the man slumped on a park bench, sorrow or despair in every line of his body, at the end of *Men, Women and Dogs.* There are animals everywhere, especially dogs, in all sorts of attitudes. A characteristic scene shows two dogs standing tail to tail, one sniffing a flower, the other almost nose-to-nose with a friendly bird. These are modest and unassuming sketches, but they are attractive because they show Thurber's appreciation of the beauty of common things.

Beginning with *Is Sex Necessary?* and continuing throughout the 1930's, Thurber poured out a steady stream of illustrations of his own essays and stories. The best of these appeared in *My Life and Hard Times,* where the originality of the draughtsmanship and the eccentricity of his characters

[23] Undated letter, probably 1936.
[24] Quoted in Morsberger, *James Thurber,* p. 164.

complemented each other perfectly. What could be more expressive than the drawing of Cousin Briggs Beall sitting up in bed under the illusion that he is about to suffocate? Or of Uncle Zenas and the trees drooping with the chestnut blight? Or of the old lady who was certain that electricity escaped from empty light sockets? Or of the botany professor in "University Days" quivering with rage, or—best of all—poor dumb Bolenciecwcz trying to think? These are classic visual representations of a world of comic fantasy, and never again did Thurber so perfectly match his talent as a draughtsman with his art as a wordman. He occasionally illustrated books written by other people, usually personal friends (most notably *How to Raise a Dog*, 1938, by Dr. James R. Kinney and Ann Honeycutt, and *In a Word*, 1939, by Margaret Ernst), and he did a considerable number of sketches for advertisers, beginning with a series for the French Line in 1933. His fresh and lively treatment of subjects usually handled with timid imitativeness won him a special award from the Advertising Club of New York for the "most artistic continuity in 1938 advertising."

It is one measure of Thurber's quality as an artist that he seldom allowed himself to be trapped into a convention or formula even of his own making. Beginning with a series titled "James Thurber Presents William Shakespeare" in the magazine *Stage*, in 1935, he started experimenting with more complicated relationships between drawing and title or caption.[25] The Shakespeare drawings are wicked visual parodies of famous characters and scenes, in which the cartoons totally destroy the romantic images created by the language and by theatrical tradition. He improved on the possibilities of the method in "Famous Poems Illustrated," in 1939, and in "A New Natural History," in 1945–46, he explored far more subtle and unexpected ways in which drawings and titles might interact. Paradoxically, this most original of his ventures as a draughtsman was virtually his last. His eyesight began to deteriorate badly in 1939, and by 1946 he had so little vision left that he had to give up all but an occasional sketch. For a time, in the late 1940's, *The New Yorker* ran some of his old drawings with new captions, reversed some cuts, broke up others and rearranged the figures, re-used old spots, and so on, but Thurber discouraged this, feeling reluctant to accept money for secondhand work.

The drawings reveal Thurber's imagination in its purest form. The sad, baffled, and apprehensive men, the predatory and threatening women (as one British critic observed about Thurber's females, "Inside every Little

[25] The series began in *Stage*, XII (September, 1936) and ran through XIII (December, 1936).

Nell there lurks a Lady Macbeth" [26]), the innocent animals and the country landscapes dotted by large trees and simple flowers—these are the essential elements of Thurber's imaginary world. It has its origins in the real, but it is the real world suddenly transformed into the dream-like and the fantastic. Thurber generates a wild and original humor out of this vision, but it is the kind of humor which springs not so much from genial high spirits as from neurosis, anxiety, and apprehension.

[26] Undated transcript of a BBC broadcast after Thurber's death, featuring Michael Ayrton and other British artists.

9

Columbus Remembered:
My Life
and Hard Times

FROM THE POINT OF VIEW of the literary historian, Thurber's career, like that of his hero, Henry James, can be seen as falling into four main stages. The labels and the dates are, of course, purely arbitrary, but they help to point up the fact that Thurber's work did grow and change over the years. First, there is the Period of Apprenticeship, beginning with his years on the *Dispatch* and extending until 1927, when he joined *The New Yorker*. Next is the Period of Early Success, spanning the decade of the 1930's, from *Is Sex Necessary?* (1929) to *My World and Welcome to It* (1942). Thurber's talent flowered during these years: his drawings brought him international fame, and his writings included *The Male Animal, My Life and Hard Times,* and his most famous story, "The Secret Life of Walter Mitty." The third period, extending from the early 1940's, when he lost his sight, into the early 1950's, might be labeled Blindness and Reassessment. It was a time of personal tribulation and creative experiment, and out of it came such collections as *The Thurber Carnival* (1945) and *The Beast in Me* (1948), as well as the remarkable fairy tales and *The Thurber Album* (1952). Finally, there is the period of the distinctive Later Manner, covering the years 1955–61. It is best characterized by some of the late pieces in *Alarms and Diversions* (1957) and by *Lanterns and Lances* (1961).

Each of these periods is marked by a preference for certain subjects and

comic techniques, reflecting Thurber's changing view of the world. The
major themes of his earlier work cluster around the conflict between the
individual (free, spontaneous, eccentric) and the system (ordered, repressive, conventional). His view of life is romantic, liberal, optimistic. His basic
form is the narrative anecdote, revealing oddities of character and behavior.
After his blindness, he begins to create his comedy out of extravagant
word-play rather than out of action and character. The change is gradual,
but it is clearly evident in *The Beast in Me*. Accompanying this change
in artistic method is a growing pessimism and misanthropy, as personal
frustrations and a despairing concern over the state of the world upset his
precarious psychic balance.

The peak achievement of Thurber's early career is *My Life and Hard
Times*. For many readers it is his one unquestioned masterpiece. Dwight
MacDonald called it the best humor to come out of the entire post–World
War I period.[1] Ernest Hemingway, in a letter to the publishers reprinted
on the dust jacket, called Thurber's work as a whole "the best writing
coming out of America." Of *My Life and Hard Times*, he said, tongue well
implanted in cheek, "I find it far superior to the autobiography of Henry
Adams. Even in the earliest days when Thurber was writing under
the name of Alice B. Toklas we knew he had it in him if he could get it
out." In spite of the heavy clowning, Hemingway's letter is a remarkable endorsement of a comparative unknown by one of the great modern styl-
ists.

The book is the definitive image of Thurber's special comic world. Here
the eccentric characters, chaotic situations, and the strange blend of the
realistic and the fantastic which are the hallmarks of his work are present
in their purest and most concentrated form. It mines one of his richest
veins of subject matter—the days of his youth in Columbus—and out of
these autobiographical materials he creates a mad comic world in which
the normal order of things is constantly exploding into chaos and confusion.
In Max Eastman's *The Enjoyment of Laughter* (1936), Thurber defined
humor as "emotional chaos told about calmly and quietly in retrospect"
(appropriating Wordsworth's famous theory of poetry to justify a levity of
which Wordsworth might not have approved),[2] and no better illustration
of this theory than *My Life and Hard Times* could be imagined. The titles
of the various chapters emphasize the theme of comic disorder—"The

---

[1] Dwight MacDonald, "Laugh and Lie Down," *Partisan Review*, IV (December, 1937),
49.
[2] Max Eastman, *Enjoyment of Laughter* (New York: Simon & Schuster, 1936), p.
342.

Night the Bed Fell," "The Day the Dam Broke," "The Night the Ghost Got In," "More Alarms at Night," and so on.

Disorder and confusion are anathema to the world at large, but for Thurber they are sources of possible liberation. They are at the heart of a set of closely related values which, until his very last years, he habitually champions in opposition to the dominant ideals of contemporary society. In a world committed to logic, organization, conformity, and efficiency, Thurber stands for fantasy, spontaneity, idiosyncrasy, and confusion. Hence Thurber's fondness for situations involving eccentric behavior, elaborate practical jokes, breakdowns of communication, and the disruption of bureaucratic machinery. Hence also his fondness for original and unconventional people like grandfather, the Civil War veteran, who was never quite sure whether he was living in 1864 or 1910, and whose efforts to drive the electric automobile exhibit the family incompetence with machines and gadgets in its purest form; or Aunt Sarah Shoaf, who went to bed every night fearing that a burglar was going to get in and blow chloroform under her door with a tube, and so piled all her valuables outside, with a note reading, "This is all I have. Please take it and do not use your chloroform, as this is all I have." The whole of *My Life and Hard Times* is a celebration of what might be called the Principle of Confusion, or the Fantasy Principle. Nearly every episode shows the disruption of the orderly pattern of everyday life by the idiosyncratic, the bizarre, the irrational.

"The Night the Bed Fell," for example, deals with chaos in the domestic circle. Father's unwonted decision to sleep in the attic one night, "to be away where he could think," and mother's certainty that the old bed up there would fall on father and kill him set in motion a chain of events reminiscent of the scenes of comic anarchy in G. W. Harris's Sut Lovingood tales, or in Faulkner's "Spotted Horses." The trouble starts when the rather unstable army cot on which Thurber is sleeping tips over with a crash. Mother, convinced that the bed upstairs has collapsed on father, cries out, " 'Let's go to your poor father!' " Brother Herman, thinking that his mother is in the grip of hysterics, shouts, " 'You're all right, Mamma!' " Cousin Briggs Beall, who lived in fear that some night he would stop breathing and always kept a glass of spirits of camphor at his bedside, starts awake with the terrifying certainty that he is suffocating and pours the camphor all over himself. Choking, he throws himself at a window which is unfortunately closed. Thurber, half awake and trapped under the cot, thinks that he is entombed in a mine. " 'Get me out of this!' " he cries. Father, awakened by mother's banging on the attic door, thinks that the house is on fire and calls out, " 'I'm coming.' " Mother, more than a little confused, cries out, " 'He's dying!' " By this time, Thurber and Cousin Briggs have got out into the hall, where Rex, the family bull terrier, jumps for Cousin Briggs, apparently feeling that he is the cause of all the trouble, and Brother Roy has to wrestle Rex to the floor. Father finally appears. " 'What in the name of God is going on here?' " he asks. Things finally get sorted out, and mother, "who always looked on the bright side of things," remarks to the boys, " 'I'm glad that your grandfather wasn't here.' "

"The Day the Dam Broke" tells of chaos in the community at large. When someone shouts "The dam has broken!" during the great flood of March, 1913, the quiet orderly life of Columbus explodes into panic and hysteria. Within minutes after the cry is raised, two thousand people are rushing through the streets crying "Go east! Go east!"—away from the river. Police and firemen and army officers—guardians of order—join the fleeing mob: " 'Go east!' " cried a little child in a piping voice, as she ran past a porch on which drowsed a lieutenant-colonel of infantry. Used to quick decisions, trained to immediate obedience, the officer bounded off the porch and, running at full tilt, soon passed the child, bawling " 'Go east!' "

The fact that no one on the East Side was in any danger gives Thurber's account of "the fine despair and the grotesque desperation" which seized the neighborhood a kind of mock-epic irony. His manner as he tells the story of this day of community madness is that of the historian—detached, objective, orderly—and much of the comic value of his account lies in the contrast between this sober historian's manner and the bizarre and fantastic events being described. He once remarked that if there was one thing identifiable as a *New Yorker* style, it would be the habit of understatement, "playing it down," [3] and the combination of dream-like unreality and reportorial matter-of-factness in this description of how they got grandfather out of the house is a good example:

> We had to stun grandfather with the ironing board. Impeded as we were by the inert form of the old gentleman—he was taller than six feet and weighed almost a hundred and seventy pounds—we were passed, in the first half-mile, by practically everybody else in the city. Had grandfather not come to, at the corner of Parsons Avenue and Town Street, we would unquestionably have been overtaken and engulfed by the roaring waters—that is, if there had *been* any roaring waters.

[3] Interview with Plimpton and Steele, in *Writers at Work*, p. 88.

My Life and Hard Times is obviously a special kind of autobiography, existing somewhere between the world of fact and the world of fantasy. Mother, father, grandfather, Thurber's two brothers, some of the servants, the family dogs and local characters like the Get-Ready Man are historically real. Thurber's bed did fall down one night, there was a day of panic in Columbus during the flood of 1913, and the boys did hear ghostly footsteps on the stairs. The basic pattern of people and events is real enough, but woven into this warp of truth is a cross-pattern of absurd and fanciful details which transforms the actual into a strange world where confusion and eccentricity are the primary ways of life. Thurber pointed to this mixture as a basic characteristic of his work as a whole when he said to Robert van Gelder in an interview of 1940 that his writing was based on truth, distorted for emphasis and amusement. "Reality twisted to the right into humor rather than to the left into tragedy," he called it.[4]

Robert Thurber remembers that their father did on occasion sleep in the attic and that one night the bed did collapse on him. This domestic mishap was the germ of truth which set Thurber's imagination to work. The wonderful concatenation of events in Thurber's account of that wild night are his own embellishment of what actually happened. They represent What Ought to Have Happened, if only the world were a little more artistically organized. There was no such person as Cousin Briggs Beall, whose picturesque neurosis adds so much to the nuttiness of the proceedings, and there was no pandemonium in the hall when the bed fell. "My brother leaned heavily on his imagination in this chapter," says Robert Thurber.[5] On the other hand, some of the details of family eccentricity which strike the reader as most made up are simple truth. Aunt Sarah Shoaf and her fear of burglars and chloroform are taken from life, as is the conviction of Thurber's grandmother (in "The Car We Had to Push") that electricity leaked out of empty light sockets.

The great flood of March, 1913, was real enough. Dozens of Ohio cities were inundated, and many people were drowned. The West Side of Columbus was under thirty feet of water, bridges were swept away, municipal services were paralyzed, and thousands of people saw their homes destroyed. More than a hundred people lost their lives. A headline in the Columbus *Dispatch* of March 26, 1913, reads, SCENES OF DIRE / DESOLATION GREET / RESCUE PARTIES / ON THE WEST SIDE / HUNDREDS ARE BROUGHT TO / PLACES OF

[4] *New York Times Book Review,* May 12, 1940, reprinted in van Gelder's *Writers and Writing,* p. 55.
[5] Robert Thurber, letter to CSH, July 4, 1966.

Electricity was leaking all over the house

SAFETY BY DISPATCH / RELIEF EXPEDITION./ MANY ARE
STILL IN PERIL / MANY CLING TO TREES. The panic over the
report that the dam had broken is also a matter of historical fact. Neil
Martin, a Columbus newspaperman, recalled that memorable day in a story
on Thurber in the Columbus *Citizen*, in 1952: "I do not believe anyone
can really, wholly appreciate Thurber who didn't participate in the Great
Run on the day the Scioto River dam didn't break . . . on March 12,
1913," he wrote. "I was one of the several thousand who joined in the run
and I have reason to think that none of us ever after was able to take himself
too seriously." [6] The flood and the panic are historical facts, but almost
all the details of Thurber's account—the lieutenant-colonel of infantry,
Aunt Edith Taylor's remarkable long-distance run, and grandfather's conviction that the city was under attack by Nathan Bedford Forrest's cavalry
—are fanciful inventions designed to heighten the absurdity already implicit in the whole preposterous episode.

In one case, Thurber fictionalized the facts not to heighten the truth
but to soften it. He changed the address of the family residence from 77
Jefferson Avenue to 77 Lexington Avenue in "The Night the Ghost Got

[6] Columbus *Citizen* Magazine Section, June 22, 1952 (RTS).

In" so as not to disturb the peace of mind of later tenants. In a letter to Bill Arter of the Columbus *Dispatch*, he said, "I deliberately changed the address for the simple reason that there was a ghost. . . . The family who lived in the house ahead of us moved out because of the strange sounds, we found out later. A corner druggist near the house, to whom I related my experience, described the walking and the running upstairs before I could describe it myself. They were undeniably the steps of a man, and it was quite an experience to hear him running up the stairs toward us, my brother and me, and to see nothing whatever. A Columbus jeweler is said to have shot himself in the house after running up those steps. . . . I didn't want to alarm whoever might be living there when I wrote the story." [7]

Confusion, chaos, eccentricity—these are the qualities Thurber discovers and delights in as he looks back at the world of his boyhood, and in telling the story of those early days he consistently reshapes reality, stylizes and fictionalizes it, to bring it closer to the world of fantasy. Long before he put any of it down on paper, he was thinking about it, working it over in his memory and imagination, shaping it into anecdotes for the entertainment of his friends at parties. Thurber alludes to the dramatic origin of his stories in the opening paragraph of "The Night the Bed Fell": "It makes a better recitation (unless, as some friends of mine have said, one has heard it five or six times) than it does a piece of writing, for it is almost necessary to throw furniture around, shake doors, and bark like a dog, to lend the proper atmosphere. . . ." By the time he came to write it all down, fact and fantasy had become so perfectly assimilated to one another that there was no longer any noticeable difference between them.

The figure of grandfather, whose airy disregard of the real world contributes so much to the zany atmosphere of the book as a whole, is perhaps the best example of the way in which Thurber's comic imagination transforms the facts of history in *My Life and Hard Times*. William M. Fisher, Thurber's real-life grandfather, is the subject of one of the portraits in *The Thurber Album:* in actuality he was a well-established Columbus businessman and lived with his wife in a fine house on Bryden Road; he never saw military service, although he was a Civil War buff and a great reader of Grant's *Memoirs;* he had trouble learning to drive the car, and he had his little eccentricities, like walking to work every morning with a rose between his teeth; but he never got the past and the present mixed up, he never shot a policeman under the impression that he was a deserter from

7 Bill Arter, "Thurber's Ghost House," Columbus *Dispatch* Magazine, April 2, 1967.

General Meade's army, and he never tried to enlist in World War I.

The fire-breathing old Civil War veteran of *My Life and Hard Times*, who prefers to live in the heroic past rather than the commonplace present, is almost entirely a fictional creation. As Thurber remakes him, he is the living embodiment of the superiority of the fantasy principle. Apparently infirm of mind and incapable of coping with the world of things as they are, grandfather is in fact superior to it. He transcends it in his dream life, but he returns to it when he wants to. When the police invade the sanctuary of his attic bedroom looking for burglars on the memorable night the ghost got in, grandfather is convinced that they are deserters from General Meade's army. Clad in his long flannel nightgown and nightcap, he confronts them, disarms one policeman and wings another. The rest beat a hasty retreat. Having triumphed over the real world in the skirmish of the night, he triumphs again at the breakfast table. While the members of the family wonder whether the old man remembers what happened, he glares at Thurber and brother Herman and asks, " 'What was the idee of all them cops tarryhootin' round the house last night?' "

Throughout *My Life and Hard Times* eccentricity of character is seen as a life-enhancing value. The mild insanities and picturesque obsessions of the people Thurber remembers from the days of his youth are not only diverting examples of the human comedy, they are also something important—they represent freedom, independence, the irrepressible stuff of life which refuses to be caught in formulas and conventions. Even the household pets showed the family strain of idiosyncrasy. Muggs, the burly, brooding Airedale who bit everybody, even members of the family, gets a whole chapter to himself. In nearly every way, Muggs belied the old saw that the dog is man's best friend. Because he would bite when anyone reached toward him, even with a plate of food, the family had to put his plate on top of an old kitchen table. Thurber's drawing of Muggs at dinner, hind feet on a bench, forefeet on the table, stumpy tail erect, his great head turned back over his shoulder, a surly and suspicious expression on his face, is an unforgettable impression of eccentricity and bad temper. Mrs. Thurber felt a special maternal protectiveness toward Muggs. He was not strong, she used to say, and she once consulted a faith healer in the hope that Harmonious Vibrations could be imparted to a dog. But Muggs went on biting people until the day he died. Over his grave, Thurber placed a board on which he had written with indelible pencil, "Cave Canem."

The conflict between the unique individual and the world of institutionalized systems and regulations is the theme of "University Days." Thurber's

inability to see through a microscope in the botany lab is a challenge to
the basic assumptions of science and mass education:

> "We'll try it," the professor said to me, grimly, "with every adjust-
> ment of the microscope known to man. As God is my witness, I'll
> arrange this glass so that you see cells through it or I'll give up
> teaching. . . ." He cut off abruptly for he was beginning to quiver
> all over, like Lionel Barrymore, and he genuinely wished to hold on
> to his temper; his scenes with me had taken a great deal out of him.

Throughout his account of his college career, Thurber pictures himself in
the role of misfit and sad sack. He had trouble in economics, because it
came right after botany, and he used to get the two subjects mixed up;
in the required gymnasium course he was not allowed to wear his glasses,
and so he bumped into "professors, horizontal bars, agricultural students,
and swinging iron rings"; he flunked Military Drill so often that by his
senior year he had "drilled longer than anyone else in the Western Conference." Looking back, Thurber remembers not the heroes and achievers,
but those whose failures were somehow memorable. There was Bolenciecwcz, the mighty tackle on the football team, who also had trouble with
economics, "for while he was not dumber than an ox he was not any
smarter"; and there was the agricultural student, a would-be journalist, who,

Bolenciecwcz was trying to think

when told to get some zip into his style, came up with this unforgettable lead: " 'Who has noticed the sores on the tops of the horses in the animal husbandry building?' "

In such sketches as "University Days" and "Draft Board Nights" Thurber appears as a kind of Bartleby, the odd-ball individual whose deepest instinct is to preserve his identity against the forces which would rob him of it. Like the hero of Melville's philosophical fable, whose response to the demands of the world that he show a decent conformity was "I prefer not to," Thurber affirms the superiority of Individual Difference over the concept of the Generic. Most often, however, he pictures himself as the nervous eccentric and comic victim whose experience is a series of small misadventures and humiliations, like the night the ghost got in, and he had to explain to a couple of skeptical cops the presence of a zither in one of the upstairs closets. Clad only in a pair of trousers, he tries to make sense out of it: " 'It's an old zither our guinea pig used to sleep on,' I said."

Thurber sharpens this self-portrait in the "Preface to a Life" and "A Note at the End" which frame his account of his early Columbus years. The "Preface" invites the reader to see the book as a mock-autobiography, a parody of the great tradition represented by Benvenuto Cellini, who said that a man should have accomplished something of excellence before writing his life, and Ford Madox Ford, who said that the sole reason for writing one's memoirs was to paint a picture of one's time. This element of parody was what appealed to Hemingway, and when he jokingly compared Thurber's book to *The Education of Henry Adams,* he was doubtless thinking of the irony with which both autobiographers viewed themselves and their achievements. Thurber points out that his only notable accomplishment is his skill in "hitting empty ginger ale bottles with small rocks at a distance of thirty paces," and that the time pictured in the work of a writer of short humorous pieces would not be "Walter Lippmann's time or Stuart Chase's time or Professor Einstein's time," but a rather small and personal one, "circumscribed by the short boundaries of his pain and embarrassment, in which what happens to his digestion, the rear axle of his car, and the confused flow of his relationships with six or eight persons . . . is of greater importance than what goes on in the nation or in the universe."

He makes the same point—more indirectly—in the title of his book: the phrase "Hard Times" would remind all readers that the book was written in the middle of a great economic depression and had absolutely nothing to say about it. The historian, the scientist, and the social critic properly address themselves to the great issues of the day, but the humorist should confine himself to the common experience of the private individual, particularly to the trivia in which every man's life is hopelessly entangled. His statement in Eastman's *Enjoyment of Laughter* emphasized the origin of the humorous in the little details of everyday life: "I think humor is the best that lies closest to the familiar, to that part of the familiar which is humiliating, distressing, even tragic. . . . There is always a laugh in the utterly familiar." Throughout the 1930's he steadfastly resisted the pressure on writers to make their work socially significant. In later years he was to modify his view and to see humor as a public force, a weapon for social good, rather than as subjective experience, but at this stage of his career, he obviously felt that the state of society and the crises of history were not the best subjects for the humorist.

The "Preface" and the "Note" are Thurber's portrait of the artist as neurotic middle-aged man. This character, or persona, is the definitive version of the literary identity which Thurber found most congenial up until his last years, when his darkening view of life required the creation of a new fictional self. It was first made explicit by E. B. White, who described Thurber in the Introduction to *The Owl in the Attic* as both Conradian romantic wanderer and anxiety-ridden modern man, and Thurber adopted it, enlarged upon it, and used it again and again over the years, both as a literary device and as a convenient mask for interviews and other public occasions.

The middle-aged writer, as Thurber describes him, lives in a constant state of "jumpiness and apprehension." His work is not "a joyous form of self-expression, but the manifestation of a twitchiness at once cosmic and mundane. . . . The little wheels of [his] invention are set in motion by the damp hand of melancholy." (He made the same point, without the fictional mask, on a BBC program many years later. Humor was not a sign of balance, he said, but of counter-balance. "I don't know any American humorist, including myself, who hasn't been in some kind of pretty serious mental emotional pathological psychopathic state," he said.[8]) In "A Note at the End," Thurber portrays himself as the romantic dreamer hemmed in by the commonplace, trapped in "the pathways between office and home," exposed to "the little perils of routine living." He yearns to break out and wander the South Seas, "like a character out of Conrad, silent and inscrutable." But there is no escape. His hopelessly Ohio background and the bondage of appointments with his oculist and dentist keep the Conradian wanderer at home.

[8] "Frankly Speaking," BBC Home Service Program, December 24, 1958.

The little autobiographical essays which frame *My Life and Hard Times* are not only an effective bit of literary clowning, but they are also an important statement about himself and the world of his imagination by a writer in full command of his talent. They advance the theory of humor underlying all of his earlier work—namely, that the twin sources of the humorous are the misadventures of everyday life and the neurotic apprehensions of the middle-class American male. And they define the Thurber protagonist—a figure created out of himself, but with the neurotic and daydreamy aspects of his nature played up, and the tough-mindedness and the professional expertise left out. Shadowing everything is the image of disaster: "As F. Hopkinson Smith long ago pointed out, the claw of the sea-puss gets us all in the end."

In *My Life and Hard Times* Thurber has arrived at full artistic maturity and nowhere is this more evident than in the style. Working on *The New Yorker* and emulating the easy informality of E. B. White, he developed a style that was natural, easy, and unself-conscious. It was colloquial without being slangy (although it could be that, too), and disciplined without being stiff. It was plain to the point of invisibility—a style which pretended not to be a style at all. It had no idiosyncrasies: sentence structure and word order were unobtrusively normal, and the language seldom called attention to itself. In *My Life and Hard Times* there are a few metaphors ("The little wheels of their invention are set in motion by the damp hand of melancholy"), a few coinages, mostly for onomatopoetic effect ("Tires booped and whooshed, the fenders queeled and graked, the steering wheel rose up like a spectre"), a few malapropisms for purposes of characterization in the dialogue ("The lady seems historical"), but in general, Thurber's prose is a transparent medium, reporting action and character in the simplest possible way.

All this he had by 1929, when *Is Sex Necessary?* first identified him as a writer of consequence. The difference is that in *My Life and Hard Times* his style has become not only a versatile comic instrument but a highly personal mode of expression as well. In *My Life and Hard Times* Thurber has developed a vocabulary and a pattern of phrasing which reflect his own unique temperament and cast of mind. Take the description in "University Days" of the tactical exercises given the students in Military Drill:

At 11 o'clock each morning thousands of freshmen and sophomores used to deploy over the campus, moodily creeping up on the old chemistry building. It was good training for the kind of warfare that was waged at Shiloh but it had no connection with what was going on in Europe. Some people used to think there was German money behind it, but they didn't dare say so or they would have been thrown in jail as German spies. It was a period of muddy thought and marked, I believe, the decline of higher education in the Middle West.

The passage is mock-heroic, one of Thurber's basic angles of vision. The comedy lies in the incongruity between the subject and the style, as in the opening sentence, where the language of military tactics ("At 11 o'clock each morning thousands . . . used to deploy") seems out of keeping with the facts that it is freshmen and sophomores who are deploying and that their objective is the old chemistry building. The method might be called "destruction by inflation," making something appear absurd by treating it in a language inappropriately grand, heightened, or conceptual. The last sentence, for example, makes the ineffectuality of R.O.T.C. drill at Ohio State all the more ridiculous by linking it to a portentous historical event, "the decline of higher education in the Middle West." The special flavor of the passage, however, is given by the adverb "moodily." Many humorists might make comic capital out of the irrelevance of the military science programs at our land-grant universities, but only Thurber would describe the cadets as "moodily creeping up on the old chemistry building." "Moodily" invests the whole scene with the slightly neurotic atmosphere which is the essence of his special world. It is one of his favorite words, along with *gloomy, jumpy, murky,* etc.,[9] all of which reflect his sense that life is full of booby traps and disappointments, and that a man has to make his way with caution.

For all its subtlety of effect, the passage looks easy, almost conversational. Appearances are deceptive: such ease came hard to Thurber. He slaved over his prose with the passionate perfectionism of a gem cutter, grinding, polishing, reshaping, until every word and every phrase was right. Writing, he often said, was for him a matter of rewriting. He rewrote most things from five to ten times, all the way through. "It's part of a constant effort . . . to make the finished version smooth, to make it seem effortless," he said to George Plimpton and Max Steele. His first drafts were always terrible; he couldn't explain it, he said, but the first or second draft of everything he wrote read as if it had been "turned out by a charwoman." [10] Describing his method of composition to Robert van Gelder, he said, "I rarely have a very clear idea of where I'm going when I start. Just people

[9] Richard Tobias, *The Art of James Thurber* (Athens, Ohio: Ohio University Press, 1969), p. 179.
[10] Interview with Plimpton and Steele, *Writers at Work,* p. 88.

and a situation. Then I fool around—writing and rewriting until the stuff jells." His first draft is " 'just for size.' " " 'That draft isn't any good; it isn't supposed to be; the whole purpose is to sketch out proportions.' " After that, he begins to revise and polish.[11]

His passion for perfection extended even to the appearance of his copy: if he made a typing mistake, he redid the entire page. He rewrote "The Secret Life of Walter Mitty" fifteen times, and it took him eight weeks, "working day and night," he told Alistair Cooke.[12] He could remember only one story that came quickly and easily—"File and Forget," which he did in a single afternoon, but even then, he confessed, the last part took him a week. "It was the end of the piece and I had to fuss over it," he said.[13] At times he envied the fluent writers whose first drafts were virtually finished copy—people like Elliot Paul, Sally Benson, and John O'Hara. O'Hara's only revising, according to Thurber, was a little " 'pencil work,' " a few touch-ups in the final rereading.[14] Still, in spite of the care and the pain, he liked the act of writing. He liked the shape of words and phrases, and he liked the look of clean copy. "Even rewriting's fun," he said to Plimpton and Steele.

[11] Van Gelder, *Writers and Writing*, pp. 53–54.
[12] *Atlantic*, CXCVIII (August, 1956), 37.
[13] Interview with Plimpton and Steele, *Writers at Work*, p. 88.
[14] Letter to Malcolm Cowley, March 11, 1954.

10

The Battle of the Sexes: The Middle-Aged Man on the Flying Trapeze

MUCH TO THURBER'S ANNOYANCE, his first real fame derived from his drawings rather than his writing. He could never take the drawings seriously, because they came without effort, but the prose was his lifeblood. Nevertheless, he was excited and flattered when Paul Nash, the English painter and critic, visiting the United States in 1931 as a judge of the Carnegie Exhibition of Modern Art in Pittsburgh, asked particularly to meet him. There was to be an elaborate luncheon in Nash's honor at the Century Club in New York. The guest list was impressive— Jonas Lie, Glackens, Hopper, Burchfield, and other famous painters were invited, as well as important critics and museum directors. Nash astounded the board of directors by requesting that Milt Gross and Thurber be added to the list. He was a great admirer of American cartoonists, and had already written an essay, on modern American humorous draughtsmen, in which he described the work of Gross, Disney, Arno, Soglow, John Held, Jr., and Thurber—whose style he had compared to that of Matisse.[1] When Nash arrived at the luncheon, "he embarrassed the hell out of me," Thurber recalled, "stopping to talk, while the others shifted uneasily and there was

[1] In a letter to Herman Miller, September 27, 1931, Thurber says that Nash's essay appeared in the London *Week-end Review*, but gives no date; in a letter to Anthony Bertram, May 4, 1951, he places it in the *English Review*, also without date; in his interview with Henry Brandon, in 1958, he has it in the *New Statesman*. The title of the essay is "American Humorous Draughtsmen," and it appeared in the *Week-end Review*, August 8, 1931.

a lot of nervous coughing." At the table, Nash insisted that Thurber should be put on his right. Between them, they put away a bottle of Scotch which they had lifted from the sideboard ("I needed more drinks to get through that amazing lunch," said Thurber) and talked happily about American comic strips. Thurber remembered one detail of the occasion with particular relish:

> Across from us sat one of the most formidable figures I ever saw, an enormous man with flashing dark eyes and a great spade beard. Paul looked at him and said, "Do you know how I could get in touch with Milt Gross?" The gentleman, probably the director of a gallery or editor of a recondite art magazine, replied gruffly, "I am sure I wouldn't have the faintest idea." Paul stared at him. "He is one of your great artists," he said, and I kicked him under the table.[2]

The next day Thurber arranged for Nash to meet Gross, and he and Althea gave a cocktail party so that Nash could meet the *New Yorker* cartoonists. (It was just before this party that Thurber got the hot water tap in the bathroom stuck.) He took Nash in to see Ross, first briefing him on Ross's ignorance of art and music and his Philistine contempt for anything he didn't understand. Ross's first words were, " 'Nash, there are only two phony arts, music and painting.' " Nash was delighted. "He thought Ross was one of the great sights of New York," recalled Thurber. The friendship between the two men developed through the years. Thurber admired the way in which Nash combined his artistic and literary talents, and he particularly liked the vein of fantasy in his work. One of his favorite Nash pieces showed the moon being approached by flowers, and carried the legend, "Last night, light and heavy hellebors attacked the mountains of the moon." This dream-like interplay between picture and text was exactly the sort of thing to which Thurber's imagination was attuned. When Thurber and his wife Helen were in England in 1937–38, Nash was one of the first people they sought out.[3]

The Nash luncheon was Thurber's first taste of international fame, all the sweeter because so totally unexpected, and he wrote excitedly about it to the Millers: "My dear people, you should be here for the fun!! . . . I must see you some day to tell you, in greater detail, how Alice in Wonderland it all was." When Smith College put on an exhibit of his drawings along with those of George Grosz in the winter of 1933, and when his

[2] Thurber tells of Nash's visit in his letter to Herman Miller, September 27, 1931, in his letter to Anthony Bertram, May 4, 1951, and in *The Years with Ross*, pp. 64–65.
[3] Thurber tells of his regard for Nash in his letter to Bertram of May 4, 1951. .

one-man show at the Valentine Gallery in New York in 1934 was widely discussed and reviewed, it was clear that he had arrived as a comic artist.

Recognition from such prestigious sources was slower in coming to his writing, although his books always got good reviews and sold well. With the success of *My Life and Hard Times* in 1933, he was doing well enough financially to quit his job as a full-time member of the *New Yorker* editorial staff and to devote the major portion of his time to his own writing. He continued to do "The Talk of the Town" for two more years, and this was worth a steady $100 a week. *The New Yorker* had first refusal on anything he wrote, and under Ross's complicated system of payment, he was guaranteed a basic yearly income if he turned in at least four stories a year. In any case, he no longer had to edit copy and spend all day at the office.

In the meantime, he was becoming known not only as a humorist but as a "character" and a celebrity. Practical jokes flourished at *The New Yorker* in the early days, and Thurber played a leading role in the horseplay that gave life at the magazine a continuous holiday air. Once, when the office was over-run with workmen and the air was filled with the sound of hammering and destruction as Ross tore down partitions and rearranged work space in his unending search for the Ideal Order of Things, Thurber hung a sign outside the elevator reading, "Alterations going on as usual during business." Another time, in a gesture reminiscent of his attack on the Public Library in Columbus, he rolled a number of big water bottles around in the corridor. When Ross heard the rumbling and crashing, he said to Bernard Bergman, the new managing editor, " 'Go out and find out what the hell is happening. But don't tell me.' " [4]

St. Clair McKelway recalls what was perhaps Thurber's most spectacular practical joke on the *New Yorker* premises: he had been irritated for some time by the habit of one of the copy editors, R. E. M. Whitaker, of making corrections in red ink on the proofs of his "Talk" pieces, and so one day he appeared in front of Whitaker's desk, staring wildly and holding a revolver. " 'Are you the S.O.B. that keeps putting notes in red ink on the proofs of my Talk stories?' asked Thurber. Whitaker nodded. Thurber pointed the revolver at Whitaker's chest, pulled the trigger, and there was a click. Whitaker fainted. When he recovered consciousness, Thurber had left his office and Whitaker never again used red ink on his proofs." [5] Now and then—but rarely—the jokes extended even into the magazine itself. Once when White was on vacation, Thurber invented a newsbreak and got it past Ross. He had done this sort of thing to the Paris and Nice

[4] *The Years with Ross*, p. 140; Kramer, *Ross and The New Yorker*, p. 178.
[5] "Salute to Thurber," *Saturday Review*, XLIV (November 25, 1961), 16.

editions of the Chicago *Tribune* in the freewheeling days in France, but Ross was not amused. " 'Goddam it, Thurber, don't kid around with the newsbreaks,' " he said.

When *Fortune* did a long feature on *The New Yorker* in August of 1934, a large part of the article was devoted to the personalities and achievements of Ross, White, and Thurber. Of Thurber, *Fortune* said, "For seven years he has shared with White the distinction of being the magazine's No. 1 contributor-editor," and then went on to observe that "It would not be unfair to say that if Ross created the body, Thurber and White are the soul of the New Yorker." [6] Much of the comment on Thurber emphasized his unconventional behavior and his practical jokes, like the time he allegedly terrified the security-conscious Ross by getting hold of the office master key and having dozens of duplicates made which he then handed out to his friends. Interviewing Thurber in the *World-Telegram* on the occasion of the Valentine Gallery show, Joseph Mitchell portrayed him as mildly eccentric, absent-minded, basically incompetent in the face of the practical demands of life. Such observations as, "His apartment at the Algonquin is full of drawings and old shirts. . . . When he needs a clean shirt he goes out and buys one," show Thurber (with Mitchell's help) creating a public character for himself, half real, half make-believe.[7]

His home town was understandably proud of him, and the Columbus *Citizen* paid him tribute in a long two-part article, the first of a series on Columbus authors, entitled "We Knew Him When." [8] Other authors in the series were Donald Ogden Stewart, Dorothy Canfield Fisher, and W. R. Burnett. By 1934 he was well enough established as a humorist and a character to be featured in a radio show. He had appeared as a guest on a number of programs ever since his debut as a published author in 1929, but early in 1934 CBS planned a weekly series for Thurber in which he could exercise his talents as a reminiscer and anecdote-spinner. This series never materialized, but what was to have been the opening broadcast produced some fine moments. Alton Cooke, the *World-Telegram* radio editor, reported that with the help of Jap Gude, then head of publicity for CBS, Thurber threw a scare into the network officials just before the first broadcast by pretending to be too drunk to go on, and Robert Thurber recalls that he sustained the suspense once he got on the air by worriedly fishing in his pockets, as though looking for his notes, then dropping them on the floor—apparently by mistake—all the while telling his stories in his casual, offhand, flat-voiced Midwestern style. That night he talked about his cook, his dogs, and finally about Sam Langford, the fighter, drawing on the rich vein of memory he had already tapped in *My Life and Hard Times* and was again to draw on in *The Thurber Album* twenty years later.[9]

It was during the winter of 1934–35 that he did his famous drawings on the walls of Costello's Bar and Grill on Third Avenue. Costello's had become Thurber's home away from home by this time, and nearly every night he dropped in for drinks and conversation with other regulars. One legend has it that every night he would decorate the wall of the booth he was sitting in with his fencing men, threatening women, contemplative dogs, his seals, penguins, and all the other creatures of his imagination. Costello was quick to see the value of what was happening, and had a preservative coat of varnish put on the wall every morning after Thurber had been drawing. The story goes that Costello maneuvered Thurber into a different booth each night without Thurber realizing what was going on, and so, by the end of the winter, had his entire wall covered with Thurber originals at no cost to himself.[10] It is a good story, but the plain facts seem to be that Thurber did Costello's entire wall in ninety minutes one evening, and that Costello then put on his coat of varnish. A few years later the drawings were obliterated when Costello had the place repainted and forgot to tell the painters to spare Thurber's wall. Thurber did a whole new set, and these drawings survived Costello's move next door in 1949. In moving to larger quarters, Costello made sure that the old booths and the wooden panels decorated with Thurber's figures were transferred intact to the new location.[11]

Most of Thurber's friends during these years were fellow *New Yorker* writers. His companions at Tony's and other oases patronized by writers in the late Twenties and early Thirties were likely to be Benchley, White, Gibbs, Dorothy Parker, Robert M. Coates, Morris Markey, Ralph Ingersoll, and John Mosher, the fastidious editor who had turned down all his manuscripts in 1926 and early 1927. A little later, there were John McNulty and Joel Sayre, Thurber's friends from old Columbus days, and St. Clair McKelway. Perhaps his best friends were John and Helen Gude. Gude was his business agent and confidant for thirty years, and, with E. B. White, knew him better than anyone else.

[9] Alton Cooke, "Jim Thurber Hurls a Scare," New York *World-Telegram*, April 20, 1934.
[10] Budd, "Personal Reminiscences of James Thurber."
[11] New York *Herald Tribune*, October 4, 1949, and "Aphorist for an Anxious Age," *Time*, November 10, 1961.

Although outsiders often spoke of "the *New Yorker* group," Thurber and his friends never felt themselves to be part of a circle or a special community in the way that the wits who made the Algonquin Round Table famous obviously did. Personal relationships on *The New Yorker* were individual and haphazard. Ross hired and fired people capriciously and often, and when a new employee joined the staff, no one showed him around or introduced him to anyone else. In the early days, newcomers had to wander around on their own even to find office space. Ross tried to avoid becoming personally involved with his writers and artists (probably because he knew himself to be a sentimentalist), and so there were no general meetings of the staff to talk things over, nor were there any efforts to promote camaraderie. St. Clair McKelway had been with the magazine three months before Thurber met him, and Lillian Ross had worked there for a couple of years before someone introduced Thurber to her. Ross did once try to set up a private speakeasy close to the office, in emulation of Punch's famous weekly tea-meetings, but neither Ross nor his staff was enthusiastic about establishing institutional friendships, and so the project died.[12]

This pattern of relatively casual and limited friendships suited Thurber. He was a gregarious man, sympathetic and helpful to others, but at the same time, he always held himself somewhat aloof. There were a few people with whom he was genuinely close—the Gudes, the Whites, the Millers, and the Nugents—but for the most part, he preferred the more or less conventionalized associations of the office and the neighborhood bar to more demanding relationships. For all his love of parties and good conversation, he kept himself to himself. Whether it was a kind of fastidious reserve, or the self-protective wariness of the artistic ego, he was afraid of intimacy.

Like many essentially private people, Thurber loved to have a crowd around, and at parties he was always the center of the group. He was a notable mimic and raconteur, and his remarkable memory for the details of his life in Columbus, Paris, and New York gave him a nearly inexhaustible supply of material. He told his stories "with wit, with perfect timing, and a great sense of dramatic climax," said Frank Sullivan. Old friends who recall Thurber acting out the anecdotes which later made up *My Life and Hard Times* were not in the least surprised at his success as a performer in his own *Thurber Carnival* on Broadway in 1960. St. Clair McKelway recalls that at parties in Greenwich Village in the early 1930's Thurber would play all the parts as he dramatized his stories about his eccentric family in Columbus. "One after another, and sometimes more or less

---

[12] *The Years with Ross,* pp. 166–67; Kramer, *Ross and The New Yorker,* p. 108.

simultaneously, he would play the parts of his mother, his father, his grandfather (offstage), his brother Roy, his brother Herman, and a dog named Rex, in addition to playing himself. It was a long time . . . before Thurber got around in 1933 to putting his family story down in words on his typewriter." [13]

Most of his impromptu entertainments never got down on paper, and those lucky enough to have seen Thurber in action feel that this was a major cultural loss. Helen Thurber speaks with particular regret of "the glorious tale of Miss Naddy's Dancing Academy of Columbus, Ohio." "This was a favorite Thurber recitation," she recalls, "and I will never forget the picture of that dancing class, over a bowling alley very much on the wrong side of the tracks and so delightfully different from the prim, white-gloved school where I learned to one-step." The clientele was tough, and so was the teacher. " 'All right, now we'll try another moonlight waltz,' she would yell, after three previous attempts by candlelight had failed, ending in what could hardly be called waltzing, 'and this time I want you guys to stay out from behind them palms.' " [14] Others remembered best his imitations of characters from literature and life. His impersonation of Harold Ross was a notable piece of caricature, according to those who saw it, capturing perfectly the nervous movement of the hands, the raucous voice, and the generally harassed manner. His most famous performance was his rendition of Jeeter Lester, the central character in Erskine Caldwell's *Tobacco Road* Wolcott Gibbs once observed that "people who have witnessed his interpretation of Jeeter Lester can have no doubt that they have seen great acting." [15]

If the atmosphere was not right for recitations, Thurber would often show off his extensive repertoire of old ballads. "Bye, Bye, Blackbird" was his special favorite, along with such standards as "Who" and "Melancholy Baby" (both well suited to the mood of wee-hours quartets); but what he liked best was to do solos of obscure and improbable songs no one else had ever heard of, like "She'll Be True to Him in Monkey Doodle Town." Then there were the parlor games he excelled at, like flipping cards into a hat, and pitching pennies. His real passion was reserved for complicated word games, however, and it was a rare evening when Thurber did not introduce anagrams or some brain-twisting variant of it into the proceedings. He loved words as things in themselves, and after he began to lose his sight in 1940, his enthusiasm for word-play amounted to an obsession. No oppor-

[13] "Salute to Thurber," p. 16.
[14] "Foreword," *Credos and Curios* (New York: Harper & Row, 1962).
[15] Review of "Three by Thurber," *The New Yorker*, March 19, 1955.

tunity for ringing some unexpected changes on familiar words and phrases was too trivial. When the minister in Cornwall, the Reverend Richard K. Beebe, and his wife were expecting a child, Thurber suggested that they nickname it Booboo, so that after greeting mother and child, he could take his leave by saying, "Bye bye, Booboo Beebe baby." [16]

Wherever Thurber appeared, he brought a touch of fantasy to the occasion. Once, after a few drinks at Tony's he had trouble getting the number he wanted on the telephone. Instead of calling the operator for help, he called the president of the telephone company. The president, alert even at that hour to the importance of good public relations, got in touch with the appropriate supervisor and saw to it that Thurber got his call through. Donald Ogden Stewart recalls another evening at Tony's in the late 1920's:

> The reunion once more was a joyful one and once more included "The Old Mill Stream," in which Robert Benchley and Dorothy Parker enthusiastically joined. Sometime around three in the morning Thurber, beginning to worry that Althea might think he was out somewhere drinking, departed in the direction of home.
>
> Three minutes later he was back at our table, with what might be described as a rather exalted look on his face. "Elephants," he announced happily, in the same awed tone in which one might report one's first impression of the cathedral at Chartres or a performance by Eleonora Duse. "Elephants . . . walking west along 52nd Street, holding each other's tails." We welcomed his seemingly imaginative contribution to our own crazy world with enthusiasm; it was only when he appeared doubtful that Althea would accept this as an excuse for his late return that we went to the door and witnessed a procession of Ringling Brothers animals on their way from the New York Central railroad yards to Madison Square Garden, where the circus was to open the following Monday.

"Thurber's world was like that," said Stewart, summing it all up.[17]

The other, darker, side of Thurber's nature also showed itself in the drinking sessions at Tony's and the parties in the Village. The extravagant clowning was the genial aspect of a wildness which often erupted into violent arguments and cruel personal abuse. Thurber quarreled with almost

---

[16] Peter De Vries to CSH; De Vries recalls many examples of Thurber's impromptu entertainments; Robert M. Coates recalls others in his memoir in the *Authors Guild Bulletin*, December, 1961.
[17] "Death of a Unicorn."

everyone, at one time or another, but his deepest hostility was reserved for women, and most particularly for wives. "Jim hated wives," said one old friend, and while the statement is obviously an exaggeration, it does point up the fact that the anti-feminism in Thurber's work is not simply a convenient comic device, but a deeply rooted bias in his own inner life. Friendly and amusing as he was most of the time, after a few drinks he could become unaccountably hostile. "He's the nicest guy in the world up to 5:00 P.M.," said a long-time *New Yorker* colleague.[18] Next morning he was always contrite, and would invariably follow up the explosion of the night before with an equally extravagant act of generosity.

Although this was the period in which Thurber first won the recognition he wanted, his private life was in a turmoil. His marriage was turning out badly, and in 1929 he and Althea separated. During the next couple of years he spent a good deal of time prowling the speakeasies in company with his *New Yorker* friends, and occasionally doing the nightclub rounds with Humphrey Bogart, Franchot Tone, Burgess Meredith, and other theater people. Harold Ross, whose own married life was difficult, sometimes joined them.[19] Two off-again-on-again love affairs only added to the emotional conflict and confusion of these years.

The loneliness and uncertainty of his situation proved to be too much for him, and in 1931 he and Althea were reconciled. Hoping to find security and permanence in old-fashioned domesticity, he bought a hundred-and-twenty-five-year-old farmhouse on twenty acres of land near Sandy Hook, Connecticut, and their daughter Rosemary was born there in October of 1931. The move to the country was good therapy for the Thurbers. Thurber threw himself into the role of family man and country gentleman, and for a time things ran smoothly. A long relaxed letter to the Millers in September reveals both his contentment and his underlying restlessness. "Althea is unquestionably the world's most patient and finest mother-expectant," he observed, and he went on to describe the tranquillity of life in the country.

> Meanwhile, outside, there is the intermittent fall of apples from my apple trees, and the curiously unnerving raspberry which my neighbor's sheep hand me, and the sounds of my five female dogs, two of them in heat (I inadvertently let Jeannie loose one day and she didn't show up till next morning, with seven of the finest specimens of manhood among the shepherd dogs of this country following her, each

[18] Sayre, "Priceless Gift of Laughter."
[19] *The Years with Ross*, p. 183.

trying to outdo the other in ardor of attention). I have twenty acres and a house a hundred and twenty-five years old, and a view over a valley to a Connecticut town that was flourishing when Washington was seducing the Mount Vernon chambermaids. I also have arranged a series of croquet wickets so that they make a golf course running completely around the house. Every few hours I get out and struggle trying to make the course under twenty-three, which is my record so far. It is maddening to me, my wife, her mother, the cook and the dogs. But nothing so completely holds me as competitive endeavor.

In this frame of mind he could talk easily about his private life and his creative frustrations. He confessed that he was at a standstill in his work, and had been meditating on "the probability that I shall never write anything really as good as I should like to, and so on. You know: the thoughts of a man of thirty-six." He had started a novel to be called *Rain Before Seven*, but had dropped it after one chapter: "I am afraid all of my novels would be complete in one chapter, from force of habit in writing short pieces and also from a natural incapability of what Billy Graves would call 'larger flight.' " He went on to speak to the Millers of his reading: he was just going through Evelyn Waugh's two books ("my favorite two books"), and *Crime and Punishment*, and the letters and the first novel of Frances Newman. "Kind of a mixed lot," he noted, "I don't suppose it has helped my thought processes any."

Then in the most revealing passage of the letter, he takes a look at his own hopelessly romantic temperament. This half-comic, half-serious bit of self-analysis shows very clearly the two poles of his imagination. He confesses to the charm of the idea of "sitting in a speakeasy on a rainy evening with somebody else's wife," and then, seeing himself with some detachment, he adds, "I sometimes wonder at just what age I will get over my until now, secret desire for and belief in fairly clandestine monkey-business." Trapped in the romantic illusion, but aware that it is, after all, only an illusion, he looks forward to the time when "I can view tranquilly and, please God, with more humor than I have been able to thus far, the sad, sweet, mixed-up pulsing of sex and beauty and drink and unfair kisses." Then, alluding to a novel Miller was planning on the misadventures of a romantic personality, he adds ruefully, "Herman, you should have taken notes on me."

Neither the pastoral charm of country life nor the presence of Rosemary was enough to preserve their shaky marriage, and by 1934 it was obvious that he and Althea would have to separate permanently. They were divorced in 1935. During this period of final breakup Thurber lived alone at the Algonquin in the classic disorder of the married man trying to make it alone. In the evenings, the need for companionship drove him out to the bars and nightclubs of the city and to the apartments of his friends. Malcolm Cowley remembers him "wandering about the city in taxis." "When he visited friends," said Cowley, "he usually stayed until three or four in the morning, as if putting off the moment when he would have to open the door of an empty room. Once inside the room he might spend the rest of the night typing a letter." [20]

On one of these excursions, in the spring of 1934, he met F. Scott Fitzgerald, another lonely wanderer in the night. Thurber recalls the episode in his warm and revealing portrait of Fitzgerald, "Scott in Thorns." It was at Tony's, on 52nd Street. They drank and talked for five hours, during which Fitzgerald was, as Thurber remembers him, "witty, forlorn, pathetic, romantic, worried, hopeful, and despondent, but . . . quiet and pleasant, too, and not difficult." Thurber goes on to say, "I should like to report that of the four or five eminent writers of the Crazy Decade with whom I have spent the night hours drinking, Scott was the best behaved, the least menacing, and the quietest, and he held his liquor better than any of the others." Fitzgerald refused to talk about *The Great Gatsby*, one of Thurber's favorite books, insisting instead that they talk about the soon-to-be-published *Tender Is the Night*, which he called, rather melodramatically, "My Testament of Faith." [21]

Fitzgerald was, of all contemporary authors, Thurber's special favorite. He often spoke of the artistic economy of *The Great Gatsby* and the grace of Fitzgerald's treatment of the romantic personality, which struck a responsive chord deep in his own nature. His account of their one and only meeting, on that night in 1934, emphasizes the doomed romantic quality in Fitzgerald—the charm and basic decency, the frustrated talent, the inner desperation. Speculating on how different things might have been for Fitzgerald if Zelda had only recovered that spring, and his novel had been well received, Thurber sums it all up: "He never had any luck."

Thurber wrote the unhappiness of these years into two highly autobiographical stories, "The Evening's at Seven," in 1932, and "One Is a Wanderer," in 1935. Kirk, the protagonist of "One Is a Wanderer," is a forty-year-old recently divorced writer who finds his lonely life almost

[20] "Salute to Thurber," p. 14.
[21] "Scott in Thorns," *Reporter*, IV (April 17, 1951), 35–38; reprinted in *Credos and Curios;* Thurber gave a briefer version of this meeting on the BBC program, "Frankly Speaking."

insupportable. He tries to dull the ache, to keep from remembering. He walks the streets of the city on a dark winter evening, trying to avoid going back to the hotel room piled with loose papers and dirty shirts. "He had had too many nights alone." He goes to a bar and drinks with some acquaintances until after three o'clock. On the way back, the cab driver is philosophical—drinking at these places is O.K., he says, " 'But when a man gets fed up on that kind of stuff, a man wants to go home. Am I right, Mr. Kirk?'

" 'You're absolutely right, Willie,' he said. 'A man wants to go home.' "

Back in his hotel room he sings softly to himself the last part of "Bye, Bye, Blackbird" as he gets undressed—" 'Make my bed and light the light, for I'll be home late tonight. . . .' " The story shows the influence of two writers for whom Thurber always had the highest regard, Hemingway and Fitzgerald. Its objective presentation of the mind and feelings of Kirk is reminiscent of the method of Hemingway, while the subject matter, the pain of lost love, is closer to Fitzgerald.

In spite of the discontents of his private life, the early 1930's were extraordinarily productive years for Thurber as a writer and artist. He was doing "The Talk of the Town" and the "Tennis" column, his cartoons were becoming one of the most talked-about features of the magazine, and he was turning out a steady sequence of brilliant short stories and sketches —pieces like "If Grant Had Been Drinking at Appomattox," "Something to Say," "The Greatest Man in the World," and "The Black Magic of Barney Haller." The best of these he collected in *The Middle-Aged Man on the Flying Trapeze* (1935), without question one of his most impressive books.

Thurber's drawing on the dust jacket of the book is a perfect visual image of the theme and tone of the whole. It shows a typical middle-aged Thurber man, complete with moustache and pince-nez, flying through the air, having just let go of his trapeze, his arms stretched out expectantly toward his lady partner, who is swinging up toward him, knees hooked securely to her trapeze bar, arms hanging down instead of stretching out toward the man, a smile of wicked intent on her face. It is an admirable image of the state of mind of most of Thurber's protagonists in this book. They are, for the most part, lonely, frightened, and inadequate males threatened and victimized by their more self-confident women, and forced to find their triumphs in small, secret ways. Often they are pursued and defeated even in the innermost recesses of their fantasy lives. These are very different people from the self-confident eccentrics of *My Life and Hard Times*, and their experience, anxious and conflict-ridden, is a very different sort of experience from that encountered by the characters in Thurber's recollections of his boyhood.

In no other single collection does Thurber deal so obsessively with the incompatibility of Man and Woman, and his preoccupation with this subject is an obvious projection of his feelings at the time his own marriage was breaking up. Two stories, "Mr. Pendly and the Poindexter" (1932) and "Smashup" (1935), show the archetypal elements of his battle-of-the-sexes pieces in their simplest form. In both, there is the timid, emasculated husband and the overpoweringly self-confident wife; and in both there is the ordeal challenging the husband's masculinity. As in so many Thurber stories, the ordeal involves the automobile: mastery of the car is the symbol of mastery in marriage. In both stories, the husband wins a victory of sorts, although Mr. Pendly's is a small private one.

Mr. Pendly is an early version of Walter Mitty: humiliated by his self-confident wife and an aggressive car salesman, he reshapes the painful realities of failure into an imaginary scene of triumph. In his daydream, he solves a complicated mechanical problem, tinkering with a couple of rods, tightening a winch gasket, and blowing softly into a valve. Just as Mac, the big mechanic, is congratulating him, his wife interrupts his reverie:

> "What's the matter; are you in a trance or what?" asked Mrs.
> Pendly, pulling her husband's sleeve. He gave her a cold, superior look.
> "Never mind about me," he said.

Here, as so often in Thurber, fantasy and daydream are a source of strength, enabling the dreamer to survive outer defeat and win inner victory, and as so often in Thurber, the male is the dreamer and the hero, and the female is the realist and the antagonist.

"Smashup" is not as artistic as "Mr. Pendly and the Poindexter," but it has a special interest because of the clarity with which it shows the autobiographical origins of this basic Thurber anecdote. Tommy Trinway and his wife Betty are obviously Thurber and Althea, and the story is his view of their marriage just at the time it was falling apart. Tommy is shy, studious, and nervous. In 1909, at the age of fifteen, he has an accident driving the family surrey. He is not allowed to drive after that, although his younger brother is. His confidence shaken, he takes to reading books instead of playing games with the fellows. When the family buys a Rambler, he dreams of driving it fast, like Barney Oldfield, but mostly he dreams of accidents. He never gets up enough nerve to learn to drive it.

At twenty-eight, he marries Betty Carter, an ambitious, self-confident girl who saw something "deep, if not profound, behind Tommy's moody silences." (Thurber was twenty-eight when he married Althea.) Betty is an expert driver. "She drove very fast herself, with keen concentration, quick reflexes, and evident enjoyment. . . ." Tommy learns to drive, but he is timid and unsure of himself, and after a while, Betty does all the driving. The ordeal by auto comes when Betty sprains her wrist, and Tommy has to drive them from Cape Cod to New York. In the nightmare of New York traffic, an elderly woman steps in front of the car. Without knowing quite how he has done it, Tommy finds that he has avoided her and saved the car from smashing into an "L" pillar. " 'Nice piece of drivin', mister,' " says a policeman.

The last scene closely anticipates Hemingway's "The Short Happy Life of Francis Macomber." In both stories, the woman-dominated male passes an ordeal which enables him to break the woman's hold over him and emerge into manhood. Over a drink at the hotel, Tommy is full of new confidence. Betty, as usual, tries to put him down, but for the first time, Tommy fights back. Betty is shaken: " 'What's the matter with you?' she asked. . . . 'Nothing is the matter with me,' said Tommy. 'I'm fine.' She stared at her husband over the cigarette, and striking another match, still stared. He stared back at her." He tosses off his drink, and steps over to the hotel desk, where he requests two single rooms instead of the usual double. Then he walks out into the street, whistling.

Sometimes the rebellion of the husband against the wife takes strange forms and results in defeat or, at best, a Pyrrhic victory. Good-natured Charlie Deshler, the protagonist of "The Curb in the Sky," cannot stand his well-meaning wife's habit of interrupting his anecdotes and correcting his mistakes. He retreats into a world of schizoid fantasies where he can have things his own way, but there is no escape. His wife pursues him even to the sanitarium, where she sits by his bedside, happily correcting his dream-tales. Mr. Bidwell is another fugitive who tries to escape from his wife into a private inner world and ends up a victim of mental breakdown. In neither "The Curb in the Sky" nor "The Private Life of Mr. Bidwell" is fantasy a refuge, a source of strength, or a redeeming value, as it is in so much of Thurber's work. Both Charlie Deshler and Mr. Bidwell flee from reality and both pay too high a price for their escape. Thurber did not often write about the world of fantasy in this way, but there is a little cluster of stories, like "The Remarkable Case of Mr. Bruhl," "The Whip-poor-will," and "A Friend to Alexander," in which he represents its dark and destructive side.

The battle of the sexes, psychological conflicts of various kinds, the tensions and anxieties of modern life—these are the dominant subjects of

The Middle-Aged Man on the Flying Trapeze. In sharp contrast to these painful and unsettling areas of experience, there are a number of reminiscence pieces which recreate the simpler, kinder world of Thurber's Ohio boyhood—"Portrait of Aunt Ida," "The Luck of Jad Peters," "Snapshot of a Dog," and "I Went to Sullivant"—and there is a particularly strong group of parodies and satires. Among the best of these are "Something to Say," "If Grant Had Been Drinking at Appomattox," and "The Greatest Man in the World."

The target of "Something to Say" is Henry James's story about the paradoxes of the artistic temperament, "The Coxon Fund." [22] James's Frank Saltram is a man of great intellectual gifts but few of the virtues expected of ordinary men in private life. To complicate matters, his genius displays itself chiefly in conversation. His actual production is pitifully small, and when he comes into a handsome endowment, he ceases to produce altogether. (In his notebook, James said that he had Coleridge in mind as the model for his Genius-Talker.) Thurber takes hold of the comic possibilities of the story—the artist as cad and bounder—and pushes them into wonderful absurdity. His Elliot Vereker (the name comes from another of James's artist stories, "The Figure in the Carpet") is a boor, an oaf, a self-proclaimed genius who never writes anything, but who is extravagantly admired by a little circle of disciples. "His entire output . . . consisted of only twenty or thirty pages, most of them bearing the round stain of liquor glasses. . . ." The story is told by an incredibly naive observer, a hero-worshipper who takes Vereker at his own evaluation, and the contrast between Vereker's actions and the narrator's view of them gives the whole tale a wonderful comic enlargement.

Thurber's parody is particularly effective because it retains the basic elements of James's own story, and with only a slight distortion, makes them ridiculous. Vereker is one aspect of James's Saltram, pressed to the outer limits of caricature, and the narrator is the sympathetic Jamesian observer transformed from an intelligent man of the world into a fatuous simpleton who gets everything wrong. A year later, in "Recollections of Henry James" (*New Yorker*, June 17, 1933), Thurber parodied James once again. He imagines an occasion on which James tells the plot of *The Bat*, the popular mystery play, to a company of literary notables. The target this time is the famous Jamesian style—the circumlocutions, the qualifications, the parenthetical interruptions, the finicky playing with words in the effort to capture the finest nuances of meaning. The piece is brilliantly done, but

[22] Edward Stone, *The Battle and the Books* (Athens, Ohio: Ohio University Press, 1962), gives an illuminating account of Thurber's imitations and parodies of James.

he did not include it in *The Middle-Aged Man*, doubtless feeling that one James parody was enough for any collection.

As a parodist, Thurber had a special fondness for targets selected from popular culture. "If Grant Had Been Drinking at Appomattox" is one of his most successful ventures of this kind. *Scribner's Magazine* had published a series of three historical fantasies in 1930 and 1931—"If Booth Had Missed Lincoln," by Milton Waldman, "If Lee Had Won the Battle of Gettysburg," by Winston Churchill, and "If Napoleon Had Escaped to America," by H. A. L. Fisher. Churchill's essay is noble in thought and language; it is an exercise in historical idealism. Thurber's parody offers a delightfully "low" version of these historical speculations, turning the heroes and the great events of the past into broad farce. His General Grant is a drunken clown so befuddled that when Lee rides into Appomattox he cannot remember who is surrendering to whom.

A more serious attack on popular culture is "The Greatest Man in the World," a Ring Lardner-like satire on heroes and hero-worship. A cultural crisis of major proportions occurs when Jack ("Pal") Smurch, an unsavory former garage mechanic from Iowa, becomes the first man to fly non-stop around the world. Smurch is everything a hero must not be: he is surly, contemptuous, crude in speech and manner. " 'Nobody ain't seen no *flyin'* yet,' " he announces before taking off, "carrying with him only a gallon of bootleg gin and six pounds of salami." His true character turns out to be so awful that at a secret conference of government officials and editors it is agreed that only drastic measures can save the country, and a former tackle at Rutgers pushes the unacceptable Smurch out a ninth-story window.

The broad irony of the conclusion recalls Lardner in its contemptuous exposure of the gap between American myth and American reality: "The funeral was, as you know, the most elaborate, the finest, the solemnest, and the saddest ever held in the United States of America. The monument in Arlington Cemetery, with its clean white shaft of marble and the simple device of a tiny plane carved on its base, is a place for pilgrims, in deep reverence, to visit."

In fact, the structure and theme of "The Greatest Man in the World" are very close to Lardner's famous story "Champion." Lardner was a hero to American comic writers in the 1920's and 1930's and he was a contributor to *The New Yorker* in the early days. Thurber had tried his hand at the Lardner manner several times without much success ("The Funniest Man in the World," in *The Middle-Aged Man*, is an example), but here, he sees things through Lardner's eyes, and what otherwise might have been a genial spoof like "If Grant Had Been Drinking at Appomattox" becomes a harsh judgment on the falsity of the ideals which dominate American public life. Thurber was to venture more and more often into direct social criticism of this kind, but his satire is almost always what Juvenal, the Roman poet, called "laughing satire," as opposed to "biting." It is tolerant, good-natured, humane. The bitterness of tone and the contempt for popular values which mark "The Greatest Man in the World" are rare in Thurber's early work.

The most original piece in *The Middle-Aged Man on the Flying Trapeze* is "The Black Magic of Barney Haller." Barney is the hired man on Thurber's country place. He is good-natured and obliging, but his heavy Teutonic accent transforms the most commonplace statements into a mysterious and frightening nonsense language. When Barney comes by one hot summer day and says, " 'Dis morning bime by . . . I go hunt grotches in de voods,' " Thurber's over-active imagination is filled with unsettling possibilities. He visualizes grotches as "ugly little creatures, about the size of whippoorwills, only covered with blood and honey and the scrapings of church bells," and he has a vision of Barney, deep in the woods, "prancing around like a goat, casting off his false nature, shedding his hired man's garments . . . repeating diabolical phrases, conjuring up grotches." Nervously, he quotes Frost to Barney, hoping that the White Magic of Frost, the poet of daylight, plain statement, and common sense, will protect him against the Black Magic of Barney's mysterious utterances. The reality, of course, turns out to be considerably less than Thurber's imagination had made it. "Grotches" are, it develops, "crotches," forked saplings which Barney cuts down to use as supports for the heavy-laden peach boughs. Nevertheless, just to make sure, Thurber counters with his own brand of Black Magic, reciting Lewis Carroll, the great master of nonsense language, while Barney retires in alarm and confusion.

Here, for the first time, Thurber plays with language as the gateway to the world of fantasy, as he was to do later in "What Do You Mean It *Was* Brillig?" and in the word-game pieces of the 1940's and 1950's. Much of the success of this sketch lies in the effectiveness of Thurber's favorite persona. The contrast between his picture of himself as the nervous intellectual who reads Proust and tries to defend himself by quoting Frost and Lewis Carroll and the stolid Germanic Barney generates comedy of a high order.

The Middle-Aged Man on the Flying Trapeze is impressive evidence of the many-sidedness of Thurber's talent. There are the more familiar areas of subject-matter—the bitter comedies of domestic warfare, the nostalgic memory pieces, and the parodies—but there are new developments as well—the comedy of language and garbled communication, the tragicomedy of neurosis and psychological breakdown, and the serious treatment of the romantic experience in "The Evening's at Seven" and "One Is a Wanderer." Throughout *The Middle-Aged Man* the dark side of Thurber's imagination is more evident than before—broken marriages and neurotic protagonists dominate the fictional scene, and it is significant that Thurber chose to conclude the collection with "A Box to Hide In," an unsettling first-person sketch about a neurotic and fear-driven man who is obsessed by fantasies of hiding away from life in a large box.

The book was praised by the reviewers. Charles Poore, writing in the New York *Times* (November 24, 1935), emphasized the Freudian predicaments of Thurber's characters, and in a wonderfully perceptive comment, he described Thurber as "a Joyce in false-face," whose characters "take their subconsciouses out on benders." Writing to the Herman Millers, Thurber rejoiced in the favorable reception of the book. He was particularly gratified by William Soskin's review in the New York *American*, he said with deadpan gravity, because it "came out with the truth: namely that the book is better than 'Of Time and the River,' 'The Green Hills of Africa,' and 'It Can't Happen Here.' Those lads have got a long way to go," he said, "but they have promise." In a brief comment on his own favorites in the collection, it was clear that the new material pleased him most: the Millers had liked "A Box to Hide In" and "The Evening's at Seven." Thurber said that he liked them too, but that his special favorite was "The Black Magic of Barney Haller." [23]

---

[23] Undated letter to the Millers, 1935.

11

Second Marriage

I N J U N E O F 1 9 3 5 Thurber married Helen Wismer, a tall handsome
girl he had met four years earlier at a party in the Village. She was
a minister's daughter, a graduate of Mount Holyoke, and a highly successful
editor of pulp magazines. At one time, she was getting out two at once
(*Sky Birds* and *Flying Aces*), handling all the editorial chores herself. She
was intelligent without being an intellectual, she was witty and gregarious,
and she was practical and well organized, although she managed to under-
play this side of her nature. Ross was initially opposed to the marriage,
primarily on the grounds that adversity had apparently been good for
Thurber as an artist, and that a happy marriage might take the bite out
of his stories and drawings. He got Benchley to try to dissuade Thurber,
but after Benchley met Helen, he changed his mind. " 'Why don't you
marry the girl?' " he asked. " 'What are you waiting for—Ross's permission?' " [1] Ross, too, capitulated once he met Helen, and before long she
became one of the few women he allowed into his private office (he had
fired one editor some years earlier for bringing his wife into the inner
sanctum). Ross was further reassured when Thurber's drawings showed no
mellowing in his view of the human condition, and his next collection of
stories, *Let Your Mind Alone*, included two bitter comedies of domestic

[1] *The Years with Ross*, pp. 188–89.

warfare, "The Breaking Up of the Winships" and "A Couple of Hamburg-ers."

The marriage was notably successful from the very beginning. Helen gave Thurber the love and emotional security he needed ("He always needed a mother," said one old acquaintance), and she gave him the kind of easy companionship that men generally expect to find only with other men. She took him as he was, without trying to improve him—except for his taste in clothes. Thurber was notoriously unfashionable and unkempt in dress, but after his marriage, the cheap ill-fitting suits and impossible neckties were replaced by a stylish and quietly elegant wardrobe. Helen would drink with him at Costello's, stay up all night talking, if that was what he wanted, and go with him on odd, spur-of-the-moment excursions. She became a second mother to his daughter Rosemary and managed over the years to preserve a friendly relationship with Althea. In her quietly efficient way she took care of the thousand details which complicated Thurber's life as he became more and more a public figure. After he lost his eyesight, in the 1940's, she was simply indispensable—"My seeing-eye wife," he often called her. She became, in fact, his other self, directing all her talents and energies to keeping her husband happy as a man and productive as an artist.

The years just after his marriage and before his blindness were the happiest period of his life. His letters to the Millers in 1935 and 1936 are full of joy and exuberance. "We are an ideal couple and have not had a harsh word in the seven weeks of our married life," he wrote. He was not to change this opinion: eight years later he wrote the Millers, "Helen and I were married eight years ago yesterday, and she is prettier and sweeter than ever, like my friendship for you." [2] They spent part of that first summer on Martha's Vineyard, near the Gudes. Thurber's happiness and good humor glow in every line of a long letter to the Whites: his marriage is perfect and the past is behind him, he says. The future holds "the promise of elms and unexpected lakes and mountain coolness over the rise," and "the hold of 21 and Tony's has been broken, headlock though it was."

He tells of the way he has met the challenge of driving a car—an accomplishment which, partly because of his bad eyesight, always had a special significance for him. They had bought a secondhand Ford V-8, and Thurber describes with mock hubris how after a few weeks of practice on the island, he got back his "old easy driving style, reminiscent of the days when I was the terror of the roads in Ohio and my mother wouldn't drive

[2] June 26, 1943.

with me because I went around the wrong side of street cars and shouted at the motormen." On the way to Colebrook, Connecticut, where they were to spend the rest of the summer, they had to drive through Providence and Hartford, and contrary to Bob Coates's warning about Providence, Thurber reported that he made it "gracefully and calmly." To highlight this tale of triumph, he ends the letter with a wonderfully comic account of the mishaps encountered by Jap Gude when he drove an ancient Packard from New York to Martha's Vineyard and ended up driving it over a three-foot stone wall in back of his own cottage.[3]

The Thurbers spent the fall and winter of 1935–36 in an apartment at 8 Fifth Avenue. They entertained at least twice a week, and went out as often. They still dropped in at Costello's of an evening, and they also went often to Bleeck's, the famous old bar which catered especially to newspapermen. There they would talk with Richard Watts, Stanley Walker, and such *New Yorker* friends as John McNulty, Wolcott Gibbs, and John Mosher. In addition to the parties and the informal gatherings at Costello's and Bleeck's, there were usually house guests. The pace was exhausting, and in the spring of 1936 Thurber took Helen to Bermuda, where they settled into a quiet and healthy life, going to bed early, getting up at eight, eating three meals a day, and playing tennis. Thurber had always been a tennis buff, but this was the first time he had tried to play, and he found it frustrating that he could not "walk up to the service line and serve like Stoefen." Still, he reported to White, "I am much better every time I play," and he noted that one day he had got to four games–all with Helen. They began what turned into an enduring friendship with Ronald and Jane Williams, an attractive young couple whom Thurber had met on a previous visit to the island. Williams was editor of the *Bermudian* magazine, and a great admirer of Thurber, White, and *The New Yorker*. The four of them spent a memorable evening at dinner with Sinclair Lewis, who was monumentally drunk, and alternately kind and bellicose. Lewis turned out to be a Thurber admirer and recited most of *The Owl in the Attic* from memory —"The only drunken writer I ever met who said nothing about his own work and praised that of another writer present," Thurber observed to White.

In their cottage were all of Benchley's books, and Thurber took the opportunity to re-read them. "There is no doubt that Benchley is our No. 1 humorist," he reported to White. "He has simply said everything. I think his 'Pluck and Luck' published in 1924 or thereabouts, is the best collection of humorous pieces in the country. . . ." In the same letter he speaks of his own writing, and thanks White for "getting some action" on the Jake Kilrain and Gertrude Ederle pieces in the new "Where Are They Now?" series. *The New Yorker* had been slow to make up its mind, and Thurber had been discouraged. Now he is confident and enthusiastic. He will keep the series going, he assures White, and he adds, "I know it will be a big hit." [4]

Thurber worked better in the country than in the city, and that summer he and Helen moved back to Connecticut and rented a house in Litchfield, where he settled down to work on *Let Your Mind Alone.* Connecticut was always one of his favorite places. He loved the physical beauty of the land and the picturesque charm of the villages, but most of all he loved the sense of being surrounded by history. Still, he liked the excitement of the city, particularly the theater. He and Helen went to plays often and they cultivated theater people. In October of 1936 they journeyed to Boston to see the opening of Noel Coward's *Tonight at Eight-Thirty,* and Thurber wrote an enthusiastic feature story on the plays, with illustrations, for *Stage* magazine.[5] They met Coward and began a friendship which, while never close, lasted throughout the years. Each man admired the other's comic skill, and Thurber was particularly envious of Coward's facility. Writing to the Millers about it, he said, "We had dinner with Coward, just the three of us, a lovely time, a swell fellow. I loved his plays, too, and he dashed them off all this summer."

In December, they visited Columbus, and spent a legendary evening with Carl Sandburg, talking, story-telling, guitar-twanging, and singing. Sandburg was appearing on a concert series sponsored by Capital University in Columbus, and the Thurbers went to hear him. After Sandburg's performance, they went up to talk to him, and the two men hit it off at once. Thurber recorded the occasion in a pair of drawings—"The Reading Hour," showing Sandburg and himself seated in armchairs, each reading aloud, while three guests have fallen asleep in the background, and "After-Dinner Music," in which Sandburg, playing his guitar and tapping his foot, towers over Thurber, who, ukelele in hand, looks up timidly at the great man. "These are," Helen Thurber has written, "only pale reflections of what really went on that night." [6]

In the spring of 1937, the Thurbers went to Europe, where they stayed for more than a year. The immediate occasion for the trip was a one-man

[4] Undated letter of 1936 (EBWP).
[5] "Tonight at 8:30," *Stage,* XIV (December, 1936), 56–57.
[6] Introduction, *Thurber and Company* (New York: Harper & Row, 1966).

show of Thurber's drawings at the Storran Gallery in London, in May of 1937, and the Thurbers decided to make this moment of professional recognition the excuse for an extended honeymoon. They got off to an unpromising start when Thurber lost most of their passage money playing the match game at Bleeck's, but the trip was in fact a great success. Thurber was already well known in London—his books were all in print in English editions, published by Hamish Hamilton, and the art exhibit was one of the events of the spring season ("The hallmark of sophistication is to adore the drawings of James Thurber," said the *Daily Sketch* for May 25, 1937).

Most of the reviewers were struck by the Freudian, surrealistic quality of the drawings. The *Daily Sketch* spoke of the "wild nonsense through which gleams a nightmare logic" in such cartoons as "That's my first wife up there, and this is the *present* Mrs. Harris," and the London correspondent of the *Manchester Evening News* observed that the point of Thurber's humor usually bypasses the intellect and is to be found "somewhere in the subterranean territory of the unconscious." Thurber explores "hitherto untouched combinations of incongruities, including some that properly belong to surrealism, the dream or the madhouse," he continued, and cited the seal in the bedroom, the lady on the bookcase, and such wonderful expressions of pure eccentricity as the little scene captioned, "I thought you'd enjoy Miss Perrish, darling. She has a constant ringing in *her* ears, too." [7]

One reviewer, more enthusiastic than accurate, assured his readers that Matisse had said that Thurber was the only person in America whom he would be interested in meeting. This was a garbled version of Paul Nash's comment, some time earlier, that Thurber apparently began his drawings with no particular idea in mind and let them develop as they would, much in the manner of the early Matisse. Matisse happened to be in London at the time of Thurber's exhibition, and one of the gallery owners, excited by the possibilities of this endorsement by one of the masters of modern painting, called him in the hope of arranging a meeting between the two artists. Matisse's secretary informed the gallery man that Matisse had never heard of Thurber *or The New Yorker.* Seeing a chance to needle Ross, Thurber cabled him the secretary's remark. "Ross had never heard of Matisse, so that evened things up," he observed some time later.[8] The success of the art show was confirmed for Thurber when two of the draw-

---

[7] Clippings from the *Daily Sketch*, the Manchester *Evening News*, and a few unidentified magazines, in RTS.
[8] Brandon, "The Tulle and Taffeta Rut," *As We Are*, p. 260; also *The Years with Ross*, pp. 64–65.

ings were stolen. "I was pleased mightily that anybody would risk arrest . . . for stealing some of my drawings. After all, if you have your drawings stolen, you're made," he said to Henry Brandon.

It was during this same visit to England that he received his first international recognition as a writer. His books had been successful on both sides of the Atlantic, and they had been well reviewed, but always in the indulgent, casual way reserved for popular entertainers as opposed to serious writers. Now, in the *Observer*, David Garnett made the English publication of *Let Your Mind Alone* the occasion for a general assessment of Thurber as a literary figure of importance.[9] He called him "the most original and humorous writer living," briefly reviewed his work to date, praised *Let Your Mind Alone*, and then warned Thurber against a strain of anti-intellectualism in his work. "It is fatally easy for the humorist to turn from attacking half-baked ideas to attacking ideas as such," he noted, and then, sounding more than a little like Matthew Arnold, he added, "I utter this solemn word of warning thinking of the terrible fate of Mark Twain, whose genius was deflected into ridiculing history and all forms of art everywhere." He need not have worried, for while the plain man's common sense is one of Thurber's weapons against pretentiousness, no humorist ever valued art and intellect more highly than Thurber did.

He was, of course, a humorist, and while he was in London he played his role. For the *Sunday Referee* he did a page of miscellaneous comment, touching on such out-of-the-way subjects as the existence of an American literary shrine on British soil, the house called Felicity Hall, in Somerset, Bermuda, where Hervey Allen wrote *Anthony Adverse*. Although it is now the private home of Mr. and Mrs. Ronald Williams, he wrote, it is over-run with tourists and sightseers. When Thurber visited the Williamses, he often worked at the old desk which Allen used when he wrote his novel. Once he looked up to see two men and two women staring in the window at him: " 'What are you doing?' one of the women asked. 'I am writing *Anthony Adverse* backwards, madam' I told her simply, and they went awe-stricken away, to tell it in Gath and Kansas and Ohio." [10]

In the spring of 1937, before going to London, they had visited Paris, where they saw such good friends as Janet Flanner, the "Genêt" of "Letter from Paris" in *The New Yorker*, and Aristide Mian, the French artist, whom they had known in New York, and his American wife, Mary. In the fall they went back to the Continent, rented a villa at Cap d'Antibes, and explored southern France and Italy by car. The return to France touched

[9] Undated clipping, with Robert Thurber's notation, "October, 1937" (RTS).
[10] *The Sunday Referee*, July 11, 1937 (RTS).

Thurber's imagination, and he did a series of eight travel sketches that winter and spring (he collected them later, in *My World and Welcome to It*) on the people, the places, and the oddities of life in Gaul. France had always had a special magic for him—it was, after all, the place where, full of the aesthetic idealism of James's *The Ambassadors,* he had discovered a larger life than that available in Columbus, Ohio. "Since France, whenever I was there, made my heart a lighted place, these . . . random essays are neither searching nor troubled," he wrote in the "Foreword" to the travel group in *My World and Welcome to It.* The Spanish civil war raged to the south, but that was not what he wanted to write about. His essays were "merely pieces of the color and pattern of the surface which is to me the loveliest in the world." His romantic response to the history and beauty of the land glows in the spare poetry of passages like this, from "Journey to the Pyrenees":

> Winding up back of Toulon, we got into moist spears of snow that turned to lazy large flakes on the mountain top. On the other side, in "true" Provence, we came down onto dry roads under a summer sun. Here you begin to see at the branching of highways the exciting names of Avignon and Tarascon and Beaucaire. This is the land of the troubadors and the mistral, of Cezanne and bull fights, of nightingales and war. For all its blood and scars and glory it is an innocent-looking land to drive through, flat and indolent, lonely and a touch scrubby.

But France was not only romantic and beautiful to Thurber, it was also highly comic in its strangeness and differentness. He writes with relish of the incomprehensibility of French politics, the eccentricity of French guidebooks, the madness of French auto drivers, the unpredictability of life in Nice, and the infinite possibilities for breakdowns in communication between Frenchman and foreign visitor. Thurber was a natural essayist —or, more accurately, he handled the form with such ease and mastery that he made it all seem as unstudied as good conversation. He had the reporter's eye for detail and the historian's interest in giving it significance, and he had the artist's ability to recreate people, places, and events. His essays are highly personal performances, mixing social observation, autobiography, and comic anecdote in an idiosyncratic, free-form way.

While they were in Europe, Thurber wrote long letters to White, full of anecdotes about the pleasures and frustrations of foreign travel, informal discussions on the problems of the writer, and the kind of personal comment that one good friend exchanges with another. The letters describing their auto trip through Provence are full of enthusiasm for the history, the beauty, and the gastronomy of the country. "We are full of snails, poulet a la crème, chateaubriand, ducks soaked in wine, pheasant, wild boar, partridge, paté, mousse au chocolat, red, white, and rosé wine," he reported happily.[11] They were in Naples for Christmas, and Thurber wrote to invite the Whites to come and stay with them in the Villa Tamisier in Antibes, "with the constant inspiration of our big genial Maria and her husband, the Russian gardener, a Mr. Smessoff" (the originals for Maria and Olympy in "A Ride with Olympy"). He and Helen came down from Rome over the Hannibal route, "a route I've always wanted to follow—like the Custer route in our West," he said, and he went on to tell about the serio-comic difficulties of driving in Europe.

In a long postscript to this letter, he turned to the subject of writers and writing, particularly the question of self-discipline. Joel Sayre is writing a play and has virtually dropped out of sight. Thurber has little patience for this sort of self-indulgence. Why do playwrights think they are different? he asks. "A novelist, comment-writer, casual writer, historian, or poet can do his work and get a lot else done, but playwrights think they must shut themselves away from the business of living completely while writing a play." "Here I am," says Thurber, "traveling all over Europe, monkeying with a car in foreign strands, writing casuals, Talk, reporters, Onwards and Upwards, drawing pictures and keeping up with *fourteen families* steadily. . . . Take it in my stride, too." Anyway, he says, being deliberately outrageous, one need not be a writer to write plays. "Hence play*wright*—like wheelwright." Plays are made up of phrases and fragments, "but it isn't writing unless you deal in sentence structure that leads into and out of paragraphs and involves balance, tone, mood, and unity of effect. . . ."[12] He is partly joking, but the value he attached to style and verbal craftsmanship was very real.

The year gave Thurber a chance to take stock and to look at things a little more objectively than he could at home. His letters to White show him thinking through certain problems and articulating some of his basic attitudes toward life. This mood of reflection and assessment is particularly strong in the long and rambling letter he wrote from the Villa Tamisier on January 20, 1938. The central theme is his view of life as hard, confused, and unmanageable, and his scorn for those writers and intellectuals who think that changing the economic and political system will change the essential conditions of existence. "Our everyday lives become, right after

[11] Letter to White, November 14, 1937 (EBWP).
[12] Letter to White, December 22, 1937 (EBWP).

college, as unworkable as a Ford in a vat of molasses," he observes, stating
what was to him a primary and universal truth. "Everybody is monkeying
with the superstructure of economics, politics, distribution, etc.," but it
will do no good, because a world in which there are hundreds of millions
of people is simply unworkable. "If you get more than six people in a room
it won't work," he said, revealing his old-fashioned Midwestern individualism.

Turning to personal matters, he lectures White for writing for the
Saturday Evening Post ("That's not your audience"), and adds that it is
his "studied opinion that the New Yorker is the best magazine in the
world." White had been in a fallow spell, and Thurber urges him to
write—"Anyone who can write the way you do has to keep on writing,"
he insists. It is a matter of moral obligation. As for himself, he has decided
that New York City life is destructive. Too many of their friends are going
back and forth to sanitariums. "It rather scares me. . . . God knows it got
me," he says of their New York life, and he sketches an unflattering image
of himself as he was: "I can see that tall, wild-eyed son of a bitch, with
hair in his eyes, and a glass in his hand, screaming and vilifying, and it's
hard for me to recognize him." He is aware that "a steady life in New York"
would bring back this dark wild self, now locked up for good, and so he
will never live in New York again "for long at a time, just run down for
a visit now and then." [13]

The long European holiday was a highly satisfactory experience for the
Thurbers—England and France spoke to their imaginations, and they were
to return often after World War II—but they came away oppressed with
the sense of impending disaster. The willful blindness of comfortable middle-class people to what was happening in Austria and Czechoslovakia in
1937 and 1938 appalled them: walking in Hyde Park on a sunny spring
day, they overheard expressions of concern about England's loss of a football match to Switzerland, and the dim prospects for the Davis Cup team
at Zagreb, but "Nobody was talking about Czechoslovakia." [14] Like many
other people in that brink-of-war era, Thurber brooded over the darkening
future, and out of this concern came his parable in pictures, *The Last
Flower*, in 1939.

In the fall of 1938 they returned to the United States and settled in
Woodbury, Connecticut, for the winter. For the first time, Thurber felt
like an outsider, "possibly a hasbeen," at *The New Yorker*. "I feel pretty
far away from the arms, the councils, and the understanding of the New

[13] Letter to White, January 20, 1938 (EBWP).
[14] "Journey to the Pyrenees," *My World and Welcome to It*, pp. 274–75.

Yorker," he complained to White. He no longer had an office, and in addition, he was feeling his age. "There is an air of college halls about the place; people bow to you," he said. "It's not the place I worked for years ago, when you and I removed Art Samuels' rugs and lamps in order to draw pictures and write lines for Is Sex Necessary." [15]

In spite of this temporary depression of spirits, 1938 was a good year for Thurber. Country life suited them. He wrote to White in the fall that after a trip to New York in the course of which he had run into Gibbs, McKelway, Mosher, Coates, Lois Long, and other New Yorker friends in the lobby of the Algonquin ("You find yourself drinking," he reported), it was "nice to be back under the 200-year-old maples and apple trees." At their country place, cows came into the yard whenever he left the gate open and ate the apples. "One morning . . . I heard a cow eating apples under my bedroom window. It was 7 o'clock. After she had eaten 27, by actual count, I got up and chased her home in my nightgown." In the same letter he told White of a pleasant afternoon he had spent with his seven-year-old daughter, Rosemary, complimented his friend on two recent pieces in Harper's ("The Sat Review is right when it says you are among the great living essayists"), and talked about some of his own current plans.[16]

At this moment in his life, Thurber was at the top of his creative powers, and he was full of projects. Among them was a play, a comedy of domestic life in a Midwestern setting, and he outlined the idea in a letter to Nugent, who was now living in Hollywood, and suggested that they do it together.[17] Two years later, Thurber claimed to have got the initial idea for the play while standing on top of his garage in Connecticut, and to have wired Nugent, "You and I are going to do a play together," and to have received this answer: "No, we're not"; but this anecdote is fairly obviously one of Thurber's improvements on prosaic truth.[18] The play, of course, was to become one of his most popular successes, The Male Animal.

In November of 1938, the Thurbers made another of their frequent trips to Columbus, where they visited family and friends, went to the Ohio State–Purdue football game, and were interviewed at length by the local press. Back in Columbus, surrounded by the people and places of his youth, Thurber's conversation and attitudes took on a strong Midwestern coloring. He told reporters that he didn't really miss America during their year abroad, because America went right along with them. The first license plate

[15] Undated letter to White (EBWP).
[16] Letter to White, November, 1938 (EBWP).
[17] Helen Thurber remembers the letter, but it has been lost.
[18] Thurber, "Roaming in the Gloaming," New York Times Theater Section, Sunday, January 7, 1940.

they saw in Carcassonne was from Cleveland. " 'You just can't outrun Ohioans,' " he said with satisfaction. He also told of the American ladies who mistook him for a Frenchman and said to him that he spoke good English. " 'I ought to,' " he told them, " 'I spent forty years in Columbus, Ohio, working on it like a dog.' " These same anecdotes appear in "Journey to the Pyrenees," but there they are cited as examples of the mildly irritating ironies of travel abroad; here, re-telling them over coffee at the Mills Buffet in Columbus, Thurber alters their emphasis, so that they become reassuring instances of the fact that an Ohio boy is really never very far from home.[19]

In January of 1939 Nugent came to New York, and he and his father joined the Thurbers at the Algonquin, where for two weeks, the writers, aided by the suggestions of the elder Nugent and Helen Thurber, hammered out the basic structure of their play. Both men had commitments which kept them busy for the next few months, but in June the Thurbers arrived in Hollywood (characteristically, they came by ship, through the Panama Canal) ready to devote the summer to writing the play. They stayed with the Nugents at first, while Thurber and Nugent were still talking over the scenario, and then moved into a small furnished house in Beverly Hills when it was time to begin work in earnest.

Thurber was already well known in Hollywood for his stories and his drawings, and he was received as a celebrity from the first. Two members of the movie colony, however, were not as clear on his identity as they might have been: Jack Warner persisted in addressing Thurber as "Mr. Ferber," and Charlie Chaplin, congratulating Thurber for having written one of his favorite short stories, proceeded to describe a well-known piece by Robert Benchley. Thurber was particularly irritated by Warner's garble of his name, and for years afterward, a stock character in his sketches is the dimwit who calls him "Mr. Thurl," "Mr. Thurb," and other unattractive variations on the family name.[20]

During his stay in Hollywood, Thurber was interviewed often, and he used these occasions to try out the autobiographical anecdotes which had become his stock in trade as both writer and conversationalist. Talking with Arthur Millier, the art critic of the Los Angeles *Times,* he recalled his brief and confusing tenure as managing editor of *The New Yorker,* he told the story of the seal drawing which got him started as a *New Yorker* cartoonist, and of the consternation at Harper & Brothers when he and White insisted

[19] "Thurber Returns to Old Haunts," *Ohio State Journal,* November 5, 1938.
[20] Nugent, *Events Leading Up to the Comedy,* chapter 24. Helen Thurber remembers the Chaplin anecdote as having to do with a story by E. B. White, rather than by Benchley.

that his illustrations for *Is Sex Necessary?* were not "rough ideas" but the finished product, and he told the story of how, in response to Ross's insistence, he tried to re-draw the early sketch of a seal on a rock, and ended up—quite unintentionally—with the seal in the bedroom.

He was to tell these stories over and over through the years, and to feature them in *The Years with Ross*, but he gave them their first public airing in these interviews of 1939. At the same time that he was enlarging his repertory, he was perfecting his distinctive style of delivery—a rapid-fire, unemphatic, ceaseless flow of anecdote and comment in the great tradition of American deadpan humor which sometimes left the listener floundering. About his "real" private life and history he was evasive and defensive. When Millier wanted more, he said, " 'If you want my biography, look up the introduction E. B. White wrote for my book, 'The Owl in the Attic.' It covers my known history very thoroughly down to the year 1931. If you want anything later than that, why not make it up yourself? It will save me the trouble.' " [21]

Thurber's Hollywood stay was productive—he and Nugent finished the play in September—but it was not particularly happy. The fabled Southern California climate did not appeal to him—for one thing, the intense sunlight hurt his eyes, and as Nugent said, "he longed for the cool green shade of Connecticut and the smoky gloom of Bleeck's." [22] He drew some figures on the walls of the men's room at Chasen's restaurant one night, and a vigilant attendant scrubbed them off before morning. Nothing went quite right. He detested Hollywood as a symbol of the money-hungry vulgarization of artistic talent, and he used to stay up nights berating Nugent for having sold out. "He had planned this play, at least partially, to save me from the Philistines and to restore me as a creative writer and actor," said Nugent. Over highballs with Helen and the Nugents, he would heap scorn upon the values of his hosts: " 'Look at the two of them,' he'd say bitterly to Helen. 'All Norma thinks about is private schools for the girls and Packards and Sheffield silver and eighteenth-century sideboards. And all Elliott thinks about is movies and tennis and swimming pools.' " [23]

In addition, he was worried about his health. He had begun to have trouble with his one good eye during the sea voyage to California, and although his doctor in New York referred him to an outstanding ophthalmologist in Pasadena, his sight began to deteriorate steadily. He was understandably short of temper, and once, at a party at the Nugents', when a

21 Interview with Arthur Millier, Los Angeles *Times*, July 2, 1939.
22 Nugent, "Notes on James Thurber, the Man, or Men."
23 Nugent, *Events Leading Up to the Comedy*, p. 141.

self-important man asked Thurber to explain what was funny about his drawing, he snapped back, " 'When I was younger and more patient . . . I might have gone along with you and said that I don't think they are so funny myself. But right now my eyes are troubling me and I don't have time to talk to dumb sons-of-bitches.' " [24]

Thurber's writing during the period from 1935 to 1939 shows considerable variety, ranging all the way from the parody of the mental-health books in *Let Your Mind Alone* (1937) to the picture parable *The Last Flower* (1939). In addition to his regular output of fiction and humorous essays for *The New Yorker*, between 1936 and 1938 he did the remarkable "Where Are They Now?" series, under the pseudonym of Jared L. Manley, as well as a number of book reviews for the *New Republic*, the *Nation*, and the New York *Herald Tribune*.

"Where Are They Now?" is the kind of journalism Thurber did best— the human-interest story or character study, where there is a good deal of latitude for personal interpretation and dramatic recreation, as opposed to strictly factual reporting. Most of the pieces deal—as the title implies— with people who were once in the limelight and who are now forgotten but still alive. There are figures from the world of sport, like Jake Kilrain, the great prize fighter of the 1880's and 1890's, the man who went seventy-five rounds against John L. Sullivan in a bare-knuckle free-for-all that lasted two hours and sixteen minutes. The Kilrain profile suggested the "Jared L. Manley" name to Thurber: the "Manley" stood for the manly art of self-defense, and the "Jared L." derived from the first two initials of Sullivan's name.

There were figures from the world of national history and military action, like Rear Admiral Richmond P. Hobson, who, as a young naval lieutenant during the Spanish-American War, led the expedition which sank the collier *Merrimac* in the harbor of Santiago, Chile. Some of the best in the series are sketches of people who figured prominently in famous crimes just long enough ago to have faded from the public mind. "A Sort of Genius," for example, is a memorable character sketch of Willie Stevens, a central figure in the Hall-Mills murder case of 1922. The murder of the Reverend Edward W. Hall and his mistress, Mrs. Eleanor Mills, wife of the sexton of Hall's church, is one of America's most famous unsolved mysteries. Thurber (with the help of Edward O'Toole, of the *New Yorker* staff) dug back into the tangled court records to recreate the highlights of the case, particularly the courtroom drama of the testimony of Willie Stevens, Mrs.

[24] Ibid., p. 138.

Hall's eccentric brother. Stevens, along with another brother, Henry, and Mrs. Hall, was indicted for murder on the basis of the highly dubious evidence of "the pig woman," Mrs. Jane Gibson, who claimed to have seen the defendants in the lonely spot where the murder was committed.

Willie Stevens was a shy bachelor who spent most of his time at the local firehouse, and who was generally more at ease with children than with adults. He had little formal education, but he read technical books on metallurgy, botany and entomology. He was unprepossessing in appearance, and because of his child-like manner and odd habits, he was often referred to as "Crazy Willie," and made the butt of jokes. It was widely assumed that the prosecuting attorney would destroy him on the stand, but he conducted himself with such openness and unself-consciousness that the prosecution could not establish its case, and all the defendants were acquitted.

For Thurber, the center of interest in the case was the strange character of Willie Stevens. He saw him as a sort of Pudd'nhead Wilson—the eccentric misfit who is scorned by the community at large, but who in reality is stronger and more intelligent than those who mock him. The case also appealed to him as a piece of social history, a significant bit of the recent American past. Thurber was a history buff throughout his life, and he particularly liked the small events and forgotten characters which, when looked at again, seemed to stand as indexes of the temper of the times. The "Where Are They Now?" series did just that, reviving the heroes, the scandals, and the mores of the very recent past in the careers of such people as Howard Scott, the prophet of Technocracy, A. Sumner Rowan, the man who actually carried the message to Garcia, and Virginia O'Hanlon, the little girl who wrote the editor of the New York *Sun* in 1897, asking him to tell her if there really was a Santa Claus, and thereby inspired the famous editorial, "Yes, Virginia, There Is a Santa Claus."

Thurber was always irritated that Ross never asked him to review for the magazine, and it is surprising that he was not invited to do so, since he was, as his reviews elsewhere showed, an extremely perceptive and articulate critic. His intellectual seriousness, his good sense, and his easy, unpretentious manner are best shown in his long review of Joseph Freeman's polemic anthology, *Proletarian Literature in the United States*, in the *New Republic* for March 25, 1936. Freeman's book was intended to be a manifesto, guide, and sampler of literary Marxism in America. Thurber took a dim view of the whole Marxist movement. For one thing, he was disturbed by the harsh and strident tone of the Marxist advocates. Their tendency to substitute insult and invective for reason and logic he saw as a dangerous symptom. In his review, Thurber was temperate and sensible, but in a letter to Malcolm Cowley he denounced the over-simplifications and distortions of Marxism in what Cowley described as "3000 sometimes obscene and always pertinent words." [25]

The center of Thurber's review is a discussion of the danger of propaganda to art. "Art does not rush to the barricades," he says, and makes a plea for the virtue of artistic detachment instead of the fashionable involvement ("oh, my friends, and oh, my foes, in detachment there is strength, not weakness"). He praises the excerpt from Dos Passos' *1919* for its simplicity and honesty, but too many of the stories, he says, seem to have been made up to fit the needs of Marxist argument rather than to truly represent life. "You don't believe that these authors *were there,* ever had been there. . . . They give you the feeling that they are writing what they want these people to have said." Thurber's critical principles were those of late-nineteenth-century realism: like Twain and Howells, he distrusted whatever was false or affected. Commenting on the strained effort of one writer to give his story an air of revolutionary novelty through typographical pyrotechnics, Thurber observes, "I was reminded, in trying to read it, of what an old English professor of mine, the late Joseph Russell Taylor, used to say: you can't get passion into a story with exclamation points." And in criticizing a badly overdone satiric effort, he says, "Even burlesque must keep one foot on verisimilitude." [26]

Thurber kept generally clear of the swirl of controversy over the social responsibility of the artist which muddied the literary waters of the mid-Thirties, but as this review shows, he knew exactly where he stood, and he wanted to have his say at least once. He told Malcolm Cowley that he rewrote the review some fifteen or twenty times. "It came out to be a thing I had to do, and do right," he said. The problem was still on his mind throughout his stay in Europe. Writing to White from Paris in the fall of 1937, he argued that the current assumption that only the social or the ideological subject was worth writing about was all wrong. The great subject for the writer is the individual plight, he said. It is the personal and the intimate that touch us most closely; the current concern with political forms is simply nonsense.[27]

He knew his strengths and his limitations as a writer, and he trusted his own instinct rather than the voices of intellectual fashion. He made his feelings clear in a letter to Katharine White. Since coming to Paris he had

[25] Malcolm Cowley, in "Salute to Thurber."
[26] Thurber, "Voices of Revolution," *New Republic*, March 25, 1936, pp. 200–01.
[27] Undated letter to White, 1937 (EBWP).

got into a lot of arguments about politics and the civil war in Spain, he said. Vincent Sheean wanted to take him to Spain, and after two scotches he said yes; but on second thought (which he confessed was really not much clearer than first) he decided not to. After all, he said, Spain, politics, and war were not exactly his field—either for writing about or for wandering around in.[28] The subject comes up again and again in his correspondence. In a long letter to White from the Villa Tamisier in January of 1938, he deplores the fact that "a frenzy has come upon writers," and that people like Lillian Hellman and even Hemingway have become "so socially conscious" that they have lost all sense of proportion. He realizes that life is not a comedy, and he refers to his own manic-depressive cycles by way of illustration, but he argues that there are always things to laugh at, even now, and that those who can laugh should keep on doing so, to restore a little sanity and balance.[29]

What disturbed Thurber most about literary Marxism was its intolerance of other points of view. When Mike Gold and other leftists attacked contributors to *The New Yorker* as "evaders of life, and . . . 'college punks,' " in 1935, Thurber expressed his concern and indignation in a letter to Cowley: "If these men . . . should ever get in control, do you think there wouldn't be a commissar of literature who would set us at work writing either poems in praise of the American Lenin or getting up time tables for work trains? If you do, you are missing a low, faint, distant rumbling." On the other hand, he had no truck with those who saw the country in imminent danger of revolution from the left: "I don't think the revolution is here or anywhere near here. . . . I believe the only menace is the growing menace of fascism. I also firmly believe that it is the clumsy and whining and arrogant attitude of the proletarian writers which is making the menace bigger every day." [30]

Thurber was essentially an old-fashioned individualist and rationalist who believed in each man's right to speak his piece. Twenty years later, he was equally outraged by Senator McCarthy and the super-patriots of the right, who wanted to forbid the circulation of all ideas they considered leftist. His basic position was that a writer should write, and that violent political factionalism was a threat to the writer's obligation to tell the truth.

Let Your Mind Alone is Thurber's collection of his best work between 1935 and 1937. While it does not match the sustained high level of *The Middle-Aged Man on the Flying Trapeze*, it offers an interesting mixture

[28] Letter to Katharine White, May 15, 1938 (EBWP).
[29] Letter to White, January 20, 1938 (EBWP).
[30] Quoted by Malcolm Cowley in "Salute to Thurber."

of the familiar and the new, and some of the individual pieces, like "The Wood Duck," are as good as anything he ever wrote. The first third of the book is a satiric attack on the popular psychology and how-to-succeed books which were crowding the publishers' lists in ever-increasing numbers. Thurber had reviewed *Be Glad You're Neurotic*, by Dr. Louis D. Bisch, in the *Saturday Review* for November 21, 1936, and Dale Carnegie's *How to Win Friends and Influence People* in the January 30, 1937, issue, and he found them both badly written and intellectually flabby. Thurber always detested uplifters and inspirationalists because of the inherent falsity in the picture of life they offer. He and White had ambushed the sex-and-psychology books in *Is Sex Necessary?* back in 1929; here, in *Let Your Mind Alone*, Thurber returns to the battle. Speaking about the book some years later, he noted the American weakness for silly fads of one kind or another, and said, "I've always liked to take hold of a piece of tripe or balderdash and try to expose it but to keep it comic, too." He selected as his special targets, in addition to Bisch's and Carnegie's books, *Streamline Your Mind* (Dr. James E. Mursell), *How to Worry Successfully* (David Seabury), *Wake Up and Live!* (Dorothea Brande), and *How to Develop Your Personality* (Dr. Sadie Myers Shellow). All of them offer simple formulas which promise peace of mind and worldly success, and all of them assume that life is something that can be dominated if only one has the key. Thurber's satire is directed at the fallaciousness of these promises and assumptions. The dominant themes of his book are the inadequacy of all systems and formulas as guides to life, the superiority of fantasy and daydream to logical thought, and the threat of technological culture to the spiritual well-being of man.

His basic method is to subject the slick generalizations and the too easy examples of the psychology books to the test of the way things really are. "Destructive Forces in Life," for example, exposes the fatuity of the idea that if we train our minds properly (that is, in the language of the Mental Efficiency books, if we attain Masterful Adjustment), we can make life what we want it to be. It tells of what happened to Harry Conner, a disciple of Mental Efficiency, whose well-ordered life is thrown into a shambles by Bert Scursey, a wag and practical joker who "enjoyed fantasy as much as reality, probably even more. . . ." Scursey is an accomplished mimic, and one afternoon he telephones the Conners and without really intending it, sets in motion a chain of disastrous misunderstandings which the well-organized Conner is powerless to control. The moral of this little tale is clear: Scursey represents the spontaneous, unpredictable forces in life (the principles of fantasy and confusion) which the disciples of Masterful Adjustment ignore at their peril. "Hardly anybody goes through life without encountering his Bert Scursey," says Thurber, and the tidy little formulas of Mental Efficiency are worse than useless when we are faced with the unexpected. In fact, "The undisciplined mind . . . is far better adapted to the confused world we live in today than the streamlined mind."

"The Case for the Daydreamer" makes an explicit principle out of Thurber's most precious fictional value—the power of the daydream to transform outer defeat into inner victory. "In a triumphant daydream, it seems to me, there is felicity and not defeat," he says, recalling his fantasy triumph over a Mr. Bustard, a large, overpowering man who had refused him a pass to a dog show. Throughout the rest of the afternoon, Thurber enjoyed one imaginary victory after another over the arrogant Bustard. By the end of the day, he was in excellent psychological trim. All the success books warn that a person who indulges in "fantasy, reverie, daydreaming, and woolgathering" will never get anywhere, but Thurber says in reply, "I have had a great deal of satisfaction and benefit out of daydreaming which never got me anywhere." And he points out that Browning's "Oh, to be in England now that April's there" is "a dream line," and that it is more famous than anything the poet wrote about actually being in England.

To see things through the glass of fantasy is to see them more richly and more aesthetically than we usually do. Thurber develops the point in "The Admiral on the Wheel," a humorous sketch in which he describes the strange and wonderful world revealed to him when he broke his glasses: "I saw the Cuban flag flying over a national bank, I saw a gay old lady with a gray parasol walk right through the side of a truck, I saw a cat roll across a street in a small striped barrel, I saw bridges rise lazily into the air, like balloons." It is a more interesting world than the world of everyday reality. "With perfect vision, one is inextricably trapped in the workaday world, a prisoner of reality, as lost in the commonplace America of 1937 as Alexander Selkirk was lost on his lonely island." Without his glasses, Thurber enters into a world of fantasy: "The kingdom of the partly blind is a little like Oz, a little like Wonderland, a little like Poictesme." [31]

[31] Thurber described the real-life origin of this experience in a letter to the Millers in the summer of 1935. Speaking of his problems in driving a car at night, he said:

> You know my sight of old, perhaps. I once tried to feed a nut to a faucet, you know, thinking it was a squirrel and surely I told you about the time I ruined my first wife's tomato plants by riddling the white paper sacks she had put over them to keep off the frost. I thought they were chickens pecking up the garden and I let them have it with a barrage of stones. (The faucet was in the statehouse grounds.) A further peril of the night road is that flecks of dust and streaks of bug blood on the windshield look to me often like old admirals in uniform, or crippled apple women, or the front end of barges and I whirl out of their way, thus going into ditches and fields and up on front lawns,

Let Your Mind Alone casts doubt not only on the kind of thinking advocated by those who would streamline our minds, but upon conceptual thought in general. "Thinking of any kind is bound to lead to confusion and unhappiness," says Thurber in "A Dozen Disciplines"; "Fantasy is the food for the mind, not facts." Such assertions are, of course, deliberate comic over-statements, but they reflect a basic distrust of the intellect as opposed to the imagination, and of stereotypes as opposed to direct experience, which was always a part of Thurber's way of looking at things. This attitude is particularly strong in his works of the late 1930's and 1940's, when World War II cast considerable doubt upon the value of man's reason. It is an important theme in *Let Your Mind Alone, The Last Flower, The Male Animal,* and *Fables for Our Time.*

If one were to list the classic predicaments in which Thurber characters find themselves, the first would doubtless be marriage, but high on the list would be the un-mechanical man faced with a contraption or gadget he does not understand. "With the disappearance of the gas mantle and the advent of the short circuit, man's tranquility began to be threatened by everything he put his hand on," he writes in "Sex ex Machina." The menace of the machine is one of Thurber's great comic subjects, but like the battle of the sexes and the celebration of the fantasy principle, it also makes a serious comment on contemporary life. In the short story "The Wood Duck," Thurber treats the theme as part of the larger subject of the alienation of modern mechanized man from the world of nature. The story has a strong E. B. White flavor: on the surface, it is a little human-interest anecdote about a wild duck which unaccountably settles down at a farmer's roadside stand for a few weeks, and about the strange concern felt by the farmer, several onlookers and the narrator and his wife when the duck is hit by a speeding car. In reality, it is a parable in which all the details weave a pattern contrasting the mechanized and the natural.

The New Milford road is concrete, "black in the center with the dropped oil of a million cars," and the heavy traffic moves fast. In the farmer's yard are people buying cider, hunting dogs, and the duck, who seems content in his surroundings. When he survives his near-fatal brush with a car and flutters his way to a nearby woods, the people on the scene are drawn together by a feeling they find hard to put into words. The beautiful wood duck obviously represents a value almost lost in the modern world: the farmer, the hunters, and the narrator and his wife recognize this in an intuitive, inarticulate way; the speeding motorists on the concrete highway,

---

endangering the life of authentic admirals and apple women who may be out on the roads for a breath of air before retiring.

on the other hand, are completely unaware of it. As Robert Elias has pointed out, the duck "confers a distinction on the farm he has adopted," and when he is struck by the car and goes off into the woods, "something precious is lost." [32]

The battle of the sexes is a distinctly minor theme in *Let Your Mind Alone*, reflecting, no doubt, the inner change brought about by his happy second marriage; but two bitter comedies of marital discord, "The Breaking Up of the Winships" and "A Couple of Hamburgers," show that Thurber was not going to completely abandon what was, after all, one of his richest subjects. There is an impressive variety of humorous essays in the collection, ranging from "Nine Needles" and other pieces in the Benchley tradition of the ineffectual American male to the more original "Wild Bird Hickok," an account of the French paperback novels of the Wild West *(contes héroïques du Far-Ouest)* which he discovered and collected during his 1925 stay in Paris. Thurber loved these tales for their confusions, anachronisms, and "imaginative abandon." For him, they were another gateway to the pleasure-world of fantasy.

"After the Steppe Cat, What?" develops the leitmotif of the collection as a whole—the decline of man. Thurber had played with the theme of imminent cosmic disaster in the Preface to *My Life and Hard Times*, but here he broods with melancholy relish over the inevitable downfall of man and all his works, and the accompanying take-over by nature and her creatures. The evidence is accumulating: an item in the New York *Times* on recent changes in the natural environment of Germany—a plague of rodents in Silesia, and the appearance of steppe animals and plants as a result of big land-reclamation projects elsewhere—points to the day when the smaller creatures will inherit the earth. "Among the 'unmistakable steppe animals' that will trot into Berlin is the steppe cat, a small wildcat," Thurber writes, and he reinforces his point with a beautiful drawing of a steppe cat crouched low, in the classic hunting position. There are also drawings of other little-known creatures who will take part in "the Great Invasion"—the aardvark, the bandicoot, and the wombat. These are not the lumpy, fanciful animals which appear in most of Thurber's work; they are firmly and accurately drawn in the style of the plates in books of science. Thurber's model here was Lydekker's *Natural History*, a classic illustrated encyclopedia which Helen had given him in London. It remained one of his favorite books, along with his dictionary and his thesaurus, and he used it as a source of inspiration for his drawings again and again.

[32] Robert Elias, "James Thurber: the Primitive, the Innocent, and the Individual," *American Scholar*, XXVII (Summer, 1958), 359.

The Last Flower (1939), Thurber's philosophical fable in pictures, rounds out a decade of artistic and personal growth and change. Written just after the Germans invaded Poland, it is an effort to state a personal credo or philosophy of life at a time when western civilization seemed to be sliding toward the abyss. In form, it is a prophetic fantasy: at the beginning of the story, World War XII is destroying civilization. The opening scenes show charging, howling soldiers, frightened civilians, ruined towns, dead forests, trampled gardens, and broken statuary. All the good things in life are gone. Human life stagnates—people sit around in catatonic attitudes, doing nothing. Dogs leave their masters, and large aggressive rabbits attack the human population. In one scene, the man sits listlessly on a rock, and the woman—so dynamic in "The Race of Life"— lies flat, her eyes shut, indifferent to the world around her; the little daughter stands in a trance-like posture nearby, and a hostile-looking bird swoops down to inspect them.

Love has disappeared from the earth, the boys and girls only stare blankly at one another when they meet. Then a girl discovers the last flower left in the world. The only other person interested is a young man, and together they nurture it. One day a bee and a hummingbird come, and "Before long, there were two flowers, and then four, and then a great many." Nature reawakens, love returns, children are happy, the dogs come back, people rediscover the skills and arts they had forgotten, and society rebuilds itself. Along with the sculptors and wheelwrights, however, are the soldiers and the politicians, or "Liberators," as Thurber ironically calls them. The people in the valleys want to be in the hills, and the people in the hills want to be in the valleys—and the Liberators play on their discontent. Before long, the world is at war again, and the climax is a prophetic scene of total destruction in which aerial bombs seem to be blasting the whole world to bits. The next scene shows what is left of the world in a single horizontal line; expanding the view, the next shows a man and a woman looking dubiously at each other across the wasteland; and the last shows a flower, drooping, but alive.

The best commentary on *The Last Flower* is the essay "Thinking Ourselves into Trouble," which appeared in the *Forum* in June of 1939.[33] Like the fable, it is an attempt by Thurber to say something about the meaning of life at a time when the future of man seemed very much in doubt. Thurber did not often commit himself to direct statements of his philosophic and religious beliefs. In 1953 he put off Raymond Gram Swing, who

[33] *Forum,* CI (June, 1939), 309–11.

wanted him to speak on the "This I Believe" radio program, saying that what the public obviously wanted was something reassuring, and that since he felt that faith was "a sterner thing than that," and that the 1950's were not "a time of affirmation," he thought he had better not say anything.[34]

"Thinking Ourselves into Trouble" is a serio-comic statement of religious skepticism which leaves the door slightly ajar, just in case. Thurber begins by rejecting the possibility that the ultimate questions about life will ever be answered: man has tried love, poetry, alcohol, philosophy and religion, and none of them has brought him the assurance he looks for. His much-vaunted reason has been worse than useless.

> In giving up instinct and going in for reasoning, Man has aspired higher than the attainment of natural goals; he has developed ideas and notions; he has monkeyed with concepts. The life to which he was naturally adapted he has put behind him; in moving into the alien and complicated sphere of Thought and Imagination he has become the least well-adjusted of all the creatures of the earth and hence, the most bewildered.

Sounding more than a little like the later Mark Twain, Thurber concludes that "Man . . . is surely further away from the Answer than any other animal this side of the ladybug."

Like *The Last Flower*, the essay sees man as essentially a destructive creature. The only justification for his intellect is Art—"the one achievement of Man which has made the long trip up from all fours seem well advised." As to man's divine origin, Thurber says, "Just now I am going through one of those periods when I believe that the black panther and the cedar waxwing have higher hopes of Heaven than Man has." On the other hand, he quotes his favorite Browning's Bishop Blougram, who makes a case for the "grand Perhaps." At the end, he retreats to fable, where he always felt safest: "A monkey-man, in the eolithic times, wandering through the jungle, came upon a jewel and stuck it into his head. Since that day, his descendants have given off light, sometimes a magic and blinding light. The question whether the jewel was carelessly flung off from a whirling star or carefully planned and placed by a supernatural hand . . . will go on and on."

"Thinking Ourselves into Trouble," with its skeptical attitude toward abstract thought and formal religion, and its faith in instinct, art and nature, is a very romantic document, and it is a significant reminder of the

---

[34] Letter to Raymond Gram Swing, November 4, 1953 (Thurber Collection).

extent to which Thurber's mind was shaped by the late nineteenth-century values which dominated the cultural scene during his university years.

The Last Flower, like "Thinking Ourselves into Trouble," is equivocal, but it is fundamentally more optimistic than the essay. The cyclic pattern of the fable suggests that the life-force is stronger than man's destructive instinct, that the ritual of renewal will be enacted again. It is only a suggestion, however, not a confident affirmation. The potential is there, but we do not see it being realized. Whatever the possibilities may be, Thurber sees them as lying in Nature and her creative force, not in the social order or in religion or in ideology of any kind. As he always did, Thurber put his faith in the natural and the spontaneous as opposed to the structured and the formularized.

The pattern of the cycle was the perfect vehicle for his view of life, since it could accommodate both his realistic recognition of all that was wrong with human nature, and his cautious optimism about the cosmic process as a whole. Significantly, he dedicated the book to his eight-year-old daughter, Rosemary, "In the wistful hope that her world will be better than mine." In the fall of 1939, with the world plunging once again into war, he could hope for better things, but he could not promise them.

12

Apogee:
The Male Animal
and Walter Mitty

Then MALE ANIMAL WAS ONE of Thurber's happiest ventures. It was an immediate hit in 1940, and when it was revived in 1952 it seemed to have grown in stature and significance. It made Thurber and Nugent a good deal of money and it quickly established itself as a part of the classic American repertory. Nugent directed a very successful screen version in 1941, and little theater companies have played it over and over through the years. The collaboration was a particularly fortunate one: Nugent was not only an experienced and successful playwright, actor, and director, he was an old and sympathetic friend; Thurber had a passion for the theater, but he was short on professional experience and unsure of himself when it came to the tight formal demands of dramatic structure. "It is very hard for a man who has always just sort of started to write pieces and begun to make scrawls on paper, wondering what they were going to turn into, to encounter what is known as the three-act play," he wrote in the New York *Times* shortly before the play opened. "The three-act play has sharp, concrete edges, rigid spacings, a complete dependence on time and more than a hundred rules, all basic. 'You can't run a first act fifty minutes'; 'you can't have people just sitting and talking'; 'you can't play comedy in a dim light'; . . . 'if you have trouble with your third act there is something the matter with your first act.' " [1]

Thurber is making fun of his difficulties, but they were real enough. He always had trouble with structure, and this is the reason that he never really tried the novel form after that abortive first effort in France, and that he never followed up the success of *The Male Animal* with another play. He worked at two or three different plays off and on throughout the 1940's and 1950's, but although he wrote dozens of good scenes, he could never pull them together into unified single wholes. In the interview with George Plimpton and Max Steele in the *Paris Review* in 1955, he recalled that Nugent always thought in terms of structure and plot, but that he himself had to work in an entirely different manner. "Nugent would say, 'Well, Thurber, we've got our problem, we've got all these people in the living room. Now what are we going to do with them?' I'd say that I didn't know and couldn't tell him until I'd sat down at the typewriter and found out." [2]

Reminiscing about their collaboration, Nugent recalls that at the beginning, the domestic comedy plot was Thurber's and the theme of academic freedom was his (contrary to what many people might assume), but that they worked together so closely that at the end it would have been impossible to say who was chiefly responsible for which parts. Their original plan was for Thurber to do the first draft of each act, so that, as Nugent said, the play would have "a genuine Thurber flavor," and for Nugent to edit and revise as necessary. But when Thurber, working in his slow meticulous way, turned out only ten pages in the first two weeks, they decided that Nugent should start writing Act II, or they would never finish by September. The upshot was that each of them had a hand, either as originator or as reviser, in all but two scenes of the play: the scene at the beginning of Act II, where Joe Ferguson demonstrates a football play using the Turners' cups and saucers as markers, is Nugent's, and the drunk scene where Tommy Turner develops the male animal theory is Thurber's.[3]

Their collaboration was punctuated by the usual clashes of opinion, and since both men were highly theatrical, some of the arguments were spectacular. On one occasion, Thurber stalked out of Nugent's house vowing that he would never sleep under his roof again. Half an hour later, Nugent found him in the garage, asleep in the car. At another time, after the West Coast tryouts, they had a bitter quarrel, after which it was Nugent's turn to walk out. Thurber memorialized some of these shouting matches in a

[1] "Roaming in the Gloaming."
[2] Interview with Plimpton and Steele, in *Writers at Work,* p. 87.
[3] Nugent, *Events Leading Up to the Comedy,* pp. 137–38.

cartoon entitled "Second Act Trouble," in which two Thurber women labeled "Helen" and "Norma" gesticulate angrily at one another, and two men, "Jim" and "Elliott," dispute loudly, while in the background "Bob and Betty" (Robert Montgomery and his wife) look on with amusement.[4]

Shortly after *The Male Animal* opened, when the tensions and exacerbations of getting the play into the theater were all behind them, Nugent described the unpredictable drama of Thurber's moods in a brilliant little character sketch for the New York *Times*. "Unstimulated," wrote Nugent, "he is one of the mildest of men. . . . I have seen strangers poking at him to find the gleam that is in his writing, the cock-eyed twist and humor of his drawings, and getting nothing in response but conventional monosyllables, muttered politely or glumly, sometimes even cheerfully. Even with friends he is shy and reluctant to disagree, when in this mood of low vitality." When he is physically becalmed in this way, says Nugent, people may outrage his most cherished principles with impunity.

The whirlwind comes later. . . . Suddenly the mild, patient Thurber is gone like a forgotten zephyr, and a new, piercing hurricane is upon you, piling up waves of argument and invective, racking you, springing your seams, forcing gallons of cold saltwater through your fondest pretenses. Listing badly, you man the pumps, you head your nose into the gale, you mix up a new batch of metaphors. . . .

Next day, while you are patching your sails and cutting away wreckage, Thurber appears in a canoe, bearing fruit and flowers.

"Was I bad last night?" he mutters, with a sheepish smile.

Too weak to hurl your last broken harpoon, you invite him aboard and borrow his ukelele.[5]

While they were still working on the play in California, Nugent arranged with Arthur Beckhard, a New York producer at that time running a stock company in Santa Barbara, to give it a brief trial run in San Diego, Long Beach, Santa Barbara, and Los Angeles. Nugent had not planned to act in the play himself, although Thurber had tried all summer to get him to agree to do the part of Tommy Turner, but when Myron McCormick dropped out during rehearsals, Nugent stepped in—and went on to one of his greatest successes as an actor. In another last-minute emergency, his father, J. C. Nugent, took over the role of Ed Keller, the reactionary trustee, just two hours before the opening in San Diego, and played it to great applause throughout the West Coast run. Mary Astor played the professor's

[4] Nugent includes the drawing in *Events Leading Up to the Comedy*, facing p. 147.
[5] Nugent, "Notes on James Thurber, the Man, or Men."

wife, Leon Ames played Whirling Joe Ferguson, and Ivan Simpson was Dean Damon. The tryout was highly successful, but the play obviously needed more work. After a limited run, they closed it and went to New York to rewrite and to find a producer.

In November, after a few weeks of polishing and revising, they read the play to Herman Shumlin. Shumlin had made his reputation producing and directing serious plays, but he liked the blend of domestic farce and social comment in the play and agreed to take it on. Thurber and Nugent had had a disconcerting moment in Los Angeles, when Marc Connelly, whose advice they had asked, told them that the theme of academic freedom was the heart of the play, and that they should throw out the domestic comedy. Thurber was badly shaken by this opinion, especially since most of the comic material was his, but Nugent encouraged him to stand firm. Shumlin's confidence in the play as they had written it gave them an important psychological lift as well as the financial support they needed. Nugent was so convinced that they had a success on their hands that—in partnership with his friend Robert Montgomery—he put up forty percent of the capital. He urged Thurber to buy a share of this forty percent, but Thurber did not have enough cash, and he was reluctant to risk what little he had on anything so uncertain as a play.

For the New York production they made a number of changes in the cast. Ruth Matteson replaced Mary Astor, who had a picture commitment, Matt Briggs replaced J. C. Nugent, and two new young people, Gene Tierney and Don DeFore, took over the roles of Ellen's younger sister, Patricia, and her football-hero suitor, Wally Myers. Nugent, Leon Ames, and Ivan Simpson continued in the roles they had played on the West Coast.

The play was to have a single tryout performance in Princeton, and then a week's break-in period in Baltimore. After the dress rehearsal in Princeton, everyone was depressed. The weather was cold and raw, the McCarter Theater was bleak and empty, and it seemed impossible that anything could take life in that dreary vastness. Nugent, Thurber, and Shumlin walked back to their hotel with "snow blowing down our necks," as Nugent recalls it.

"I'm sorry we only have one week in Baltimore," Herman muttered finally. "That isn't nearly enough time to do all this play needs before New York. . . . But we're trapped now—and I'm very worried."

I was silent.

"I'm worried, too," said Jim. "I'm worried about all those laughs we're going to get tomorrow night. They'll make the play run thirty or forty minutes too long."

They then joined Leon Ames in his room, where they "drank up all the available Scotch. Jim even finished up the available gin as well, since he did not have to get up early."

Thurber was right—the Princeton tryout was a great success. In Baltimore they made their final revisions (Thurber stayed up all one night streamlining the first act) and then they were ready to open at the Cort Theater in New York on January 9, 1940. The opening-night audience was enthusiastic, and backstage, after the curtain had rung down, there was happy pandemonium as friends, backers, and well-wishers congratulated the authors, the producer, the cast and one another. There were several parties afterward, one of them given by the Robert Montgomerys at the Waldorf. When these were over, Thurber suggested that they all go to Bleeck's for a final round. Nugent was aghast: " 'But that's the hangout of newspapermen!' " he protested. " 'Suppose we get bad notices—the morning papers will be out pretty soon.' " Thurber's confidence was greater than ever: " 'How could we get bad notices?' " he replied. " 'I just want to see if we're going to win the Pulitzer Prize.' " [6]

The play did not win a Pulitzer Prize, but the critics were friendly and the audiences were happy. Most of the reviewers noted a basic incompatibility between the farcical and serious elements, but almost all of them felt that the play transcended its shortcomings. Brooks Atkinson described it as "three acts of insane hubbub" which sent the audience out of the theater "in a spirit of dazed hilarity," but he also noted that there was more to the play than this. Beneath the surface, he said, one could see a basic Thurber theme—"the general helplessness of the civilized man in a world dominated by primitives." [7] Burns Mantle selected it as one of the ten best plays of the year, and described it as "the third knockout comedy success of the 1939–40 season," along with *The Man Who Came to Dinner* and *Life with Father*. It ran for a highly profitable 244 performances in New York.

Joseph Wood Krutch described *The Male Animal* as "one-fourth . . . Thurberian madness, and one-fourth mild social protest," and the remainder as "skillful domestic farce of a thoroughly American kind." [8] There is really very little Thurberian madness in the play (the dogs, gulls and

[6] Nugent describes the early history of *The Male Animal* in chapters 25 and 26 of his autobiography, *Events Leading Up to the Comedy*.
[7] Brooks Atkinson, "The Play," New York *Times*, January 10, 1940.
[8] Joseph Wood Krutch, "Lucid Interval," *Nation*, January 20, 1940.

demented souls who make up his private fantasy world are not in evidence here), but there is social criticism and there is that affectionate treatment of the everyday problems of middle-class life which represents the other, or common-sense, side of Thurber's imagination. As John Mason Brown observed, the play is essentially a family comedy of the type represented by Frank Craven's *The First Year* and Nugent's own earlier success *The Poor Nut* (which also made use of the college-town setting).[9] It is full of stock situations and characters—the worm who turns, the kindly old absent-minded professor, the rah-rah college students, the big bad businessman, and so on. It celebrates tolerance, liberalism, and the basic decencies of middle-class life.

The materials of the play are familiar and traditional, but they carry the stamp of Thurber's own view of the American scene. Tommy Turner, for example, is one of Thurber's mild-mannered, bookish males who must struggle to survive in a world full of aggressors. The plot consists of two challenges to Tommy's adequacy as a man. The first threatens his role as husband, when "Whirling Joe" Ferguson, the great football star of ten years ago, and his wife's former boyfriend, returns for the homecoming game; the second threatens his integrity as a teacher, when Ed Keller, a Philistine Red-hunting trustee, demands that he give up his announced intention of reading to his class the famous letter of Vanzetti, the condemned anarchist, or risk losing his job. Both challenges require resolute action, and much of the comedy of the play lies in the reluctance and awkwardness with which Tommy assumes the hero's role.

Both Joe Ferguson and Ed Keller are aggressive extroverts, successful businessmen, Babbitts and Philistines. Joe is fundamentally good-natured and kind-hearted, while Keller is all suspicion and self-righteousness, but their fundamental values are the same—they stand for the status quo and what Keller calls "Americanism." Their minds are paralyzed by the slogans and clichés of their social and economic class. They have no interest in the intellectual life, and no understanding of the nature of a university. When Tommy announces that he plans to read the Vanzetti letter to his class, Keller and Ferguson are outraged ("You better deny it quick, Turner," says Keller, "I'll call the papers in the morning"; "Tommy'd better deny this," says Joe) and the women—all common sense and practicality—cannot see why Tommy should jeopardize his career over a little thing like reading a letter. Initially, he has no intention of making an issue out of the affair ("I'm not standing up to anyone," he protests to Michael

9 John Mason Brown, "Two on the Aisle," New York *Post*, January 29, 1940.

Barnes, the editor of the student paper), but Keller's crude threat to the principle of free discussion at the university forces him to take a stand. "I know I am not a tiger," he says, "but I don't like to be thought of as a pussy-cat either," and at a homecoming week-end party he challenges Keller. "Americanism is what we want taught here," says Keller. Tommy answers that "a college should be concerned with ideas. Not just your ideas or my ideas, but all ideas." "No, sir!" shouts Keller. "That's the *trouble* —too many ideas floating around. . . ." After this exchange, Tommy knows that he must read the letter.

Tommy's effort to save his marriage parallels his struggles to preserve his professional integrity. In a great comic scene, in which he and Michael get philosophically drunk, he develops the theory that since all the male creatures of the world fight for their mates—the wolf, the tiger, the penguin, the sea lion—man, too, should take direct, primitive action. For a brief moment, under the inflammatory influence of the whiskey, Tommy becomes the male animal and fights the astonished and unwilling Joe. The value of his warlike gesture is equivocal, however, since he suffers a concussion when Joe accidentally knocks him into a garden bench. Talking it over the next day, Tommy sees the episode only as a defeat, and he quotes to Ellen from Hodgson's poem "The Bull"—it is "the story of the defeated male," he says gloomily. Ellen recognizes the reason for his action. "I rather liked you as a sea lion," she says.

In spite of the prominence of the theme of academic freedom, the dominant mode of the play is that of light comedy and farce. Its high points are such moments as the famous drunk scene and the scene in which Joe makes a shambles of Ellen's table setting as he tries to demonstrate an unbelievably complex football play to two women who cannot make head or tail of what he is doing. There are wonderfully comic moments in the dialogue, like Ellen's irritable retort to Tommy, "Oh, you and your mind! I have to go through such a lot with your mind!" which sounds like a caption for a Thurber cartoon; and the play is full of inventive bits of strange business dramatizing man's essential helplessness in a baffling world, such as the moment when Michael, trying to make a dramatic exit, pulls off the doorknob, and the door opens to reveal Tommy standing on the other side with the other doorknob loose in his hand. Shumlin directed the play in the slam-bang style of the old vaudeville routines on which Thurber and Nugent drew for some of their details.[10] The result is that the problem of academic freedom comes through as little more than a

10 Brooks Atkinson, "James Thurber and Elliott Nugent See the Comic Side," New York *Times*, February 11, 1940.

temporary disturbance in the Turner household, an issue no more serious than the misunderstanding between husband and wife.

The Male Animal is one of Thurber's most optimistic works. At the end, Tommy's future is very much in doubt, but he has saved his self-respect as a man and a scholar, and he has saved his marriage. He has also discovered that neither intellect nor instinct alone is a reliable guide to life. What a man needs, obviously, is some sort of combination of the two. In this comedy of the reluctant hero, Thurber shows more faith in the hidden possibilities of the timid American male than he usually does, and the victory by the forces of liberalism, enlightenment, and openness to life over those of reaction, prejudice and fear is much more emphatic than the victory of the life cycle in *The Last Flower.* Part of the reason may be that the tradition of theatrical comedy to which he and Nugent had committed themselves demanded a more affirmative point of view than either man held privately. One would guess that *The Last Flower* is closer to expressing Thurber's view of life in 1939–40 than the more reassuring *The Male Animal.*

The setting of the play is obviously Ohio State, but neither Thurber nor Nugent admitted it publicly until some years later, "to avoid libel suits or mayhem," as Nugent put it.[11] Just before the play opened in Columbus in January of 1941, both authors renewed their reassurances that "Midwestern" was in no way to be equated with Ohio State, although their denials were more than a little ironic. They had used certain Ohio place-names, wrote Thurber, and they had drawn on the famous Dean Denney, but "as for the bad trustee, it goes without saying that no Ohio State trustee, past or present, was in our minds. Just bear in mind that the good people in the play are Ohio State and the trustee belongs only to Midwestern." [12]

After a most successful season in New York, the play went on the road and finally closed in the spring of 1941. Later in the year Nugent directed a film version for Warner Bros., with Henry Fonda and Olivia de Havilland as Tommy and Ellen, and Jack Carson as Joe Ferguson. The adaptation to the screen was generally well handled, although Warner Bros. insisted that some new dialogue be added to show that Professor Turner was clearly anti-Communist, and the ending was rewritten to make Tommy's triumph more emphatic. Ten years later, Warners remade the story into an outstandingly bad musical called *She's Working Her Way Through College,* with Virginia Mayo and Ronald Reagan. Thurber and Nugent were out-

[11] Unpublished manuscript of a speech to an alumni gathering of Ohio State Phi Psi's, May 26, 1967 (Thurber Collection).
[12] Letter to the editor, Columbus *Dispatch,* Sunday, January 5, 1941.

raged, but they had sold their film rights, and there was nothing they could do about it.[13]

In 1952, during the height of the McCarthy panic, *The Male Animal* was revived, and its obvious relevance to the contemporary situation made it an even greater success than it had been back in 1940. The authors briefly considered rewriting the play to make it more topical, but then wisely decided to let it speak for itself. It opened in Washington, then moved to the New York City Center for a brief run, and finally settled at the Music Box, where it ran for nearly a year. Nugent played Tommy again, Martha Scott was Ellen, and Robert Preston was Joe Ferguson. The reviewers were unanimous in saying that the play seemed even funnier and more significant than it had in 1940, and more than one observed that this was a sad comment on the times. "What seemed an attractive though lightweight comedy in 1940 turned up as one of the brighter spots of 1952," said Walter Kerr in the *Herald Tribune*.[14] Excited by its timeliness, a number of little theater companies did the play, and the impact of its old-fashioned liberalism on some communities was electrifying. When the Laguna Beach Playhouse in California put it on in 1954, the *South Coast News* attacked the production in a review entitled "Americanism Ridiculed in Playhouse Attraction." The review went on to complain that "college trustees, administrators, and even realistic faculty wives" were being shown as lacking in ideals and as subservient to "the ogre of big business." [15]

A friend sent Thurber a clipping of the review, and Thurber, obviously relishing the chance to score another point against the professional patriots of the day, took over Walter Kerr's column in the New York *Herald Tribune* (July 18, 1954) to answer. The reviewer had charged that the comic elements in the play disguised a great deal of subtle anti-American propaganda. Quite right, said Thurber: he was indeed trying to undermine the security of the United States. His principal message was that "freedom of thought is a good idea and should be preserved," but his "hellish over-all purpose included the effort to destroy America's faith in realistic wives, whom I can't abide," as well as an attack on stadium-building and the competence of Republican presidents, "which shows up in the line, 'Hoover can't write as well as Vanzetti.' " He added, "Many people who laughed at that line later thought it over seriously and joined the party,

[13] Nugent, *Events Leading Up to the Comedy*, pp. 157–59, and Morsberger, *James Thurber*, pp. 150–51.

[14] Walter Kerr, New York *Herald Tribune*, May 1, 1952. Brooks Atkinson, in the New York *Times*, and Richard Watts, in the New York *Post*, made the same point.

[15] "Offstage," *Theater Arts*, XXXVIII (October, 1954), 15; and Thurber, "Thurber Unmasked," New York *Herald Tribune*, July 18, 1954.

either the Democratic, or the Communist, or the one going on at 21 after the play."

In 1939, Thurber began one of his most original and artistically successful ventures—a series of fables in the tradition of Aesop and La Fontaine, and in September of 1940 Harper & Brothers published *Fables for Our Time and Famous Poems Illustrated,* a collection of twenty-eight fables with accompanying drawings and nine irreverent treatments of popular nineteenth-century poems, all of which had appeared in the pages of *The New Yorker* during 1939 and 1940. The fable was a particularly congenial medium for Thurber because of its brevity (he was usually at his best in the shorter forms), its indirect didacticism (like most humorists, he was a moralist in disguise, but he disliked preachiness) and its vein of fantasy (in the comic mingling of human and animal worlds he could give free rein to the antic side of his imagination). He told Alistair Cooke that he liked the fact that the fable was the oldest form of literary expression, and that within its compact limits it could say "a great deal about human life: the little flaws and foibles and vanities of a man and his wife, or the larger political scene, or anything else." [16] In fact, it was the adaptability of the fable to the contemporary scene which attracted him most, and he was angered when *The New Yorker* rejected "The Bears and the Monkeys" (later included in *Further Fables for Our Time*) on the grounds that the political subject was too familiar. Writing to the Whites about his disagreement with the magazine, he pointed out that a concern with politics had always been an important part of the fable-writing tradition. "Fables should reflect the temper of their times," he said. [17]

Thurber's fables differ from those in the classic tradition in that they are given sharply contemporary settings. His animals and birds are not simply universal human types—although they are that, too—but they are very twentieth-century American figures as well, and they speak in the colloquial American style. The philandering crow, for example, who has fallen for a lady oriole, has these words for his wife: " 'Tush,' " he says. " 'You are simply a jealous woman.' He tossed her a few dollars. 'Here,' he said, 'go buy yourself some finery. You look like the bottom of an old teakettle.' And off he went to look for the oriole." The idiom of the know-it-all Scotty who goes to the country and tries to beat everybody up is that of the American street-corner scrapper: when the farm dogs warn him about the porcupine he says, " 'Lead me to him. . . . I can lick anything that doesn't wear horseshoes.' " When they point out the porcu-

---

[16] Interview with Alistair Cooke, *Atlantic,* CXCVIII (August, 1956), 40.
[17] Letter to the Whites, April 2, 1956 (EBWP).

pine he says, " 'A clown . . . a pushover,' " and he moves in, "leading with his left and exhibiting some mighty fancy footwork."

This modernity of tone in Thurber's fables underlines a basic modernity in point of view: the dominant motif of the collection as a whole is the repudiation of the folk wisdom of the past as it appears in the old fables and proverbs. The fables of Aesop, La Fontaine and Gay are essentially reassuring—they are store-houses of traditional wisdom and they reinforce conservative moral values. Thurber's fables move in exactly the opposite direction. They show the world to be an uncertain and precarious place where there are no reliable guide-lines beyond one's own direct experience. Like *Let Your Mind Alone* and *The Male Animal, Fables for Our Time* mocks fossilized knowledge—the neat little formulas and unexamined assumptions which offer misleading pictures of reality.

Thurber rewrites some of the classic fables, exposing their essential falsity. In his version of "Little Red Riding Hood" the little girl is more than a match for the wiliness of the wolf. The moral is: *"It is not so easy to fool little girls nowadays as it used to be."* The accompanying illustration gives a wonderfully comic emphasis to the difference between Thurber's conception of the scene and the traditional one: the wolf is a genial ruffian (as unlike any grandmother as could be imagined), and the little girl is a woman in miniature; she is no sheltered innocent, but a skeptical, frowning and dangerous female. The story of the swallow in "The Glass in the Field" shows that *"He who hesitates is sometimes saved,"* and the unsettling moral in the case of the Fairly Intelligent Fly is that *"There is no safety in numbers or in anything else."* Many of the fables mock the slogans and the values of the American success ethic and Puritan morality generally. In "The Shrike and the Chipmunks" the wife's demand that the husband go out and make something of himself leads to disaster. Moral: *"Early to rise and early to bed makes a male healthy and wealthy and dead."* The reformed bear in "The Bear Who Let It Alone" creates as much havoc in his zeal for temperance as he ever did when he came home full of mead. The moral: *"You might as well fall flat on your face as lean over too far backward."*

One significant group of fables reflects Thurber's growing concern with political and social issues. The instability and paranoia of the mass mind is the subject of "The Very Proper Gander," in which an overheard remark ("There is a very proper gander") starts a series of rumors that destroy an innocent creature. In "The Owl Who Was God" the gullibility of the herd is seen as self-destructive as well. In this bitter fable the creatures conceive an irrational admiration for the owl because he can see in the dark, and—ignoring the fox, who asks, " 'Can he see in the daytime, too?' "—they follow him down a busy highway in broad daylight to their doom. These political fables say that the world is a dangerous place and that the people in it are either fools, aggressors, or victims. Behind them all is Thurber's apocalyptic vision of the oncoming war.

Although Thurber's fables are distinctly modern in subject and in tone, they are at the same time universal, as all fables ought to be. "The Scotty Who Knew Too Much," "The Crow and the Oriole," "The Tiger Who Understood People," and others dramatize the classic themes of pride and fall, the folly of trying to be what you were not meant to be, and man's unlimited capacity for error, and they do so with a liveliness and fullness of detail which make them seem completely original. To the modern taste, at any rate, Thurber is a far better fable-writer than his illustrious predecessors. He himself found most of the classic fables dull: writing to White in 1956, he said that a good fable should "explode," and that too many of Aesop's had no fuses. La Fontaine, he said, "has some that sparkle, some that go off, and a few that just lie there." [18] His own little narratives are constructed with a sure sense of climax (or artful anti-climax), and unlike the generalized tales of Aesop and La Fontaine, they are filled with sharply observed details of speech and behavior which give them dramatic life.

His most memorable and most original fable, however, is "The Unicorn in the Garden." One could imagine someone else writing "The Little Girl and the Wolf," for instance, but not "The Unicorn in the Garden." It springs from a deeper, more private imaginative level than the other fables, and it is such a quintessential expression of Thurber's themes and values that it could well stand as an introduction to his work as a whole. The gentle poetic husband, who sees the unicorn eating the lily in the garden, and the coldly rational wife, who scorns her husband's vision and tries to have him put in "the booby hatch," are archetypal figures in Thurber's world. Here, two of his richest themes, the battle of the sexes and the conflict between fantasy and reality, are blended into a delightful (and malicious) fable. The unexpected triumph of the man and of the fantasy principle is only a more spectacular version of the little victories won by Thurber's other hen-pecked dreamers.

"Famous Poems Illustrated" is one of Thurber's most original comic inventions. He had experimented with the possibilities of an unconventional kind of interplay between picture and text in "The Pet Department" series, back in 1930, and in his "James Thurber Presents William Shake-

---

[18] Letter to White, April 16, 1956 (EBWP).

speare" series in *Stage,* in 1935. Here, he provides irreverent illustrations for nine poems from the popular repertory of the nineteenth century. Most of the poems are standard anthology pieces of the kind everyone in Thurber's day had to learn in school—Longfellow's "Excelsior," Scott's "Lochinvar," Tennyson's "Locksley Hall," Whittier's "Barbara Frietchie"; a few are memorable as monuments of Victorian bathos, like Rose Hartwick Thorpe's "Curfew Shall Not Ring Tonight." They are all poems of uplift and romance, and for thousands of people to whom they offered encouragement, consolation and emotional experience, they were what was meant by the term "literature." To the modern taste, of course, most of them seem naive, sentimental, and irritatingly preachy. Thurber's deliberately crude and simplistic drawings take all the glamor out of the romantic gestures and the high-flown language of the poems, and make them more than a little ridiculous.

Longfellow's "Excelsior," a poem that generations of idealistic and ambitious young men had by heart, exists only in the world of daydream and inspiration; to picture it literally and realistically is to make it preposterous. Thurber's illustration of the opening scene is a good example of his method throughout the whole series. Longfellow's lines run:

> The shades of night were falling fast,
> As through an Alpine village passed
> A youth, who bore, 'mid snow and ice,
> A banner with the strange device—
> Excelsior!

Thurber's youth wears a business suit, a bow tie, and a determined expression, and he strides with exaggerated vigor along a snowy village street, holding aloft a staff to which is attached the Excelsior banner. Two townspeople wearing fur hats and ear muffs turn in a startled way to look at the strange spectacle.

The reductive effect of Thurber's primitive drawings on these tales of noble aspiration and heroic action is devastating. The method works best on second-rate poems, where it heightens what is already faintly ridiculous, but it is also effective in pointing out the possibilities for unintended humor in the greatest masterpieces. Among the 1935 illustrations of famous scenes from Shakespeare, for example, are a wonderfully loony Ophelia scattering flowers, and a minstrel-show Black Sambo of an Othello about to strangle Desdemona in her bed. Ophelia and Othello have always been difficult for the modern imagination, and after seeing these two ludicrous versions of their pathetic fates, no theater-goer will ever again be able to suspend his disbelief as willingly as he once did.

Between September of 1940 and July of 1941 Thurber did a twice-weekly column, "If You Ask Me," for the newly established liberal paper, *PM*. Ralph Ingersoll, his old friend from the early *New Yorker* days, was the editor and publisher, and he offered Thurber a free hand if he would take on the job. Harold Ross read a few of the columns and objected to Thurber, saying, " 'You're throwing away ideas on *PM* that would make good casuals,' " but Thurber liked the freedom from the *New Yorker* formulas, and as he said in *The Years with Ross*, he needed the hundred dollars a column that Ingersoll paid him. The offer came at a providential time: he was having serious eye trouble in 1940, and he was virtually unable to work; the loose undemanding form of the column was easy to handle, and at the same time, the assignment kept him from feeling totally helpless and inadequate. For a period of ten months it was the only writing he did, but in July of 1941 his health was so bad that he had to give up even this light commitment.[19]

There are few surprises or new departures in "If You Ask Me," and most of the columns come out of the second drawer. There are some exceptions, however, like the piece on Will Rogers' *Letters of a Self-Made Diplomat to His President* (1926), a report to President Coolidge on the comedian's visit to Mussolini. Thurber resurrects this obscure and eccentric little book from its well-deserved oblivion and discusses it as a document in American social history. He sees it as a fascinating example of the popular American faith in the superiority of the semi-educated rural intelligence to European guile and sophistication. "Will, the shrewd, the kindly, the comical, was fondly believed by his publishers, his public and perhaps his President (Calvin Coolidge) to be able to see through the nature and intentions of European statesmen with the same keen eye with which he was wont so neatly on occasion to see through the monkey shines of Western congressmen." What the book actually shows is Rogers' incredible naiveté. "This grinning Yankee at King Victor Emmanuel's court was bound to make a fool of himself," observes Thurber, accurately linking Rogers to Mark Twain's comic abroad. Thurber makes allowances for the date of the book, but his quotations are devastating: " 'Of course,' " wrote Rogers of Mussolini, " 'I don't think he is as great as Roosevelt, but this Gent is a kind of cross between Roosevelt, Red Grange, Babe Ruth when the Babe is really good, the older La Follette, a touch of Borah, Bryan of '96, Samuel Gompers, and Tunney.' " [20]

Thurber's commitment to intellectual and aesthetic over popular values shows up in two book reviews he did for the *New Republic* early in 1942

[19] *The Years with Ross,* p. 121.
[20] "If You Ask Me," *PM,* September 19, 1940.

("Taps at Reveille," a review of Fitzgerald's *The Last Tycoon*, and "What Price Conquest?," a review of Steinbeck's *The Moon Is Down*).[21] Discussing *The Last Tycoon*, Thurber praises Fitzgerald's craftsmanship and adds that the book is "not for everyone; it is for the writer, the critic, the sensitive appreciator of literature." He did not care for the sentimentality of Steinbeck's book. He objected to the air of unreality which pervades the whole story. The setting and the characters come straight out of familiar theatrical conventions. "If these are German officers, if they are anything else but American actors, I will eat the manuscript of your next play," he says. The central theme of Steinbeck's tale, "that there are no machines and no armies mighty enough to conquer the people," is simply wish-projection, he argues, as the facts of the German conquest of Poland make clear.

The review provoked a lively response in the Correspondence Column of the *New Republic*. Marshall Best, Managing Editor of the Viking Press, which published Steinbeck's book, called Thurber's review "a slap in the face for all the decent people who have been moved by the book's shining sincerity." He went on to lump Thurber with "parlor intellectuals" whose "cynicism . . . might yet lose us the war." Thurber replied by referring Mr. Best to a New York *Times* summary of a Polish White Paper on the German conquest. He will send a clipping of this article to Mr. Best, he says, "by whose fuzzy mental distress and public heartbreak I am approximately as deeply moved as I would be by the tears of a real-estate agent." [22]

My World and Welcome to It, Thurber's collection of his best essays and sketches between 1938 and 1942, culminates an important stage in his artistic development: after 1942 his world and his work would be different. The showpiece of the collection is "The Secret Life of Walter Mitty." This little story (it is only about four thousand words) is a curious phenomenon: comic in substance, elegant in form and style, it is a work of art in its own right; but it has also become, through one of those mysterious cultural transubstantiations, a part of our modern mythology and folklore. Like Sinclair Lewis's Babbitt, Mitty is a genuine culture figure, a character whom we immediately recognize; and in his predicament and his absurd daydreams we see a comic image of our own impotence and desperation.

Mitty's name, like Babbitt's, is now a part of our language ("He's a real Walter Mitty," we say), but it was during World War II that his impact

[21] "Taps at Assembly," *New Republic*, CVI (February 9, 1942), p. 211; "What Price Conquest?" *New Republic*, CVI (March 16, 1942), p. 370.
[22] "Correspondence," *New Republic*, CVI (March 30, 1942), p. 431.

on the American imagination was greatest. The story was reprinted in the *Reader's Digest* in 1943, and the troops immediately made it their own: there was a Mitty International Club in the European Theater and a Mitty Society in the South Pacific. Bomber pilots in the South Pacific made "Ta-pocketa-pocketa-pocketa" an official password, and painted the Mitty Society emblem—two crossed Webley-Vickers automatics—on the noses of their planes.[23] In a 1944 letter to Peter De Vries Thurber told a story about the Mitty cult which Lieutenant Joseph Bryan, a *Saturday Evening Post* editor and occasional *New Yorker* contributor just back from the South Pacific, had told him: "A young pilot from Augusta, Ga., cruising around in the night heard over the radio the voice of a strange American pilot dreamily droning 'Ta pocketa pocketa pocketa.' The Georgian, giving his identification—say 'Albatross, 7310,' said 'Come in, Walter Mitty, Over.' The other pilot asked for the Georgian's direction and location and presently showed up alongside in a P-38. The Georgian was a Navy flier, the other man proved to be Lt. Francis Parker of Chicago, an Army pilot. The two men landed their planes and introduced themselves." [24] It is interesting to speculate on the reasons for the special appeal of the story to men at war, but fundamentally, they identified with it because they, like Mitty, felt trapped and helpless, and Mitty's secret breakouts provided them with an emotional comic release.

The story of Walter Mitty is not only an archetype of contemporary experience, it is an intensely personal tale as well. Mitty is Thurber's image of himself as romantic daydreamer. It was this side of his nature which identified with Conrad's Lord Jim, that other romantic who lived in a dream of heroic action. He first revealed it in that class prophecy for the eighth grade at the Douglas School, where he was the cool daredevil who hung by his feet and disentangled the rope from the curobator to save the seairoplane from disaster. He returnedto the character again and again in the stories of the 1930's: Mr. Monroe, Tommy Trinway, Mr. Pendly and all the other mild-mannered ineffectual men who carry on an intense fantasy life to compensate for their inadequacy in the real world are descendants of that eighth grade self-portrait and ancestors of Walter Mitty.

The central theme of the story is the conflict between the world of fantasy and the world of reality and, as in "The Unicorn in the Garden," this is seen as a part of the conflict between husband and wife. The male is always associated in Thurber's imagination with fantasy, the female with

---

[23] Morsberger, *James Thurber,* pp. 45–46; also undated clipping of interview with Thurber in *PM,* sometime in 1945 (RTS).

[24] Letter to De Vries, April 4, 1944.

logic and common sense. In reality, Walter Mitty is inadequate to the demands of the real world: his wife bullies him, the parking-lot attendant sneers at his awkward efforts to park the car, he cannot remember the shopping list. But in his secret world of fantasy, derived largely from bad movies, he triumphs over the humiliating forces of the actual.

Mitty's daydreams are the veriest claptrap, made up out of the clichés of popular fiction and movies, and their triteness serves to underline the pathos as well as the comedy of his situation, but at the same time, they are a source of strength, the means by which he makes his life significant. By the standards of the world, Mitty is a pathetic and inadequate figure, but as the closing image of the story suggests, he is in a deeper sense triumphant:

> "To hell with the handkerchief," said Walter Mitty scornfully. He took one last drag on his cigarette and snapped it away. Then, with that faint, fleeting smile playing about his lips, he faced the firing squad; erect and motionless, proud and disdainful, Walter Mitty the Undefeated, inscrutable to the last.

Much of the brilliance of the story is the result of Thurber's mastery of style. Three levels of language interplay throughout. There are the melodramatic clichés of the dream-sequences (" 'The new anesthetizer is giving way!' shouted an interne. 'There is no one in the East who knows how to fix it!' 'Quiet, man!' said Mitty in a low, cool voice"); contrasting sharply with these is the flat colloquial idiom of the scenes of real life (" 'Pick it up, brother!' snapped a cop as the light changed"); and holding it all together is Thurber's own narrative style—economical, lightly ironic, and wonderfully expressive ("Walter Mitty drove on toward Waterbury in silence, the roaring of the SN202 through the worst storm in twenty years of Navy flying fading in the remote, intimate airways of his mind"). Examples of Thurber's inventiveness as a comedian of language are everywhere, but the most notable are the mock-technical vocabulary of the hospital sequence (" 'Obstreosis of the ductal tract. Tertiary. Wish you'd take a look at him' ") and the repetition of the "ta-pocketa-pocketa-pocketa" phrase which runs throughout the tale like a comic leitmotif.

The story is essentially dramatic, and would seem to have been meant for the stage, but because of its brevity, it proved difficult to adapt. Robert Benchley did a radio version in 1945 which Thurber and Helen always felt was the best of the efforts to translate it into dramatic terms. Samuel Goldwyn made a lavish two-hour showcase for Danny Kaye out of it in 1947, but in the process of shaping it to the particular talents of the star and broadening it to appeal to the taste of a mass audience the theme and tone of the original story were lost. The Cincinnati Conservatory of Music put on an operatic version in 1953, but the venture apparently never got beyond the campus. In 1960 Thurber himself adapted it to the stage for *A Thurber Carnival.*[25]

"You Could Look It Up" is a very different sort of story for Thurber, and the fact that it was published in the *Saturday Evening Post* says something about the nature of the difference.[26] It is a "popular" story, an imitation of Ring Lardner's baseball stories without Lardner's acid, but with a strong measure of Thurber's taste for the bizarre and the wild instead. Like Lardner's stories, it is told in the first person by a semi-literate narrator, and so the texture of the prose is full of the humor of malapropism and mangled grammar (" 'We was now in first place by a margin you could a' got it into the eye of a thimble' "). The plot has to do with what happens when the manager of a big-league ball club hires a midget and puts him into a crucial game to draw a walk. The climax is right out of the great tradition of the American tall tale:

> I know you never seen a midget ketched, and you prob'ly never even seen one throwed. To ketch a midget that's been throwed by a heavy-muscled man and is flyin' through the air, you got to run under him and with him and pull your hands and arms back and down when you ketch him, to break the compact of his body, or you'll bust him in two like a matchstick. I seen Bill Lange and Willie Keeler make some wonderful ketches in my day, but I never seen nothin' like that center fielder.

Harold Ross was much taken by the story, and he wrote Thurber that Grantland Rice had talked to him about it throughout two innings of a World Series game, and had said that it ought to be made into a movie. "By God, I do, too," wrote Ross. "Do you want me to start selling it?" Nothing came of the suggestion, but baseball followers will recall that shortly thereafter, Bill Veeck, the owner of the St. Louis Browns, created a minor furor when he signed a midget and used him as a pinch-hitter. It was a clear case of life imitating art: Veeck acknowledged that he got the idea from Thurber's story, and that he had tried it out as a publicity stunt.[27]

"You Could Look It Up" shows Thurber working within the well-

---

[25] Morsberger, *James Thurber,* p. 152.
[26] *Saturday Evening Post,* CCXIII (April 4, 1941).
[27] "Midget Story Given New Twist by Veeck," *Sporting News,* August 29, 1951 (RTS).

established conventions of American humor; "What Do You Mean It *Was* Brillig?" bears the stamp of his unique imagination so unmistakably that it would be impossible to confuse it with the work of anyone else. Like the earlier "The Black Magic of Barney Haller," it shows how a slight distortion of ordinary language can create an Alice-in-Wonderland world where ordinary rational communication is transcended and the real gives away to the surreal. Della the cook has her own way with words, and to talk with her is to enter a strange and mysterious land. " 'Do you want cretonnes for the soup?' " she asks. She has a brother who works "into an incinerator where they burn the refuge"; he has been working there "since the Armitage"; another brother has just passed his "silver-service elimina-tions"; and her sister got "tuberculosis from her teeth and it went all through her symptom." Only Lewis Carroll could have understood Della, says Thurber, and the reference is significant, for Carroll was the presiding genius over the fantasy side of Thurber's imagination, and his nonsense poem "The Jabberwock" was always a touchstone for Thurber, the defini-tive example of the creation of a surreal world through language.

Della's announcement that " 'They are here with the reeves' " sends Thurber to the dictionary.

> "Are they here with strings of onions?" I asked. Della said they were not. "Are they here with enclosures or pens for cattle, poultry, or pigs; sheepfolds?" Della said no sir. "Are they here with administrative officers?" From a little nearer the door Della said no again. "Then they've got to be here," I said, "with some females of the common European sandpiper." These scenes of ours take as much out of Della as they do out of me, but she is not a woman to be put down by a crazy man with a dictionary. "They are here with the reeves for the windas," said Della with brave stubbornness. Then, of course, I under-stood what they were there with; they were there with the Christmas wreaths for the windows.

Thurber values these mind-bending excursions with Della, he says, because they are "the most satisfying flight from reality I have ever known."

Nevertheless, like so much of his fantasy, the origin of Della and her word-magic is the real world. Writing to White in the fall of 1938, Thurber noted that their cook, Margaret, was a perfect subject for a *New Yorker* casual: "She says one of her sons works into the incinerating plant where they burn the refuge; has had the job since the Armitage. I'm going to have to combine her with another lady of the vicinity who pointed out a flock of fletchers on her lawn and who also told me of a young man who had passed his civil service eliminations." [28] In a BBC interview in 1958 he said in answer to a question about these details that he would not have dared to make them up. If he had, he said, "somehow the validity would go out of the thing." His humor was based on truth, he always insisted, but truth "slightly distorted for emphasis and amusement." [29]

The humorous essays and autobiographical anecdotes which make up the bulk of *My World and Welcome to It* include Thurber's lightly malicious survey of thirty years in the life of that great institution of British humor, *Punch* ("Backward and Downward with Mr. Punch"), and his international comedy of imperfect communication, "A Ride with Olympy," in which he tells what happened on the Cap d'Antibes when he tried to teach a Russian émigré who spoke no English how to drive a Ford. More significant, because it expresses a set of values of special importance to him, is "Memorial," his tribute to Jeannie, the black poodle who epitomized for him the innocence and natural dignity of the canine nature. The piece is in Thurber's sentimental-nostalgic vein, but the sentiment is controlled and lightened by humor. Jeannie was beautiful, and once won best of breed in Madison Square Garden, but she was happiest prowling the countryside in her natural shaggy state. Riding in a car made her sick, and Thurber used to put a red rubber bib on her and sit with her in the rumble seat. He told and re-told the story of the time when it began to rain and he put up a green parasol to protect her. They stopped for gas along the way, and one of the attendants took a look at the strange tableau in the rumble seat and muttered to his companion, " 'Hey, Mac, get a load of this.' "

Jeannie sometimes seemed to have an intuitive understanding of life that surpassed our reason; and when death came to her, she accepted it "with a grave and unapprehensive resignation." Like "The Wood Duck," "Memorial" develops the contrast between the closeness of the other creatures to the ways of nature and man's alienation from them. The uncaptioned drawing on the last page, showing a dog gazing thoughtfully at a gravestone, says in line what the memoir says in words—all the innocence and intuitive understanding which for Thurber were the special possessions of the animal world are suggested in the dog's posture and expression.

[28] Undated letter (EBWP).
[29] "Frankly Speaking," BBC Home Service Program, December 24, 1958.

13

Blindness and
Fairy Tales

Between 1935 and 1940 everything seemed to be going Thurber's way. He had made a happy second marriage and he had established himself as one of the leading humorists in the English-speaking world. The success of *The Male Animal* promised still another exciting world to conquer. Then, in the spring of 1940, he began to go blind. He had had trouble with his one remaining eye on the way to Hollywood in the summer of 1939, and in June of 1940 he was operated on for a cataract. The next year was a nightmare. Glaucoma followed, then Grade A iritis, and a series of other complications, and between June of 1940 and June of 1941 he underwent five operations. At the end, it was obvious that he was going to have very little vision—if any—for the rest of his life. He had been living on borrowed time all along, as it turned out. The specialists who examined him were amazed to find that he had been seeing without the normal apparatus of vision for forty years. The infection which had followed his accident ("sympathetic ophthalmia," the doctors called it) had been lying dormant all this time. Now it had started in again.

After the summer of 1941 he could no longer read, and this was a severe deprivation for a man to whom books had always been a necessity. Even worse, he was no longer able to see well enough to use the typewriter. Like most newspapermen, he was a hunt-and-peck typist, and without vision, he was lost. Slowly and painfully he had to learn to compose in longhand, using soft pencils on yellow copy paper and writing large—about twenty words to a page—and, as his sight worsened, to compose by dictation.[1] In 1946 he told Earl Wilson that he had about one-eighth of normal vision, and that it came and went in cycles. "A mist covers the eye part of the time," he said.[2] By 1947 he could no longer see well enough to draw, except for occasional experiments with special equipment, like the illuminated board made for him by General Electric, or the Czechoslovakian mechanical pencil that produced a line that glowed like neon tubing. A friend from Simon and Schuster brought him some black paper and white pastel chalk in the summer of 1950, and with these materials and the aid of a powerful microscope called a Zeiss loop, which he wore like eyeglasses, he was able to do a few drawings for the first time in three years.[3] His sight was not good enough to continue, however, and a self-portrait for the cover of the July 9, 1951, issue of *Time* was his last published drawing. For this he used black paper and a special crayon sent him by an almost blind admirer in Manchester, England.[4]

The onset of blindness was a traumatic experience for Thurber. He was a forty-five-year-old writer, utterly dependent, so he thought, on his eyes for his living. It was through his eyes that he knew the world, and he needed his eyes to put it all down on the typewriter. The prospect of having to discover not only a new method of composition but a whole new way of coping with the world brought on what he later called a "five-year nervous crack-up." [5] For nearly two years he was able to work only occasionally. He did a book review or two, and he kept up his *PM* column until July of 1941, but the falling-off in his productivity can be measured by the fact that between March of 1940 and January of 1942 he published only three pieces in *The New Yorker*—"The Man Who Hated Moonbaum" (March 16, 1940), "The Whip-poor-will" (August 9, 1941), and "A Friend to

[1] Sources for the history of Thurber's blindness: Helen Thurber, conversations with CSH; Thurber, letter to Elmer Davis, May 18, 1956; letter to Edmund Wilson, May 25, 1959; Sayre, "Priceless Gift of Laughter,"; article in *Harper's Bazaar*, November, 1950 (RTS); interview with Harvey Breit, "Mr. Thurber Observes a Serene Birthday," *New York Times Magazine*, December 4, 1949; Brandon, "The Tulle and Taffeta Rut," in *As We Are*.
   Thurber described his adjustment to his affliction in many interviews. Among the most important are those with John Ferris, "Thurber Has Own Brand of Humor," Columbus *Citizen*, Sunday, November 8, 1953; with Plimpton and Steele, reprinted in *Writers at Work;* and with Alistair Cooke, *Atlantic*, CXCVIII (August, 1956).
   [2] Interview with Earl Wilson, Columbus *Dispatch*, October 13, 1946.
   [3] Thurber, New York *Herald Tribune* Book Review, October 8, 1950; and article in *Harper's Bazaar*, November, 1950.
   [4] Brandon, "The Tulle and Taffeta Rut," *As We Are*.
   [5] Letter to Frank Gibney, October 31, 1956.

Alexander" (January 10, 1942). The next few years were better, but the entire period from 1940 until 1947 was a time of struggle and discouragement for Thurber. Heroically, he turned out some of his best work during this time—stories like "The Cane in the Corridor" and tales like *The White Deer*—but his output was severely limited. Then, in 1947–48, he experienced a resurgence of creative energy and confidence and began to turn out the sort of pieces which made *The Beast in Me* one of his most interesting collections.

He revealed something of the deep depression of spirit against which he was struggling in a letter to the Whites in June of 1941. He keeps hoping to hear from them, he says, and he adds, with understandable self-pity, that it is easier for them, because they do not have to try to write in the dark, as he does. His new glasses are thick and uncomfortable, but they bring everything closer, and he can even see the faint track of the pencil as it moves across the page, although he cannot make out the words. After this brief lapse, he goes on to talk cheerfully of everyday matters. He has just finished the first draft of a fairy tale, he says, and he hopes that it might make a good Christmas book, with colorful illustrations. (The story was *Many Moons*, and he did not complete it until more than two years later.) He also has a couple of good anecdotes about life on Martha's Vineyard. One, showing the proud insularity of the islanders, particularly caught his fancy. The twelve-year-old son of a family which had lived on Martha's Vineyard for some two hundred years was asked by his teacher to do an essay on Mussolini. The boy identified Mussolini at once: Mussolini was an off-islander, he said. Thurber hoped to make a "Talk of the Town" anecdote out of that one.[6]

This letter to the Whites is written with a soft pencil on yellow paper, and nothing could illustrate the sudden change in Thurber's situation more dramatically than the change in his handwriting. He had always written a neat, firm, and vigorous style as a penman; here, in his blindness, the letters are large and somewhat uncertain, and the words and lines are widely spaced, much as they are in the writing of a child. As his sight deteriorated, the letters became larger and more irregular and disconnected, and about 1947, when he got so that he could no longer see the lines at all, he gave up trying to carry on his personal correspondence in longhand, although he continued to rough out parts of his stories in this painstaking way for a number of years longer.

In spite of his efforts to keep a grip on himself, the physical and psychic

[6] Undated letter to the Whites, probably June, 1941 (EBWP).

strain of five operations and the frightening prospect of total blindness proved to be too much, and in mid-summer of 1941, shortly after his letter to the Whites, he suffered a severe nervous breakdown. For a few weeks he was in a state of uncontrollable panic. He had hallucinations and he feared for his sanity. When his old friend Jap Gude came to see him, he gripped his arm and whispered, "Promise me that you won't let them put me away." The paralyzing anxiety lasted only a short time, however, and with the help of Dr. Ruth Fox, a psychiatrist who summered on Martha's Vineyard, his indefatigable wife, Helen, and his friends the Gudes, the Coateses, and Joel Sayre, all of whom came to give him support and encouragement, he pulled himself out of the hole before the summer was over.

Late in the summer, when the worst was behind him, he wrote the Whites about it. It is a remarkable letter in every way, and what comes through most strongly is the honesty and tough-minded optimism with which he faces his situation. "I have been in a tail spin and power dive combined which was awful," he wrote. "I simply cracked wide open and it has been frightful, almost insupportable, but now I'm fighting back." He is taking massive injections of Vitamin B-1, he says, and will probably have to have further psychiatric help. His eye has had a set-back, but luckily Dr. Knapp, who had consulted with Dr. Bruce on Thurber's case, was vacationing on the island, and so he is well looked after. He is pleased with the selections of his work made by the Whites for their anthology, *A Sub-Treasury of American Humor.*

Then he turns to a subject which was to be much in his mind for the next several years. He has "a swell idea for a play," he says. "I need someone to help me on it, though. I want to do most of the actual writing, but talking it out with someone is important to me, especially now." He thinks the idea "has more stuff than *The Male Animal* and will be funnier." He may get a secretary in to dictate to, he says, but what he really wants to do is work with White: "I wish I could sit around and tell the idea to you. It is a little hard to do it in pencil in semidarkness." He also wants White to look at the fairy tale he did just before his crack-up.

He had managed to turn out one story, "The Whip-poor-will," after his breakdown, and he was naturally proud of it. It was quite an achievement, he said, since he had to write it in longhand, using up eighty sheets of yellow paper, and since he had to use a totally new method of composition, writing and rewriting in his head before putting anything down. He and Helen did a little cutting later, but no rewriting was necessary. He added that Ross was so impressed that he wrote him an eight-hundred-word letter about it—an extraordinary burst of prose from the usually telegraphic editor.

He talks about domestic topics: regretfully he refuses the offer of a dachshund puppy, although it has long been their dream to have a house in the country and six or eight dogs, including a water spaniel, a poodle, and a dachshund. He goes on to tell the Whites about a wonderful black poodle named Hugo at their rented place on Martha's Vineyard who fetches the ice bucket from the kitchen at cocktail time. At the close, he comes back to the subject of his determination to get well. He has been down in the bowels of terror, he says, but he has pulled himself out with what Dr. Fox considers remarkable speed. Writing the letter, like turning out "The Whip-poor-will," was good for him. It was the first piece of writing of any kind he had been able to finish in two weeks, he said, and it gave him back some of his confidence to sit at his writing table again. A quick postscript catches up the two main themes of the letter—the optimism and the fear: "There is nothing pathological about me, babies, just nerves. I used to think nervous breakdowns were not so terrible. I know now how wrong I was." [7]

The best gauge of his state of mind during the terrible summer of 1941, however, is "The Whip-poor-will." It "came somewhere out of a grim fear at the back of my mind," he said to Plimpton and Steele, and it obviously had a therapeutic value for him. The act of writing the story proved that he *could* work, in spite of everything, and the translating of his private terrors into fictional form was a way of triumphing over them.

It is a tale of obsession, mental breakdown and death. Kinstrey, the protagonist, is a middle-aged man very much like Thurber, living in a New England village with his wife and a servant couple. The insistent call of the whip-poor-will outside becomes part of an early-morning nightmare and wakes him up. His nerves are bad, and he has trouble getting back to sleep. At breakfast, his wife, cool, calm, and well rested ("She did not believe anyone had to toss and turn"), says that she did not hear it. She tells him to take hold of himself. "Use your will power," she says. The next morning the bird does fifty-three whips without stopping. Kinstrey thinks to himself, " 'I suppose, like the drops of water or the bright light in the third degree, this could drive you nuts.' " The servants say that they have heard that a whip-poor-will singing near the house is an omen of death. All through the day the rhythm of the bird's song beats obsessively in his mind, but now to the phrase "fatal bell, fatal bell"—a fragment from *Macbeth* that had lain long forgotten in the bottom of his memory.

[7] Undated letter to the Whites, probably September, 1941 (EBWP).

He tries to pull himself together, but the nightmares get worse and the bird call keeps running through his head, carrying with it darkly suggestive phrases like the refrain of Poe's "The Raven"—"nevermore, nevermore, whip-poor-will, whip-poor-will. . . ." The final nightmare is the worst of all—he is in a hospital "filled with poor men in will chairs," and then he is trying to play tennis, and Madge is "the umpoor in the high chair beside the court, holding a black umbrella over her head," and she cries "whip him now, whip him now!" Kinstrey finds himself in the kitchen, a carving knife in his hand, still halfway between dream and reality. When Arthur, the manservant, appears, he whispers, " 'Who do you do first?' "

From June of 1940 until the summer of 1942 Thurber was in serious physical and psychological trouble, but by the fall of 1942 he had turned the corner and accepted his new situation. He was writing regularly again, and in the 1942–43 season he did two of his best stories, "The Catbird Seat," which was chosen for *Best Stories of 1943*, and "The Cane in the Corridor," which made the *O. Henry Memorial Collection* the same year. His courage and optimism glow warmly in his letters to his old friends the Herman Millers. In May of 1943 he is busy and active in his own affairs and anxious to help Miller get started as a writer. He is seeing a little better, he says, and is drawing with the aid of a special Zeiss lamp. He is getting together a book of drawings *(Men, Women and Dogs)* and he is also getting his children's story, *Many Moons*, ready for publication.[8] In June of 1943 he takes pleasure in calling attention to the success of "The Catbird Seat" and "The Cane in the Corridor." His nerves are better, he says, but he is "not very productive right now." He is trying to do a play about *The New Yorker*, he says. He talked about this project for the rest of his life, but he never completed it.[9]

The extent of his psychological recovery can be seen in the letters he wrote his friends after he had undergone an emergency appendectomy in Hot Springs, Virginia, in December of 1944. "At fifty—yesterday—I feel that I have just begun to write. I spit on the grave of my awful forties," he said, and he urged Herman Miller to take heart and begin to write.[10] He took an active interest in Miller's efforts to get started as a writer, not only because he was an old friend and a man of talent, but partly because he was middle-aged. John McNulty did not begin until he was forty-eight, he reminded Miller in a subsequent letter. "It is a good age to get going seriously. The older the American male is, the better, say I, who am just

[8] May 28, 1943 (Thurber Collection).
[9] June 26, 1943 (Thurber Collection).
[10] December 9, 1944 (Thurber Collection).

beginning." [11] Age had always been a phobia with Thurber, and he played on the subject with melancholy relish throughout his life. He adopted the fictional role of the middle-aged man when he was still in his thirties, and in his letters and conversation one of his favorite veins was what might be called the comedy of debility. Writing to his friend John Parker, in 1939, he said, "Your letter found me in the midst of death, illness, funerals, loss of sight, diminishing sex desire, hyperthyroidism, etc., also a hundred thousand things to do to keep my baby in shootin dice and drinkin liquor." [12]

After his blindness and breakdown, however, his attitude changed. In an interview with Harvey Breit he said, "When I was 30, I felt that the next day I was going to be 40. When I was 40, I felt that the next day I was going to be 50. Now it is different. Now I think: I have five long years to 60. . . . Now I have got over my middle age. I have gone past it into something better." [13] He began to take pride in his durability: lying in the hospital in Hot Springs, after his appendectomy and peritonitis, he boasted of his remarkable recovery in a letter to the Sayres and McNultys.

> When I got onto the operating table I told the docs I was in fine shape. When they whisked off the hospital shirt, they must have wondered what it's like when I'm in bad shape. I was picked for a "breakdown" of the incision and 2 weeks more in bed, but the chief said my recuperation was "remarkable." He ought to see Mama and Robert and Uncle Jake who lost 9/10 of his insides and sold pamphlets about it for 35 years.
>
> I told Dr. Emmett that my great-grandfather could lift a horse, and he said, "The effect of those hypos will wear off in a few days now." [14]

By 1949 he could speak of his affliction cheerfully and philosophically. He told Harvey Breit with understandable pride that he had written more than forty pieces in the last two years ("A hell of a lot more than I'd written in the five years before that"). He had learned a whole new method of composition, a blend of dictation and writing in longhand, he said. Relying on his unusual memory, he was able to get about five hundred to fifteen hundred words in his head before he started writing; then he either wrote it in longhand (getting about twenty words to a page) or dictated it to a secretary. For a time, he liked to write out the narrative and descriptive

[11] March 10, 1945 (Thurber Collection).
[12] April 29, 1939 (Thurber Collection).
[13] Interview with Harvey Breit, New York Times Magazine, December 4, 1949.
[14] Undated letter.

passages and to dictate the dialogue.[15] In later years, as he became more adept, he learned to compose almost entirely by dictation. "I still write —occasionally—in the proper sense of the word—using black crayon on yellow paper," he said to Plimpton and Steele in 1955. "My usual method, though, is to spend the mornings turning the text over in my mind. Then in the afternoon, between two and five, I call in a secretary and dictate to her. I can do about two thousand words. It took me about ten years to learn." [16]

His accommodation to blindness was remarkable in every way. As time went on, he could even point out that there were compensations for the blind writer. Alistair Cooke asked him in his interview of 1956 if blindness were not a great handicap to his contact with life and his imagination as a writer. Thurber said no, because "the imagination doesn't go blind." Besides, he said, "A blind writer does not have the distraction of the writer who can see. I can sit in a room and I don't look out the window; I don't become distracted by flying birds or the breeze or a pretty girl walking by. Of course I can still *hear* a pretty girl." As he put it on another occasion, "When I write now . . . I am not handicapped by vision." [17] He took an understandable pride in having met this personal and professional challenge, and there is a tough Midwestern Puritan belief in the positive value of hardship and deprivation just below the surface humor of his remark to Frank Gibney of *Newsweek*, in 1956: "I have got out twelve books since my fifth eye operation in 1941. During those fifteen years I had cataract, glaucoma, sympathetic ophthalmia, two pneumonias, ruptured appendix, peritonitis, and toxic thyroid. What a writer needs is handicaps." [18]

He learned to handle himself socially with grace and ease. Interviewers nearly always remarked on the fact that he did not move with the cautious uncertainty of most blind people, but that, with his wife Helen on his arm, he stepped forward boldly, as though he knew where he was going. When he talked to a person, he looked right at him as though he could see, and he seldom missed an ash-tray or upset a highball glass.

He liked to talk to people about his blindness. "When someone doesn't bring up the subject I usually do. . . . When you're blind you naturally take a great interest in eyes," he said in an interview with Eddy Gilmore in 1958.[19] In a letter of encouragement to his friend Elmer Davis, who

[15] Interview with Harvey Breit, *New York Times Magazine*, December 4, 1949.
[16] Interview with Plimpton and Steele, *Writers at Work*, p. 96.
[17] Interview with Alistair Cooke, *Atlantic*, CXCVIII (August, 1956).
[18] Letter to Gibney, October 31, 1956.
[19] "Call Me Jim," A.P. interview in London, reprinted in the Columbus *Dispatch*, August 3, 1958.

was seriously ill, he described his own affliction. It wasn't really so bad, he said, because it had come upon him gradually, and because, much to his astonishment, he had discovered that total blindness is not darkness but light: "The totally blind live in a soft light, without shadow or figures or landscape, but light nonetheless. . . . It didn't bother me at all, because of its slow approach and because I like light." [20] Sometimes he joked about it. In his conversation with Harvey Breit, he said that he had a theory about Bernadette of Lourdes and her vision of the Virgin. Blind people see spots before their eyes called phosphenes, and these spots assume definite shapes. "I have a bright blue shape these days," he said. "At one time my phosphenes used to take the definite shape of the face of Herbert Hoover. Of course, it wouldn't make history."

He was particularly fascinated by the medical aspects of his blindness. All his life he had been interested in the world of ailments, symptoms, doctors and doctor-talk, and his own misfortune made this subject doubly fascinating to him. Peter De Vries recalls that Thurber's mind was full of bits and pieces of medical lore, particularly about the eye. At parties he would give impromptu lectures on such topics as the suprising toughness of the eye ("It's the toughest thing in the body") or the odd fact that the eye is the one part of the body that is the same size at birth as in maturity. ("That's why all babies are beautiful.") He found it oddly satisfying that his case had baffled the best ophthalmologists in the country. He liked to describe the exact nature of his condition and to recapitulate the efforts of the doctors to account for it. Writing to Edmund Wilson in 1959 about ghosts, miracles, and the inexplicable, he recalled that Dr. Gordon Bruce had told him in 1938 that it was a miracle that he had been seeing at all. "According to him, there have been 30,000 recorded cases like mine, and only three of us did not go stone blind," he said. Dr. Bruce could not explain it. " 'God couldn't have wanted you to draw, could he?' " he asked Thurber.[21] It doubtless helped him to bear the loss of sight to know that his case was one for the medical history books, and that he had had almost forty years of vision to which—according to all medical knowledge—he was never really entitled.

Thurber made a remarkable adjustment to his affliction, but his blindness had a profound effect on his work, nevertheless. The immediate impact of this dramatic change in his whole relation to the world was to drive him inward into the world of fantasy and backward into the world of childhood imagination. It is no accident that he begins to write his fairy tales in the period just after the painful series of eye operations which cut him off from

[20] May 18, 1956.
[21] Letter to Edmund Wilson, May 25, 1959.

everyday life and forced him into seclusion. The fairy tales are in part an escape from an uncomfortable and threatening present, and in part a disguise for a good deal of introspection and self-examination. Like the fable, the fairy story allows the author to confess or to preach without seeming to do so, and in *Many Moons* (1943), *The Great Quillow* (1944), *The White Deer* (1945), *The Thirteen Clocks* (1950) and *The Wonderful O* (1957) Thurber is talking about himself and affirming certain values that had come to have a new importance to him.

All the fairy tales tell the same story: as each one opens, a sickness, an evil or an insoluble problem lies like a blight upon the scene. In *Many Moons* the little Princess lies ill of "a surfeit of raspberry tarts," in *The Great Quillow* the giant Hunder threatens to destroy the village, in *The White Deer* no one knows whether the beautiful young girl so strenuously wooed by King Clode's three sons is really a princess or a deer, in *The Thirteen Clocks* the cold Duke has driven life, love and warmth from his domain, and in *The Wonderful O* the pirate Black takes over the island, banishes the letter "O" and with it all the good things with "o" in them, like *cellos, houses, hope,* and *love.*

In each tale, the royal councillors, the lawyers, the scientists, the men of affairs fail to cope with the problem. In *Many Moons* the Princess will get well only if she is given the moon. The King calls in the Lord High Chamberlain, the Royal Wizard and the Royal Mathematician, but he gets nothing but pretentious evasion. " 'Now let me see,' " says the Royal Mathematician. " 'I have figured out for you the distance between the horns of a dilemma, night and day, and A and Z. I have computed how far is Up, how long it takes to get Away, and what becomes of Gone. I have discovered the length of the sea serpent, the price of the priceless, and the square of the hippopotamus.' " But as for getting the moon, that is quite impossible. King Clode, in *The White Deer,* runs into the same problem. Neither the Royal Recorder nor the Royal Physician is any help. The town council's plans for dealing with the giant in *The Great Quillow* are both unimaginative and impractical, and the professional men in *The Wonderful O* prove to be timid and ineffectual. In every case, the kinds of men most esteemed by the world turn out to be inadequate.

And who is it who breaks the spell, wards off the evil and renews life? The court jester in *Many Moons,* the little toymaker in *The Great Quillow,* the poetical son in *The White Deer,* the minstrel-prince in *The Thirteen Clocks,* the poet in *The Wonderful O.* In short, the man of imagination and love is the only true savior.[22]

[22] Richard Tobias points out this pattern in his excellent discussion of the fairy tales in chapter 7 of *The Art of James Thurber.*

The fairy tales are thus in the mainstream of nineteenth-century Romanticism, the cultural movement which shaped so many of Thurber's literary and personal values. They all celebrate the pursuit of the ideal, the superiority of the artistic imagination over the practical intellect, and the redeeming power of love. Coleridge and Shelley would have felt at home in them. These romantic values were of special importance to Thurber in the difficult period when his future as a man and as an artist was very much in doubt. In the fairy tales, Thurber is not only creating a delightful fantasy world for children and adults who have not forgotten how to dream, but he is also reassuring himself that the artistic talent and the grace of love can triumph over any disaster. He identifies—sometimes strikingly—with the poet figure in each of the tales. Like the hero in the old folk tales, the poet in Thurber's stories is taken lightly by the world—he is the court jester, the third son, the little toymaker, the wandering minstrel—but only he has the power to save. Here, in a more sophisticated form, is the fantasy of the Unpromising Hero which first appeared in Thurber's work in his Eighth Grade Prophecy at the Douglas School in Columbus.

The full significance of the fairy tales is best seen in *The White Deer* (1945) and *The Thirteen Clocks* (1950). In *The White Deer* King Clode is a bluff, irascible but good-hearted ruler with three sons. The older two, Thag and Gallow (the names seem deliberately ugly), share their father's passion for hunting and the active life; the younger son, Jorn, is a poet and a servant of love. While the King and Thag and Gallow drink and sleep and roughhouse, Jorn sings "that love, not might, would untie the magic knot." Jorn is sensitive; the others see only the surface of things. The King tells his sons the story of their mother's early death:

"Perhaps she died of a fall," said Thag.
"Perhaps she died of a surfeit," said Gallow.
"Perhaps she died of a look," said Jorn.

The King hurls a tankard at Jorn for his typically odd remark, and Jorn catches it in mid-air.

The parallels here to Thurber's own family background are suggestive. He was one of three sons, and although he was in fact the middle one, his childhood accident, which forced upon him the role of observer, made him feel like the traditional third son of the folk tales. His brothers were active in the normal way of boys (Robert was an outstanding baseball player at East High), and Thurber fiercely compensated by developing his talent for humor, for writing, and for games which required precision and dexterity, like pitching horseshoes or tossing cards into a hat. In the folk tales, it is to the rejected and the misfit that magic is given: to Thurber it was the magic of the Word, the deftness of the Hand, and the Eye that saw beneath the surface.

Many of the details of the story reflect Thurber's personal concerns: the figure of Tocko, the Royal Clockmaker, for example, is obviously a projection of his sense of himself as a blind man. Formerly, Tocko was the Royal Astronomer, but when he got so old that he could not see the planets very well and began to report that everything was going out, he became the Clockmaker. He makes sundials, which he sets in the shade, and on them he carves gloomy legends, like "After this brief light, the unending dark," "It is darker than you think," and "This little light and then the night." The theme of time runs strongly throughout all of Thurber's work, but after his blindness it is more insistent than ever. Sometimes it is felt as the destroyer, sometimes it is the symbol of life. In *The White Deer* it is associated with blindness and death.

The White Deer is a story of quest and search. King Clode and his sons bring a white deer to bay, and it suddenly turns into a beautiful dark princess. There is the mystery of her identity—is she a deer turned maiden, or a maiden turned deer and now a maiden again? She has no memory of her previous existence and can tell them nothing. The three sons woo her, and she sets a task for each of them. Prince Thag is sent to kill the Blue Boar of Thedon Grove in the Forest of Jeopardy and to bring back its golden tusks; Prince Gallow is to kill the Seven-Headed Dragon of Dragore and bring back the Sacred Sword of Loralow; the task set Prince Jorn seems insultingly easy—to vanquish the Mok-Mok (a figure made of clay and sandalwood, a sort of glorified scarecrow) and bring back a thousand cherries from the Orchard of Chardor.

The dangers facing Thag and Gallow turn out to be fraudulent, and the apparently easy mission of Jorn to be a real test of wit and nerve. He has to face the Black Knight, "the tallest and strongest Black Knight that the young Prince had ever seen." He is frightened, but he does battle and conquers his awesome opponent, who then turns out to be a little old man wearing a huge suit of armor. When Jorn cries out despairingly that he has been cheated, the Black Knight says, " 'You fought the fearful thing I seemed to be, and that's the proof and test of valor. . . . When all is dark within the house, who knows the monster from the mouse?' " When Jorn asks, " 'What's there to trust?' " the knight says, " 'Ah, trust your heart . . . trust love.' "

Valor and trust in love break the spell binding the Princess and win for her Jorn.

"I knew her," said the King, "by the manner of her speech and the carriage of her head."

"I knew her," said the Royal Recorder, "by the smallness of her foot and the slimness of her ankle."

"I knew her," said Tocko, "by the highness of her forehead and the brightness of her eye."

"I knew her by the singing in my heart," said Jorn.

This story of the ordeal of the sensitive third son and of the courage, fidelity and insight which help him triumph over the deceptions and confusions of life indirectly expresses many of Thurber's feelings about his own very recent personal struggle. In *The Thirteen Clocks*, five years later, Thurber takes a more detached and self-critical look at himself. Here, he identifies not only with the wandering minstrel-prince, the seeker after love, but with the cold-hearted Duke, who has rejected life and human warmth. The Duke wears a velvet patch over one eye (he had lost the eye in a childhood accident), he is always cold, he wears gloves (lacking the human touch), and he is sadistic ("His nights were spent in evil dreams and his days were given to wicked schemes"). He holds the Princess (Love) a prisoner, and as a result of some unspecified trauma, he has stopped all the clocks in the castle. He is afraid of Now because it is alive; he prefers Then because it is dead. Throughout the tale, clocks and time represent life lived; the Duke is afraid of it and tries to deny it. The figure of the Duke can be seen as the embodiment of a set of possibilities within himself which Thurber both feared and wanted to exorcise, and the Prince, the brave minstrel and lover, as representing the nobler qualities he aspired to.

Like *The White Deer*, *The Thirteen Clocks* is the story of a quest. The Duke sets the Prince an impossible task—to bring back a thousand jewels within ninety-nine hours. With the aid of the Golux, a somewhat absent-minded wizard, but a man of magic and imagination nevertheless, and guided by a rose (the symbol of love), the Prince tracks down Hagga, the old woman who weeps jewels instead of tears. The jewels of laughter last only a fortnight, but the jewels of sorrow last forever. After some fruitless efforts, Hagga weeps jewels of laughter for them, and they give these illusory valuables to the Duke. The warm hand of the Princess starts the clocks, and the iron spell is lifted through the magic of love. At the end, the Duke is left bathing his hands in the jewels, and the Prince and Princess start off for Yarrow, the Prince's homeland. The Golux bids them farewell and says, " 'Remember laughter. You'll need it even in the blessed isles of Ever After.' "

The Thirteen Clocks is another tale of the triumph of imagination and love, and it is much more equivocal than *The White Deer*. It is shadowed throughout by the awareness that pain and evil are inescapable, and that even our most cherished values—like laughter—may be only illusions after all. Thurber seems to be saying that life is made up of both the tears of laughter and the tears of sorrow, but like Melville's Ishmael, for whom *Ecclesiastes* was the truest of all books, he feels that the tears of sorrow are more "real."

The fairy tales are serious—Thurber was always most serious when he was being most fanciful—but they are also delightful works of art, full of romantic beauty and playful humor. In these tales the fantasy side of Thurber's imagination creates a never-never land of kings and princesses, of castles, giants, and magicians, of strange enchantments and dangerous journeys, where nothing is quite the way it is in real life, and the improbable and the impossible occur as a matter of course. King Clode and his sons hunt the beautiful white deer through a dream-like artificial landscape— "through the green forest . . . past the barking tree, across the musical mud, in and out of a flock of wingless birds . . . through a silver swamp and a bronze bog and a golden glade"—and they encounter wizards, spells, and strange metamorphoses.

If the warp of the fairy tales is the world of romance, the woof is the substance of everyday comic reality. King Clode inhabits a world of magic, but his nature is earthy and familiar. When the Royal Wizard suddenly appears in a cloud of smoke, the King complains.

> "I thought I told you not to appear in a cloud of smoke any more," growled the King. "The smell of powder spoils the fragrance of the wine. I told you that."
> "I forgot," said the Wizard.
> "Just come in the room like anybody else," said the King.
> "Yes, Sire," said the Wizard, and he began to juggle seven little crescent moons made of gold and silver.

King Clode is one of those people to whom life is an unending series of small irritations and exasperations. He comes, in fact, from Harold Ross, the testy editor of *The New Yorker*, as Thurber acknowledged in *The Years with Ross*. King Clode, like Ross, is good-hearted but short of fuse, and he goes through life feeling constantly harassed. When the Royal Astronomer (who wears rose-colored glasses) reports that a huge pink comet has just missed the earth, King Clode complains, " 'They aim these things at me. . . . Everything is aimed at me.' " One of Ross's favorite expressions at the *New Yorker* office was " 'Nobody ever tells me what anything is.' " The King's encounter with the Royal Recorder brings out his impatience of spirit in its purest form. The Recorder is pedantic, legalistic, and verbose; the King cannot abide all this flummery. " 'Babble, babble, babble,' " says the King. " 'Blither, blither, blither. I have no time for sophistries and riddles.' "

The style of the fairy tales is markedly different from that of Thurber's fiction and journalism. It is highly wrought and ornamental, full of carefully balanced constructions, internal rhymes, alliteration, assonance, and other poetic devices. It is a style that calls attention to itself, and it is a style addressed to the ear rather than the eye: "Twenty hoofs thundered hotly through a haunted hollow of spectral sycamores hung with lighted lanterns and past a turquoise tarn and along an avenue of asphodel that turned and twisted down a dark descent which led at last to a pale and perilous plain." It is part poetry, part prose. Often the prose slides accidentally, as it were, into the regular patterns of verse, like this: "He bowed and sighed and bowed again and watched the Princess cross the grass like summer rain and vanish through a portal." Little poems and scraps of verse appear frequently in the text. At the close of *The White Deer* Tocko recites a romantic couplet for Prince Jorn and his newly won bride:

> "As slow as Time, as long as love:
> The rose, the fountain, and the dove."

The general effect of this heightened language is to deepen the atmosphere of strangeness and romance in the tales, to give them an air of far away and long ago. But the language of the fairy tales is also an effective vehicle of comedy. Often the romantic atmosphere of the fairy-tale world is shattered by the intrusion of vigorous colloquial speech. In *The Thirteen Clocks* the villagers are warning the minstrel-prince against the Duke: " 'He will slit you from your guggle to your zatch,' " says one: " 'He breaks up minstrels in his soup, like crackers,' " says another. Much of the comedy of the fairy tales—and of *The White Deer* and *The Thirteen Clocks* in particular—is the comedy of word-play. Thurber had always loved verbal games and the humor of word-garbling, but with the exception of "The Black Magic of Barney Haller" and "What Do You Mean It *Was* Brillig?" he had never before played so fancifully with language. Prince Thag encounters a roundish balding man in the crotch of a tree in the enchanted forest and engages in this tongue-twisting exchange:

"I wonder what type it is?" said Prince Thag.

"It's sick thirsty," said the man, "or half-past hate or a quarter to fight. I'm in no moon for questions."

"You're in no *mood,*" said Thag.

"First he accosts me, then he tells me what I'm not in," said the man. "I crutch in the crouch of this tree to avoid troublemakers like you, riding on their nagamuffins."

Thag wants to get things straight:

"You crouch in a crotch, but you have no crutch," said Thag.

The man burst into tears. "That's right," he bawled, "laugh at a man because he has no crutch." He shook his fist at Thag and cried, "A plague on both your horses." Four redbirds in a tangle bush sang "verti verti verti go . . ."

It is in *The White Deer* that Thurber began to indulge his taste for small half-hidden verbal jokes, like spelling names backward, and working in unacknowledged scraps of popular songs or bits of familiar poetry. Prince Gallow asks the way to the Seven-Headed Dragon of Dragore, and a man tells him that it is " 'Down and down, round and round, through the Moaning Grove of Artanis.' " (References to Frank Sinatra occur a number of times in Thurber's later work.) The man goes on: " 'fear not the roaring of the dreadful Tarcomed, nor yet the wuffing-puffing of the surly Nacilbuper, but ride straight on.' " And then what, asks the Prince. " 'Turn to the right and follow a little white light,' " says the man.

Writing *The White Deer* was a release for Thurber—"Most fun I ever had," he said to the Millers.[23] White was enthusiastic about it, and called it "Exhibit A in the strange case of a writer's switch from eye work to ear work. I can't believe that anybody could make such a switch and live. The King is a magnificently funny character, I think, and ought to last forever. . . ." [24] He was right in calling this fairy tale a turning point in Thurber's artistic method. As Thurber adjusted to his blindness, he came to live in a world where words were the primary reality. In the last of his fairy tales, *The Wonderful O* (1957), language is not only the medium but the subject itself. The tale is nothing more than an elaborate demonstration of what would happen if the letter "O" were banned from the language. " 'We shall have mantels but no clocks, shelves without crocks, keys without locks, walls without doors, rugs without floors,' " says one character.

23 Letter to the Millers, December 9, 1944 (Thurber Collection).
24 Undated letter from White to Thurber, probably December, 1945 (EBWP).

" 'We can't tell rot from root, or owed from wed,' " says another. In this shift from a visual to a verbal world, Thurber's experience closely parallels that of Joyce, whose blindness turned him from the richly observed physical world of *Ulysses* to the fantasy and word-play of *Finnegans Wake*. And—to stretch the parallel a little—one cannot help thinking of the effect of Milton's blindness on the style of *Paradise Lost*.

14

Recovery and
The Beast in Me

I N   T H E   S P R I N G   O F   1 9 4 3, Harper & Brothers suggested that
Thurber and White revise *Is Sex Necessary?* Thurber was unenthusias-
tic. He observed rather wearily to White that in 1929 he was thirty-four
years old and able to see; now, he was neither so light-hearted nor so
unaware of the state of the world as he was then.[1] At the same time, he
kept after White to collaborate with him on the *New Yorker* play, even
though White had bowed out early, saying, "The only way you and I could
write a play would be the way we wrote Is Sex Necessary? which was to
get thinking about the same thing in the same way and then each withdraw
into our separate orbits and write it. Only in the case of a play, you would
probably have to do the whole thing because I can't seem to think of
anything for anybody to do on the stage." [2] Thurber was undaunted, and
in May of 1943 he wrote that he had finished the first act and that it was
very funny. The second act would be even funnier, he said; all the improbable things that ever happened at *The New Yorker* would be in it. It would
end, he said, with Ross holding a Scotty with a red rubber bib while

[1] Letter to White, March 20, 1943 (EBWP). Eventually White did a new introduction,
and the book was reissued in 1949. It is still in print and has been translated into more than
eight languages.
[2] Letter to Thurber, September 1, 1942 (EBWP).

pneumatic drills hammered offstage, and crying out, "God, how I pity me!" [3]

His letters to White in 1943–44 are warm and affectionate, and as full of wit, energy, and ironic observation of the human scene as ever. He wanted to dedicate Men, Women and Dogs to White, who had picked his doodles up off the floor and forced them down a few people's throats, he said.[4] It was either accept the dedication or write the introduction, or both. White took the dedication. The New Yorker was constantly on his mind, and in nearly every letter he passed on an anecdote or an oddity or an idea for a department. He was always ready to help talented young writers get started, and in 1943 he asked the aid of the Whites in getting The New Yorker to publish Mary Mian's delightful sketches of domestic life in France. Her talent was a new and rare thing and ought to be encouraged and appreciated, he said.[5] The melancholy strain in his temperament shows itself in occasional brooding comments on the passing of time and our common mortality. In one letter he listed all the people they knew who had died in the past six years. Their generation was dropping off like flies, he concluded gloomily.[6] On the other hand, he always made light of his own misfortune: when White complimented him on his bravery, he passed it off as a joke. He couldn't very well call his own bravery wonderful, he said, because everyone would think of him as proud-ass Thurber, the guy who calls himself Whattaman.[7]

When he got lobar pneumonia in September of 1944, he made a characteristically entertaining story out of it when he wrote to White. He was stricken at the baptism of his god-daughter Dinah Jane Williams (the daughter of their old friends Ronald and Jane Williams, of Bermuda) at the Sampson Naval Training Station. He reported that the Navy doctors who knocked out his 105 degree fever with sulfa said that it was the first time on record that a godfather failed to rally after a baptism. He then discussed his symptoms in detail, and talked about sulfa and penicillin. He had one chill violent enough to rattle the plates in the rack downstairs, he reported, but added reassuringly that pneumonia was now nothing more than a nuisance. Sulfa was no longer toxic, he went on, and no one pees pink any more. As for him, he peed amber through the whole ordeal. In the age of wonder-drugs, we will all live to be a hundred and thirty. The

[3] Letter to White, May 15, 1943 (EBWP).
[4] Letter to White, June 12, 1943 (EBWP).
[5] Letter to White, June 9, 1943 (EBWP).
[6] Letter to White, May 15, 1943 (EBWP).
[7] Letter to White, June 9, 1943 (EBWP).

only thing to worry about, he said, is the Mok-Mok, a weapon about to be invented for World War III. He went on to develop one of his frightening apocalyptic fantasies, outlining the shape of things to come with uncanny accuracy. Four Mok-Moks will blow up the U.S., he prophesied, and warned White to look out for KM 10, the terrible ZU58, and the Zo-Zo-40, which makes no sound as it flies. To be killed in Maine by something which explodes in Michigan is an unsettling prospect, he concluded.[8]

An essay in *Harper's* by Huxley, classifying the various kinds of human physique, provided him with the perfect opportunity to tease White about his hypochondria. According to Huxley's classification, Thurber says, White is the type to last—a cerebretonic ectomorph, a man of mighty sexual potential, a man whose hair will not fall out, and a man who will endure. In spite of dizzy spells and buzzings in the head, he will outlast the Lou Gehrigs, the Christy Mathewsons, the Young Striblings, the Red Granges, the Joel Sayres, and the Bob Coateses. Pale he may be, and unsteady, but he will live to carry the coffin of many a mesomorph and endomorph, says Thurber, concluding his analysis with a hearty exhortation to cheer up.[9]

In the spring of 1944 he met Peter De Vries, whose talent so impressed him that he made it his personal mission to get the younger man a position on *The New Yorker*. De Vries was the editor of *Poetry* and a Thurber admirer. In the December, 1943, issue of the magazine, he had published a perceptive critical essay on Thurber (the first serious discussion of Thurber in the United States) entitled "James Thurber: The Comic Prufrock," in which he showed the kinship between Thurber's apprehensive protagonists and T. S. Eliot's famous archetype of modern man. Thurber wrote an appreciative letter to De Vries, in the course of which he reported with pardonable pride that Eliot had praised *My Life and Hard Times*, particularly the self-portrait in the Preface.[10] In the spring of 1944 De Vries asked Thurber to give a talk in The Modern Arts Lecture Series in Chicago to help out *Poetry*. Thurber rather nervously agreed. Although he was a notable living-room entertainer, the prospect of a formal public lecture filled him with misgivings. "Last night I got to fussing so profoundly about my coming ordeal that I developed a sharp pain in my stomach. Sensing that I was going around in a panicky circle, Helen woke up in the middle of the night, got pencil and paper, and wrote down some ideas for me. Her notes, together with your letter and some thoughts of my own

[8] Letter to White, September 30–October 5, 1943 (EBWP).
[9] Letter to White, undated, 1944 (EBWP).
[10] Letter to De Vries, November 19, 1943.

have helped me to work out a kind of plan which I think will get me through this," he wrote De Vries shortly before he was to go to Chicago. He would talk for a few minutes to start with, he said, then he would answer questions and tell some anecdotes about himself and *The New Yorker*. "I will certainly want you up there on the platform beside me," he wrote. He hoped that there would be a lectern "to kind of hide behind and lean on since this would give me added confidence and help me to stand up for an hour." [11]

To make sure that the questions would lead to his anecdotal strengths, he and De Vries cooked up a number beforehand (sample: "Is it true that your little daughter really does the drawings for you?"), and the day before the talk, in Chicago, De Vries put them on slips of paper of different sizes and colors in an elaborate effort to make it seem as though they had come from the audience. They need not have taken all that trouble, De Vries recalls, because once Thurber faced the audience, his nervousness disappeared, and "with the first question he took the bit between his teeth and galloped off on as fine a formal lecture as the audience had ever heard, and they had heard Frank Lloyd Wright, Robert Penn Warren and Rudolph Ganz." [12] He talked about his blindness, his drawings and their "accidental" origins, how he got started on *The New Yorker*, his stint with the Paris and Nice editions of the Chicago *Tribune*, and ended up with the definition of humor he had given in Max Eastman's *Enjoyment of Laughter*.

De Vries recalls that after a few minutes he retreated backstage and dumped the carefully prepared questions into the wastebasket, realizing that he was in the presence of "one of the great monologists of our time." Thurber was "a story teller, mimic, fantasist, realist, running commentator and mine of information on every subject under the sun. . . . He never to my knowledge mounted a public platform again, but he occupied one just long enough to show that he might have borne comparison with Mark Twain on that score too, had he cared to add it to his list of accomplishments," he added. [13] The occasion must have been a memorable one, since De Vries provided an introduction so full of wit and outrageous puns (he described Thurber as an artist who "hits the male on the head") that many in the audience thought that he was Thurber. [14]

[11] Letter to De Vries, April 4, 1944.

[12] Peter De Vries, "Introduction," *Lanterns and Lances* (New York: Time Reading Program Special Edition, 1962), pp. xvi–xvii.

[13] Ibid.

[14] Thurber's talk and De Vries's introduction were reported in the Chicago *Tribune*, April 16, 1944; and in the Chicago *Sun*, April 16, 1944.

The two men hit it off from the beginning, and after he got back to New York, Thurber asked De Vries for some samples of his work, which he immediately showed to Ross, bypassing the various department editors. Ross was, as usual, suspicious: " 'I'll read it, but it won't be any good,' " he grumbled, but a half hour later he called Thurber in and exclaimed " 'Jesus Christ, it *is* good!' " and wanted to hire De Vries at once. Thurber then wrote the younger man a long avuncular letter, full of all sorts of advice: "put each art idea on a separate sheet with your name and address and mark it 'art idea.' . . . . Casuals, or fiction as they used to be called, should not go to Ross first—but to me or to Gus Lobrano, a tall, sweet guy you will like. . . . always keep carbon copies of everything you send in to compare with their edited copy." He hesitates over the question whether De Vries should take a full-time editorship or a part-time position on the magazine, the danger in the former being that Ross would decide he was "God, Donald Nelson and Barney Baruch all in one" and make him the new Miracle Man. A part-time job, on the other hand, would give him more freedom to do his own work. Whatever happens, he says encouragingly, he has unbounded confidence in De Vries's talent and success. Besides, he adds, he himself will be around "like a mother dog, to snap and snarl in your defense." [15] De Vries decided on a part-time position— which he still holds—and went on to make an outstanding career as a novelist and playwright. He and Thurber remained warm friends throughout the years, and in their letters they punned and played the word games which both of them enjoyed as a sort of mental gymnastics.

In 1943 Harper & Brothers offered another idea to Thurber: what would he think of getting together an anthology of his own work? He was skeptical at first, particularly of the title suggested by the publisher, "A Thurber Sampler." He had for some time been scornful of what he regarded as Harper's stodgy old-fashioned ways, and the term "sampler" epitomized everything he objected to. The title was pure Harper, he wrote to White, and he sketched out a little fantasy about the editors sitting around drinking madeira and winding their watches with little keys while they thought it up.[16] Thurber's impatience with Harper went back to 1939 and a series of frustrations in connection with *The Last Flower*. To begin with, the publishers had let *Life* run a double-page spread of the drawings (almost the whole book, he observed bitterly) for which *Life* offered Thurber the princely sum of $350.

In Thurber's view, the old firm was hopelessly genteel and naive about

15 Letter to De Vries, June 14, 1944.
16 Letter to White, June 9, 1943 (EBWP).

business matters. It was too bad that nice people like Harper were so bad at promoting books; they couldn't sell a drink to a thirsty man, he protested to White in a letter of 1939. Simon & Schuster, on the other hand, would probably sell a hundred thousand copies of his book. Harper's low-keyed advertising campaign infuriated him. The Harper ad rather cautiously described *The Last Flower* as "The Book That Captured a Hundred Over Night," and Thurber complained to his editor that placing this on the same page with extravagant boasts by other publishers was like saying that fifty people jammed Carnegie Hall to hear Gluck. As a result, the *Times* Book Review gave him only an unsigned review under Children's Books. You have to choose between publishers who know the best places to eat and those who know how to sell your books, he wrote to the Whites.[17] As for the projected anthology, 1943 was the wrong year, he said, since he was already coming out with *Many Moons* and *Men, Women and Dogs* (neither of them published by Harper).[18] Nevertheless, he kept thinking about the idea, and in 1944 he set to work on it.

The Thurber Carnival appeared in February of 1945 and turned out to be his greatest single artistic and financial success. Like a retrospective art show, this collection of Thurber's best work over a fifteen-year period demonstrated his stature and significance in a way that the separate *New Yorker* cartoons and casuals and the individual collections appearing over the years had never quite done. The reviewers were unanimous in pointing out, sometimes with an air of surprise, that Thurber was not simply a clever *New Yorker* writer, but a major comic artist. "The man, or at least his work, is here to stay," wrote Dan Norton in the New York *Times;* "We can no longer be content simply to laugh at what he produces; we must make a determined effort to understand him as man and artist." Thomas Sugrue, in the *Herald Tribune,* said that the *Carnival* showed that Thurber was a modern master, "a satirist and prophet, a Jeremiah in fool's cap, a mixture of laughing gas and deadly nightshade," and compared him to Ring Lardner as a great observer of the American social scene. *Time* saw the Thurber Male as a significant image of modern man, belonging with Joyce's Bloom and Mann's Hans Castorp, and the drawings as "a psychic distorting mirror" which reflects the reality locked in our sub-consciousness. E. B. White, reviewing the book for *PM,* spoke on the range and variety of Thurber's work, and especially of its fundamental humanity. "His characters and his ideas are developed with sympathy, with love, with compas-

[17] Undated letter to the Whites, fall, 1939 (EBWP).
[18] Letter to White, June 9, 1943 (EBWP). One sheet of this letter was mistakenly sent with a letter of June 12.

sion," he observed.[19] The *Carnival* was a Book-of-the-Month Club selection and it remained high on the best-seller lists for nearly a year.[20]

Thurber dedicated the book to Harold Ross, "with increasing admiration, wonder and affection." In the Preface he offered another of his half-comic, half-serious self-portraits: "James Thurber was born on a night of wild portent and high wind in the year 1894, at 147 Parsons Avenue, Columbus, Ohio. The house, which is still standing, bears no tablet or plaque of any description, and is never pointed out to visitors." The persona is that of the Preface to *My Life and Hard Times*—the writer as nervous middle-aged man. Now, at fifty, he "goes on as he always has, walking now a little more slowly, answering fewer letters, jumping at slighter sounds." The one change that the years have made is that Thurber no longer describes himself as the romantic Conradian wanderer, but as a Jamesian seeker for the ordered and the traditional. "In the past ten years he has moved restlessly from one Connecticut town to another, hunting for the Great Good Place, which he conceives to be an old Colonial house, surrounded by elms and maples, equipped with all modern conveniences, and overlooking a valley." As so often with Thurber, fiction reflected fact, and in 1945 he and Helen bought a house in West Cornwall.

The book included six new pieces, among them the two prize-winning stories, "The Cane in the Corridor" and "The Catbird Seat." Both are variations on standard Thurber themes: "The Catbird Seat" pits the mild little man against the aggressive and threatening woman and tells of his secret triumph; "The Cane in the Corridor" is one of those comedies of neurosis and veiled psychological warfare which Thurber perfected in *The Middle-Aged Man on the Flying Trapeze*. "The Cane in the Corridor" tells how Joe Fletcher gets even with George and Nancy Minturn for not having come to see him when he was in the hospital. The three are drinking brandy after dinner, and as the evening wears on, the edges of reality and fantasy become more and more blurred and the conversation becomes more and more bizarre. Fletcher plays on the guilty feelings of the Minturns with a wild and subtle inventiveness, and by the end of the story, he has won a sadistic victory over his friends.

It is a brilliant story, one of Thurber's best, and it represents a vein of humor about which neither he nor his admirers had much to say. Thurber

[19] Dan Norton, *New York Times Book Review*, February 4, 1945; Thomas Sugrue, New York *Herald Tribune* Book Review, February 4, 1945; "Books," *Time*, February 12, 1945; E. B. White, *PM*, February 4, 1945.
[20] Some measure of the financial success of *The Thurber Carnival* can be taken from the fact that in 1945 Thurber complained to the Whites that the government was trying to collect $74,000 in taxes from him.

spoke of fear, anxiety, humiliation, and melancholy as sources of humor, but he was curiously silent about aggression. The mild-mannered Mr. Martin plans to murder the awful Mrs. Ulgine Barrows in "The Catbird Seat," and Fletcher makes Minturn pay dearly for his dereliction of friendly duty. One of Thurber's most successful forms is the comedy of manners in which the traditional civilities begin to dissolve under the influence of alcohol and late hours, and the hidden antagonisms which are the truth of the situation rise to the surface. "Am Not I Your Rosalind?," "The Waters of the Moon," "The Interview," and "Midnight at Tim's Place" are all comedies of this kind; anything like a complete list would be a long one. The form was congenial to Thurber for many reasons, but the most important was that it was the perfect outlet for his own frustrations and resentments, the artistic transformation of those occasions on which he would attack his friends, throw drinks at the wall, and give vent to the dark wild self within. As a matter of biographical fact, the creative impulse for this story was Thurber's sense of injury over the fact that his friend Wolcott Gibbs did not come to see him when he was recovering from one of his many eye operations.

The success of the *Carnival* brought with it a multitude of new claims upon his time, as radio and film producers sought the rights to his work, and his already considerable correspondence swelled to barely manageable proportions. No matter how busy he was, however, he kept in constant touch with his family and friends in Columbus. He and Helen went back to visit his mother on her eightieth birthday. There was a big party at the Deshler-Wallick Hotel to honor the old lady, and it would have been even bigger, Thurber confessed to reporters, if his mother had had her way. "She was equal to it, but we weren't," he said. When reporters asked him if the party wouldn't keep his mother up too late, he laughed. Five years ago, he said, she had visited him and Helen in New York, and they had done the nightclubs until about 4:30 in the morning. A couple of hours later, he noticed a light under his mother's door, and he found her reading a detective magazine.[21]

He wrote the Millers regularly. He enjoyed Herman Miller's comment on their home state: "Come back to Ohio, where no news is practically the only good news." His brother Robert, the family historian, kept him pretty well posted on Columbus affairs, he said, especially "the flux of coaches at Ohio State." He reported on his health (as he did to all his friends) and he kept on urging Miller to write, reading his manuscripts and

[21] Columbus *Dispatch*, January 14, 1946.

offering suggestions. When Miller sent him the draft of a short story in the spring of 1945, Thurber replied, " 'The Winter of Curly's Shadow' is one of the most gratifying occurrences since the day Roosevelt first took office. I greet it with hallelujahs for it shows what I have known all along: the hand of a true writer. It is beautifully imagined and written and you must get at that typewriter all the time." [22]

The dominant subject of his letters to the Millers in 1946–48, however, is Henry James. Late in 1945 he began an ambitious parody of James, and he struggled with it for the next two years. It finally emerged as "The Beast in the Dingle," and was first published in Cyril Connolly's *Horizon*.[23] Herman Miller was a great Jamesian, and it was only natural that Thurber would turn to him for sympathy and encouragement on the James project. On January 22, 1946, he says that he is sending the third or fourth draft "of my pastiche, or whatever it is, on Henry James." He has been working on it night and day for four months, he says, but it still is not right. He also wants Miller's view of the possibility of adapting *The Ambassadors* to the stage. The next day he sent a long letter about this new project. He has been thinking about it for twenty years, he says. The novel has "most of the essential characters for a play," he insists, but the focus would have to be shifted from Strether's interpretation of what is going on to "the relationship between Chad Newsome, Madame de Vionnet and the girl who shows up from Woollet. . . . The subsidiary characters, such as the girl's relatives, Senator Waymarsh, little Bilham and a few others are perfect parts for comedy." The possibility of dramatizing James was never far from his mind, and he was enthusiastic about *The Heiress*, which, he said, "put a sharper point on *Washington Square* than the old master ever did, but it is not much of a distortion and the best play we have seen in some time."

A few months later he writes that he has abandoned "the incredible idea of making a play out of *The Ambassadors*.[24] The James piece is still giving him trouble—"I may be working on it when I die," he observes ruefully. His spirits were always mercurial, but they were particularly so during the period in which he was adjusting to his blindness. In March, he is in a good frame of mind: "I actually have a paunch, and weigh 163 after lunch. Aside from sweaty palms, cold feet, and a touch of nervous apprehension for a day or two as the result of fretting about my case history, the state of the world, and chiefly the illnesses of friends—almost all of whom are down—I

[22] Letter to Miller, March 10, 1945 (Thurber Collection).
[23] *Horizon*, XVIII (September, 1948).
[24] Letter to the Millers, March 7, 1946. (Thurber Collection).

am fine!" But in December he is frustrated and depressed. He feels like "one of those charred carbon sticks we used to pick up under street lamps in the days when all technics were still clumsy and life was fun." He has not been able to write "a god damn thing for months," he says, "which combined with a cold and gloomy view of man, makes me feel like an empty raspberry basket, frail, stained, and likely to be torn to pieces by a little child." [25]

Miller had not been in good health for a number of years, and in April of 1949 he died. Thurber's letter to his widow, Dorothy, is a warm and generous expression of what Miller's friendship had meant to him. Herman was "my oldest friend, and in so many ways my closest," he wrote. "There was no other man who knew me so well, and I took pride and comfort in his sensitive understanding." He spoke appreciatively of his friend's "good old Henry James awareness and his fascinated analyses of Joe and Esther Taylor, Billy Graves, Althea-and-me, and others. Helen delighted him like a Christmas gift, because he saw she was made to order for me—and a tough order that is." [26] A few months later he wrote to Dorothy that he wanted to dedicate his forthcoming book to Herman's memory, and *The Thurber Album* (1952) is dedicated "To Herman Allen Miller, October 25, 1896–April 20, 1949, whose friendship was an early and enduring inspiration."

In 1946–47 Thurber found himself involved in a painful comedy of misunderstanding and frustration with Samuel Goldwyn. Goldwyn had bought "The Secret Life of Walter Mitty" and "The Catbird Seat" in 1944, and he wanted to use "Mitty" as a vehicle for Danny Kaye. Expanding a very short story into a two-hour motion picture which would effectively show off Kaye's versatile talents required an almost total revision of Thurber's original story. Apparently convinced that the American public did not go to the movies to see the humdrum, Goldwyn and his writers substituted a wildly melodramatic plot for the scenes of everyday life in the story, completely washing out the ironic contrast between dream and reality which is the heart of Thurber's tale. In addition, there were substantial changes in the dream-sequences, and new scenes were added, many of them totally out of character. One in particular, in which Mitty imagines himself as Anatole of Paris—a scene introduced so that Kaye could do Sylvia Fine's clever song—outraged Thurber. No man dreams of being a milliner, he grumbled. [27]

[25] Letter to the Millers, December 4, 1946 (Thurber Collection).
[26] Letter to Dorothy Miller, April 21, 1949 (Thurber Collection).
[27] Morsberger, *James Thurber*, p. 152.

Thurber never saw the script until Goldwyn brought the already completed scenario to New York in December of 1945 and asked if he had any suggestions. Goldwyn assured Thurber that the screenplay was fine except for the last hundred pages, which he said were "too blood and thirsty." Thurber read the whole script, and was "horror and struck," he reported.[28] He and Ken Englund, one of the writers of the screenplay, saw eye to eye on the central problem, and they worked for ten frantic days in New York, trying to tone down the melodrama and bring the story closer to Thurber's original conception.

Meanwhile, Thurber fans had got wind of what was happening, and a small protest movement began to form, headed by Frank Sullivan, the humorist and friend of Thurber, who organized the "Walter Mitty Association." Ken Englund said that "threatening letters used to come in every morning from Thurber fans warning us not to touch a hair of Walter's head." [29] The New York *Times* reported on August 25, 1946, that sacrilege was being done, and Thurber was moved to write the *Times* on September 23 and explain that he was not responsible for the outrages. "I think we improved the script by tinkering with it, but there was never any question of my taking the thing over and writing it myself," he said. He added, "I think the picture which I tampered with here and there will be an interesting one, but I have no hope that the daily life of Walter Mitty as presented in the film will meet with the entire approval of the little group who make up the Walter Mitty Association. . . ." [30]

Life reviewed the film on August 4, 1947, emphasizing the changes which had been made in the story and reporting Thurber's unhappiness with the result (he is supposed to have said, after attending the opening, "Did anyone catch the name of that picture?"). Goldwyn, fearing the impact of Thurber's widely reported disapproval, wrote a nervous and defensive letter to *Life*. The letter, obviously composed by studio public-relations men, is a tissue of carefully selected quotations from Thurber's letters and memoranda designed to make it appear that Thurber was pleased with the screenplay and grateful for the opportunity to work with the Goldwyn organization.

Life invited Thurber to reply, and he did so, setting the record straight. Never once during the original writing of the scenario was he consulted, he said. He described the last-minute emergency treatment which he and

[28] "Two Communications: Goldwyn vs. Thurber," *Life*, August 4, 1947.
[29] Ken Englund, "A Scenarist Mumbles to Himself," New York *Times* Theater Section, August 10, 1947.
[30] "Mr. Thurber Comments," New York *Times* Theater Section, September 23, 1946.

Englund had tried to give the play, and pointed out rather bitterly that in the final script, "almost everything that I had written, suggested and fought for was dropped." His new dream-scenes were cut, the RAF sequence was ruined by Goldwyn's insistence that Danny Kaye do one of his famous scat songs instead of the more appropriate "Molly Malone," which Thurber, Englund and others wanted, and Goldwyn worked in "a bathing girl incident which will haunt me all the days of my life." He closed his letter with a generous salute to "the gifted but overwhelmed Ken Englund, the skillful Everett Freeman, long since in the doghouse for a brave, face-to-face appraisal of the Goldwyn sense of humor, and the sensitive but frustrated director, Norman McLeod." He added, "Sorry, Walter, sorry for everything." [31]

The film was, of course, not all that bad. It had Danny Kaye in it, and as many reviewers pointed out, his presence made up for many of the inadequacies of the screenplay. Some of the individual dream-sequences were excellent comedy, and for an audience not previously devoted to Thurber, the whole enterprise would have been highly diverting. The uproar over the transformation simply shows to what an extent Thurber's tale had become a part of popular culture, and hence as untouchable as any of our other myths.

Thurber was particularly sensitive over the "Mitty" issue because at the same time, he was having trouble making a film adaptation of "The Catbird Seat." When he sold the story to Goldwyn for $30,000, he also accepted a $10,000 advance to do the scenario. According to the agreement, he was to keep the $10,000 if he turned in 15,000 words by a certain date. As the time approached, he began to have his doubts. He had the 15,000 words, but they did not suit him. He wrote the Millers in March of 1946 that he was diving "into the preposterous adventure of a movie treatment for Goldwyn—a Baudelairian experience among the dark flowers." [32] He struggled with the story for months and then gave it up as a bad job. He returned the $10,000 advance and destroyed the manuscript of the screenplay. [33] One of the great frustrations of his life was his inability to repeat the success of *The Male Animal*. For all his passion for the theater, his gifts as an actor and his wonderful ear for dialogue, he was never able to construct a play. With *The Male Animal* he had the help of Elliott Nugent, and *A Thurber Carnival* was a revue, an anthology of separate pieces which presented few structural problems. Eventually, in 1959, a British company

[31] "Two Communications," *Life*, August 4, 1947.
[32] Letter to the Millers, March 10, 1946 (Thurber Collection).
[33] Thurber described his problems in a letter to Paul Nathan, "Books into Films," *Publishers' Weekly*, CLVI (October 8, 1949), 1671.

made an excellent film of "The Catbird Seat, entitled *The Battle of the Sexes*. Monja Danischewsky did the screenplay, and Peter Sellers, Robert Morley and Constance Cummings played the leading roles.

In the post-war years Thurber became increasingly concerned over the quality of American life, which seemed to him to be deteriorating in every respect. In the era of the Bomb and the Cold War, the country seemed to have lost its bearings and to be buffeted every which way by demagoguery and unreason. In addition, he deplored the general change in manners and morals which followed the war. Elliott Nugent felt the same way. Looking back, Nugent said to an alumni group in Columbus: "the two great flashes over Japan did something to the eyesight and the nerves and spirit of the more civilized, sensitive, thoughtful and humorous people . . . and this change was reflected in literature, drama, music, art and politics." He saw Thurber and himself as casualties, or at least symbols, of that tense period in history.

> By 1949 my friend Thurber was going through a really bad time. Although he was more famous than ever before, his eyesight was completely gone and he had to fight long periods of depression, broken by occasional short periods of rebellious temper.

In a strangely parallel experience, he himself had eye trouble followed by a nervous breakdown. "My periods of self-assertion . . . lasted longer than Thurber's, gave me more pleasure and caused my lawyers, my wife, my doctors, and my friends . . . more trouble," he confessed. "There is no doubt that Thurber excelled me as a writer, but for several years I was way ahead of him as a middle-aged hell-raiser." [34]

Nugent may have colored the picture a little highly, since Thurber had put his worst years behind him by 1949, but there is no doubt of the fact that a combination of personal troubles and concern over what was happening to the country had shaken him profoundly. The uneasiness with which he regarded the changes taking place in the world comes through in the series of letters he wrote between 1947 and 1949 to Miss Sarah B. Whitaker, the headmistress of the Northampton School for Girls, where his daughter Rosemary was a student. These letters show the conservative strain in Thurber's values: here he is not the humorous iconoclast or the political liberal, but rather the worried parent, trying to offer guidance in a confusing and frightening world.[35]

[34] Nugent, unpublished manuscript of a speech to Phi Psi alumni at Ohio State, May 26, 1962 (Thurber Collection).
[35] These letters were printed in "James Thurber on the Perplexities of Educating a Daughter," Chicago *Tribune* Magazine, Sunday, May 2, 1963.

In his letter of May 13, 1947, he speaks rather sadly of the lack of intellectual interest on the part of American schoolgirls. (In other moods and on other occasions he treated the intellectual shortcomings of the American woman as a prime comic subject.) It is only after they leave school that they develop any desire for knowledge, he says. He suggests that "the tempo of our life, our remarkable technological achievements, our love of gadgets and entertainment, and various other factors militate strongly against a desire for study." He is even more concerned, however, about the psychological impact on young people of living in a world balancing precariously on the brink of war. "From talking to a number of girls in their teens, I have discovered the indisputable fact that world unrest, threats of conflict, radio broadcasts, and newspaper stories have built up a background of apprehension which amounts in some degree to insecurity. In my own day, when I was Rosemary's age, the greatest threat to the world was Halley's comet."

A year later he returned to the subject. He wonders whether sufficient efforts are being made to reassure young people and to explain to them that war with Russia is not inevitable. "Accenting the dark side of the situation" is dangerous, "since fear can lead to panic and disastrous nervous states in young girls and boys who in this country seem to have no natural aptitude for understanding politics." Teachers should represent "security and anchorage" for students, he says, obviously worried about what young people were hearing in the classroom about the world outside.

The last two letters have to do with Rosemary's future, and they are interesting because of what they show of Thurber's ideas about education and his literary taste. Rosemary wanted to go to a dramatic training school rather than to college, and Thurber was disappointed. He said that his old friend Herman Miller ("one of the best amateur actors I have ever known") always claimed that "the best actors and actresses were the product of life and literature, rather than of merely technical study." With that in mind, he was giving her, as a graduation present, a list of twenty books, all of them short, "to supply the lack of a general arts course in college." It is not a list of Great Books, he said: it is a highly personal list of short novels "that interested, inspired, or excited me," and, most important of all, "affected me as a writer." He hopes that they will stimulate a young lady's interest in good writing.

Here are the books: *Babbitt*, by Sinclair Lewis, *Daisy Miller*, by Henry James, *Gentle Julia*, by Booth Tarkington, *Linda Condon, Java Head, Wild Oranges*, by Joseph Hergesheimer, *The Wanderer*, by Alain Fournier, *The Great Gatsby*, by F. Scott Fitzgerald, *The Sun Also Rises*, by Ernest

Hemingway, *Invitation to the Waltz*, by Rosamond Lehmann, *This Simian World, God and My Father*, by Clarence Day, *The House in Paris*, by Elizabeth Bowen, *A Lost Lady, My Mortal Enemy*, by Willa Cather, *A Handful of Dust, Decline and Fall*, by Evelyn Waugh, *Heaven's My Destination, The Cabala*, by Thornton Wilder, *February Hill, The Wind at My Back*, by Victoria Lincoln, *Blue Voyage*, by Conrad Aiken, *The Bitter Tea of General Yen*, by G. Z. Stone, *Lady into Fox*, by Edward Garnett, *How to Write Short Stories*, by Ring Lardner, *The Return of the Soldier*, by Rebecca West, *Miss Lonelyhearts*, by Nathanael West. Rosemary has already read a number of these books, Thurber adds, "including E. B. White's *One Man's Meat*, whose perfect writing should be on every reading list."

The problem of reading for young people is difficult, he said, and he was thinking about doing an article in *Harper's* about it. There is the question of sexual content: most schoolgirls of seventeen have read the sexy parts of *God's Little Acre* and *Appointment in Samarra*, he says, "exchanging books in which pages are marked, never beginning or ending the books." He offers no solution, but he implies that giving young people free access to books is better than trying to proscribe the dangerous ones. His list, however, is notably free of titles which might be questionable. A greater problem, however, is student resistance to assigned reading. Rosemary had no desire to read *My Ántonia* because it was on a reading list; but looking back, Thurber acknowledges that he was not so much different: "I was a great reader from the time I was 10, but most of my enthusiasms in high school and college I found outside class. I am a rabid antagonist of the 'Silas Marner' kind of required reading. Neither this, nor 'The Spy,' nor 'The Talisman,' nor 'The Return of the Native' stirred my interest as a writer and appreciator as much as the good books I read for myself."

Even though his list is addressed to the needs and interests of a teen-age girl, it contains most of the touchstones of Thurber's own literary taste. Most obviously, it shows his passion for brevity and the concentrated effect. He told Fred Millett in 1940 that his special favorites were *The Great Gatsby, Lady into Fox, My Ántonia, My Mortal Enemy* and *A Lost Lady*—"Which will indicate that I like the perfectly done, the well-ordered, as against the sprawling chunk of life." [36] He liked to quote Scott Fitzgerald's remark to Thomas Wolfe, "You're a putter-inner and I'm a taker-outer," and it was obvious that he preferred the taker-outers. He never liked Cervantes, and the reason was undoubtedly the unwieldy

[36] Fred B. Millett, *Contemporary American Authors* (New York: Harcourt, Brace and Comapny, 1940), p. 613.

prolixity of *Don Quixote.* Wolfe irritated him at a cocktail party once by saying that he didn't know what it was to be a writer. Thurber's wife, Helen, said, " 'But my husband *is* a writer.' " Wolfe was surprised. " 'He is?' " he asked. " 'Why, all I ever see is that stuff of his in *The New Yorker.*' " For Wolfe, to be a writer was to write long novels; Thurber's brief sketches hardly qualified.[37]

An illuminating picture of Thurber at the end of the decade is given in the long birthday interview with Harvey Breit ("Mr. Thurber Observes a Serene Birthday," *New York Times Magazine,* December 8, 1949). It is a different Thurber from the melancholy, angry man described in Nugent's speech; here, the dominant and public side of his personality reveals itself, and he is cheerful, rational, tolerant and ironic. He spoke candidly about the problems of adjusting to middle age and blindness. He talked about the dog which was the trademark of his drawings; although to begin with, the dog was simply a device to give compositional balance to a scene, he gradually became an important figure, " 'a sound creature in a crazy world,' " said Thurber. He expanded on one of his favorite subjects, man's unwarranted sense of superiority to the other animals. And he spoke about Woman. Since Man has failed to run the world, " 'Woman must take over if the species is to survive.' " This reversal of his carefully established role as America's best-known woman-hater was a position he was to return to again and again during the next ten years. In a world coming apart at the seams, Woman was the only hope for a troubled humanity. " 'I would like to see a matriarchy,' " he said, noting that girls are getting bigger all the time, and that nature may be working out the problem in her own way.

He went on to speak of the effect of the frightening world situation on the young and on the practice of humor. The best humorists got started in the Twenties, he said; very few have come up since, because the depression and now the threat of atomic destruction have had a shattering effect on people. " 'There is a grim turn to the stories today, even to humor.' " The writers of the Twenties were without this sense of doom. " 'The sense of doom . . . that they had was more legendary than real. They were the lost generation, but they were lost in Paris, and having a pretty good time. All of them had a good twenty or thirty years to look ahead to. There just wasn't the sense of another war to look forward to then, as there is now.' "

Turning to the lighter side, he told one of his favorite anecdotes, about how he came to illustrate a book on brussels sprouts which President Roosevelt sent to Winston Churchill shortly after the Quebec Conference.

---

[37] Interview with Plimpton and Steele, *Writers at Work,* p. 94.

Roosevelt, in a moment of waggishness, had told Mrs. Churchill that brussels sprouts were the great American vegetable and that there were thirty-four ways to cook them. Continuing the gag, he had a pamphlet made up entitled *Thirty-four Ways to Cook Brussels Sprouts* and got Thurber to draw the cover. Roosevelt wanted the drawing to show the long line of eager-looking people with forks in their hands descending upon a bowl of brussels sprouts with human faces. Not liking the cannibalistic overtones of Roosevelt's idea, Thurber put the vegetables with human faces in a border design and placed a dog in the center.

Not long after, Thurber heard that the following conversation took place between Mrs. Churchill and John Winant, the American Ambassador to Great Britain. " 'I understand the brussels sprout is the great American vegetable, Mr. Winant.' 'Oh, no,' said Winant, 'it is a dreadful vegetable.' 'But,' exclaimed Mrs. Churchill, 'your President himself told me that it is the great American vegetable.' It was a tough spot for a diplomat, but he got out of it. 'Oh, the brussels sprout!' he cried. 'Of course, I guess I was thinking of the parsnip.' " Thurber's rendering of President Roosevelt's bizarre conception doubtless confirmed Winston Churchill's low opinion of his talent as a draughtsman. Vincent Sheean reported that a few years earlier, when he mentioned Thurber in a conversation with Churchill, the great man groped for a moment, and then said, " 'Oh yes, that insane and depraved artist.' " [38]

The Beast in Me (1948), Thurber's first collection of new work since his blindness, is full of innovations and fresh departures. Among them are two new forms, which might be called, for lack of traditional labels, the word-game comedy and the conversation piece. Both show the turn from "eye-writing" to "ear-writing" which accompanied Thurber's gradual loss of sight. The word-game comedy is a fictional or essayistic anecdote which provides the occasion for bravura displays of dictionary learning, wit, and verbal acrobatics. The setting is usually a half-drunken conversation uninhibited by the restraints of logic and custom, or an insomniac monologue during the lonely hours waiting for sleep, when the mind plays fast and loose with whatever it contemplates.

In "Here Come the Tigers," for example, two tipsy friends invade Thurber's apartment just as he is about to go to bed, announcing that they have discovered "a new dimension of meaning" in a variation of the old

[38] Breit gives the highlights of the anecdote in his piece in the New York *Times*, but Thurber told it in fuller detail in a letter to Breit, November 22, 1949. Helen Thurber recalls that the Churchill-Sheean exchange took place in 1938.

game of anagrams. The great new insight is that "the mood and tone and color of a word are echoed in its component parts," says Hayes. " 'You guys are stiff,' " says Thurber. " 'Let me unwrap stiff for you,' " says Jordan. " 'Stiff, tiff, fists, fits.' "

The key to the game is in the haunting quatrain:

> There are lips in pistol
> And mist in times,
> Cats in crystal,
> And mice in chimes.

Hayes and Jordan help themselves to more drinks, over Thurber's protests, and pursue the animals hidden in familiar words—the wolf in flower, the gander in danger, the frog in forget, the ant in autumn, the wren in winter, and the pig in spring. Hayes says that there are three six-letter words with tiger in them, but that it won't be easy to think of them. While Thurber follows the trail of the tiger, his guests go on, opening up the bewildering variety of realities locked within the conventional forms of language. They discover a startling constellation of entities in the single word crystal: salt, slat, cyst and cart, as well as star, cry and satyr. " 'There's practically a sentence in woman,' " says Jordan, and Hayes demonstrates—" 'Woman: moan now won wan man.' " Thurber finally gets rid of his friends, and at the end, he is tossing restlessly in bed, hunting for the tiger in three six-letter words. At dawn he gets it: gaiter, goiter, aigret. Then he goes to sleep.

Thurber had always been a word-gamesman, but after his blindness his passion for word-play amounted to an obsession. He took to playing elaborate games with friends like Jap Gude and Peter De Vries at parties, by mail and over the telephone. Once, in 1947, De Vries challenged him to list as many words as he could think of which had all the vowels in them. Thurber wrote back, listing sequoia, discourage, precaution, precarious, auditioned, and some others; then added, "I got six or eight more last night, but they left me. Damn Roueché and you for bringing this up!" He threw in two five-vowel names for good measure—Louise Macy and Benjamin Clough. "God!" he exclaimed. Then, as though unable to keep it all in, he added, "I'm going nuts. Nuts! do you hear? Nuts he he he he he he." [39] A sophistication of this game—finding words which had all the vowels in order—drove both men to the far edge of sanity.

The conversation piece is similar to the word-game comedy, but it is not

---

[39] Letter to De Vries dated "September, 1947."

quite as specialized in subject. The action is the give-and-take of dialogue in which all sorts of fantastic variations are played upon a central theme. The setting is usually a party or other convivial occasion, and the talkers are reckless and expansive, creating out of the play of wild generalization, false example, garbled quotation and outrageous pun a strange and dreamlike world. The scene of "The Waters of the Moon," for example, is a literary cocktail party. In the swirl of pretentious intellectual talk ("I had broken away from an undulant discussion of kinetic dimensionalism and was having a relaxed moment with a slender woman . . . who described herself as a chaoticist . . .") Thurber encounters an intense, self-important editor who is determined to trap him into a discussion of "the male American writer who peters out in his fifties."

Thurber retaliates with an elaborate hoax, playing a series of deliberately absurd variations on the editor's theme. There is the case of "poor old Greg Selby," for example, " 'whose first wife claimed to have discovered that his last book, 'Filiring Gree,' was his next-to-last book, 'Saint Tomany's Rain,' written backward.' " Or there was Douglas Bryce, who ran out of creative ideas and spent his last years planning grandiose projects like " 'Translate Lippmann into Latin' " and " 'refute Toynbee.' " The climax of the hoax involves an esoteric joke based on a line from Browning ("Let twenty pass and stone the twenty-first"); the editor recognizes it and realizes that he has been had. " 'I happen to be familiar with Browning,' " he says, drawing himself up with alcoholic dignity, and the game is over. A number of readers were delighted and impressed by Thurber's new comic mode, and Maxwell Anderson wrote Katharine White that for sheer virtuosity in style and structure, "The Waters of the Moon" was the best thing he had ever read in *The New Yorker*. [40]

Thurber's heightened interest in virtuoso effects of language and style shows itself in the two literary imitations, "A Call on Mrs. Forrester (After rereading, in my middle years, Willa Cather's 'A Lost Lady' and Henry James's 'The Ambassadors')" and "The Beast in the Dingle (With quite the deepest of bows to the master, Henry James)." Both are "imitations" rather than parodies, since their intention is not so much to make fun of as to recreate the world of their famous originals. In "A Call on Mrs. Forrester" Thurber interweaves the settings, characters, and language of his two authors so skillfully and appreciatively that the reader feels that he is simultaneously looking at Henry James through the glass of Willa Cather and at Willa Cather through the glass of Henry James. "The Beast

[40] Letter from Maxwell Anderson to Mrs. E. B. White, March 7, 1947 (Thurber Collection).

in the Dingle" is a pastiche made up out of elements of "The Beast in the Jungle" and "The Turn of the Screw," and while it is impressive evidence of Thurber's ability to think and write like Henry James, it is a little too studied, too respectfully literary, to be altogether successful. Harold Ross was baffled by it. He read it and handed it back to Thurber with a sigh. " 'I only understood fifteen per cent of the allusions,' " he said, but he liked "A Call on Mrs. Forrester," and printed it, because it was " 'about a man and two women, and it comes over.' " [41]

Two of the five sections of *The Beast in Me* are devoted to drawings. These are of particular interest because they are virtually the last he did, and because they show him at his best. The most interesting and original are his drawings of animals, both real and imaginary. "A Gallery of Real Creatures" is a series of studies based on Lydekker and other source books, but its bold simplification of form marks it as unmistakably Thurber's. The style is essentially realistic, but the subjects are exotic and unusual, like Bosman's Potto, a small tree-dweller with large, haunting eyes. "Nature is ever more fanciful than the artist," Thurber observes in the Foreword, "and I envy her the creation of Bosman's Potto." His gallery is full of such creatures, strange in appearance and picturesquely named, like the Rock-Jumping Shrew, the Spider Muck-Shrew and Common Shrew, the Tasmanian Devil, and the Hoolock, or White-Browed Gibbon.

In "A New Natural History" Thurber invents a set of non-existent birds, plants, and animals, and describes them in captions which have only an oblique and fanciful connection with what is pictured. The effect on the observer is to make him feel that he is looking at a whole new order of reality. The creatures pictured exist only in the world of imagination, and the vocabulary of the captions is wildly inappropriate to the subject of natural history, although it has a sort of dream-like plausibility. Essentially, Thurber is playing an elaborate game of word-association, in which the caption represents the denotative or logical meaning, and the drawing represents the surprising suggestions called up by the auditory or visual connotations of the word. For example, a fish feeding in the weeds is captioned "The Dudgeon." Here, the drawing is the visual image of an association triggered by the sound of the word—"dudgeon" rather easily becomes "gudgeon," a species of fish. The same principle is at work in the drawing of a small raccoon or fox-like animal and a scaly prehistoric creature captioned "The Femur (left) and the Metatarsal." "Femur" suggests "lemur" (a small nocturnal member of the monkey family with a foxy face),

[41] *The Years with Ross*, p. 77.

and "Metatarsal"—by a stretch of imagination—sounds as though it might be the name of some ancient saurian.

More surprising and fanciful associations are involved in "A Trochee (left) encountering a Spondee," which shows two almost identical creatures standing nose to nose. The drawing adds a meticulous touch of authenticity in representing the Trochee as an animal whose hind legs are shorter than his forelegs, while the Spondee's legs are all the same length. And in perhaps the most wonderfully improbable association of all, two strange creatures looking out of the high grass are described as "A Scone (left) and a Crumpet, peering out of the Tiffin." Harold Ross was delighted with the natural history series. He urged Thurber to continue, and he even offered some ideas of his own—"the Blue Funk," for example—but Thurber felt that he had pretty well exhausted the possibilities, except for a few like " 'a man being generous to a fault—that is, handing a small rodent a nut.' "

A Scone (left) and a Crumpet, peering out of the Tiffin

These elaborate games of word-association are the sort of thing a nearly blind man might play. Thurber could see just well enough to do his drawings, but he was to all intents and purposes cut off from the visible world; living in a world of sounds, he would let words reverberate in his imagination and listen to the strange echoes they sometimes made. In his unexpected conjunctions of drawing and caption, he is—like Joyce—remaking language, allowing the pressure of subconscious associations to force new meanings onto familiar words and phrases, and in effect, transforming the real into the surreal.

"Soapland," a long five-part essay on radio soap opera, shows Thurber in a very different role, that of social historian and critic of popular culture. As his sight deteriorated, he began to listen more and more often to the radio, and he became fascinated by the soap opera as a sociological phenomenon. His essay is, he says, "the record of a year's sojourn in the strange and fascinating country of daytime radio serials." He did a great deal of research on the project, not only listening but writing to and interviewing many of the producers, writers and actors who worked in that highly special world. His account of "this deeply rooted American institution" is comprehensive, lively, and full of sharp insights into American popular values.

In the best New Yorker manner, Thurber avoids making overt judgments in his essay, but it is obvious that he finds soap opera a depressing phenomenon. His discussion of the relationship between the sexes in soap opera is particularly acute, because in the serials he saw his own reading of American domestic life corroborated. The inferiority of the male is shown in a variety of ways: the weak men are always confessing to the good women, who then reform them and make them gratefully dependent; the good men frequently suffer paralysis of the legs or some other crippling disease. "The man in the wheel chair has come to be the standard Soapland symbol of the American man's subordination to the female and his dependence on her greater strength of heart and soul."

"A Miscellany" is a gathering of some of Thurber's last—and best—drawings. The anti-feminist strain was always more prominent in his drawings than in his writings, and "A Miscellany" is full of scenes in which woman appears as threat and menace. She is the huntress in "Let me take your hat, Mr. Williams" (over the fireplace are crossed guns, heads of deer, and in the center, the mounted head of a middle-aged man); and she stares down death itself in "Death comes for the dowager." Husbands and wives are apathetic or bickering. "Sunday Morning," a curiously haunting sketch, shows a bedroom cluttered with shirts and shoes, a man in bed, his expression vacant, a woman seated undressed in a chair, absent-mindedly holding a stocking, the whole scene a depressing image of emotional emptiness. Courtship is a species of warfare: the leering suitor brings the lady to bay on the sofa, and asks her, "Where did you get those big brown eyes and that tiny mind?"

Thurber's sharp view of man and his kindlier opinion of dog is beautifully shown in the scene in which a man and a dog hover fearfully on the edge of a forest on a wild and stormy night; the man gestures roughly and shouts

"Comb the woods!" while the gentle dog, already turning back, looks up at him unbelievingly. A much harsher comment is made in "American Folk Dance," which shows a riot in progress. In the foreground a policeman and a berserk woman are locked in a ballet-like pose; in the background, men beat each other without mercy. In the 1930's Thurber's crowd scenes were cocktail parties or people fleeing natural disasters, like the Columbus flood; now, in the mid-1940's, he sees American society as at war with itself.

American Folk Dance

The last section of *The Beast in Me*, "Time Exposure," is a collection of pieces done for "Talk of the Town" between 1928 and 1936. Like "Soapland," they show the rational, common-sense side of Thurber's talent, as opposed to the eccentric and the fantastic. Thurber was always proud of his ability and experience as a reporter, and these *New Yorker* pieces, done when he had his sight and could explore the city at will, doubtless had a special value for him in the first years of his blindness. They include visits to such places of contemporary interest as the yet-unfinished Empire State Building (1930) as well as to historic landmarks like the places once frequented by O. Henry. Most of them show his fondness for history and his sensitivity to the passage of time. In all of them are the sharp eye for significant detail and the clean economy of phrase which were the special trademarks of *New Yorker* reporting.

15

Escape to the Past:
The Thurber Album

THE LATE 1940'S AND EARLY 1950'S were anxious times for Thurber, as they were for many Americans. He worried about politics, about the fate of humor, about the decline of standards, and most of all, he worried about man's chances of survival. In addition, his health was not good, and he was often weak, moody, and depressed.

He was outraged by the demand for political orthodoxy which swept the country after the war. When the New York *Herald Tribune* stated in a 1947 Thanksgiving Day editorial that all employees should be required to state their political beliefs in order to hold their jobs, White, Roger Angell, Coates, and other writers sent letters to the editor, protesting this idea as a violation of basic constitutional rights. The *Herald Tribune* replied to White's letter on December 2, dismissing it as eccentric and quixotic and potentially dangerous. Thurber joined the battle with an angry letter to the newspaper in which he said that its editorial could be used as a preface to a book on how to set up a totalitarian state under the guise of protecting the security of the nation. "This is the familiar way in which all such states have been established," he said. "Your editorial clearly suggests Chapter I for the handbook I have mentioned: How to Discredit Liberals as Dangerous Elements Who Imperil the Safety of the Nation and the True Meaning of Its Constitution, and Who Stand in the Way of the New Freedom and the Greater Security." [1]

[1] Letter to New York *Herald Tribune*, December 3, 1947.

He became more and more disturbed as the signs of fear multiplied, and America seemed to be inviting a dictatorship of the right. The general approval of the House Un-American Activities Committee seemed to him a particularly dangerous sign. In a letter to Miller and Nugent in October, 1948, telling them that he would not have his *New Yorker* play ready for the fall season after all, he talked more about the political climate in America than about his dramaturgic problems. The two were related, however: he had taken his swipes at a right-wing Congressman in the play, and Nugent had warned him that any satiric treatment of a Congressman, however justified, ran the risk of being called un-American in the present state of violently inflamed opinion. Thurber agreed, adding that he did not want to write a play on any subject which would invite the judgment of a people currently in the grip of hysterical fear.[2]

His understanding of the dangers of the popular mood in America which was soon to bring Senator McCarthy to the center of the stage is eloquently expressed in the closing paragraph of the letter. The greatest threat in communism, he said, is its belief that any means can be justified by the end. If we begin to follow the same doctrine we will be destroyed just as surely as if the Bomb had been dropped on us. Ruefully, he confesses that he would love to stand up and say this, but that he realizes that in this worst of all moments in our history it would not be safe to do so. Looking ahead apprehensively, he wonders whether things will be any better in the Dewey administration.

In his important interview-conversation with George Plimpton and Max Steele for the *Paris Review* in 1955, he looked back on the period "when all the American Congress seemed to do was to investigate writers, artists, and painters" as the low point in American history. It was a difficult time for all writers, but it was particularly hard on humorists. "In the years 1950 to 1953 I did very few things, nor did they appear in the *New Yorker*," he said. Disheartened by the present, he turned back to the past, and in 1948–49 he began the series of nostalgic memoirs which ran first in *The New Yorker* and then appeared as *The Thurber Album* in 1952. "The *Album* was kind of an escape—going back to the Middle West of the last century and the beginning. . . . I wanted to write the story of some solid American characters, more or less as an example of how Americans started out and what they should go back to—to sanity and soundness and away from this jumpiness," he said to Plimpton and Steele.

In returning to the past, Thurber was not only escaping from a demoral-

[2] Letter to Miller and Nugent, October 28, 1948 (Thurber Collection).

ized present and searching for values which America had lost somewhere along the way; he was also making a journey of self-discovery, calling up the figures of his family ancestry and the Columbus community who had some special meaning for him. And so, although the book is about other people, it reveals a great deal about Thurber himself. Part of what he was looking for can be seen in his portraits of such figures as his great-grandfathers Judge Stacy Taylor and Jake Fisher.

Stacy Taylor came west to Ohio when it was still Indian country, made and lost a fortune in real estate (at one time he and another man bought from an Indian chief a tract of land on which the city of Fort Wayne now stands), studied his law books by candlelight, and was elected to the State Legislature. He knew much of Shakespeare and all of Burns by heart, and when he died, in 1893, "full of scars and honors . . . he had lived all but thirteen years of the American nineteenth century." Jake Fisher, a blacksmith and prosperous farmer in Franklin County, was a man of prodigious strength, warm heart, and simple, clear-cut beliefs. He fought over a thousand fights in his time. He fought chiefly to protect women, dumb animals, Republican principles and the Scriptures, according to his son, Mahlon Taylor, the family historian, and he never lost a fight and never held a grudge. He used to eat dinner with his Negro hired hands, and to those people who objected, he said, " 'If a man's good enough to work for me, he's good enough to eat with me.' " He lived to be seventy-seven, and when the minister asked him as he lay dying if he didn't wish to forgive his enemies, he smiled and said, " 'I ain't got none . . . I licked 'em all.' " In these men Thurber saw the strength, independence of spirit and moral integrity which modern man has lost. Living in the early days of Ohio history, they are figures of legend, bigger than life, and "a far lesser breed of men" has succeeded them.

Thurber's love of history dominates the entire book, but it is especially strong in the early chapters. He liked to set the details of personal and family life against the background of historical events: he notes that Grandfather Fisher, for example, was married "the year the Civil War started, and died, at the age of seventy-eight, the year the First World War ended," and he observes with a touch of awe that Stacy Taylor and his son Mahlon (still vigorous at the age of ninety-four) between them cover "one hundred and forty-six years of American history, beginning in 1806, when Thomas Jefferson was President of the United States, and extending to the administration of Harry S. Truman."

If his pioneer ancestors represented strength and colorful individuality to Thurber, Grandfather and Grandmother Fisher and the tribe of aunts

and uncles and cousins of which Kate Fisher was the acknowledged ma-
triarch stood for family security and solidarity. Grandfather's big house on
Brydon Road, the leisurely Sunday breakfasts and dinners attended by
Fisher connections of all ages, and the Jackson family reunions in Sugar
Grove expressed a way of life in which the family was the center and
everyone knew where he belonged. The unspoiled beauty of the Ohio
countryside was the perfect setting for this world of deep roots and strong
family ties. Thurber's description of the Fourth of July reunions down in
Sugar Grove is pure pastoral—a hymn to the serenity and abundance of
a vanished rural past:

> The deer came down from the thickly wooded hills surrounding the
> farm, unabashed by the horns and headlights of the first Hupmobiles.
> Ten acres of blackberry bushes yielded a wagonload of berries in every
> season, and an enormous bin in the barn held nuts in the fall that
> fell from six different kinds of trees. The woods were filled with
> wintergreen, laurel, and rhododendron, and in a genuine deep-tan-
> gled wildwood lived the biggest blacksnakes in the county.

There was usually a banquet at noon to start things off: "fried chicken and
turkey, potato salad and a dozen other salads, as many as forty layer cakes,
and enough pies, blueberry, lemon, mince, and cherry, for half a dozen
Keystone comedies." In the evening, there would be enough sky rockets,
aerial bombs, Roman candles, and pinwheels to light up Fairfield County
for miles around. Grandfather Fisher sometimes spent as much as a thousand dollars to supply the fireworks.

Thurber's portraits of his mother and father and of Aunt Margery Albright are nostalgic and affectionate, softened by family piety but lightened
by humor. His vivid account of Aunt Margery's folk remedies stirred the
memories of many readers who had grown up in rural areas, and he received
hundreds of letters adding to the list. He reprinted some of them in "Loose
Leaves," at the end of the book. One lady recalled that in the Ozarks
dogwood was an emetic if scraped up, a cathartic if scraped down; another
lady remembered that in New Hampshire sixty years ago, one of the
standard herbs was thoroughwort, "a horrible tasting tea for breaking up
a cold." Thurber, his love of esoteric lore aroused, did some research on
thoroughwort and reported that it was also known as "boneset, wild hoar-
hound, and agueweed," and that it was once valued for its "diaphoretic
and tonic properties."

About half the portraits in the *Album* are of people outside the family
circle who were either important influences on Thurber or stood for certain

qualities he admired. There are brief sketches of Frank James, the dynamic coach and manager of what must have been the strangest baseball team in America, and of Mr. Ziegfeld, the philosophical old carpenter with whom Thurber shared a small voting booth when they were both registrars in the Taft-Wilson election; but the most important are the six devoted to the professors and newspapermen who shaped Thurber's early intellectual and professional life.

The sketches of Taylor, Graves, and Denney show Thurber's ambivalent feelings toward Ohio State. These were the great teachers who had introduced him and the students of his generation to the world of literary study: he wanted to pay tribute to them, but at the same time he wanted to say something about the narrowness and provincialism of the university itself. The periodic threats to freedom of speech at the university disgusted him, and in his portrait of Denney, the champion of academic freedom, Thurber worked in some harsh political comments about the quality of Ohio State. Throughout the 1950's he felt estranged from the university and from Columbus generally. When he went to see his ailing mother in 1953, it was his first visit since 1950, and he wrote Dorothy Miller in 1957 that he had not been back since his mother's death in 1955, and had no desire to go back again. It had become a sprawling, vulgar, and depressing city, he said.[3]

The portraits of Graves and Denney were the hardest of the entire *Album* to do, chiefly because he did not like Graves and did not know Denney well enough. He worked on these two chapters for over a year, and rewrote each one a dozen times. He exchanged long letters with his friend Professor James Fullington, who knew both men well; but at the end, he felt that he had missed the mark in both cases. The inner truth of these complex personalities had somehow eluded him in spite of his remarkable memory and all the research he had done. "You are right about personality being hard to get down on paper," he said in answer to a letter in which Fullington had objected that he had not done justice to Graves. "After more than three years on my book, I have come to the conclusion that nobody is simple and that everybody is complex, each in his own way," he said. "I have found keys to people but for some reason they don't open the doors, or all of the doors, anyway." [4] Interestingly enough, he found Taylor, Billy Ireland, and Bob Ryder comparatively easy to do, because he could view them in relatively simple terms: Ireland and Ryder were "fascinating and almost without flaw," he said to Fullington, and Taylor "was

[3] Letter to Dorothy Miller, May 15, 1957.
[4] Letter to Fullington, March 18, 1952 (Thurber Collection).

perfect too." [5] For the purposes of the *Album*, obviously, admiration was the necessary basis for characterization.

Thurber concludes his retrospective excursion with three portraits of Columbus newspapermen who had influenced him in the early days. The ghost of Kuehner still haunted him, but at the same time he had developed a perverse affection for the hardboiled city editor and in his sketch of Kuehner, it is the affection that comes through strongest. Ireland and Ryder, on the other hand, were totally benign presences. Billy Ireland, the genial *Dispatch* cartoonist, whose Sunday "The Passing Show" was a national institution, represented in his life and in his work the small-town Midwest which Thurber was trying to recapture in the *Album* as a whole. He was born and raised "in the nostalgic era of horses and buggies, covered bridges, and dusty country roads that mired carriage wheels in the rainy season," and his cartoons pictured the vagaries of life in places like his native Ross County, Ohio. His work was plain and craftsmanlike ("Nobody else could draw a weather-vane, or a rocking chair, or an old-fashioned ice-cream freezer with his fine affectionate touch"), and it was often enlivened by a vein of fantasy, as in the cartoon showing a mouse-faced dirigible threatened by an enormous cat-shaped storm cloud.

Ryder was important not only as a literary influence, but as an ideal of personal culture as well. He was a student of the classics and of the contemporary political and domestic scene. His temperate, enlightened editorials made him the intellectual conscience of Columbus, and his witty, low-keyed paragraphs delighted a much wider audience. In Ryder's courtesy, civilized values, and professional skill, Thurber saw the best qualities of an older generation.

Thurber worked hard on the *Album*. He wrote hundreds of letters to scores of people, and he confessed to Fullington, in a letter thanking him for his help, that he was "fagged at the end"; but at the same time, he liked the challenge of digging up the facts and bringing the past to life. Like his old friend Harold Ross, he was a stickler for accuracy in research and writing. No fact was too small to be worth checking. He kept after his Columbus friends to supply him with such details as whether Ryder drove an electric runabout or a Cadillac, what his address was on Franklin Avenue, whether his father-in-law, Colonel Wilson, was a "cherry-pie man" or a "pumpkin-pie man," and so on. He was irritated when he found that some of his informants had misled him in reporting that Ryder favored black bow ties rather than blue, and that when he retired he lived in a house

---

[5] Letter to Fullington, January 31, 1952 (Thurber Collection).

overlooking "Oakland Bay" rather than San Francisco Bay. He was particularly disappointed in the famed *New Yorker* checking department. He complained about it in a letter to Dr. James E. Pollard. "The New Yorker under Ross didn't make that many mistakes in two years," he said. The name of Joseph E. Myers, for many years the head of the journalism department at Ohio State, had been spelled "Meyers," and the *New Yorker* copy editors had tried to spell "Chic" Harley's name "Chick," but Thurber had spotted this last outrage in time to prevent it.[6]

Most readers found Thurber's gallery of Ohio characters highly engaging. E. B. White called the *Album* "an amazing blend of madness and affection," and he wrote to Thurber that it was something of an imaginative shock to discover that all these people, "most of whom from long acquaintanceship had achieved a sort of mythical quality," were, after all, real. Looking at the collection of photographs at the end of the book was something like seeing a high school graduation picture of Lewis Carroll's Alice, he said, and he went on to complain that there were no such wonderful characters in his own home town.[7] Orville Prescott, in a perceptive review in the New York *Times*, however, took a different view. The book was "mildly amusing" and expertly written, he said, but the character sketches were slight and revealed relatively little about their subjects. "Mr. Thurber has not dug deeply into character or bothered with much biographical material. It is characteristic quality of personality which he has sought to recapture, the quality which stuck in his memory, softened by affection, romanticized . . . by time and distance." [8]

The point is well taken, although it fails to add that this was exactly Thurber's intention. His method as a biographer and memoirist was always highly personal, informal, and impressionistic. He preferred the quick sketch, the lively surface art of the *New Yorker* profile, to the fully developed character study, just as he found the very short story more congenial to him than the novel. He was always suspicious of generalization and auctorial commentary, and in his biographical sketches he depended primarily upon anecdotes, concrete images of the surface of life, to bring out the special quality of character he saw in each person. It is a deliberately limited art, but Thurber's wonderful memory, his eye for detail, and his remarkable ear for speech give these portraits an extraordinary vitality.

Some Columbus readers expected more biographical "reality" than

[6] Letters from Thurber to Pollard, October 8, 1951; January 26, 1952; February 5, 1952; February 9, 1952 (Thurber Collection). Also, Pollard's biographical essay, "Thurber," in *Ohio Authors and Their Books*, pp. 633–36.
[7] E. B. White letter to Thurber, July 13, 1952 (EBWP).
[8] "Books of the Times," New York *Times*, May 28, 1952.

Thurber offered, and complained that he idealized his figures too much, but this was to miss the point of the book, which was to be frankly and deliberately nostalgic. He was writing about family and friends, and he wanted to talk about their virtues, not their shortcomings. "I had to soften the book a little, because of the people involved, especially my mother and brothers who wanted everything tinted like photographs taken at Buckeye Lake," he wrote Carey McWilliams in August of 1952.[9] He carefully filtered out all references to the intellectual limitations and private disappointments of his idol, Joseph Russell Taylor, for example, although his correspondence with James Fullington shows that he was well aware of them. He was afraid that his realistic treatment of Billy Graves might provoke a storm from sentimental alumni, but he was pleasantly surprised to receive only a few angry letters from that quarter.

He was totally unprepared, however, for his brother Robert's bitter outburst over the portrait of their father. To Robert, the implication that Mr. Thurber was not a success in his career was a betrayal of family loyalty, and when "Gentleman from Indiana" appeared in *The New Yorker* in June of 1951, he sent Thurber a long and angry letter. Thurber was badly shaken, particularly since he had been at such pains to avoid giving offense to anyone. He wrote to White, seeking reassurance and describing Robert's inexplicable reaction. In view of what had happened, he was particularly worried about how his mother would take the portrait of her due to appear in *The New Yorker* in the next issue. He had Gus Lobrano send her a proof, together with a letter praising the piece. Then he wrote to Robert, and followed this with a note containing quotations from people like Frank Sullivan who admired the sketch. Joel Sayre, who was doing a feature story on Thurber for *Time*, helped out by inserting a sentence saying that Thurber had just completed an affectionate piece about his father.[10]

The misunderstandings were eventually smoothed over, but the whole affair left a bitter taste in Thurber's mouth, and he swore that he would write only about imaginary people from now on. Real ones took too much out of him, he said to White. "The emotional debris was terrific," he wrote Carey McWilliams, "since Columbus is the heart of evasion and fatty degeneration of criticism. Said my mother: 'It wouldn't go down very well with the young man of today if you reported that your grandfather sent a substitute to the Civil War.' Said a man named Opha Moore out there years ago: 'The story of Chic Harley does not point a good moral.' (Chic had become a mental case in his senior year.) Said the city attorney of

9 Letter to McWilliams, August 13, 1952.
10 Letter to White, June 12, 1951 (EBWP).

'Jurgen,' after thinking a moment: 'Why do writers write books that offend people?' " He was fed up with Columbus and he was fed up with nostalgia, and so when William S. Schlamm wrote a rather unsympathetic piece in the *Freeman*, in July of 1952, arguing that Thurber's humor was fatally tied up with homesickness and nostalgia, he was irritated. "As for Schlamm's theory about homesickness and humor, his buttons are twisted," he said to McWilliams. "I have done only two out of nineteen books that could be called nostalgic," he said. "I'd much rather write a piece about 'The Cocktail Party' or Sam Spade on the radio, or the sloppy way publishing houses are run than delve into the Columbus past. . . . My unfond memories would fill a bucket." [11]

The effort to transcend the conflicts of the present by recreating an idealized past proved to be only partially successful; the past turned out to be—in its own way—as troublesome as the present. Besides, the present could not be shut out indefinitely. The paranoid fear of communism which he saw as a danger-sign in the 1940's was by now sweeping the country like a grass fire, and he felt it was a matter of duty to take a public stand in defense of the freedom to think and speak according to one's conscience.

The role of political spokesman went against the grain, because he still felt as he had in the 1930's that literature and politics were a bad mixture. His letters to Malcolm Cowley in the early 1950's show him struggling with the problem. The humorist (and by implication, the artist generally) ought to stay clear of political commitments, he argued. "I ought to figure but slightly in the history of humor on the barricades," he wrote in 1952. "I have to write what I have to write, and I don't give a damn what anybody says about it. I wanted to be on the New Yorker, and I wanted to make money, and I wanted to sell books. I am a writer . . . because I couldn't do anything else." [12] He was always skeptical of causes and ideologies: "I keep thinking how basically inept American writers are in doing much with the political field," he wrote in a letter of 1954. Fitzgerald "damned near ruined 'The Last Tycoon' by wedging that labor leader into it," he said. "Same thing happened to Hemingway toward the end of 'To Have and Have Not.' . . . This was the same Hemingway who wrote at the end of 'Death in the Afternoon' the paragraph that begins 'Let those who want to save the world. . . .' " [13]

Nevertheless, in spite of his theoretical objections to political involvement for the writer, his own work during this period became markedly more

[11] Letter to McWilliams, August 13, 1952.
[12] Letter to Cowley, July 31, 1952.
[13] Letter to Cowley, May 21, 1954.

political in content. In addition to *Further Fables for Our Time*, such pieces as "A Holiday Ramble," "Exhibit X," and the long, unfinished satire called "The Spoodle" show his effort to come to the barricades in defense of freedom of thought.

As always, his position was a common-sense liberalism based on a belief in reason and education and a free press. The growing suspicion with which Americans were beginning to regard one another, and the consequent demand for security checks and loyalty oaths and investigations into people's opinions he saw as a frightening threat to the very basis of a free society. His most eloquent comment on the fear which was infecting American life is the essay "Look Out for the Thing," which first appeared in the October, 1950, issue of the *Bermudian* (and was also included in the posthumous collection *Credos and Curios*). Near his house in Connecticut, he writes, there is an ominous sign pointing to the woods and reading, "Look Out for the Thing"—a practical joke which does not seem quite so funny now, because there is a Thing abroad in the land, "older than the Questing Beast, uglier than the Loch Ness monster," which has a terrible effect upon "the rational mind of Man. It enlarges his credulity by magnifying peril, exaggerating fear, and inventing danger." It can turn him upside down so completely that he will try to protect free speech by denying it, "so that it cannot be used by such dubious citizens as the Accused, the Exonerated, and the Acquitted." Thurber warns the reader not to challenge the Thing single-handed. "It is armed and dangerous, and what is worse, it has a lot of friends."

When Ohio State adopted its speaker-screening rule, Thurber was so outraged that he refused the offer of an honorary degree which the university had planned to give him at the December convocation and took one from nearby Kenyon College instead. (Professor James Pollard, University Archivist, notes that this was the first time in Ohio State history that anyone had done so, and that no mention of the episode is to be found in the Trustees' minutes or the official correspondence of the period. [14]) In a letter to his friend Pollard, Thurber vented his scorn and indignation. He pointed out that it was hardly likely that an Ohio audience would be swayed by communist speakers, and that "if we are in such danger of being politically debauched, then all we have in the Western Conference is the greatest football area in the world." [15]

He spoke out in interviews and newspaper articles whenever he had the

[14] James E. Pollard, "With Honor, Not Without," text of unpublished talk to the Kit-Kat Club of Columbus, October 20, 1964 (Thurber Collection).

[15] Letter to Pollard, quoted in Pollard's "Thurber," *Ohio Authors and Their Books*, p. 635.

chance. During the successful revival of *The Male Animal* in the summer of 1952 he talked to Harvey Breit about the damage done by the constant investigation of writers and artists. " 'If we don't stop suspecting all writers,' he said, 'it will be a severe blow to our culture. I think all writers, even the innocent ones, are scared.' " People ask him why there aren't any more free and exuberant comedies like *The Male Animal,* he said, and the answer is that it is impossible to write comedy of that kind any more " 'because we're living in the most frightened country in the world.' " [16] Thurber was not exaggerating the danger. During this period, Congress was indeed examining books and interrogating authors at a frightening rate. Congressional hostility to writers was neatly summed up in the comment by Roy Cohn, chief counsel for Senator McCarthy's sub-committee, when he was asked about the choice of speakers for a television program: " 'Any writer is out.' " [17] When the State Department lifted Arthur Miller's passport, and a Congressman asked Miller, " 'Do you really believe that the artist is a special person?,' " Thurber protested in the New York *Times* that "A nation in which a Congressman can seriously ask: 'Do you think the artist is a special person?' is a nation living in cultural jeopardy." [18]

In a long article entitled "Dark Suspicions," in the New York *Times* for July 27, 1952, Thurber returned to the attack. The Congressional intimidation of writers "has seriously depressed literature in America," and the theater "is lying at death's door," he charged. The essay is a vigorous defense of writers as practitioners of an art worthy of respect, which is more than one can say of most politicians. Whittaker Chambers is not a writer, he says, nor is Richard Nixon. "A writer is a man who devotes his entire life to writing and who has an intense respect for the English language, which almost all politicians abuse," he said, anticipating a theme he was to develop frequently in the coming years. "They do not know its quiet, precise, and loving uses and they handle it profanely, as if it were a twenty-five cent ball bat." Demagogues of both the right and the left fear and distrust humor, he pointed out, and any society which cannot tolerate humor is in trouble. However, voices of sanity like that of Elmer Davis are beginning to be heard and there are signs that perhaps Americans are ready to laugh again. And with the revival of humor, there might be a revival of the theater, "the primary evidence of a nation's culture."

The moral and social value of humor, as distinct from the aesthetic, was

[16] Interview with Harvey Breit, New York *Times* Book Review, June 29, 1952, reprinted in Breit, *The Writer Observed* (Cleveland and New York: The World Publishing Company, 1956), p. 256.
[17] Malcolm Cowley, *The Literary Situation* (New York: Viking Press, 1954), pp. 221–22.
[18] Morsberger, *James Thurber,* p. 144.

much on Thurber's mind throughout the decade of the Fifties. "Every time is a time for humor, especially now, because the communists set out long ago to knock it off, and writing it is doing battle in one small corner of the field," he said in a 1951 letter to E. B. White, who really needed no convincing, having taken a similar position in a "One Man's Meat" column, "Salt Water Farm," back in 1939. In a statement which reveals many of his personal values, he went on to say that he wrote humor for the same reasons that the surgeon operates—because it was a demanding skill, because he liked it, and because he hoped that it might do some good. Humor, for him, was an active force, and that is why he always objected to Dorothy Parker's famous epigram, "Humor is a shield, not a weapon." Commenting on this to White, he says that he remembers how in the Gallic wars, the soldiers of the Tenth Legion banged the enemy silly with their shields after their swords were gone. He took pride in recalling Robert Benchley's statement that the treatment of the trustee in *The Male Animal* was more effective than a dozen lectures.[19]

The importance of humor to the life and health of a nation is the theme of his speech of acceptance when he was awarded the Sesquicentennial Medal by the Ohioana Library Association in the fall of 1953. The association gives awards to distinguished Ohioans each year, and on the 150th birthday of the state, it struck a special medal for Thurber, "In appreciation of . . . your priceless gift of laughter, boon to disturbed mankind." [20] Thurber was unable to attend the meeting in Columbus, and his speech was read by his old *Dispatch* colleague George Smallsreed.

On this occasion Thurber elected not to entertain, but to preach. The great tradition of humor in America is in danger, he said. Comedy is resilient, but it "sickens in the weather of intimidation and suppression, and such a sickness could infect a whole nation." The art of rough-and-tumble political satire as practiced by H. L. Mencken, Will Rogers, William Allen White, and "our own unforgettable Bob Ryder" has grown rusty through disuse. During "the free and untrammeled Twenties . . . humorists were a dime a dozen. There are not many left, alas, and only a handful coming up." We can ill afford the loss, for comedy is one of the necessities of civilized life. "Let us not forget the uses of laughter or store them away in the attic," he said. "If a thing cannot endure laughter, Professor Joe Taylor used to say, it is not a good thing." We will always need humor because, as E. B. White put it, " 'humorous writing, like poetical writing,

[19] Letter to White, April 24, 1951 (EBWP).
[20] Citation in *Thurber on Humor*, the Martha Kinney Cooper Ohioana Library Association (Columbus, 1953) pamphlet containing the presentation statement and Thurber's response.

has an extra content. It plays, like an active child, close to the big hot fire which is Truth.' " [21]

His hero during these years was Elmer Davis, whose low-keyed common-sense ironic comments on national and international politics were a haven of sanity in those panic-stricken years. Like Thurber, Davis was a Midwest-erner, and his flat voice, plain style, and liberal principles were for Thurber an image of the old-fashioned American virtues we all lost somewhere along the way. Thurber dedicated *Further Fables for Our Time* (1956) to him: "To Elmer Davis, whose comprehension of people and persons has lighted our time, so that we can see where we are going, these fables are dedicated with admiration, affection, and thankfulness." A few years after Davis's death, Thurber wrote to Roger Burlingame what Davis had meant to him and to the country at large: "His radio program was a pillar of American strength, light, soundness, learning, intelligence, and wit. He was, as I have often said, my favorite American of this century." [22]

In May of 1956, when Davis was seriously ill, Thurber wrote him a warm and encouraging letter which reveals many of his own private values. The theme of the letter is courage, and Thurber, with his characteristic empathy for those who were suffering, shared his friend's distress. "Only a few of us are left in our sixties," he says, "and I now wake up each morning earlier than usual, and lie there brooding and trying to be brave and remembering Conrad's 'The best we can hope for is to go out nobly in the end,' and Hemingway's 'Nothing ever happens to the brave.' " Like Davis, Thurber detested humbug of every kind, and he says that he has often thought of a book "containing not the usual inspirational crap, but some of the strong and truly reassuring things good men and good minds have written, about life and its burdens and death and its whatever-you-call-it." What brought this to mind, he says, "is the unquestionable success of almost any book about Positive Thinking, the conquest of Fear, usually trash, money-making trash, written by trashy men. Maybe this is true: Nothing ever happens to the trashy." Apologetically, he adds, "I didn't set out to lecture, but here I am." [23]

Thurber himself was in poor health, and his concern for what was happening to American society at large was paralleled by a number of personal anxieties. He had had thyroid trouble off and on for many years, and in 1951–52 the problem became acute. He was nervous and irritable and unable to work effectively. He wrote White in October of 1952 that

[21] *Thurber on Humor,* pp. 9–14.
[22] Letter to Roger Burlingame, July 25, 1960.
[23] Letter to Elmer Davis, May 18, 1956.

his metabolism had been up to twenty-four and then had dropped to three. His energy was down to zero. He had to sit down to shave, he could no longer tie his shoes, and sometimes he was too weak even to brush his teeth. He found it difficult to read or write, and he had not finished a casual so far this year, he said.[24]

At the same time, he worried constantly about the health and well-being of friends, and his letters to the Whites are full of commiseration, medical advice, and news about the health of others. A letter to the Whites in 1951 opens with the statement that he and Helen arrived in New York to find themselves in the midst of all kinds of problems and illnesses, and goes on to report on the condition of Ross, who was cheerful, but coughing con-stantly, Gertrude Sayre, and Elliott Nugent. In 1954 he told White that he had been writing letters to sick and disabled friends because he realized the psychological boost this gives to people who can no longer get around. The thought that death was thinning out their generation depressed him profoundly. He used to count his dead friends and former associates like prayer-beads, he said, but he has decided to give it up.[25]

When Helen suffered a displaced retina in August of 1953, the impact on Thurber was severe. She was wife, secretary, amanuensis, and business manager to him, and this threat to her left him badly shaken. He rushed her from West Cornwall to the Columbia-Presbyterian Medical Center, and took a room in the hospital adjoining hers. He wanted to get Dr. Gordon Bruce, who had operated on him back in 1940–41, but Dr. Bruce was fishing in Colorado, and there was a telephone strike. Meanwhile, two of the best eye surgeons in New York were in attendance. Finally, with the help of two telephone companies and the Associated Press, Thurber got hold of Dr. Bruce, who assured him that Helen was in good hands. She was operated on successfully, and Dr. Bruce did not have to cut short his vacation after all; but Thurber's dramatic search for him made headlines in many cities ("Thurber's Seeing-Eye Wife Faces Emergency Surgery to Save Sight," read the New York *Times* for August 26).

In October he wrote the Whites about it, and launched into one of his characteristic lectures on the eye. They were back in the country and Helen's retina was sticking well, he reported. The human eye was unbeliev-ably tough. It is almost impervious to infection from the outside, and it can stand three drops of atropine, only one of which would dry up a person's mouth for weeks. If you get something in your eye, you can take it out by making a circle out of a hair from your head and pulling it across your

[24] Letter to White, October 14, 1952 (EBWP).
[25] June 12, 1951, and February 20, 1954 (EBWP).

eyeball. In the old days, people licked foreign objects out of one another's eyes with their tongues. If you wake up and find your eye completely red, it is only a broken vein and will be all right in a few hours. Almost all cataracts are operated on successfully. You cannot get eye-strain from reading in a bad light. You may get a muscle-strain, but the eye will quickly recover. Retina operations are usually spaced three weeks apart, but Helen had two in twelve days. She is an indestructible Scot, he said, and astonished the doctors by her calmness through the whole ordeal.[26]

The death of Harold Ross in 1951 was a severe blow to Thurber. Ross was not only the living incarnation of *The New Yorker*, he was one of Thurber's closest friends. He never really reconciled himself to the loss, and although the magazine continued to flourish under the able leadership of William Shawn, Thurber became more and more critical of it as time went on. For one thing, it had been getting too serious, he thought, and with Ross gone, the trend began to accelerate. What happened to a projected feature story on Houdini was a case in point. He had given Ross a pile of notes on Houdini, and Shawn had turned them over to one of the new writers on the magazine. The new man, a serious intellectual type, came to talk to Thurber about the project, and Thurber was disgusted because the only thing the new man could find of interest in Houdini was the fact that he was a great exposer of spiritualism. Thurber protested that he was interested in the great man's tricks, his famous escapes, and everything else there was to know about him. Ross made *The New Yorker* great by staying away from intellectuals and the intellectual approach, he said to White, and if the magazine was going to become a journal of opinion, he would rather write for the *Partisan Review*.[27]

Even the cartoons showed signs of declining into formula, now that the vigilant eye of Ross was no longer there to keep up standards. "There is too much stuff about the man and woman on the raft and the two beachcombers," he complained to De Vries in a letter of October, 1952. "There is a definite carelessness at the New Yorker, for the fear that comes out of true respect is gone," he continued. "The best thing the New Yorker has done in comic art is the probable or recognizable caption dealing with the actual relationships of people in our middle-class society. All of us have had a fling at fantasy and formula, but they should never predominate," he said, stating one of his favorite principles, that comedy should be rooted in the real. What with his blindness and his low spirits he has had few good cartoon ideas lately ("I can't do anything now, since my humor sounds like

[26] Letter to the Whites, October 20, 1953 (EBWP).
[27] Letter to White, July 18, 1952 (EBWP).

that of an assistant embalmer"), but he passes along a few possibilities anyway. In one, there is "a double page spread of cows moving from left to right, and then another double page, and then another single page, all moving from left to right. The right half of the third spread shows the leader of the cows, a defeated biblical king who is presenting the cattle to a victorious biblical king, as reparations after a long war. The defeated king is saying, 'Oh, I thought you said payment in kine.' " [28]

He was never quite reconciled to the inevitable change in his relationship to the magazine and the staff which took place when he decided to be a free lance. He wanted his independence, but at the same time he missed the cameraderie of the old days. He wrote gloomily to Gibbs, "Ross used to send a note reading 'Jesus Christ, that was a swell piece.' All you get now, if you insist on finding out what happened to a manuscript is a telegram saying 'Piece bought, money deposited.' " He and White, when they come to the office, wander around like a couple of ghosts, he said. "The only person who stops me in the corridor now is old Whitaker" (the copy reader whom Thurber pretended to shoot one day many years ago).[29]

As time went on, he felt himself more and more out of sympathy with the tone and editorial standards of the magazine. In a 1956 letter to White, he had a number of sharp things to say about the famous *New Yorker* style. If *The New Yorker* has a major fault, he said, it is its passion for smooth writing. White's clarity and precision are individual and inimitable, but too many people have tried to imitate him notwithstanding. As a result, with the exception of John McNulty's pieces, the magazine almost totally lacks grittiness and roughness of edge in its style and language. There have been attempts at boldness, as in the story in which a man and a woman are in bed and the man talks to the woman's husband on the telephone. This is a situation straight out of French farce, Thurber observes, and it cannot be made realistic by piling up phrases like "Jesus Christ," "For God's sake," and "Jesus Christ Almighty." Here the desire to shatter the idol of good taste has been fulfilled all too well. It reminds him of a line in Don Marquis, "I'll show 'em how to repent," he said; "the New Yorker will show 'em roughness, come what may." [30]

Readers may recall that the story about the man and woman in bed was Salinger's "Pretty Mouth and Green My Eyes."

[28] Letter to De Vries, October 16, 1952.
[29] Letter to Gibbs, February 8, 1956.
[30] Letter to White, April 16, 1956 (EBWP).

16

Thurber Country

FROM THE PUBLICATION OF *Is Sex Necessary?* until the end of his life, Thurber enjoyed the admiration of both the popular audience and the critics; and in the 1950's the honors and awards came in from every side. He was given an honorary degree by Kenyon College in 1950, another by Williams College in 1951, and another by Yale in 1953. In 1953 he also received the Sesquicentennial Medal from the Ohioana Library Association, and in 1957 the American Library Association gave him its Liberty and Justice Award for *Further Fables for Our Time.* Among other public and institutional awards were the T-Square Award of the American Cartoonists' Society in 1956, and the Antoinette Perry Award from the American Theater Wing for *A Thurber Carnival* in 1959–60. He was an international figure, and wherever he went, in England as well as in America, he was interviewed and written about and invited to appear on radio and television programs. For the last ten or fifteen years of his life, he was the closest thing we have had to a national humorist-spokesman since Mark Twain and Will Rogers. His style and personality were different from theirs, to be sure, and were keyed to a different moment in history, but his voice was felt as representative by millions of Americans and Britons.

Blindness and middle age failed to slow Thurber down or to tame the wildness of his spirit. The comments of his friends testify to the fact that he was as dramatic, as gregarious and as disputatious as ever. "He loved midnight wrangles," wrote Peter De Vries, "and the good pugnacious sociability of Tim Costello's saloon as much as he did the word games and old song titles with which he outwitted the laudanum hour and whiled away the long stretches of insomnia." [1] His old friend and Connecticut neighbor Professor Kenneth MacLean has vividly described how he would become "super-alive" at night, "offering to his friends not just conversation but a complete show—talking in every form of American dialect, now going through his nose in Brooklynese, now coming through his lips in good old labial Southern negro speech—now acting out scenes from the life of his Erskine Caldwell character Thee—reciting now a high school graduation-speech covering the history of the introduction of music into tuneless, tone-deaf New England." As a change of pace, he might recite "fifty completely original limericks." "Thurber's talk is as brilliant as his writing," added MacLean, "and will remind us that all the literature of America is not in the printed word." [2]

Red Smith, the sports columnist for the New York *Herald Tribune*, recalls that if Thurber was an introvert he did not show it at parties, "where he was almost sure to be the center of attention." He often directed his wit and humor against himself, and Smith tells a nice anecdote about how Thurber turned an embarrassing accident at a party into a joke:

> "Your drink's here, Jamie," Marc Simont, his artist neighbor in West Cornwall, Conn., said one night, setting a highball at his elbow. Jim said thanks, and a little later, groping for the glass as he talked, he knocked it over. He made no more of that than a person would who could see, but when it happened again with a fresh drink he sprang to his feet and delivered an impassioned protest to an imaginary House and Rules Committee about the untidy habits of this member Thurber, who persistently loused up the club premises on the flimsy pretense, the hollow excuse, that he was blind.

"His witty eloquence made it funny," said Smith, "and like all his humor, it was also bitterly poignant." [3]

There was something awe-inspiring about his tall bony figure and the restless energy with which he spoke and gestured. "There is a touch of powerful authenticity in the sight of James Thurber, hair tumbling over

---

[1] Peter De Vries, "Introduction," *Lanterns and Lances*, pp. xvii–xviii.
[2] Kenneth MacLean, "James Thurber—A Portrait of the Dog Artist," *Acta Victorana*, LXVIII (Spring, 1944), 6.
[3] Red Smith, "Jim Thurber," New York *Herald Tribune*, November 3, 1961.

forehead, raising his 6 feet 1½ inches awkwardly from a chair and flopping his long arms about like a scarecrow in Hydra-Matic drive, as he duplicates the nasal platform delivery of long-dead Ohio politicians," wrote an interviewer in 1957.[4] Peter De Vries recalls that there was a preternatural acuteness and intensity about Thurber. "He always put me in mind of a praying mantis," he wrote. "About his elongated form there hovered the same air of something delicate and improbable, of almost eerie sensitivity, of tactile grace and predatory caution. . . . Thurber's forepaws, too, lay folded in repose only when they were not tearing something to shreds, be it a handkerchief, the sash of a dressing gown or a personified tendency of modern life." [5]

The subjects of Thurber's conversation were varied, ranging from politics to literature to sport, but his favorite topic was the American Woman, and he mounted his attacks on her with all the imaginative and rhetorical power at his command. In his role of wife-scourge, he liked to quote Clarence Day's poem,

> Who drags the fiery artist down?
> What keeps the pioneer in town?
> Who hates to let the seaman roam?
> It is the wife, it is the home.

"When he started explaining women as he often did, no force on earth could stop him," said Lewis Gannett, another of his Connecticut neighbors. If any of the ladies present contradicted him, "the resultant explosions were memorable," but so were his acts of contrition the next day. After an evening in which Mrs. Gannett had been the target of his satiric wrath, he sent her a book inscribed, " 'Once upon a time there were two Gannetts, a male and a female, fortunately . . . With love, Jim.' " [6] During many of these performances, Thurber was not only entertaining the company, he was trying out ideas and phrases for his writing. After his blindness, when he could no longer see the words on the page, he needed to hear what they sounded like, and the Saturday-night parties in Cornwall or the get-togethers in New York were often in the nature of stage rehearsals for his work. "He needed listeners," as Lewis Gannett said.

In other moods, he would sit quietly in a gathering, composing in his head, and he would withdraw so far into his private world that Helen would

[4] "Up with the Chuckle, Down with the Yuk," Newsweek, LI (February 4, 1957), 53.
[5] De Vries, "Introduction," Lanterns and Lances, p. xvii.
[6] Peter De Vries recalls Thurber's fondness for Day's poem; it is in Thoughts Without Words (New York and London: Alfred A. Knopf, 1928), p. 26. Gannett's remarks are in "James Thurber, 'Pre-Intentionalist,' " New York Herald Tribune Books, November 12, 1961.

have to say, "Stop writing. People want to talk to you." Often he would lie awake at night, polishing his sentences, constructing his paragraphs, shaping his thoughts for the next day. As a rule, he composed during the mornings and dictated to his secretary in the afternoons, but sometimes, when an idea took possession of him, he wrote on into the night, after going to bed. He liked to tell interviewers that even in the middle of the night Helen could sense when he was writing instead of dreaming, and would wake up and tell him to quit working and go to sleep.[7]

Between 1949 and 1954 Thurber did a series of pieces for the *Bermudian* magazine, under the title of "Letter from the States" (he did two pieces earlier, but it was not until 1949 that he began contributing more or less regularly). They are brief and informal treatments of the major themes and subjects which concerned him during the late 1940's and early 1950's. Many of them were obviously preliminary versions of essays which appeared, revised and enlarged, in *The New Yorker* or other magazines later on. A number of pieces underline his concern over politics in the late 1940's and 1950's. "Winter Thoughts" (February, 1951) comments harshly on the fierce intolerance of failure in America, and our compulsion to find scapegoats, as in the case of the hue and cry raised against Secretary of State Dean Acheson. Acheson had had his successes, Thurber observes, "but he failed to stop the rise of Communism in China, and, as one English newspaper pointed out, he had also not prevented the eruption of Mt. Etna." In a lighter vein, there are critical comments on the inanities of radio, some nostalgic recollections of people and events in Columbus, Ohio, an eloquent defense of the poodle as one of nature's noblest creatures, two excursions into classical and American Civil War history, and a variety of personal anecdotes and reflections. One of the best is a meditation on growing old entitled "How to Be Sixty," in the June, 1954, issue.

The heart of the essay is a comic contrast between himself and Ernest Hemingway as aging writers. Hemingway had recently written in *Look* (May 4, 1954) about his state of mind now that he was in his mid-fifties, and he reported that in one of his dreams he was engaged to a lioness, who not only hunted for him, but cooked and served the meat " 'in a manner worthy of the Ritz in Paris.' " Hemingway obviously found the dream reassuring in its implication that his spirit was still young and bold, but Thurber suggests that it reveals something that Hemingway apparently does not recognize: "This dream plainly proves that Ernest Hemingway is getting a little old for big game hunting, and yearns for the creature

[7] "Thurber Doing Play on Ross," interview in New York *Herald Tribune*, April 24, 1960.

comforts of life—the warm room, the well-cooked dinner, the napery and silver, the prompt and efficient service. In a word, what he now wants is a waitress and not a lioness." The point is that the prospect of age is a threat to a writer like Hemingway; for a man of sedentary habits, like Thurber, it should be easier—as indeed it was, because Thurber was always able to see himself with humor.

> The writer who is sixty usually finds that non-fiction has become easier than fiction, and he turns from the creative to the reflective. If he is still going at sixty-five, he customarily plans to set down his memoirs, under some such title as "If Memory Serves" or "Before I Forget It." He then finds to his consternation that he has not only forgot it, but for the life of him can't remember where it was held or who was there, let alone why it was given or how he came to be asked.

He liked to bait Hemingway, partly because he admired him, and partly because Hemingway's public image was so comically antithetic to his own, and a couple of years earlier he had managed to work a Hemingway-Thurber contrast into an exchange of letters with Laura Z. Hobson. Writing in the "Trade Winds" column of *The Saturday Review* (October 6, 1952), Miss Hobson had reported that Mary Welsh Hemingway had done the first of a series for *Today's Woman* in which wives of famous men would write about their husbands, and that among those who would contribute was Mrs. James Thurber. Thurber replied in mock-dudgeon that there wasn't enough money in the world or wild horses in hell to get Helen to do a piece on him. "I would never have married a woman who would write about me while I'm alive or when I'm dead. I am repelled by husband-evaluaters," he said. Then he added this oblique reference to Hemingway: "If I lived in Cuba I probably wouldn't give a damn."

There are no new departures in *Thurber Country,* Thurber's collection of short pieces written between 1948 and 1953, but the quality of the fiction, parodies, and sketches is uniformly high. The turn to the comedy of sounds and word-play characteristic of the fairy tales and *The Beast in Me* is notable in several pieces, but the major changes in tone and method which his work was shortly to undergo are not much in evidence. In one important respect, however, *Thurber Country* is very representative of his later work, and that is in its concern with the problem of communication. As blindness narrowed his world and made him dependent as never before on the spoken word, Thurber became extraordinarily sensitive to the possibilities of misunderstanding involved in even the simplest transaetions.

Breakdowns in communication, confusions and misunderstandings of all kinds had always been one of his richest subjects for comedy, but in his later years, the act of communication took on a special importance for him.

In "The Case Book of James Thurber" it is the telephone which is the instrument of confusion: there was the girl named Sherlock Holmes who turned out to be Shirley Combs; and there was the time in Columbus, back in 1922, when Mary, the maid, reported to Mrs. Henderson that her husband, a well-known prankster and reveler, was bringing home a cock-eyed Spaniard, who later turned out to be a four-month-old cocker spaniel. The difficulty of communication in the modern world is most spectacularly demonstrated in "File and Forget," an exchange of letters between Thurber and his publisher in which he tries to get his address straightened out and to explain that he did not order thirty-six copies of a book called *Grandma Was a Nudist*. Misunderstanding piles on misunderstanding until at one point, Thurber is threatened not only with thirty-six copies of *Grandma* but thirty-six copies of his own book, *Thurber's Ark*, as well. In desperation he writes an old friend at the company, but all he gets in reply is a falsely hearty letter from a stranger, which introduces a whole new set of confusions.

Thurber tries to stem the tide, but it is no use. Everybody's place is taken by someone else, no one understands anyone else, and each exchange of letters lifts the situation a little bit farther from the level of reality. He is caught in a Kafka-like comic nightmare of incompetence, misconception and non-sequitur. At the end, his secretary writes that after receiving thirty-six copies of *Grandma* and thirty-six copies of his own book, Thurber has had "one of his spells," and says that he intends to burn all seventy-two in the middle of U.S. Highway No. 7. The story bears the unmistakable stamp of Thurber's imagination. It not only makes a pointed comment on the plight of the individual in a highly organized and depersonalized society, but it does so in terms of his special comic vision, which was always of the disruption of order, the collapse of structure, the onset of chaos. The heart of the comic, for Thurber, lay in the moment when things began to get out of hand.

Failure of communication is the implicit subject of "The Interview," an ironic comedy about the unsuccessful attempt of a reporter to interview a famous writer. Lockhorn, the writer, is an embittered alcoholic. He has moved beyond the polite hypocrisies of ordinary social intercourse, and his answers to Price's questions are deliberately outrageous and unusable. He makes his notes and outlines after his books have been published, not before, he says; then he hides them around the house for his literary executor to find. His conversation veers wildly from topic to topic, and as he talks, he gets drunker and drunker. His wife, all cool competence and disapproval, finally gets him to take his nap. As he goes, he quotes Joyce to his visitor: " 'Is love worse living?' " and he stomps up the stairs shouting out the names of his four previous wives.

At the end, Price is left with nothing. He has learned a good deal during the interview, but not what he came to find out. Lockhorn has obviously been driven to cover by too much success, too many interviews, and too much marriage, and he no longer communicates with the world in the usual ways. The story is full of brilliant details, and in its distillation of the latent humor in neurotic behavior, it is like another of Thurber's little master-pieces, "The Cane in the Corridor."

Three satiric pictures of the literary life play with the possibilities for obfuscation and misunderstanding in the practice of criticism. "The American Literary Scene" parodies Geoffrey Gorer's critique of American culture, *The Americans* (1948), and Stephen Spender's "The Situation of the American Writer"; "What Cocktail Party?" spoofs the mania for explicating T. S. Eliot's enigmatic play which swept through American intellectual circles during the theater season of 1949–50; and "A Final Note on Chanda Bell" plays absurd variations on the theme of Henry James's story about the writer whose works nobody could understand, "The Figure in the Carpet."

This last of Thurber's parodies of James is remarkable for its use of Joycean language. Chanda Bell, the eccentric and unintelligible genius, speaks in mind-spinning puns and garbles: she refers to her lawyer as Strephon, " 'a young mad I cussed in the sprig,' " and she says to the narrator, " 'You have the scaffold touch of a brain certain.' " She loves surrogate words with ambiguous meaning like the words in dreams—"rup-ture" for "rapture," "centaur" for "sender," "pressure" for "pleasure." Thurber's interest in Joyce was of long standing: he had tried to parody him in a *New Yorker* sketch back in the 1920's, and in 1953 he told an interviewer that he was having *Finnegans Wake* read aloud to him (although the experience was so frustrating to his secretary that she threw the book across the room).[8] It would be too much to claim Joyce as an important influence, but the fantastic word-play of *Ulysses* and *Finnegans Wake* obviously struck a responsive chord in Thurber's imagi-nation.

Another literary comedy involving the failure to communicate is "A

[8] "Thurber Has His Own Brand of Humor," interview with John Ferris, Columbus *Citizen*, November 8, 1953; also Helen Thurber letter to CSH.

Friend of the Earth." Thurber's work seldom derives from traditional American folk humor, but this story, like "You Could Look It Up," is an exception. It is a modern-day version of the standard nineteenth-century folk anecdote in which the sly rural character defeats the city feller. Thurber, the representative of modern urban wit, pits himself against Zeph Leggin, the self-appointed town character and cracker-barrel philosopher of the Connecticut village the Thurbers are living in, and suffers a galling defeat. Both are comedians with reputations to uphold, and they try to best each other whenever they meet. Much of the humor of the tale lies in the fact that the duels of wit between the two champions are all of a painfully low order (" 'Fella goes into this grocery store,' " says Zeph, " 'and sez to the man, "What you got in the shape of bananas?" "Cucumbers," sez the man' "), and also in the fact that the character of the shrewd old rural philosopher—a stock figure in American folklore—is viewed with positive dislike. Everyone else in the village cherishes Zeph's lame jokes and cranky ways, but for Thurber he is anathema. In *Fables for Our Time* Thurber had turned the proverbial wisdom of popular culture upside down; here, he rejects another popular stereotype, while at the same time acknowledging its power.

There are many fine stories and sketches in *Thurber Country*— "Teacher's Pet," a moving story about a middle-aged man's recollection of a painful episode in his childhood, and "The White Rabbit Caper," a highly original blending of the hardboiled detective story and the animal fable—but the showpiece of the collection is "Do You Want to Make Something Out of It?," an exercise in word-making which shows Thurber's linguistic wit and inventiveness at their best. To begin with, Thurber describes Superghosts, a sophisticated version of the old spelling game, in which the players start in the middle and spell backward and forward. It is not so much a game as it is an addiction: "The Superghost aficionado is a moody fellow, given to spelling to himself at table, not listening to his wife . . . wondering why he didn't detect, in yesterday's game, that 'cklu' is the guts of 'lacklustre' and priding himself on having stumped everybody with 'nehe,' the middle of 'swineherd.' " The expert players like to call each other up and set such problems as " 'Get out of "ightf" twenty ways' " (Thurber tossed and turned all one night and came up with ten).

Challenged to do something with *sgra*, he exhausts the possibilities sanctioned by the dictionary with *disgrace, crossgrained,* and *misgraff,* and then, leaving the realm of the actual behind, he begins to invent, offering a list of what he calls "bed-words," make-believe *sgra* words which have come to him in the small hours of the night. All of them are combinations of familiar everyday words into fanciful compounds, and Thurber presents them in mock-dictionary style:

PUSSGRAPPLE. A bickering or minor disturbance; an argument or dispute among effeminate men. Also, less frequently, a physical struggle between, or among, women.

KISSGRANNY. 1. A man who seeks the company of older women, especially older women with money; a designing fellow, a fortune hunter. 2. An overaffectionate old woman, a hugmoppet, a bunnytalker.

BLESSGRAVY. A minister or cleric; the head of a family; one who says grace. Not to be confused with praisegravy, one who extolls a woman's cooking, especially the cooking of a friend's wife; a gay fellow, a flirt, a seducer. *Colloq.*, a breakvow, a shrugholy.

FUSSGRAPE. 1. One who diets or toys with his food, a light eater, a person without appetite, a scornmuffin, a shuncabbage. 2. A man, usually American, who boasts of his knowledge of wines, a smugbottle.

And there are such other expressive coinages as *cussgravy, bassgrave, hossgrace,* and *tossgravel.* All of these comic compounds show Thurber's passion for dictionary lore and his love of remaking language, playing with the relationship between sound and meaning, pushing back the limits of the familiar, and transforming the terrain into something strange and new.

The immediate origin of the essay was an evening in Bermuda, in the spring of 1951, when Mr. John Young, proprietor of the Ledgelets, where the Thurbers often stayed, put the *sgra* challenge to Thurber. Young, in turn, had got it from the Thurbers' friend Mrs. Ronald Williams. After the piece appeared in *The New Yorker,* Thurber was deluged with mail from word-play enthusiasts, pointing out real words he had missed, like *grosgrain,* and offering him further challenges, like *msh* ("almshouse").[9] The best letter was from Richard Haydn, the English actor, who passed on some further bed-words based on *sgra,* among them "PRESSGRAP-PLER (A celebrity who resents being photographed when entering or leaving nightclubs, City Halls or an apartment tenanted by one of the opposite sex; [Colloq.] a smackbrownie [Am.] a bashbeaton [Brit.])"; and "PRISSGRAMMAR (1. One who deplores slovenly speech in others. A pedantic fellow. 2. A wife who, at social gatherings, kills the punch line of her husband's stories by correcting his English; an ainthater, a talkdainty.

---

[9] "Letter from the States," *Bermudian,* December, 1951, pp. 21, 43.

3. One who is acutely discomforted by certain Anglo-Saxon words or risqué stories; a smutwince.)" [10]

As Thurber moved into middle age, he began to think more and more about the writer and his special problems, particularly what happens to him as he gets older. His letters to Malcolm Cowley are full of these concerns. In an exchange of 1953–54 the two writers talked about style: Cowley distinguished two levels, the intoning and the plain, and said that Thurber used the plain style better than anyone since Mark Twain. Faulkner, he said, was the great master of the intoning style.[11] Cowley was at work on his illuminating study "A Natural History of the American Writer," and in it he confessed that he was using some of the jargon of the social sciences, like "provenience" and "affective." Thurber, always interested in discussions of words and their proper use, replied that "affective" was "one of those great big words, or tortured synonyms, with which psychiatry has infected the language, so that a page of type sometimes looks like a parade of Jack Johnsons wearing solid gold teeth and green carnations in the lapels of their electric blue morning suits. What could be worse than 'eroticize'? "

Cowley's psychological-sociological study of the American writer fascinated Thurber, and to a letter of 1954 he appended a three-page single-spaced postscript of questions and comment on the subject of the writer and the mysterious processes of creation. He asks Cowley if he has interviewed any writers "who are going through change of life or of religion or of viewpoint," and adds, "In our neurotic world the late middle age or sunset of the writer is becoming more tangled than the female climacteric. This may be because women are giving up something they no longer want, whereas men feel everything slipping away." He has always been fascinated by the case of Hervey Allen (who wrote *Anthony Adverse* in Bermuda), he says, because his sudden success and equally sudden decline show the potential fate of every artist. He asks about writers who need a certain kind of setting to work in: James Ramsay Ullman (another writer associated with Bermuda), like Hemingway, goes in for dangerous and violent physical activity between books; others, like D. H. Lawrence, are "forever looking for The Place." Former newspapermen, like himself, can work anywhere, he says.

The topic which most interested him, however, was the creative process, and the problem of the writer who has run dry. He notes that he has just read a monograph by a psychiatrist on the subject. He finds that he gets a great deal of help from dreams. He has read Eric Fromm's *The Forgotten*

[10] Letter from Richard Haydn, October 5, 1951 (Thurber Collection).
[11] Letter to Thurber, December 16, 1953.

Language, a study of dreams, myths, and fairy tales, and is much impressed with Fromm's view that we often get a truer version of things in our dreams than we do in real life. "I have found this to be true," he says, and no wonder. Few artists have drawn more consistently and profitably on their fantasy lives than Thurber. "One recurring dream tries to help me, but I don't yet know what it's talking about, since it deals with either the chopping away or the falling off or the burning of the limb of a tree." Although its meaning would seem to be primarily sexual, he is convinced that its real reference is to his work.[12]

Even though he was depressed and irritable much of the time during the late 1940's and early 1950's, in his personal relationships he showed his old humor and ebullience. He cracked jokes and played word games with White and De Vries: in a letter to White he asks what a man does standing up, a woman sitting down, and a dog with one leg raised; the answer—they shake hands.[13] Writing to De Vries about compulsive word-players, he recalls that his brother Robert suffered from the disease and was given to puns like "Many are cold, but few are frozen"; and he brings up the old one about the court case in which Elihu Root represented the Budweiser breweries, and the opposing lawyer said, " 'It used to be Hires' root beer, and now it's beer Hires Root.' " He speaks of the plight of the word-player when a phrase takes possession of him and begins to run through his mind over and over, and of "the meaninglessness of words like 'spool' when repeated all night, and all the Freudian tricks that pop up in nightmares—one of mine was 'as important as the "r" in shirt.' " [14]

A letter to White on his daughter Rosemary's imminent marriage is an ironic and high-spirited commentary on changing attitudes toward marriage and the unfair burden thrust by social custom on fathers of brides. Developing the theme that people today marry much younger, he observed that most of Rosemary's married friends were still in college. This meant that few wives had chosen their husbands on the basis of their promise in a career; a girl could have three children before discovering that she has married a funeral director, he said. After claiming that their own generation was more cautious, he admits that he himself had little to offer. When he married Helen he had three pints of rye and was $3500 in debt, but the difference was that he had proved that he could make money if he put his mind to it.[15]

[12] Letter to Cowley, May 20, 1954.
[13] Letter to White, July 1, 1953 (EBWP).
[14] Letter to De Vries, January 16, 1953.
[15] Letter to White, December 22, 1952 (EBWP).

Although Thurber looked at the American scene with an unsympathetic eye during this period, his reputation was growing steadily, and he was full of plans and projects. He took particular pleasure in his British following. "I have had some small serious attention from the British, where humor and fantasy in our language began and is not considered merely 'zany' or 'crackpot,'" he wrote to Cowley. "God, how I love a grownup country!" he exclaimed.[16] T. S. Eliot was a Thurber admirer, and occasionally sent him clippings from the papers which he called "Thurber items." When *Time* ran a cover story on Thurber in 1951, Eliot had this to say about his work:

> It is a form of humor which is also a way of saying something serious. There is a criticism of life at the bottom of it. It is serious and even somber. Unlike so much humor, it is not merely a criticism of manners—that is, of the superficial aspects of society at a given moment —but something more profound. His writings and also his illustrations are capable of surviving the immediate environment and time out of which they spring. To some extent, they will be a document of the age they belong to.

Thurber prized this comment on his work above all others. He told Cowley that Auden and Eliot used to astonish Edmund Wilson by their aficionado's knowledge of minute details in his prose and drawings (" 'Do you know the difference,' Auden asked Wilson, 'between the wall maps in GHQ men and GHQ women in "The War Between Men and Women?", Wilson spluttered that of course he didn't. 'There is no Florida on the map in GHQ women,' said Auden severely and accusingly' "). He received many fan letters from British writers and intellectuals: Wilfred Taylor, the Scottish journalist, after hearing him on a BBC broadcast, wrote him in 1952 that for many Scotsmen, he and E. B. White stood for "the real America." "Your quiet and witty and sane voices more than make up for the raucous and rather strident voices that sometimes reach us here," he said. Taylor met Thurber a few years later, and contributed an appreciative essay on him to the *Rothmill Quarterly*. When A. L. Rowse, the noted historian, lectured at Ohio State in 1956, he said that Thurber was by now "part of the English landscape." [17]

The *Time* essay gave a laudatory and detailed biographical portrait of

---

[16] Letter to Cowley, July 31, 1952.
[17] Wilfred Taylor, letter to Thurber and White, spring, 1952 (EBWP); Taylor's essay appeared in *Rothmill Quarterly*, Autumn-Winter, 1958, pp. 94–101; Rowse's comment was reported in the Columbus *Dispatch*, January 20, 1956.

Thurber, and it included, in addition to Eliot's comment on his importance as a humorist, a statement by E. B. White which is probably the best critical description of Thurber's unique imagination ever made:

> When I first knew him, his mind was unbelievably restless and made him uncomfortable at all hours. Now, almost 25 years later, I can't see that it has relaxed. He still pulls at his hair and trembles all over, as though he were about to sell his first piece. His thoughts have always been a tangle of baseball scores, Civil War tactics, Henry James, personal maladjustments, terrier puppies, literary tide rips, ancient myths and modern apprehensions. Through this jungle stalk the unpredictable ghosts of his relatives in Columbus, Ohio.

Throughout the 1950's there were innumerable plans and efforts to adapt Thurber's work to the theater, the film, television, and even the dance. Anything like a complete listing would be tedious, but among the projects conceived of or tried out between 1950 and 1955 would be the ambitious plan of UPA productions (the creators of the imaginative cartoons "Gerald McBoing-Boing" and "Mr. Magoo") to do a feature-length film of Thurber stories and cartoons which would blend live action and animated drawings. Originally titled "Thurber Carnival," and then "Men, Women, and Dogs," the film was to open with a lecture by Thurber on the battle of the sexes, illustrated with Thurber cartoons; then there would be animated versions of "The Unicorn in the Garden" and "You Could Look It Up," followed by live scenes from the Mr. and Mrs. Monroe stories, then a series of cartoons about animals, and finally "The White Deer." [18] The project unfortunately never materialized, although UPA did make an excellent "Unicorn in the Garden" in 1961. Commenting in *Publisher's Weekly* (August 6, 1952) on a report that there were plans to do *My Life and Hard Times* and *The Thurber Album* on television, Thurber said, "There are always a lot of prospects but most of the time nothing happens. I don't even think about it."

There was an emasculated version of "The Greatest Man in the World" on "Robert Montgomery Presents," in 1953, and a good production of "The Remarkable Case of Mr. Bruhl" on "Omnibus," in 1954. [19] One of Thurber's few unqualified television successes was the "Motorola TV Hour" production of *The Thirteen Clocks*, with Basil Rathbone as the Duke, Sir Cedric Hardwicke as the Golux, John Raitt as the minstrel-

---

[18] Sayre, "Priceless Gift of Laughter."
[19] Dean Myers, "On the Air," Columbus *Dispatch*, January 17, 1954.

prince, and Roberta Peters as the princess. *Life* called the production "one of television's finest achievements in make-believe." [20] Thurber had better luck on the stage than in films or television. The Barter Theater did a well-received dramatic version of *The Thirteen Clocks* in 1953, and in 1955 the off-Broadway Theater de Lys presented an adaptation by Paul Ellwood and St. John Terrell of the Mr. and Mrs. Monroe stories under the title *Three by Thurber.* Brooks Atkinson, reviewing for the New York *Times*, spoke with admiration of Thurber's comic insight into the battle of the sexes, but felt that much of Thurber's wit and subtlety was lost in translating the stories to the stage. Wolcott Gibbs, writing in *The New Yorker*, felt that the sketches were too brief and too similar to stand up as a full evening's program.[21] A number of chamber operas and children's operas were based on Thurber stories, and at one time, Jule Styne planned to make a musical out of *The Wonderful O*, although the project was never completed. Doris Humphrey did a successful ballet version of "The Race of Life," and Charles Weidman's dance company performed several of the fables as well as the cartoon narrative "The War Between Men and Women." [22]

Thurber was highly productive throughout the 1950's but there were certain projects which he was maddeningly unable to finish. There was the ill-fated *New Yorker* play, which he began in 1943 and was still working on when he died. It was to be a character study of Harold Ross, and to draw on some of the farcical moments in the history of the magazine, but it was also to be a political satire, and when Governor Dewey was defeated in the 1948 election, a good deal of its point was lost. Thurber put it aside for a time and began work on a modern version of the Enoch Arden story, set in Bermuda. In 1949 the New York *Times* reported that he had decided to combine the two plays under the title "Make My Bed." In 1951 Thurber announced that he had finished parts of each of the three acts and had sent them to Nugent, who was going to co-author the play, now titled "The Moon in Aries." The collaboration never got beyond the discussion stage, and in 1952 Thurber told a *Times* interviewer that when Nugent read the script, he said, " 'What you appear to have is six-and-a-half first acts, some unrelated scenes, and four or five third acts. Also a guy whose name is

[20] *Life*, January 11, 1954; John Crosby was also enthusiastic: "Thurber Fairy Story Enchanting," Miami *Herald*, January 7, 1954.

[21] Atkinson, "Theatre: Thurberisms," New York *Times*, March 9, 1955; Gibbs, "In a Glass Darkly," *The New Yorker*, March 19, 1955.

[22] *New York Times Magazine*, June 20, 1954. Robert E. Morsberger gives a comprehensive account of the various efforts to dramatize Thurber's material in chapter 7 of his book, *James Thurber.*

changed between the first and third acts from Thatcher to Johnson, though I assume it's the same person." Talking to an interviewer in Columbus, in December of 1953, Thurber said that as soon as he finished his current project, he was going to return to the play, which he described as "a tribute to Harold Ross." [23]

In the middle 1950's, however, he had another go at the Bermuda play, now titled "The Welcoming Arms." He wrote De Vries in 1956 that he wanted it "to make some sense about the predicament of the American writer, while at the same time basically dealing with two men and a woman and two younger men and a younger woman. The man of action against the man of sensibility and thought." [24] The themes were close to Thurber's heart, but he was unable to find the right dramatic structure for them, and after 1957 he gave the whole thing up. The Ross project, meanwhile, was temporarily diverted into the biographical memoirs which ran first in the *Atlantic Monthly* and then appeared in book form as *The Years with Ross*. Nevertheless, Thurber never gave up his plans for the play. He told interviewers in 1957 and 1959 that he was working on it, and in 1960 he announced to a *Herald Tribune* reporter that he expected to have it ready for the 1961 season. The title was still "Make My Bed," and he wanted Robert Preston, who had played in the 1952 revival of *The Male Animal*, for the leading role. When the reporter asked him if he would like to play in it himself, he said, " 'Yeah, I'd love it . . . I just want to have one scene in the play, a yelling fight with Ross,' " remembering, no doubt, the time when Ross tried to bawl him out for having overstayed his vacation to look for a lost dog.[25]

Another unfinished project was the fantasy-satire originally entitled "The Spoodle." He wanted to write something that would sum up all of his moral and intellectual judgments on American life, a work that would stand as his definitive satiric statement, and he worked at it, with increasing frustration, from the late 1940's to the end of his life. It started out as a sharply focused political satire, ridiculing the House Committee on Un-American Activities and the whole confused atmosphere of suspicion, accusation, and investigation which clouded the public scene in the days of Senator McCarthy's power.[26] After a number of false starts, however, he dropped "The Spoodle," and in early 1953 he started work on another

[23] News stories and interviews in the New York *Times*, August 20, 1949, January 21, 1951, November 16, 1952; and in the Columbus *Dispatch*, December 24, 1953.

[24] Letter to De Vries, July 2, 1956.

[25] "Thurber Doing Play on Ross," New York *Herald Tribune*, April 24, 1960.

[26] He first talked about "The Spoodle" in his interview with Harvey Breit, New York *Times*, December 4, 1949.

fantasy called "The Sleeping Man," which became his major project for
the next two years. He described it to an interviewer as "a fairy tale satire
on the anxieties of the modern middle-aged married American male,"
which would include everything from "a study of domestic frustrations to
a satire on political probes." The protagonist falls asleep, and his dreams
and memories offer a kaleidoscopic image, public and private, of American
life.[27]

He worked hard on it, and he wrote Elmer Davis late in 1953 that he
thought it was the best thing he had done.[28] It included much of the
material originally intended for "The Spoodle," but it cut a much wider
swath than the earlier piece. It was full of the wild puns and garbles of
famous lines of poetry to which he was increasingly addicted. Many of those
he liked best he dug out and used in other pieces later on, like "Ah, what
a dusty answer gets the soul when hot for certain keys in this our life,"
"Loneliest of these, the married now are hung with gloom across the vow,"
and "McCarthage delenda est." [29] In fact, throughout the 1950's, he
consistently mined his unfinished manuscripts for puns, quips, and conversational exchanges.

Simon & Schuster announced the new work under a new title, "The
Train on Track Six," in their spring list for 1955, but it did not appear.
Thurber wrote Elmer Davis in 1956 that he had abandoned the whole
project, but he was working on it again in 1957 under the title "The Train
on Track Five." [30] As the years went on, he realized that he was hopelessly
entangled in the project and so he dropped it and returned to his original
idea, "The Spoodle," under a new title, "The Grawk." He gave up "Spoodle" when someone said that the word was a coinage for a dog part spaniel
and part poodle, and since the satire dealt with "an unidentified flying thing
that attacks the roofs of a city," Thurber felt that "Grawk" (a word
resurrected from his old "Pet Department") would be more appropriate.
The piece was "a serious, sometimes savage" satire, he told Rod Nordell
in 1959. He was still talking about it the following year, but under a new
title, "The Nightinghoul." [31] His continuing struggle with this project in
all its various versions shows just how intensely he wanted to make a major

[27] He described "The Sleeping Man" in interviews in the Edgartown (Mass.) *Standard-Times*, July 25, 1953; the Columbus *Citizen*, November 8, 1953; the Columbus *Dispatch*, December 24, 1953.
[28] Letter to Davis, October 28, 1953.
[29] Letters to Elmer Davis and Malcolm Cowley in 1953–54 contain a number of these puns and garbles from "The Sleeping Man."
[30] Interview with Maurice Dolbier, New York *Herald Tribune*, November 3, 1957.
[31] Interview with Rod Nordell, *Christian Science Monitor*, June 4, 1959; also "Thurber Doing Play on Ross," New York *Herald Tribune*, April 24, 1960.

book-length statement about modern life, and just how difficult the problem of structure always was for him.

Thurber was in much better spirits in the mid-1950's than he was in the early years of the decade. The country seemed to be recovering from the McCarthy sickness, and he himself was in better health than he had been. Accepting the Liberty and Justice Book Award from the American Library Association in 1957 for *Further Fables for Our Time*, he said that "Recent shadows are receding"; and he remarked to an interviewer that he did not think his new book, *The Wonderful O*, which dealt with freedom, would " 'be looked at askance, as it might have been a few years ago when the American air was thick with suspicion of non-conformity.' " " 'It seems about two decades ago that we were in such a crazy "Alice-in-Wonderland" state of mind,' " he said.[32] In the spring of 1955, he and Helen went to England and France again, and Thurber was full of energy, confidence, and good will. Helen wrote the De Vrieses from Paris in May that on a recent nightclub outing Thurber had been irrepressible, talking, drinking, singing with the band, and "dancing like mad until dawn." A few months later, in Edinburgh, he took part in a memorable all-night session of talk and refreshment with Sir Compton Mackenzie, Wilfred Taylor and other British writers. In his essay in the *Rothmill Quarterly* Taylor described the evening, and said that Thurber was even larger in life than he was in print, his conversation just as funny, as wise, and as unique as his writings. Mackenzie sent Thurber an appreciative note after the all-night session, in which he said that meeting Thurber was "one of the notable pleasures" of his life.

[32] "His Imagination Won Him Award," interview with Marian Robb, Bermuda *Mid-Ocean News*, April 26, 1957.

17

Fables and Word Games

T HE CHANGES IN THURBER'S VIEW of life and in his artistic
method which began to appear in the late 1940's become the dominant feature of his work in the mid-1950's. On the surface, his life was
secure and happy—his marriage was highly successful, he was working more
productively than ever, and he was praised and honored on every side. Yet
underneath, there were frustrations, anxieties and a deepening strain of
melancholy. Although on one level he had made a remarkable adjustment
to his blindness, the loss of his sight was a psychic blow from which he
never really recovered. In addition, the world at large outraged him daily
with examples of vulgarity, stupidity, irrationality, and self-destructiveness.
Throughout the 1950's there is an anger and desperation in much of
Thurber's conversation and writing which stand in sharp contrast to the
tolerant humor and faith in man which underlie his earlier work.

" 'I think there's been a fall-out of powdered fruitcake—everyone's going
nuts,' " he remarked in an interview.[1] The theme of such typical later works
as "The Future, If Any, of Comedy" is decline—of form, style, good sense,
"human stature, hope, humor." The great issue becomes, simply, survival
in a world of disintegrating standards. The spirit of much of his later work
is satiric rather than humorous: anger, he observed in the Foreword to

---

[1] "An Old Hand at Humor," *Life*, March 14, 1960.

Lanterns and Lances, had become "one of the necessary virtues." The humor is still there, but it is a wild dark humor, often playing on the brink of hysteria, and in its bizarre anecdotes and compulsive verbal acrobatics it suggests a world collapsing into chaos.

The later manner is strikingly evident in *Further Fables for Our Time* (1956). While at first glance they seem to be a return to the successful formula of the 1940 *Fables for Our Time,* they are in fact quite different. They take a dark and pessimistic view of the human condition, and they play with language in a wild and original way. The comedy of the earlier fables was the comedy of irreverence toward the encapsulated wisdom of the past, as in "The Little Girl and the Wolf." The comedy of the 1957 fables is the grim comedy of looking beyond the surface to the ineradicable paradoxes and limitations of life. In "The Rose and the Weed" the rose boasts of her beauty, and the weed congratulates himself on his strength; a strong wind suddenly decapitates the rose, and the hand of the gardener comes out of nowhere and pulls up the weed. The moral: "Tout, *as the French say, in a philosophy older than ours and an idiom often more succinct,* passe." The gloomy view of Ecclesiastes, that all is vanity, and that one generation passeth and another generation cometh, underlies the collection as a whole.

A strong vein of misanthropy accompanies the philosophic pessimism of *Further Fables.* " 'Man will go on forever, but you will be one with the mammoth and the mastodon, for monstrosity is the behemother of extinction,' " boasts man to the dinosaur. " 'There are worse things than being extinct,' said the dinosaur sourly, 'and one of them is being you.' " In "The Truth About Toads," the creatures are drinking and bragging at the Fauna Club. The Rooster, the Stork, and the Raven boast of their powers, and the Toad says expansively that he has a precious jewel in his head. The others scoff at him, and then, when he falls asleep, they get the woodpecker to pound a hole in his head. What they find is nothing: "There wasn't anything there, gleaming or lovely or precious." The savage moral: *"Open most heads and you will find nothing shining, not even a mind."* E. B. White called this uncomfortable fable "the best one you ever wrote," and he added, "You are the only living fable writer." [2]

In contrast to the fables of 1940, the values expressed in *Further Fables* are highly conservative. In fable after fable, folly, wishful thinking, and sentimental illusions are measured and shown up by a hard traditional moral wisdom. The wealthy young wolf who wanted to show off buys a

[2] Letter to Thurber, March 21, 1956 (EBWP).

Blitzen Bearcat and tears around town with "a speed-crazy young wolfess." He fails to make it one day when he tries to turn into Central Park "while travelling at a rate of 175 miles an hour, watching television, and holding hands." The moral: *"Where most of us end up there is no knowing, but the hellbent get where they are going."* On a deeper level, "The Clothes Moth and the Luna Moth" dramatizes the uncomfortable truth that life is less than we think it is. The amorous clothes moth batters himself to death trying to open the window for the beautiful Luna Moth, who is attracted not to him, as he thinks, but to the candle flame on the mantel-piece. Once in, she flies to the flame and is consumed "with a little zishing sound like that made by a lighted cigarette dropped in a cup of coffee." The cynical implications of the closing image are underscored by the moral: *"Love is blind, but desire just doesn't give a good goddam."*

One group of fables reflects Thurber's intense political concern during the 1950's. All of these deal with the threat to individual liberty posed by McCarthy-style accusations and investigations. Thurber's own favorite among these was "The Trial of the Old Watchdog," in which a faithful country watchdog is arrested for the murder of a lamb actually killed by a fox, and is brought to trial. The jury and spectators are all foxes, and the judge is a kangaroo. A witness says, " 'I didn't actually see this lamb-killer kill this lamb . . . but I almost did.' " The judge says, " 'That's close enough.' " The jury recommends that he be acquitted rather than hung, because having been accused, he will be suspected all the days of his life. " 'Guilt by exoneration!' " cries the prosecutor, approvingly. " 'What a lovely way to end his usefulness!' "

The growing conservatism and pessimism of Thurber's later work is paradoxically accompanied by a more and more self-conscious and experimental play with language. *Further Fables* is full of puns, rhymes, coinages, and literary allusions. The prose is carefully patterned, clause balanced against clause, and phrase against phrase, as in this description of the hedonistic bluebird: "He sat loose, sang pretty, and slept tight, in a hundred different honey locusts and cherry trees and lilac bushes." The language sparkles with comic figures of speech and unexpected coinages. The gloomy brother of the hedonistic bluebird, for example, "never flew higher than you could throw a sofa." Many of the coinages create fresh images of sound and movement: Fleder, a great-great-great-grandfather bat, "chittered, quickered, and zickered" around his cave; a primeval creature leaves the water and begins "flobbering" up the sand; the busybody female hare who wants to get everyone up and working bustles into the room, "buttocky buttocky." Other coinages show Thurber's love of Joycean word-making in the manner of "Do You Want to Make Something of It?"—the female guinea pig who has had one hundred and seventy-three young and then let herself go is a "bragdowdy," and the moral to the story of the red squirrel who has destroyed the romantic illusions of the other creatures is, *"O why should the shattermyth have to be a crumplehope and a dampenglee?"*

Language, in these later pieces, comes to be the basic principle of order in life; disaster appears as the breakdown of verbal communication.[3] "The Weaver and the Worm" makes the point with classic economy: the weaver admires a silkworm spinning his cocoon, and asks, " 'Where do you get that stuff?' " The silkworm answers innocently, " 'Do you want to make something out of it?' " They go their separate ways, each feeling that the other has insulted him. "We live, man and worm, in a time when almost everything can mean almost anything, for this is the age of gobbledygook, doubletalk, and gudda." The moral: *"A word to the wise is not sufficient if it doesn't make any sense."*

In the final fable, "The Shore and the Sea," the self-destructive panic of the lemmings is set off by a series of verbal confusions. Their stampede toward the sea is a frightening re-enactment of the comic and harmless confusion described by Thurber years before in "The Day the Dam Broke," and the difference between the two episodes says a good deal about the change in Thurber's view of life in his later years. One old scholarly lemming refuses to be panicked. He watches his fellow creatures destroy themselves, tears up what he has written, and prepares to start over.

Like *The Last Flower* and "The Last Clock," "The Shore and the Sea" is one of those cosmic-apocalyptic fables in which Thurber presented the distilled essence of his view of life, and here it is a dark and pessimistic one. The hysterical lemmings are a depressing symbol of man, and the suggestion that the life cycle will bring along a new generation carries little comfort with it. There is no last flower to stand as a token of hope, only the old scholar, ready to record the next round of folly. In earlier years, Thurber had relished life's confusions; by the 1950's he found them disturbing and frightening.

The dark tone of *Further Fables* does not represent a sudden change in Thurber. His humor was always inextricably intertwined with fear, anguish, and desperation. As far back as 1933 he observed that the source of humor was "the damp hand of melancholy"; and in 1955, when Alistair Cooke cited the old Roman saying that a man could not be a great comedian unless he was well acquainted with the sadness of things, Thurber agreed, saying,

[3] Malcolm Cowley describes Thurber's world of words in his review of *Further Fables for Our Time*, "Lions and Lemmings," *Reporter*, XV (December 13, 1956), 42–44.

" 'It's very hard to divorce humor from the other things in life. Humor is the other side of tragedy.' " He was well aware of the gloomy strain in the fables, and in a letter to White he noted that seventy percent were about death—" 'I am the deathiest of fable writers,' " he said.[4]

In later years he consistently emphasized the serious side of his work, as his desire to lecture and to moralize became stronger and stronger. "I am surprised that so few people see the figure of seriousness in the carpet of my humor and comedy," he wrote to Dr. Pollard, and he went on to say that *Further Fables* was his favorite recent book precisely because of its blend of humor and seriousness. He was proud of the fact that it won the 1957 American Library Association award for the work "in the entire field of imaginative literature that had done the most for the cause of liberty and justice." [5]

In 1957 Thurber brought out *Alarms and Diversions,* an anthology of his best prose since 1942 and of his drawings from as far back as 1931. In addition, there were ten new pieces, representing his work since 1954. The book was obviously planned as a companion volume to the earlier anthology, *The Thurber Carnival* (Harper & Brothers did in fact bring out a matched boxed set of the two in 1959), and a comparison of them points up some of the differences between earlier and later Thurber. There is less fiction in *Alarms and Diversions,* and there are fewer memorable characters, fictional or real. *The Thurber Carnival* included *My Life and Hard Times,* with its gallery of Columbus eccentrics, as well as such varied figures as Walter Mitty, Emma Inch, Doc Marlow, Olympy, and Rex, the bull terrier. In *Alarms and Diversions* there are Willie Stevens, of the Hall-Mills murder case, Aunt Margery Albright, and Thurber's mother, but the company is a small one. Broadly speaking, one can see a moving away from the comedy of character to the comedy of words and ideas in the later volume. The new pieces show this difference very clearly. There is no short story or even parody among them; for the most part, they are essays and dialogues on contemporary culture. They are less concerned with the comic predicaments of the author than early Thurber, and more with the state of the modern world.

The highlight of the new material in *Alarms and Diversions* is "The Psychosemanticist Will See You Now, Mr. Thurber," a brilliant attack on the forces destroying the precision and beauty of the English language, and a plea for traditional standards of taste and style. The American indifference to grace, harmony, and other aesthetic considerations is particularly

---

[4] Letter to White, April 16, 1956 (EBWP).
[5] Quoted in his interview with Marian Robb, Bermuda *Mid-Ocean News*, April 26, 1957.

evident in what we have done to our language, says Thurber. He parodies the symptoms of the disease in his description of it. Our fondness for vague and ponderous phrases has infected the language with an acute case of "polysyllabic monstrositis," he says; "elephantiasis of cliché" has set in, and "the onset of utter meaninglessness is imminent." Twisting Goldsmith's famous lines, he moralizes on the situation in eighteenth-century fashion: " 'Ill fares the land, to galloping fears a prey, where gobbledygook accumulates, and words decay.' "

Politicians, administrators, and psychologists are among the chief perpetrators of these outrages, but he reserves his ultimate wrath for the assaults of Madison Avenue on order and decency in language. "The conspiracy of yammer and merchandising against literate speech" reached its apogee, in his opinion, in the notorious singing commercial, "Winston tastes good like a cigarette should." In a devastating *reductio ad absurdum,* Thurber goes them one better. He has a good slogan for a brewery, he says: "We still brew good like we used to could."

Lanterns and Lances, Thurber's last collection (1961), further develops the theme that everything in the modern world is going downhill. The chief targets for his concern are the state of the language and the present condition of comedy. For Thurber, as for such social critics as Ezra Pound and George Orwell, language and culture were inseparable. If thought was timid and stereotyped, if grace, order and beauty were deteriorating in society at large, the language would show it; conversely, if the language was losing its precision and accuracy, society was in danger. He made the point over and over that in the era of the Cold War, a healthy language was more than ever a condition of survival, but wherever he turned, he encountered a growing carelessness and indifference to standards.

In "Friends, Romans, Countrymen, Lend Me Your Ear Muffs" he points to the sloppiness of pronunciation which puts an extra syllable into words like "sparkling" ("the bastard sound of 'sparkeling' is heard, day in and night out, in radio and television commercials") and the indifference to grammar which confuses transitive and intransitive verbs ("Thus a certain cigarette 'travels and gentles the smoke' ") as examples of the current breakdown of forms. He has an uneasy premonition of the future: in a dream, a woman says to him, " 'We can sleep twenty people in this house in a pinch, but we can only eat twelve.' " In "The Spreading *You Know*" he points with distaste to the latest blight to afflict the language— the sudden popularity of the phrase, "you know," as a filler or bit of verbal padding (" 'The other day I saw, you know, Henry Johnson, the, you know, former publicity man for, you know, the Charteriss Publishing Company' ' "). Depressed by the signs of linguistic decay, he says that he is currently at work on a book to be called *A Farewell to Speech or The Decline and Fall of the King's English.*

On the other hand, Thurber liked to collect the oddities of speech which identify a region or a class. For example, the characteristic sound of the American woman is "and-uh," and of the British male, "but-um-uh." The expressions sound almost the same, but they are used differently: the American woman "puts in the 'uh' because she is not quite sure what she is about to say, having got ahead of her story or lost track of it, whereas the 'but-um-uh' of the English is used as a gesture, like the waving of a lighted cigarette in the air, the striking of a match, or the lifting of a highball glass." He had a special fondness for the expressions of old country women: ladies of his mother's generation in Ohio always pronounced "laugh" as though it were "lay-uff," and an elderly Connecticut woman once said to him " 'I'll just nice up this room before the company comes.' "

He treasured such oddities because they were picturesque, but for the most part, he disapproved of deviations from traditionally accepted usage. He recognized that change is in the very nature of language, but he wanted to hold hard to the old standards and distinctions. "A living language is an expanding language, to be sure," he wrote, "but care should take itself that the language does not crack like a dry stick in the process." He deplored the disappearance of Latin from the high schools. " 'What does he know of English who only English knows?' " he asks, in one of those paraphrases of famous quotations which became a trademark of his style in later years. "In my day, Latin was taught in high schools to prepare the youthful mind for the endless war between meaning and gobbledegook," he wrote, but it was too hard, and so it became a casualty of the general abandoning of standards characteristic of the modern world.

When he looked at comedy, he found the prospect equally depressing. Throughout the decade he had been pronouncing the obituary of comedy and humor (and calling for a renewal of their powers), and the subject became one of his favorite essay topics. He saw literature and the theater as given over to formlessness and a decadent view of life. What little comedy survived was either mindless fluff or crude farce ("We are a nation that has always gone in for the loud laugh, the wow, the yak . . . the gagerissimo," rather than "the appreciative smile," he observed rather bitterly in 1960).[6] One of the causes for this retrogression in the life of comedy in America was the atmosphere of political intimidation which had

---

[6] "On the Quality of Mirth," New York *Times* Theater Section, February 21, 1960.

made all artists and intellectuals jittery and self-conscious ever since the late 1940's. But Thurber recognized that the decline of comedy was more than a casualty of politics or the Bomb: like the degradation of language, it was a symptom of a general loss of values, and this is the theme of such late essays as "The Case for Comedy" and "The Future, If Any, of Comedy, or Where Do We Non-Go from Here?"

The times are sick and confused, the indictment runs. We live in "the era of Science and Angst"; we are surrounded by "Bedlam and Babel." More and more people are suffering "from everything from the galloping jumps to the mumbling crumbles." Morbid and neurotic themes dominate the theater. Lying in bed at night, Thurber retitles some famous comedies of the past to suit the present mood: among others, he comes up with *Abie's Irish Neurosis*, *I Dismember Mama*, *Toys in the Psychosomatic*, *The Glands Menagerie*, and *Oklahomasexual*. The change in the view of human nature taken by a Freud-centered culture can be seen in what has happened to words like "funny" and "gay," which used to be happy epithets, but now have more troubling connotations. The heart, the symbol of man's inner nature, is no longer identified with his nobler qualities, but with "the disturbed psyche, the deranged glands, and the jumpy central nervous system." In a passage in "The Future, If Any, of Comedy" which reveals his own traditional stoic values, Thurber observes, "I'm not pleading for the heart that leaps up when it beholds a rainbow in the sky. . . . The sentimental pure heart of Galahad is gone with the knightly years, but I still believe in the heart of the George Meredith character that was not made of the stuff that breaks."

The delusions of the time cry out for great satire: man's foolish assumption that he is superior to the animals, the fanaticism of political ideologies ("Complete power not only corrupts but it also attracts the mad"), the impact of modern psychology and psychiatry ("I heard of one frightened woman who burst into her doctor's office crying, 'I think I have got psychotherapy!' "), the universal worship of the specialist, or the Area Man ("Every man is now an island unto himself, interested in, even obsessed by, his own preoccupation"), and the progressive dehumanization of the species are prime subjects, but no great satirist's voice is heard. Behind it all is one chilling fact: "The greatest truth of our time is both simple and awful—total war means annihilation, and the Brink of War has become the Brink of Was."

An old-fashioned Midwestern suspicion of anything abnormal or perverse, as well as an innate fastidiousness of taste lie behind many of Thurber's strictures on the modern cultural scene. The prudery which led him to object to the novels of D. H. Lawrence and to take a stand for "clean love" in his column for the Columbus *Dispatch* in 1923 shows itself again in 1961 in his disapproval of "the modern morbid playwrights and sex novelists, who are more interested in the sordid corners of human life than in the human heart." He did not care for the "sick" humor which was emerging in the 1950's; to him, humor was healthy and health-giving. His own taste—as *The Male Animal* indicates—was for the comedy of American family life, like Frank Craven's *The First Year* and Clarence Day's *Life with Father*, which found its truth and humor in the normal and the familiar. What both the theater and society needed, he argued, was a return to comedy, for in comedy there were civilizing and healing virtues—form, intelligence, and a sane and balanced view of life. He was delighted with *My Fair Lady* because it exhibited just these qualities. It was one of those rare experiences, he wrote, in which "the heart and mind are lifted, equally and at once, by the creative union of perception and grace."

In these late essays on comedy and language, Thurber is defending traditional standards and virtues, waging war against the new barbarism, building walls, as Paul Jennings said, against Chaos.[7] At the same time, however, the bold play with language in his conversation pieces and word games creates a dream-like and surreal world in which familiar reality is always in motion, dissolving, flowing, and reshaping itself into something strange and new. "Midnight at Tim's Place" is typical. The setting is a bar (obviously Thurber's favorite spa, Tim Costello's), the hour is late, and the Thurbers have just been joined by an attractive young woman and a man who moves in saying, *"Horas non numero nisi serenas."* The speakers begin to play conversational games with one another, and as they assume false names, get off esoteric puns, and engage in contests of fanciful invention, reality and fantasy begin to change places. The stranger pretends to take Thurber for Bing Crosby. " 'How are you, Bing?' " he asks. " *'Non sum qualis eram sub regno bony Sinatra,' "* replies Thurber, mixing ancient and modern cultures in an impressively learned pun on Horace's famous line.

The conversation piece was a natural form for Thurber. He loved the give and take of argument, the louder and more opinionated the better, and in the years of his blindness these dramatized dialogues became one of his favorite representations of life. Most of them are highly competitive encounters, reflecting Thurber's own aggressive spirit. The speakers meet not so much to communicate as to score points against one another.

---

[7] "Thurber: Man Against Monsters," *Observer*, November 5, 1961.

Challenges are offered and accepted, the weapons are preposterous assertions, quips, and literary allusions, and the stakes are psychological victory or defeat. In "The Lady from the Land," a lady takes the position that God is a woman. Thurber lights a cigarette and begins to develop the implications of this assertive feminism: " 'Listen my children and you shall hear of the midnight ride of Paula Revere,' " he recites, and continues with " 'The girl stood on the burning deck whence all but she had fled.' " In "The Saving Grace," when Thurber is expounding on the decline of humor, a man somewhat the worse for drink comes over and makes a lame pun: " 'the pain in Twain stays mainly in the brain.' " Thurber comes back with a better one: " 'If you prefer "I think, therefore I am," to *"Non sum qualis eram,"* you are putting Descartes before Horace.' " The man is taken aback. " 'Nuts,' " he says, and weaves away.

The Thurber who stalks through these scenes, lecturing, arguing, punning, and quoting his opponents into submission, is a very different figure from the timid and ineffective protagonist of the early stories and sketches. Until the time of his blindness he saw himself most characteristically in the role of comic victim and neurotic misfit; later, this self-portrait begins to change, and in his later work, he is most often the self-confident middle-aged author, wit, and conversationalist, a man more than equal to whatever challenges life might put to him. It is significant that in *Lanterns and Lances* and *Credos and Curios* only one piece, "My Senegalese Birds and Siamese Cats," deals in the comedy of autobiographical misadventure. This change in dramatic persona obviously reflects certain changes in the circumstances of Thurber's life. His inner struggle against the handicap of blindness obviously made a kind of aggressiveness psychologically necessary to him; then, too, middle age and success made the role of the inept American male less and less real as an expression of his own experience. His world had become the world of cocktail parties with rich and talented people in New York and London, and one of the characters he enjoys playing in the late essays is that of Jamesian gentleman, formal, polite, and master of the art of repartee (" 'Don't you think that things are getting better?' a woman asked me not long ago at a party. 'Madam,' I replied, in my courtly, but slightly edged fashion, 'things will take care of themselves. What I am interested in is people' "). He does not abandon the role of the neurotic, however; often he portrays himself as the nervous insomniac, desperately playing word games to keep the terrors of the night at bay, but the emphasis in these pieces is on his wit and learning and intellectual energy and not on his fears and weaknesses.

In "Conversation Piece: Connecticut," Thurber and a stranger who suddenly materializes in the living room (obviously an alter ego) pursue the themes of anxiety and decline into the world of language. The stranger announces that all he can think of is nervous ailments, and he broaches the subject in a flurry of puns: " 'Have you heard of the roofer who got shingles from Sears, Roebuck? Or the steeple-chase horse with the gallop-ing jumps, or the jittery cup-bearer of the gods who had the Hebe Jee-bies. . . .' " Thurber counters with a highly fanciful treatment of gram-mar, climaxing his lecture with a Joycean flourish: " 'The great good place, the lighted place, has become the lought place, so close to lost that our last link with light is—' " The stranger advises him to get away from words for a while and to put on some music, but Thurber immediately thinks of the word "music" and compulsively begins to take it apart:

> "The word is icsum and mucsi," I said. "It is also musci and scumi. If you say 'Sicum!' your dog starts barking at nothing, and if you say 'Sucim,' the pigs in the barnyard start squealing and grunting. 'Mu-ics' is the cat's miaow. Say 'imsci' and the Russians are upon you. As for mucis—my God, are you ready for another drink al-ready?"

Thurber's mind, as Kenneth Tynan once observed, was "a seething kaleido-scope" of word forms and word shapes.[8] There is something close to desperation in the restless energy with which he takes words apart, spells them backward, and rearranges them, as though he were looking for the key to reality in the structure of the word.

The most striking examples of Thurber's verbal passion are the introspec-tive word-game pieces like "The Tyranny of Trivia" and "The Watchers of the Night." Lying nervously awake at three in the morning, "gloomily staring at the mushroom-shaped ceiling," and thinking of death, he plays restlessly with words and letters. Sometimes he experiments with tongue-twisters like "We supply watchmen to watch men you want watched," and working up to "We supply wristwatches for witchwatchers watching witches Washington wishes watched." More complicated rituals include rewriting Poe's "The Raven" from the point of view of the bird instead of that of the man; meditating, like Ishmael in *Moby Dick*, on the mysteri-ous and frightening ambiguities of the word "white"; and thinking of palindromes, those words or phrases which are the same spelled backward or forward—" 'Madam, I'm Adam,' " " 'a man, a plan, a canal, Panama,' "

[8] Kenneth Tynan in a BBC tribute to Thurber, quoted in Morsberger, *James Thurber*, p. 194.

and " 'he goddam mad dog, eh?' " One night, brooding on the precarious-
ness of language, where the thinnest line separates sense from nonsense,
he toys with the possibilities of chaos inherent in the change of a single
letter in a word: " 'A stitch in time saves none' . . . 'There's no business
like shoe business' . . . 'Don, give up the ship.' "

In "The Tyranny of Trivia" he surveys the kinds of experience associated
with various letters. He recommends "N" to his doctor, a nervous man,
because it is the letter of novocain, nicotine, and narcotic, but he warns
him against slipping " 'too easily from nocturne and Nepenthe into some
such sequelae as ninety naked night nurses.' " "B" is the letter of noise
and aggression: "the bugler, braggart, blowhard . . . barker, booster,
bouncer, bruiser, and so on." "C" and "M" are the letters of antipathies:
"cat and mouse, cobra and mongoose, Capulet and Montague." "F" is a
disturbing letter, standing for "falter, foozle, flunk, flop" as well as "fake,
fallacious, flimflam, fishy, fib, fob, foist, forgery . . . and fabrication." "Its
friend is too close to fiend for comfort. . . . If its fizzle doesn't get us,
its fission may."

The style of these later pieces is self-conscious, artificial, almost rococo
in its fondness for decorative flourishes and busy detail. Puns are everywhere, ranging from the simple to the complex: on one level there is
Thurber's close friend Walter Ego, or his theory of "Elaine Vital, the
female life force," which he opposes to Bergson's Elan Vital; and there
is his comment on Khrushchev's bad manners, "Great oafs from little icons
grow"; on a more sophisticated level there is his remark on the McCarthy
years, " 'In the early 1950's, before McCarthage delenda was, I had some
terrible nightmares,' " or his description of the writer's war against illiter-
acy: " 'We battle for the word while the very Oedipus of reason crumbles
beneath us.' "

The ceaseless garbling of famous quotations, titles, and familiar adages
gives the style a strong literary flavor. Most often the familiar lines are
twisted to fit an incongruous or ludicrous situation, and the effect is that
of parody or burlesque. In "The Future, If Any, of Comedy," Thurber's
friend quotes Alfred North Whitehead's statement that if Shelley had been
born a hundred years later, he would have been a Newton among chemists.
Then he and Thurber weave a series of fanciful variations upon the theme
out of fractured quotations from Ralph Hodgson, Wordsworth, and Browning: " 'Shelley in the bells and grass, Shelley with an apple halfway to his
head,' " says Thurber, rewriting a line from Hodgson's poem "Eve"; his
friend tops this effort with "My heart leaps up when I behold a test tube
in the lab!" and " 'And did you once see Shelley plain? And was he stained

with chemicals?,' " kidnapping Wordsworth and Browning to his purpose.[9]

Twisted or straight, quotations and literary allusions are a major feature of Thurber's later style. In "The Lady from the Land," the lady argues that men are inordinately interested in the sea, and assaults Thurber with quotations from O'Casey's *Juno and the Paycock,* Tennyson's "Crossing the Bar," Robert Louis Stevenson's "Under the Wide and Starry Sky," O'Neill's *Anna Christie,* Longfellow's "The Wreck of the Hesperus," and allusions to Ibsen, Conrad, and McFee. Thurber's remarkable memory was a store-house of lines from the standard authors, particularly the nineteenth-century poets, who provided the cultural furniture of his generation. A rough count of the writers quoted or referred to in the work of his last six years puts Henry James, his favorite author, in first place, followed by Tennyson, Longfellow, Browning, Lewis Carroll, Henley, Shakespeare, Poe, Wordsworth, and Gray. Among twentieth-century writers, Fitzgerald, Hemingway, and T. S. Eliot appear most often. A complete list of literary references in these late pieces would include such diverse figures as Coleridge, Blake, Shelley, Emerson, Emily Dickinson, Stevenson, Tom Moore, Meredith, E. A. Robinson, Conrad, Bergson, Ibsen, Whitehead, O'Neill, O'Casey, Thomas Wolfe, and Tennessee Williams, not to mention a crowd of others who appear in the lists of names in sketches like "The Moribundant Life," and "The Porcupine in the Artichokes." And to this list would have to be added Ralph Hodgson, a popular minor poet in Thurber's college days, whose "Eve" took Thurber's fancy, and whose "The Bull" is referred to by Tommy Turner in *The Male Animal.*

The gloomy view of the human scene and the obsessive word-play of Thurber's later work put off many of his readers. John Updike, reviewing the posthumous *Credos and Curios* in the New York *Times* (November 25, 1962), dismissed Thurber's criticisms of contemporary culture as the cantankerousness of an "indignant senior citizen" whose disapproval of the present state of things was so inclusive as to be pointless. Thurber's "logomachia" (a fine term for the wild verbal gymnastics of the late pieces) was sometimes exciting, he said, but too often it was merely compulsive punning passed off as conversation. The enlivening humor of the earlier years was "overwhelmed by puns and dismay." There is truth in the charge, but Updike overstates it. For many people, the word-play (taken in small doses, as it must be) is an unusual imaginative experience, and the comments on

---

[9] Thurber often parodied Browning's lines from "Memorabilia,"

> Ah, did you once see Shelley plain
> And did he stop to speak to you . . .

And he was also fond of Hodgson's line, "Eve in the bells and grass."

the blight of mass culture are penetrating and prophetic. While there is a narrowing of range and a preciosity in Thurber's later work, there are pieces in *Lanterns and Lances* and *Credos and Curios*, like the long essay "The Wings of Henry James," and the two short stories "The Other Room" and "Brother Endicott," which show that he had not lost his capacity for generous appreciation or his talent as a story-teller.

"The Wings of Henry James" is an impressive example of Thurber's talent as a literary critic. The focus of the essay is *The Wings of the Dove*, which had recently been adapted for television, but in typical Thurber fashion it moves easily through a wide range of topics, including James's reputation, his failure to succeed in the theater, the history of other people's efforts to dramatize his work, a critical discussion of his fictional method, and the low state of taste represented by television. Thurber is well up on modern critical studies of James, and he discusses the contributions made by Leon Edel, Dr. Saul Rosenzweig, Gordon Ray, and Edmund Wilson. Wilson's Freudian reading of *The Turn of the Screw* interested him, but he disagreed with the view that the tale is full of unconscious meanings: for Thurber, James was the complete artist, and that meant that he was completely aware and in control of "every latent meaning that has been read into the famous story."

The essay is particularly interesting in the light of Thurber's public recantation of his devotion to James in the interview with Plimpton and Steele in Paris in 1955. At that time he said that in the era of the Bomb, James seemed somehow irrelevant; and he repeated the point in his interview with Henry Brandon, in 1958. He obviously changed his mind the following year when he went back to *The Wings of the Dove*, and he bore public witness again in 1961 when he told William Weatherby in London that he was "a great Henry James man." [10] On that occasion, what he had in mind was James's ability to portray friendship between men and women, as opposed to the modern writers' obsession with psychiatry and sex. In a time of crudity and violence, James was a citadel of civilized values, and at the close of "The Wings of Henry James," he says that he is reading *The Sacred Fount* as a refuge from the vulgarity of television.

"Brother Endicott" and "The Other Room" are the last stories Thurber wrote. Both deal with Americans in Paris: "Brother Endicott" offers a sharp satirical picture of the American as Babbitt and eternal fraternity man, while "The Other Room" gives a sympathetic portrait of the American doughboy forty years later. "Brother Endicott" is somewhat contrived, but

[10] "Antic Disposition," *Guardian*, February 2, 1961.

Thurber's romantic feeling for Paris and his sympathy for the confused middle-aged veteran of World War I from Iowa give "The Other Room" a moving reality. The plot is slight: sitting in the bar of the Hotel Continental, Mr. Barrett tells the narrator and a little group of friends of the disturbing effect of his return to Paris after more than forty years. He had been badly wounded at Fère-en-Tardenois (" 'What I seem to remember most is hospitals' ") and he had had an ambiguous experience with a French girl (" 'This girl, this Frances, gets in my dreams sometimes too. But the door is always locked, or something, or the floor to the other room is gone, like it was blown away' "), and on an afternoon in Paris, the past and present get all mixed up, and he makes a pathetic and abortive effort to pick up a girl and make contact with his vanished youth.

Neither story is representative of the main body of Thurber's later work, and neither shows him at his best, but "The Other Room" is interesting as Thurber's final effort to write a bittersweet mood piece in the Fitzgerald vein. His major talent was for a very different kind of story, but periodically, throughout his life, he dropped the mask of comedy and tried to write seriously and directly about the mixed pain and sweetness of the romantic experience—first in "Menaces in May," then in "The Evening's at Seven" and "One Is a Wanderer," and finally, near the end of his career, in "The Other Room," which draws on his nostalgic memories of Paris in 1919.

18

Last Days:
The Years with Ross
and A Thurber
Carnival

Thurber's last years were as busy and as filled with projects as ever. Between 1957 and his death in 1961 he published *The Years with Ross* and *Lanterns and Lances*, returned to the theater with *A Thurber Carnival*, worked at his unfinished projects—the play about Ross, the Bermuda play, and the satiric fantasy "The Nightinghoul"—went to England twice, and gave out countless interviews. As he grew older he drove himself harder. He said to an interviewer in London in 1961, " 'I'm 66 now, going on 50, and I expect to live and work for another 30 years.' " Later the same year he composed a brief statement for the Associated Press in which he repudiated the value of daydreaming, nostalgic reverie, and the whole escapist impulse in favor of purposeful activity—turning his back, apparently, on Walter Mitty. "When I sit silent at parties, I am not remembering the time, at my 13th birthday party, that I kissed a little girl named Eva, or my election in 1913 as president of the senior class at East High School in Columbus, Ohio, or the evening I won a zither in a rotation pool tournament," he said. "At such moments of obliviousness I am trying to write something new, and not under the name of A. I. Glatson (try spelling that backward)," he added, and he closed by paraphrasing Longfellow's "Psalm of Life" ("Let us then be up and doing").[1] Back in 1940 he

---

[1] "The Time of Your Life Is Now," August 21, 1961.

had parodied Longfellow's lines; now he was taking them at least half seriously.

At the same time, with characteristic inconsistency, he indulged in all sorts of nostalgic recollections in the wide and varied correspondence he carried on with old friends and new acquaintances. A witty and eloquent fan letter from Mrs. F. J. Acosta, in Falls Church, Virginia, brought a flood of boyhood memories to the surface of his mind. The Thurber family had spent the summers of 1901 and 1902 in Falls Church, and Thurber and Mrs. Acosta corresponded eagerly in an effort to identify the exact house on Maple Avenue (it turned out to be the one next door to the house the Acostas were living in). In the course of their exchange of letters, Thurber recalled the traumatic occasion on which his brother accidentally shot him in the left eye with an arrow, as well as a whole set of comic and nostalgic memories: it was the era when "so long" and "hot dog" were new expressions, and "The Good Old Summer Time" was the popular song; his father took him to the Senate, where he heard Senator Beveridge speak, and to the ball game, where he met Washington's first baseman, a man named Unglaub. It was in the Falls Church house, he recalled, that they had the maid who burned her finger in the steam of the kettle to test the value of the salve she had just bought at a traveling medicine show.[2]

He and E. B. White wrote less often after the middle 1950's, although when White underwent a particularly trying medical examination in 1959, Thurber tried to cheer him up with some of the clinical humor which had been part of the language of their friendship over the years. During 1959, while he was working on "The Wings of Henry James," he exchanged a number of letters with Edmund Wilson. Re-reading "The Turn of the Screw" and Wilson's provocative essay on it crystallized his intention to write a "long planned extensive essay on ghosts," he said. It would include an account of the evening he spent with Houdini's widow in the winter of 1926–27 waiting for the spirit of the famous "ghost hater and ghost breaker" to manifest itself, as well as the facts about the apparition of a young woman which appeared to friends of Thurber's living in the West Fifties, and Henry James's experience with the supernatural. "I firmly believe James himself must have had some similar experience, so I can see depths in 'The Turn of the Screw' that do not occur to me as shallow or unimportant," he said.

The essay would also tell the story of Thurber's own ghost, which walked around the dining room one night in 1915, and then ran up the back stairs,

[2] "Name-Hunting with Thurber: A Correspondence," letters in the Washington *Star*, dated May, 1959, in RTS.

frightening Thurber and his brother William out of their wits. He laughed
it off in his story "The Night the Ghost Got In," he said to Wilson, but
now, after forty-five years of examining all the possible explanations, he
said, he had become convinced that it was "a supernatural phenomenon."
He spoke of his other encounters with the inexplicable—the miracle of his
forty years of sight, which baffled all medical knowledge, his gift of total
recall ("discovered not by me, but by Professor Weiss of Ohio State's
Department of Psychology in 1913"), and even more mysterious, his ability
to communicate by mental telepathy.

As early as the age of six, he said, "it was a commonplace with me . . .
to perform what seemed to others, to my astonishment, unbelievable feats
of mental telepathy." He and his mother used to baffle people with their
telepathic communication, but his sensitivity did not depend on her. At
the age of seven, for example, he had an intuition that his brother was in
danger, and he ran all the way home from play, arriving just in time to
rescue him from a flaming bed. His mother was on the porch the whole
time and was totally unaware that anything was wrong.[3] It is doubtful that
the empirical, skeptical Thurber would have attached much importance
to any of this a few years earlier, but his blindness and perhaps his age made
him want to believe that he possessed special powers and special ways of
knowing which would compensate for the loss of physical sight.

During these later years he made his peace with Columbus. He had been
angry and alienated ever since the gag-rule episode, but when the city was
selected an "All American City" in 1959, he sent congratulations to the
mayor, as did President Eisenhower, General LeMay and Captain Eddie
Rickenbacker. When the Press Club of Ohio honored him with a Distinguished Service to Ohio Award in November of that year, he and Helen
went back to receive it in person. Thurber reminisced happily with reporters about his days on the *Dispatch* (" 'I was a helluva good newspaperman,' " he told them), and amazed them with his feats of memory. Describing the night the City Hall caught fire, he recalled the names of the
City Council and what the issue was they were considering that night, as
well as the names of every city official and member of the *Dispatch* staff.[4]

He insisted that *A Thurber Carnival* have its world premiere in Columbus and its tryout run in the Midwest rather than in Boston, New Haven,
or Philadelphia. He wanted the show to test itself in Thurber country, he
said. The climax of his spiritual homecoming was the acceptance of an
invitation to speak at the dedication of Denney Hall, the new College of

[3] Letter to Wilson, May 25, 1959.
[4] "Thurber Still Dreams of Reportorial Days," Columbus *Dispatch*, November 13, 1959.

Arts and Sciences building at Ohio State in April of 1960. On that occasion he spoke of the importance of "the Middlewest to the culture and destiny of the United States," and of his personal debt to three professors at Ohio—Taylor, Graves, and Denney. Touching on the issue which had estranged him from the university, he said that he honored Denney particularly for his courage and his devotion to the ideal of academic freedom. But the emphasis in his speech was on the positive values of Ohio State, not on its shortcomings. "I have faith in Ohio State University and the great work it is accomplishing," he said, and he went on to call the roll of the men now carrying on the good work, adding a special salute to the department of English and to the memory of Herman Miller, "who meant as much to me as any man who ever lived." [5] Thurber's feelings about Ohio State and Columbus were apt to swing violently from one pole to the other, but his speech honoring Denney shows how strong the ties which bound him to the university really were.

He suffered two painful losses during these years, with the death of John McNulty in 1956 and of Wolcott Gibbs in 1958. Writing to Dorothy Miller in the spring of 1957, he mournfully ran over the names of some of the friends and colleagues who had passed away and whom he particularly missed—McNulty, Getzloe, Cherrington, and Miller of Columbus, and Ross and John Mosher of New York. He paid formal tribute to McNulty in an appreciative introduction to a collection of McNulty's pieces, *The World of John McNulty*, in 1957. Thurber's memorial describes McNulty's special talent as a writer and observer of the human scene ("There was always, faint or sharp, in what he said or did a critical comment on our tangled civilization, a sound parody of the ways of men") and his inimitable style as a man ("Walking about the streets of any city with McNulty was to be taken on a guided tour of what William James called, in another context, unexplored experience"). Thurber loved the strangeness and oddity of McNulty's imagination, as when he said of the year 1885, in an awkward moment during a conversation with Thurber's mother and another elderly person, "That was the year the owls were so bad," and he loved McNulty's talent for elaborate deadpan jokes, like his going into a store and asking for noiseless dice, explaining to the proprietor that he wanted them for a couple of fugitives holed up in a house with marble floors.[6]

[5] "He Cast a Light: of Learning, of Scholarship," speech delivered April 1, 1960, at the dedication of Denney Hall. The text is given in *Ohio State University Monthly*, May, 1960.
[6] "My Friend McNulty," introduction to *The World of John McNulty* (Garden City, N.Y.: Doubleday, 1957); reprinted in *Credos and Curios*.

Thurber was a master of the memorial essay, partly because of his wonderful memory, which supplied him with an abundance of fresh, character-revealing anecdotes, partly because of his rare ability to bring a personality to life in a few quick sentences, and partly because of his command of tone, in which the sense of loss and the sense of life are perfectly blended. "My Friend McNulty" is perhaps the best of a genre which Thurber handled with particular mastery—the personal tribute to a fellow writer. In *Credos and Curios* Helen Thurber collected some of the others, most notably "The Incomparable Mr. Benchley" and "Scott in Thorns."

Thurber was always a restless soul—he liked to move back and forth between the city and the country, he liked to go to Bermuda, and he liked to visit England and France. As he grew older, he moved around more and more often, looking for a place (the Great Good Place, as he often called it) which would bring him the serenity he never found. In June of 1958, he and Helen went to England, where, Thurber announced, he planned to work on his Ross play. He had a special fondness for England—"I feel a sense of 'getting home' when I get to London," he told Henry Brandon —and the English reciprocated with an admiration that was little short of hero worship. One observer of the London scene said that the English could never quite reconcile themselves to the fact that Thurber was American.[7] He was, they felt, too perfectly attuned to their frequency to be anything else than British. He had many friends in England—John Duncan Miller, the former *Times* of London correspondent in Washington, Hamish Hamilton, the publisher, Peter Ustinov, and Kenneth Tynan, as well as a number of expatriate friends like Donald Ogden Stewart and Nunnally Johnson—and he and Helen were entertained and called upon constantly. In addition, there were endless interviews and radio and television appearances.

The rest and quiet the Thurbers sought proved elusive, and Helen wrote the De Vries family in July that life was "inexorably busy." Earlier in the month, Thurber received an unobtrusive but signal honor. Every Wednesday for more than a hundred years, there was a luncheon meeting of the editors of *Punch,* at which the political cartoon for the next issue was selected. Until 1958, only two outsiders had been permitted to watch the ritual—Mark Twain and Prince Philip. In a historic gesture (and a magnanimous one, since Thurber had lampooned the magazine some years earlier), Thurber was invited to sit in and to pencil his initials on the table

[7] Eddy Gilmore, "Call Me Jim," A.P. interview in London, reprinted in the Columbus *Dispatch,* August 3, 1958.

which bore, among other signatures, the WMT of Thackeray. Twain, noting Thackeray's initials, declined to add his own, saying, "Two thirds of Thackeray will do for me"; Thurber was bolder, penciling in the "Th" with which he used to sign his drawings.[8]

In England as in the United States, he was constantly being interviewed. He seldom refused a request, partly because he was an old newspaperman and sympathized with reporters, and partly because he was one of the great talkers of his time. He had opinions on everything and liked to express them; he was a superb story-teller and mimic, and he loved an audience. Over the years, he made the interview-monologue into an art form, the oral equivalent of the autobiographical essay which he had developed to perfection in his prose. It was, perhaps, the form most congenial to him as he grew older. The key to it was the balance between the casual, conversational manner—its spontaneous quality—and the basic structure of ready-made topics, anecdotes, and routines which gave it substance and coherence. Depending upon how the particular interview was going, Thurber would rely mostly on his standard anecdotes or introduce fresh material and improvise on it as the spirit moved him.

Some interviews, like those conducted by Plimpton and Steele or by Alistair Cooke, were carefully structured, wide-ranging discussions of Thurber's aims, habits, and tastes as an artist. In these conversations Thurber is the artist as autobiographer, talking seriously and entertainingly about how he got started, about the people who influenced him, about the craft of writing and his personal work habits, about his drawings, and about the fate of humor in the modern world. Most of the interviews with Thurber were, of course, more informal and impromptu performances. In these, he is chatty and gossipy, jumping from topic to topic as his fancy pleases, talking mainly about his current plans, but working in a few comments on dogs, women, his blindness, his wonderful memory, and other of the subjects which formed his standard repertory. Nevertheless, in each one there was almost always something he had not said before. In an interview with Maurice Dolbier in the New York *Herald Tribune* (November 3, 1957) there is a totally unexpected story about how Helen's critical judgment improved "The Secret Life of Walter Mitty." In the first version of the story Thurber had had a scene in which Mitty got involved in a brawl between Hemingway and an opponent at the Stork Club. Helen objected to the scene on the grounds that there should be nothing topical in the story. " 'Well, you know how it is when your wife is right,' " said Thurber

---

[8] *Time*, July 7, 1958; also the "F sharp" column in the Ohio State *Journal*, July 21, 1958.

to Dolbier; " 'you grouse around the house for a week, and then you follow her advice.' "

Thurber was interviewed so often that he repeated himself without compunction, falling back on ideas and anecdotes which he had already used in other interviews, or, even worse, already committed to print. John Updike recalls the time he went to see Thurber in London, in 1958: he was awed by the power of Thurber's presence (he was no Walter Mitty, but "a big-boned blind giant . . . and there could have been no way of anticipating the alarming way his eyes caromed around the refracting magnification of his glasses"), but he was appalled by the great man's unabashed reliance on oft-told tales even in his social conversation. "He sat, talking and drinking tea until I wondered why his bladder didn't burst. . . . Though Thurber cocked his head alertly at my poor fawning attempts to make conversation, these attempts did not appreciably distract him from the anecdotes of Columbus, Ohio, he had told a thousand times before, and that I had read 10 years before, in their definitive, printed version. Pages of 'The Thurber Album' and 'My Life and Hard Times' issued from his lips virtually intact." [9] Thurber's interviews, like his conversation, were essentially monologues, and most of those who interviewed him simply got out of the way and listened. W. J. Weatherby, interviewing him for *The Guardian* in 1961, said that Thurber "needed hardly any questions, pouring out what seemed like part of the interior monologue that has been going on now for 66 years." [10]

In the late 1950's the interviews, like his writing, become less personal and anecdotal and more didactic and critical. This change is strikingly evident in the long and revealing interview conducted by Henry Brandon in New York in 1958. The theme is Thurber's sense of change in American life. Among the objects of his disapproval:

AMERICAN WOMEN: "It became obvious to me from the time I was a little boy that the American woman was in charge. . . . I think it's one of the weaknesses of America, the great dominance of the American woman. Not because of that fact in itself, but because she is, as a Chinese woman of distinction said to me some twenty years ago, the least interested in national and international affairs and the most ignorant."

AMERICAN SMUGNESS: "We've always had a belief in push-button superiority and instant lovability—everybody must love us; why shouldn't they, we're Americans!"

[9] Updike, "Writers I Have Met," *New York Times Book Review*, August 11, 1968.
[10] Weatherby, "Antic Disposition," *Guardian*, February 2, 1961.

THE AMERICAN FEAR OF NONCONFORMITY: "The six or eight years that went by—those terrible years—when all the American Congress seemed to do was to investigate writers, artists, and painters—to me were the dreadful years."

THE DECLINE OF HUMOR: "There was a period . . . in which we were distinguished for our ability to laugh about ourselves, the days of Mencken, Will Rogers, William Allen White, and many others, with either a broadsword or a slapstick, you know, making fun of Congressmen. But then we got scared of 'em."

"In the 1920's when Ross said that humorists were a dime a dozen, they practically were. . . . We've had Peter De Vries, in the last twelve or fourteen years, and John McNulty. But the young people are not funny. . . . Everybody is getting very serious. You can just sense that change; the beginning of a kind of chill."

THE INTELLECTUAL FLABBINESS OF AMERICAN SCHOOL-CHILDREN: "But what troubles me most about today are our children. . . . Our kids have given up hard work. Every year, for instance, I get hundreds of letters from . . . students from all parts of the United States asking me for biographical material. . . . They don't want biographical material; they want us to do their homework. In one case I wrote back that I spent two years studying the facts about the Loch Ness monster before doing my story about it, but that I never wrote to it."

THE DECLINE OF THE ENGLISH LANGUAGE: "My most intense dedication now is the defense of the English language against the decline it has suffered in this century and particularly since the end of the last war. . . . So what does the President do but use 'finalize' in his State of the Union address. That awful, fake, synthetic word. . . ."

THE FOLLY AND DESTRUCTIVENESS OF MAN: "It is very hard to sustain humor . . . in a period when mankind seems to be trying on the one hand, to invent a pill or miracle drug that will cure us all of everything; with the other hand, it's inventing a machine for instant annihilation. . . ."

THE SUPERIORITY OF ANIMALS: "Often I think it would be fine if the French poodle could take over the world, because they've certainly been more intelligent in the last few years than the human being, and they have great charm, grace, humor, and intelligence."

APOCALYPSE: "We're living on the edge of the abyss."

"Every man is a moon and has his dark side," reads one of Pudd'nhead Wilson's calendar mottoes. Thurber's work showed his dark side more and more often in the 1950's, but there are two notable exceptions, *The Years with Ross* (1959) and *A Thurber Carnival* (1960). In the Ross book, Thurber turns back to one of his richest imaginative sources, the biographical and autobiographical recreation of the past. He was, above all, "a memory writer," as he often said, and Ross had been on his mind for a long time as a potential literary subject. He had been telling Ross anecdotes and doing Ross imitations at parties for years, and in June of 1954 he wrote White that he was embarked on "what looks like a series of three or more pieces about Ross." It was to be an informal portrait, "in kind of Talk of the Town style, chasing him casually from memory to memory, dealing with all his facets and maggots and prejudices, his perception, intuition, and plain ignorance, as they occur to me." [11] It had to wait on other projects, however, and it was not until Charles Morton of the *Atlantic Monthly* persuaded him in a letter of May, 1957, to do a series of Ross pieces for the magazine that he actually began to write it. The first of nine biographical sketches of Ross appeared in the November, 1957, issue, and the series was so successful that Thurber was encouraged to expand it into a book. He spent the next year and a half researching and rewriting, and in May of 1959 *The Years with Ross* appeared, full of new material on Ross, his magazine, and the talented people who wrote for it.

Thurber was not a man easily impressed, but he did have his heroes, and Ross remained his special favorite. He admired him for his independence, his mixture of eccentricity and talent, and for his success, and he was grateful to him for having created a magazine which opened up careers for so many gifted people. Without *The New Yorker*, few of them would have had the success that they did.

Ross was a strange and contradictory personality ("If you get him down on paper," Wolcott Gibbs once said to Thurber, "nobody will believe it"), and Thurber's portrait highlights the paradoxes of his character. He pays handsome tribute to Ross's genius as an editor, but at the same time he delights in anecdotes showing Ross's Philistinism and his ignorance, like

[11] Letter to White, June 30, 1954 (EBWP).

the time he inquired of his checking department, " 'Is Moby Dick the whale or the man?' " The Harold Ross that Thurber brings to life in his portrait is a pure Thurber character—apprehensive, constantly getting himself into uncomfortable predicaments, baffled and frustrated by things large and small (there is a wonderful account of E. B. White's effort to teach Ross to drive a car, which could come out of any Thurber story). This side of Ross comes through best in the incredible tale of how he was swindled out of seventy-one thousand dollars by Harold Winney, his private secretary. Winney was another Thurber character, "a pallid, silent young man," a secret horse player and expert forger, who took advantage of Ross's carelessness about money matters and almost ruined him. Thurber's view of the tragi-comic affair is summed up in his remark that anyone can be taken for twenty thousand, but "it takes a really great eccentric to be robbed of seventy-one thousand dollars right under his busy nose."

Although Thurber sees Ross as a richly comic figure, his portrait is softened by the affection he felt for his friend. Beneath Ross's gruff exterior was a capacity for warmth and sentiment, and the book is full of anecdotes showing this softer side of his nature. When Thurber was undergoing his eye operations in 1940–41, Ross came to see him often and on one occasion he growled, " 'Goddam it, Thurber, I worry about you and England.' " He clucked over White and Thurber, his favorites, like a mother hen. He wrote to Helen not to bring Thurber back to New York too early after his appendectomy: " 'Wheeling him through town might have a permanent effect on him. Also he might get cold and wet,' " he warned.[12] Thurber's affection for Ross is a major strand in the book, and his account of the last year, when Ross was close to death, while reportorial and matter-of-fact in method, is a beautifully muted expression of personal feeling.

The Years with Ross, as the title suggests, is strongly autobiographical. Thurber is writing about Ross, but he is thinking of him as a part of his own past, and there are many stories about his days as a newspaperman in France, his efforts to get started with *The New Yorker*, his early battles with Ross and the long friendship that followed, and a variety of personal ventures. There was the time, for example, when Thurber's friend and former *New Yorker* colleague Bernard Bergman was editing the "March of Events" page for Hearst's New York *American* and asked Thurber to contribute some prose and drawings. Thurber did so until Bergman received a note from Hearst himself, saying, "Stop running those dogs on your page. I wouldn't have them peeing on my cheapest rug." (Bergman

---

[12] *The Years with Ross*, pp. 18 and 300.

recalls that the facts were not quite so colorful, but the story is too good not to keep alive as an example of Thurber's ability to improve on life.) The book is also an informal literary history—in telling about Ross and himself, Thurber chronicles the rise of *The New Yorker*. He talks about the unique *New Yorker* features—the drawings, the profiles, "The Talk of the Town," the newsbreaks—and about the people who worked for it, and about the changes in the magazine that came with the depression, World War II, and post-war prosperity.

Thurber looks back on the old days on *The New Yorker* with a warmth and indulgence that are conspicuously lacking in his view of the present. In many respects, *The Years with Ross* is like *The Thurber Album*—a retreat from a disturbing present to an idealized past. The people and the events are real enough, but as refracted through the prism of Thurber's memory and imagination, they become part of a world more interesting, more delightful, more understandable, than the one we live in. Ross comes through as the embodiment of the sort of unregenerate individualism which has almost disappeared from the modern scene, and nearly all the people who worked for him are, like the people in Thurber's recollections of Columbus, divertingly eccentric. Thurber's picture of life on *The New Yorker* emphasizes the pranks, the practical jokes, the colorful characters, making it into a fabulous, comic, holiday world in which a group of talented scamps play their games around a central father figure, and at the same time turn out the best prose and comic drawing in the country.

The Years with Ross is Thurber at his best, and the reviewers and the public were quick to respond to it. It was selected by the Book-of-the-Month Club, and it remained high on the best-seller lists for some time. It was reviewed more widely, enthusiastically, and in more detail than any of his previous books. Yet, as with *The Thurber Album*, some of those close to the subject were not happy. E. B. and Katharine White felt that Thurber's discussion of Ross's problems with money and women was an invasion of privacy. Thurber was irritated, since he felt that his picture of Ross was complimentary, and particularly since, as he wrote to Edmund Wilson, he had "cut out quite a lot of cracks at the New Yorker after . . . listening to the objections of Helen and a few others." [13]

He had been taking pot-shots at the magazine ever since the death of Ross. He said to Henry Brandon that with prosperity the magazine had fallen into formula, "a tulle and taffeta rut," in which everybody was writing about "their girlhood, young womanhood, first baby, first year of

[13] Letter to Wilson, May 19, 1959.

marriage, and so on," and on Ed Murrow's "Small World" program he complained that there was little humor in the New Yorker nowadays." [14] Katharine White took Thurber's comments on "Small World" as a disloyal attack on the magazine, and a coolness fell over the friendship between the two families. After the book came out, Thurber complained to Edmund Wilson that although many people had written him enthusiastic letters about it, no one on *The New Yorker* had praised it in any way.

The stage revue, *A Thurber Carnival,* was Thurber's last important venture, and in bringing him back to the theater it realized a long-frustrated ambition. He clung to the belief that he would finish his play about Ross, but as time went on, he did more talking about it than writing on it. Other people continued to try to adapt his stories and his fables to the dramatic medium, mostly without success. There were a few exceptions—a good television production of "One Is a Wanderer," starring Fred MacMurray, in 1959, and the excellent film made out of "The Catbird Seat," *The Battle of the Sexes,* with Peter Sellers, in 1960. For the most part, however, the efforts to put Thurber into the theater were marked by good intentions and insufficient imagination. An ambitious project to make a continuing television series based on Thurber stories and characters entitled "The Secret Life of James Thurber" and starring Arthur O'Connell got as far as the showing of the pilot film, "Christabel," on the "Goodyear Theater" in 1959, but failed to arouse either critical or commercial enthusiasm. (It was revived in 1969 by Mel Shavelson, the writer-producer who first conceived it, and under a new title, "My World and Welcome to It," and with some effective new writing, it ran throughout the 1969–70 television season.)

In the early 1950's Cheryl Crawford had planned to make a stage revue out of an anthology of Thurber's already published material, but nothing came of the idea; and so when Haila Stoddard, an actress and producer, approached him with another such plan, Thurber was only mildly interested. Miss Stoddard had more than an idea, however; she had adapted a number of Thurber stories and put together a scenario, and when she finally got in to see Thurber and read him the script, he was sufficiently impressed to give her the dramatic rights to his prose and drawings. Still, the project was not his, and on the basis of past performances, he doubted that much would come of it. But when Miss Stoddard not only arranged for solid financial backing but also lined up Burgess Meredith to direct and Tom Ewell, Paul Ford, and Peggy Cass to perform, and Don Elliott to

[14] "What's with the National Funnybone?" excerpts from the CBS-TV "Small World" Program, New York *Post,* March 29, 1959.

compose the music, Thurber's friendly interest turned into enthusiasm.

He dropped all his other projects and attached himself to the show as writer and consultant. He attended rehearsals and sat in endless conferences with Meredith; he wrote new sketches and took on the task of rewriting, revising, and polishing the old ones with all his incredible energy. He was exaggerating only a little when he told a reporter in Cincinnati that the show had been rewritten twenty-eight times. The atmosphere of crisis, the last-minute conferences, and the camaraderie of backstage life in the weeks before an opening appealed to Thurber's taste for excitement, and he relished it to the full.

When the company arrived in Columbus a few days before the world premiere (January 7, 1960) at the Hartman Theater, the city was in a state of high anticipation. For two weeks, the pages of the *Dispatch* and the *Citizen-Journal* had been filled with pictures and feature articles about the great event, and when Thurber arrived in his old home town, it was, as one reporter put it, like the return of Ulysses. Governor DiSalle proclaimed James Thurber Week, and Mayor Westlake designated Thurber "A Distinguished Native Son." [15] The opening was naturally a great success, and although the reviewers agreed that the show was uneven and needed trimming, they were enthusiastic about its future. After three nights in Columbus (not nearly enough, complained one reviewer), the show embarked on its shakedown run, playing in Detroit, Cleveland, St. Louis, Cincinnati, and Pittsburgh before opening at the ANTA Theater in New York on February 26.

The "evening of words and music" which opened in New York was the joint creation of Thurber, Haila Stoddard, Don Elliott, and Meredith, whose imaginative direction gave a genuine Thurber style to the whole production. The cast featured Tom Ewell, Paul Ford, John McGiver, Peggy Cass, and Alice Ghostley, and their expert playing did much to bring the Thurber world alive in the theater. During the shakedown period dozens of different sketches were tried and discarded (Haila Stoddard said that Thurber wrote enough new material to fill four novels and two more such evenings), but on opening night the format of the show was this: Act I—"Word Dance," "The Night the Bed Fell," "Fables for Our Time" ("The Wolf at the Door," "The Unicorn in the Garden," "The Little Girl and the Wolf"), "If Grant Had Been Drinking at Appomattox," "Casuals of the Keys," "The Macbeth Murder Mystery," "Gentlemen Shoppers," and "The Last Flower." Act II—"The Pet Department," "File and For-

[15] "Thurber on the Stage," *Newsweek*, January 18, 1960; also Columbus *Citizen-Journal*, January 6, 1960.

get," "Mr. Preble Gets Rid of His Wife," "Take Her Up Tenderly," "The Secret Life of Walter Mitty," and "Word Dance." [16]

Most of the material is familiar, but some of the sketches were completely new, like "Gentlemen Shoppers" (a highly successful skit about the possible consequences of a plan by New York department stores to attract men during the Christmas season by serving drinks), and the Word Dances. The Word Dances, a wholly new form designed to dramatize Thurber's cartoon captions, were the most original feature of the show. The members of the cast danced, and at intervals, when the music stopped, they threw off a series of those enigmatic remarks with which Thurber captioned his drawings, and then resumed dancing. Most of the captions were Thurber standards ("Well, if I called the wrong number, why did you answer the phone?"), but some were newly written for the revue ("She says he proposed something on their wedding night her own brother wouldn't have suggested"). All of them had that quality of strangeness and dreamlike logic which characterized the fantasy side of Thurber's imagination.

Spring Dance

Nearly all the sketches were considerably rewritten to make them dramatic rather than narrative presentations, although Thurber wisely decided not to tamper with "The Night the Bed Fell." For that classic tale, Tom

[16] *A Thurber Carnival* (Samuel French, Inc., 1962).

Ewell sat on the edge of the stage and told the story to the audience in its original narrative form. Most of the others, however, underwent a good deal of face-lifting. In some cases the cutting, adding, and reshaping were an obvious improvement, as they were with "Casuals of the Keys," a minor piece about a traveler who meets a romantic Lord Jim-like figure on an isolated island in the Caribbean. To the traveler, the Caribbean isle is the epitome of romance; to the fugitive, the everyday life back home is exotic and wonderful. The stage version enlarges on the comic possibilities of the situation with a wonderful new sequence in which the bored romantic fugitive tells the traveler—as an example of the monotony of his isolated life—about the mermaid to whom he taught English and who bored him to death by endlessly reciting Coleridge's "The Rime of the Ancient Mariner." Generally speaking, the slighter pieces look better in their new form as stage sketches, and the classics, like "The Secret Life of Walter Mitty," lose something. Much of the richness of effect in the Mitty story lies in the way the language conveys the author's awareness of both the value of Mitty's daydreams and their inadequacy. In the dramatic version, this double view of the situation does not come across, and much of the pathos of Mitty's character is lost.

The New York critics praised the *Carnival* enthusiastically. They liked the fact that the comedy grew out of an original view of contemporary life and did not depend upon the usual gags and contrived situations. As Brooks Atkinson put it in his review in the New York *Times* (February 27, 1960), "everyone involved in 'A Thurber Carnival' has succeeded in proving that intelligence is as refreshing as showmanship, and nine educated comedians are as entertaining as a regiment of gag-men." He went on to praise the direction, saying that Burgess Meredith "has had the wit to keep the scale small but the details diamond bright," and he described the cast as a group of "expert comedians who can be funny without laughing or mugging." The revue did well at the box office, running (including a summer stint in Colorado) until November 30, but it was never a sell-out.[17] After it closed, the road company with Imogene Coca and Arthur Treacher toured successfully for several months, but it was clear that the audience for the revue was a relatively limited one.

Part of the reason was that *A Thurber Carnival* does not represent the best or the complete Thurber, but only the Thurber most adaptable to the form of the stage revue. As a result there are too many second-level pieces, like "Mr. Preble Gets Rid of His Wife." Even though some of these are better in their stage versions than they were in print, they are poor substi-

[17] Norman Nadel, "The Lively Arts," Columbus *Citizen-Journal*, June 25, 1960.

tutes for such classic short stories as "The Cane in the Corridor." The point is, of course, that not all of Thurber is suited to dramatic presentation; like his idol, Henry James, he had a passion for the theater, but his genius was for fiction, not the stage. In addition, his low-keyed, intelligent comedy did not offer the belly laughs which many audiences had come to expect in the theater. The very qualities most highly praised by the critics worked against the broad popularity of the show.

Thurber was very sensitive on this point, and throughout the run of the production he gave out interviews and wrote articles for the newspapers trying to prod and educate the public into an awareness that there are many kinds of comedy and that the best kind of laughter is not the boffola but the thoughtful laughter that comes with the recognition of truth. The week before the show opened, he discussed the taste of the American audience in "The Quality of Mirth," in the drama section of the New York *Times*.[18] The biggest problem in the theater today is how "to preserve honorable laughter in a comedy," he said. Americans have always preferred "the wow, the yak, the belly-laugh" to "the appreciative smile," he noted, and this failure in public taste is responsible, more than anything else, for "the decline of stage comedy during the last decade." He spoke of his aims as a writer of comedy, and expressed his dismay that so few people seemed to realize that comedy should have something to say. "Having tried for four decades to make some social comment, it is something less than reassuring to discover that what a jittery America wants is the boffo laugh or nothing," he wrote. If it turns out that the audience will be satisfied with nothing less, "I shall return to the dignity of the printed page, where it may be that I belong," he said.

The *Carnival* company took a month's vacation in July and then played to full houses for a month at the Central City Opera House in Colorado before reopening in New York in September. The high point of the fall run was Thurber's unexpected debut as a professional actor. Tom Ewell had left the show before it moved to Colorado, and the actor hired to replace him had not worked out. In a desperate last-minute reshuffling of roles in New York, Paul Ford and John McGiver took over Ewell's sketches, and Thurber volunteered to play himself in the "File and Forget" number. Since the scene called for him to be seated in an armchair, his blindness was no handicap, and he played the sketch with a perfect command of tone and timing. The critics and the audiences responded enthusiastically, and Thurber's presence undoubtedly extended the life of the production. For Thurber, the experience was the fulfillment of a lifelong ambition. "There

18 "The Quality of Mirth," New York *Times*, February 21, 1960.

is a great deal of ham in my family," he reminded one reporter, and he said to another, "One friend of mine put it very well when he said, 'That s.o.b. has been trying to get on the stage for 40 years.' " [19] He loved playing before a large audience and he loved the praise and the applause. Doing the role seemed to give him a new lease on life, and Burgess Meredith said that the part "lit an old fuse in him." He liked doing it so well that he stayed with it until the show closed at the end of November.

Taking a role in the theater was no great departure for Thurber, who had played the part of a "character" throughout most of his life. In his last years, the role that he found most congenial was that of the satirist and curmudgeon, cultivating his prejudices and ridiculing the follies of the age. When *Life* interviewed him in March of 1960, the play was going well and Thurber was in rare form. He took a shot at Woman: "I like to do what I can to keep the American woman—my mortal enemy—in excellent condition for the fight." He followed with an attack on the sappy sentimentality of the American cult of love. "A lady of 47 who has been married 27 years and has six children knows what love really is and once described it for me like this: 'Love is what you've been through with somebody.' "

The heart of the interview, however, was his testy correction of the popular image of himself as "mild and gentle," a libel perpetuated by reviewers who confused Thurber with some of his characters. "One thing let's get straight—I'm not mild and gentle. Let the meek inherit the earth—they have it coming to them. I get up mad at something every morning and think I should. I used to wake up at 4 A.M. and start sneezing, sometimes for five hours. . . . I get to goddaming everything and start sneezing." [20] His conversation in the last years of his life showed what had not been there before—an aggressive vanity and a frustrated sense that he was not properly understood. He saw himself as a justifiably angry man, a Juvenalian satirist, and it infuriated him when reviewers described his work as "zany and whimsical." Later in the year, he complained that only in New York did the drama critics see "the meaningful, serious, and even mordant beneath the comedy." West of the Alleghenies, his comedy was variously called "zany, pixie, wispy, quaint . . . and elfin," and he added that he had challenged the man who used the last epithet to a duel at ten paces with cold potato cakes.[21]

[19] "James Thurber in 'Carnival,' " Columbus *Dispatch*, September 13, 1960; "People," *Time*, September 26, 1960.
[20] "An Old Hand at Humor," *Life*, March 14, 1960.
[21] "State of Humor in States," New York *Times*, September 4, 1960.

After the Broadway success of the *Carnival* things went downhill for Thurber. His health began to deteriorate, he became more and more restless and irritable, and none of his projects seemed to come out right. When the show closed, he was suffering from flu and exhaustion, and he was ordered by his doctor to rest. He and Helen planned to go to England again in the spring, but decided to go in January, when negotiations for a London production of the *Carnival* began to look promising. The venture was a fiasco from the beginning. The Thurbers and Meredith thought that the basic preparations had been made and that the show would go on in the late winter or early spring. When they arrived, they found that nothing was arranged for, the British producers' schedules were full, and the actors they wanted were unavailable. Thurber wrote his old friend and agent Jap Gude that he was fed up and that Meredith was packing up and going home. A recent conference with their British producers was "like a summit conference in Wonderland, and I expected the March Hare and the Mad Hatter to show up any minute," he said. "I understand most writers, some editors, and a few publishers, but I have never had the vaguest idea what anybody in the theater is trying to say," he added. He did not want to spend the rest of his life with *A Thurber Carnival.* "Art is long and time is fleeting, and I have many things to do," he said.[22]

In addition, the pace of life in London was getting them down. "It has been the worst of all fortnights: we are worn out with fifteen interviews and a Press, Television, and Radio far more aggressive and persistent than our own," he wrote Gude after their first two weeks in England. "We are both worn thin, and have been very depressed," he concluded. "What a world, what a species!"[23] He confided in his next letter that for the first time in his life he was taking Miltown and that he felt "comparatively calm most of the time." In the course of a long and detailed postscript to Thurber's February 25 account of their frustrations, Helen told Gude that the previous night she had got to sleep before three o'clock in the morning for the first time since they left home.

Negotiations dragged on unsatisfactorily, and on March 16, Thurber wrote Gude that the production had been indefinitely postponed and that he doubted that it would ever be done in England. (A few months after Thurber's death, the *Carnival* was finally produced in England, with Tom Ewell recreating his original role. The revue got mixed notices and was distinctly less popular than it had been in the United States.) Thurber was gloomy and depressed when he wrote the De Vrieses on May 11. He and

22 Letter to Gude, February 25, 1961.
23 Letter to Gude, February 13, 1961.

Helen had been suffering "recurring attacks of Angst, the new world plague, which spreads like a virus," he went on. "It is harder and harder to tell whether one is awake or asleep in this world, and also to know the difference between one's personal state and the decline of civilization," he said, sounding a good deal like the later Mark Twain. But unlike Twain, he was determined not to give in to his pessimism. "My only solution is a high heart and a brave spirit, however hard these flags may be to flaunt in the stormy weather of today," he said.[24]

The spiritual depression and philosophical pessimism which clouded his last years come through strongly in the long and revealing interview-monologue he gave W. J. Weatherby in the Manchester *Guardian* shortly after arriving in England. Weatherby sketches an evocative portrait of Thurber at sixty-six—"a tall lean man thinned down by the worry of the war between men and women," fuming behind his glasses, "behind the little moustache that seems to bristle with indignation," handling his whiskey and cigarettes unerringly, and talking "in a constant stream that in 66 years must have added up to a whole sea." Thurber ranged widely and eloquently during their conversation, telling about his habits of composition, his memory, and his remarkable output in the ten years since he had gone totally blind, but the central theme of his discourse is the decline of civilization and the psychological desperation of people today.

" 'I don't see any hope for us unless the Western World perks up,' " he said. " 'The difference between our decadence and the Russians' is that theirs is brutal, ours is apathetic.' " People don't read any more, he said, they " 'just develop a TV mouth and a TV stare.' " Democracy seemed to him an illusory promise. " 'I don't believe in the greatest good for the greatest numbers. I believe in the most good for the greatest persons, the only ones who have ever made our getting up off all fours seem worthwhile,' " he said. Ours is the age of mental illness; " 'tranquilizers, sleeping-pills, women-chasing, and drink—everybody in the United States is trying to escape from reality.' " He concluded with a bitter comment on the public's failure to understand him. " 'I say these things and people just talk about my "charming dogs," ' " he observed, revealing what had become an obsessive frustration. " 'I have written as many savage pieces as humorous ones,' " he protested. " 'How many years will it take to convince people that I'm not a clown?' " The central paradox of the later Thurber is sharply illuminated in this interview: the view of life is more gloomy and pessimistic than ever, but as Weatherby observes, it is expressed "with such verve and

[24] Letter to De Vries, May 11, 1961.

pellmell vitality that the final impression is optimistic, of a man engaged in life to the hilt. . . ." [25]

The Thurbers returned to the States in late May with the Gudes, who had come over for a brief visit. Throughout this last year it was apparent that something was wrong with Thurber. He began to behave erratically, he picked quarrels with some of his closest friends, he drank more heavily than ever, and he was unable to settle down anywhere. He would leave the country place without warning and go down to New York, call up people and stay half the night drinking and talking, then, capriciously, pick up and go back to West Cornwall. He kept to his work schedule, however, and during the spring and early summer of 1961 he turned out five pieces (later collected by Helen in *Credos and Curios*), but he began to talk more and write less as the months went by. In retrospect it was clear that he had been suffering from a series of small strokes, but the seriousness of his condition was not apparent until he collapsed after attending the opening of Noel Coward's *Sail Away* on the night of October 4, 1961.

He was in a difficult mood that evening, and left after the first act and went to Sardi's. Helen picked him up after the show and took him to the opening-night party for Coward at Sardi's East. At the party he tried to make a speech, but he was obviously unwell, and when they got back to the Algonquin he suffered a major stroke. He underwent surgery at Doctors Hospital for a blood clot on the brain, and in the following weeks seemed to be making good progress, when he was suddenly stricken by pneumonia and died Thursday afternoon, November 2, 1961. His last words, according to legend, summed up his sometimes angry love affair with life. "God bless . . . God damn," he is supposed to have whispered.

It would be difficult to select a single work which might be labeled the quintessence of Thurber, but a case could be made for the complex and gloomy fable "The Last Clock," written in 1959. The dominant theme of the fable is the fate of a culture which worships specialization; the underlying theme is the inexorable running-out of time. It tells of an ogre who begins to eat up all the clocks he can find, and of the inability of the intellectual elite of the community to deal with the situation. The psychronologist, the clockonomist, and the clockosopher throw up their hands because the problem does not lie within their disciplines. An "old inspirationalist," representing the moral and spiritual wisdom of the community, is called in, but his inspirationalism has become "a jumble of mumble," and all he can offer is, " 'The final experience should not be mummum.' "

[25] Weatherby, "Antic Disposition."

The last clock runs down and is put in a museum, as a collector's item. Life comes to a standstill and language deteriorates into nonsense.

The close of the fable presents a comic and frightening image of the ultimate meaning of our civilization. Before long the town is buried under the sands of a nearby desert. More than a thousand years later, when explorers from another planet are digging at the site, they find a clock (whose function they do not recognize) and the papers of the old inspirationalist, which include fragments of poetry summing up the wisdom of the culture for which he was the spokesman. The last words he had put down were

> We can make our lives sublime,
> And, departing, leave behind us,
> Mummum in the sands of time.

The world of "The Last Clock" is the world reduced to non-meaning, chaos, the absurd. What more grotesque epitaph for our civilization could be imagined than a garbled fragment of a second-rate nineteenth-century poem celebrating optimism and moral uplift? This final sequence is remarkably similar to the closing moment of Ionesco's play *The Chairs*, in which the Orator, who is to put into magnificent words the significance of the life of the old man and his wife, can only utter unintelligible grunts.

Although many readers, E. B. White among them, have claimed *The Last Flower* as the truest expression of Thurber's world-view, they overlook the dark strain which was always a part of his imagination, and they ignore the extent to which it came to dominate his later work. He formed his view of life independently, but the world created in his late pieces is the same world as that seen by the modern comedians of the absurd—Ionesco, Beckett, Albee, Pinter, Heller, and all the others for whom life is so incomprehensible that it can only be represented as a surrealist dream. The kinship to Ionesco is particularly close: the apocalyptic vision, the fascination with the breakdown of communication as the primary symptom of a cosmic sickness, and the comic virtuosity are characteristic of both.

But the world of Thurber is larger than that of Ionesco. The dark fantasies and the melancholy strain in his work are balanced by a basic sanity and a positive relish of the whole human scene. The essential quality of Thurber's imagination is the tension between a strong sense of fact and a strong bias toward fantasy. In his earlier career he searched out and celebrated disorder, illogic, and confusion, feeling that these qualities were desirable counter-balances in a society over-committed to logic and organization. Later, as history changed the world he knew, and as illogic and disorder on an international scale threatened to engulf mankind, he began to champion those things which hold a society together, and his fantasies and his brilliant images of chaos became warnings and distress-signals rather than signs of revelry.

But he never lost his compensating faith in the saving power of humor and intelligence, and in this way he stands apart from the Black Humorists of the 1960's. "Let us not forget the uses of laughter or store them away in the attic," he wrote in "The Duchess and the Bugs." Comedy, humor, and laughter he saw as essential to the health of any society, because they demolish humbug and reveal the truth. The title of his last collection, *Lanterns and Lances* (1960), with its suggestion of attack and illumination, defines the role he thought comedy should play, and his basic faith in comedy, in intelligence, and in life is finely expressed in the advice he gives to the reader in the Foreword of that volume: "In this light, let's not look back in anger, or forward in fear, but around in awareness."

Thurber's death was an event of international significance, and the obituaries and tributes filled the press in England and America. The New York *Herald Tribune* summed up the general feeling in calling Thurber the greatest American humorist since Mark Twain, and like Mark Twain, much more than a humorist. "To countless thousands who read his prose and studied his drawings, he was a clear-thinking philosopher, a low-voiced commentator on the state of the world, an observer who saw clearly long after his eyes had become useless." The Manchester *Guardian* spoke of his originality and described him as "one of those rare writers with such an individual view that their books hardly need their name on the covers." Paul Jennings of the *Observer* noted that "Thurber had no more passionate admirers than his English ones," and pointed out his special relevance to the modern scene. "His humor was the first that could be regarded as a genuine literary product of an age in which the ordinary man, heir to centuries of peasant and family life, suddenly . . . is up against the fragmentation, complexity, and directionless menace of industrial civilization," he said.[26]

The *Saturday Review* of November 25 featured a "Salute to Thurber," with memorials and appreciations by such old friends as Malcolm Cowley, Peter De Vries, St. Clair McKelway, and E. B. White. De Vries quoted Malcolm Muggeridge's comment that Thurber "tells the truth," and added that he told it best in his fantasies, which were not escapes from life, but

[26] New York *Herald Tribune*, November 3, 1961; Manchester *Guardian*, November 3, 1961; *Observer*, November 5, 1961.

"a means of coping with it." E. B. White understood him best, and his eloquent obituary captures the unique quality of the man and his genius:

> His mind was never at rest, and his pencil was connected to his mind by the best conductive tissue I have ever seen in action. The whole world knows what a funny man he was, but you had to sit next to him day after day to understand the extravagance of his clowning, the wildness and subtlety of his thinking, and the intensity of his interest in others and his sympathy for their dilemmas—dilemmas that he constantly enlarged, put in focus, and made immortal, just as he enlarged and made immortal the strange goings on in the Ohio home of his boyhood. His waking dreams and his sleeping dreams commingled shamelessly and uproariously; Ohio was never far from his thoughts, and when he received a medal from his home state in 1953, he wrote, "The clocks that strike in my dreams are often the clocks of Columbus." It is a beautiful sentence and a revealing one.[27]

But the phrase which should stand as Thurber's epitaph was written by Henry Brandon, in 1959: Thurber's secret, he said, was "a warm heart and an angry mind."

[27] White's obituary first appeared in *The New Yorker*, November 11, 1961.

Acknowledgments

The Thurber drawings in *The Clocks of Columbus* are included with the generous permission of Mrs. James Thurber. They have been drawn from the following sources: drawing originally in the Ohio State *Sun-Dial* from *Thurber & Company*, copyright © 1966 by Helen Thurber, published by Harper & Row, Publishers; Stuffed Cockatoo from "The Pet Department" in *The Owl in the Attic*, copyright © 1931, 1959 by James Thurber, published by Harper & Row, Publishers—originally printed in *The New Yorker*; "Stop me!" from *The Seal in the Bedroom*, copyright © 1932, 1960 by James Thurber, published by Harper & Row, Publishers—originally printed in *The New Yorker*; "All right, have it your way—you heard a seal bark" from *The Seal in the Bedroom*, copyright © 1932, 1960 by James Thurber, published by Harper & Row, Publishers—originally printed in *The New Yorker*; drawing from *The Seal in the Bedroom*, copyright © 1932, 1960 by James Thurber, published by Harper & Row, Publishers; The Bloodhound and the Bug from "The Bloodhound and the Bug" in *The Seal in the Bedroom*, copyright © 1932, 1960 by James Thurber, published by Harper & Row, Publishers, Inc.—originally printed in *The New Yorker*; Home from *The Thurber Carnival*, copyright © 1945 by James Thurber, published by Harper & Row, Publishers, Inc.—originally printed in *The New Yorker*; Electricity was leaking all over the house from *My Life and Hard Times*, copyright © 1933, 1961 by James Thurber, published by Harper & Row, Publishers; Bolenciecwcz was trying to think from *My Life and Hard Times*, copyright © 1933, 1961 by James Thurber, published by Harper & Row, Publishers; A Scone (left) and a Crumpet, peering out of the Tiffin from "A New Natural History" in *The Beast in Me—and Other Animals*, copyright © 1948 by James Thurber, published by Harcourt Brace Jovanovich—originally printed in

The New Yorker; American Folk Dance from *The Beast in Me—and Other Animals,* copyright © 1948 by James Thurber, published by Harcourt Brace Jovanovich—originally printed in *The New Yorker;* Spring Dance from "The Race of Life" in *The Seal in the Bedroom,* copyright © 1932, 1960 by James Thurber, published by Harper & Row, Publishers.

The sources for the photographs which appear following page 114 are identified in the list of Illustrations. The author gratefully acknowledges permission to reproduce them from their several owners.

Throughout *The Clocks of Columbus* there appear numerous references to, and short quotations from, the published and unpublished writings of James Thurber. Acknowledgment of this material has been made where appropriate in the footnotes and in the Selected Bibliography. Among the non-Thurber material, the author is happy to acknowledge permission from Alfred A. Knopf, Inc., to reprint the four lines from *Thoughts Without Words* by Clarence Day, copyright © 1928 by Clarence Day and renewed 1950 by Mrs. Clarence Day.

Selected Bibliography

The following list of sources is selective, not comprehensive. The most important materials are here; a complete list would include too many minor and ephemeral items to be of value. In any case, now that Edwin Bowden's definitive *James Thurber: A Bibliography* (Ohio State University Press, 1970) has appeared, there is no need for further attempts to list Thurber's drawings and writings. I have noted one or two uncollected pieces not identified in Bowden, and I have listed some of the more important interviews in which Thurber talked about himself and his work. Robert E. Morsberger's *James Thurber* (New York: Twayne Publishers, 1964) made the first attempt to provide a bibliography of Thurber, and although it is in part superseded by Bowden, the list of secondary sources is still extremely useful. I include the best of them here, as well as a number of additional items.

The most important of my sources are the unpublished materials, most of them still unavailable for general use. The Thurber Collection at the Ohio State University Library is open to scholars, however, and it is the indispensable starting point for any consideration of Thurber's life and literary career. Much of my biographical information is drawn from informal rather than formal sources. There is as yet no official or comprehensive life of Thurber, and my account of his career depends in part upon correspondence and conversation with Mrs. Thurber and a number of long-time Thurber friends.

UNPUBLISHED MATERIALS

(1) The Thurber Collection, Ohio State State University Library. Originally the family papers given to the university by Robert Thurber, augmented in 1969 and

1971 by some of Helen Thurber's papers. In this collection are all sorts of letters and family memorabilia, as well as the invaluable scrapbooks (RTS) in which Robert Thurber kept a record of his brother's public career and reputation from 1929 until 1961. The collection includes important exchanges of letters with Elliott Nugent, Herman Miller, James Fullington, and James Pollard.

(2) The E. B. White Papers (EBWP), Cornell University Library. The papers include a correspondence with Thurber extending from 1935 to 1960.

(3) Letters to such friends and associates as J. G. Gude, Peter De Vries, Malcolm Cowley, Edmund Wilson, Wolcott Gibbs, Elmer Davis, Carey McWilliams, Harvey Breit, and Frank Gibney. Thurber was an indefatigable correspondent, and an edition of his letters would be a remarkable inside history of an era.

PUBLISHED MATERIALS: PRIMARY SOURCES

(1) Newspaper and magazine files
X-Rays (literary magazine of East High School, Columbus, 1909–13).
Makio (yearbook, Ohio State University, 1914–18).
Sun-Dial (humor magazine, Ohio State University).
Chicago Tribune, Paris and Nice editions, 1925–26.
Columbus Dispatch.
Bermudian.
PM, 1940–41.
The New Yorker.
(2) Interviews and uncollected pieces of biographical interest
"Death Takes 'Big Six' Mathewson," unsigned obituary of Christy Mathewson in the Chicago Tribune, Paris edition, Friday, October 9, 1925.
"Wills Goes Down Fighting Lenglen," unsigned account of the Helen Wills–Suzanne Lenglen tennis match at Cannes, in the Chicago Tribune, Riviera edition, February 17, 1926.
"If the Tabloids Had Covered the Famous Sport 'Love-Death' Scandal of Hero and Leander," signed "Jamie Machree," in F.P.A.'s "The Conning Tower," in the New York World, September 28, 1926.
Interview with Arthur Millier, Los Angeles Times, July 2, 1939.
Interview with Robert van Gelder, New York Times Book Review, May 12, 1940. Reprinted in van Gelder's Writers and Writing. New York: Charles Scribner's Sons, 1946.
Interview with Harvey Breit, "Mr. Thurber Observes a Serene Birthday," New York Times Magazine, December 4, 1949.
"Letter from the States," Bermudian, July, 1950.
Interview with Harvey Breit, "Talk with James Thurber," New York Times Book Review, June 29, 1952.
"Dark Suspicions," New York Times Theater Section, July 27, 1952.
Interview with John Ferris, "Thurber Has His Own Brand of Humor," Columbus Citizen, Sunday, November 8, 1953.
"Old Newspaperman Recalls Some Troubles He's Seen," Fire Island News, June 18, 1954.
Interview with George Plimpton and Max Steele, "The Art of Fiction," The

Paris Review, X (Fall, 1955), 35–49. Reprinted in *Writers at Work*, Malcolm Cowley, editor. New York: The Viking Press, 1959.

Interview with Alistair Cooke, "James Thurber in Conversation with Alistair Cooke," *Atlantic*, CXCVIII (August, 1956), 36–40.

Interview with Marian Robb, "James Thurber," Bermuda *Mid-Ocean News*, April 26, 1957.

Interview with Maurice Dolbier, "A Sunday Afternoon with Mr. Thurber," New York *Herald Tribune* Book Review, November 3, 1957.

Interview with Henry Brandon, "Everybody Is Getting Serious," *New Republic*, CXXXVIII (May 26, 1958). Reprinted and expanded in "The Tulle and Taffeta Rut," in Brandon's *As We Are*. Garden City: Doubleday and Company, 1961.

Interview with Eddy Gilmore, "Call Me Jim," A.P. interview in London, reprinted in the Columbus *Dispatch*, August 3, 1958.

Interview with Stephen Potter, "Frankly Speaking," BBC Home Service Program, December 24, 1958.

Interview with Ed Murrow, Siobhan McKenna and Noel Coward, "Small World," CBS-TV, March 22, 1959. Reprinted in condensed form in the New York *Post*, Sunday, March 29, 1959.

Interview with Rod Nordell, "Humor Is a Gentle Thing," *Christian Science Monitor*, June 4, 1959.

"An Old Hand at Humor with Two Hits on Hand," *Life*, March 14, 1960.

"Thurber Doing a Play on Ross and Writing It in His Head," New York *Herald Tribune*, Sunday, April 24, 1960.

Interview with Virginia Haufe, "Thurber Gives Advice to American Women," *Ohioana*, III (Summer, 1960).

Interview with W. J. Weatherby, "Antic Disposition," *Guardian*, February 2, 1961.

Interview with Eddy Gilmore, "Blind at 67, Thurber Still Cracks the Wit," London interview reported in the Toledo *Blade*, May 7, 1961.

"Thurber Looks Back," Columbus *Dispatch* Magazine Section, October 1, 1961.

"James Thurber on the Perplexities of Educating a Daughter," Chicago *Tribune* Magazine, Sunday, May 2, 1963. Letters from Thurber to Miss Sarah B. Whitaker, headmistress of the Northampton School for Girls, 1947–49.

PUBLISHED MATERIALS: SECONDARY SOURCES

(1) *Biographical*

Baker, Samuel H. "James Thurber: The Columbus Years." Unpublished Master's thesis, Ohio State University, 1962.

Benét, Stephen Vincent and Rosemary. "Thurber: As Unmistakable as a Kangaroo," New York *Herald Tribune* Book Review (December 29, 1940).

Budd, Nelson H. "Personal Reminiscences of James Thurber," *Ohio State University Monthly*, January, 1962.

Coates, Robert M. "James Thurber," *Authors Guild Bulletin*, December, 1961.

Cowley, Malcom. *The Literary Situation*. New York: The Viking Press, 1954.

———. "Lions and Lemmings," *The Reporter*, XV (December 13, 1956).

Gannett, Lewis. "James Thurber: 'Pre-Intentionalist,' " New York *Herald Tribune*, November 12, 1961.

Kanode, Bob. "Columbus Still Home to Thurber," Columbus *Dispatch*, June 15, 1950.

Kramer, Dale. *Ross and The New Yorker.* New York: Doubleday and Company, 1952.

Nugent, Elliott. "Brother James G. Thurber," *Buckeye Phi Psi*, April, 1962.

―――. *Events Leading Up to the Comedy.* New York: Trident Press, 1965.

―――. "Note on James Thurber, the Man, or Men," New York *Times* Theater Section, February 25, 1940.

Pollard, James E. "James Thurber," *Ohio Authors and Their Books.* William Coyle, ed. Cleveland and New York: The World Publishing Company, 1962.

―――. "With Honor, Not Without," unpublished speech before the Kit-Kat Club, Columbus, October 20, 1964.

"Salute to Thurber," *The Saturday Review*, XLIV (November 25, 1961).

Sayre, Joel. "Priceless Gift of Laughter," *Time*, LVIII (July 9, 1951).

Seeds, Charme. "Using . . . Whimsical Humor . . . Jim Thurber . . . Created a Best Seller," *Ohio State University Monthly*, April, 1930.

Stewart, Donald Ogden. "Death of a Unicorn," *New Statesman*, November 10, 1961.

Updike, John. "Writers I Have Met," *New York Times Book Review*, August 11, 1968.

Van Doren, Mark. *The Autobiography of Mark Van Doren.* New York: Harcourt, Brace and Company, 1958.

Ruth White. "Early Thurber," *Life*, VIII (April 22, 1940).

―――. "James Thurber: His Life in Columbus," Columbus *Dispatch*, March 10, 1940, and March 17, 1940.

(2) *Critical*

Benchley, Nathaniel. *Robert Benchley.* New York: McGraw-Hill, 1955.

Blair, Walter. "The Urbanization of Humor," *A Time of Harvest.* New York: Hill and Wang, 1962.

Brady, Charles. "What Thurber Saw," *Commonweal*, LXXV (December 8, 1961).

De Vries, Peter. Introduction to Time Inc., edition of *Lanterns and Lances*, 1962.

―――. "James Thurber: The Comic Prufrock," *Poetry*, LXII (December, 1943).

Eastman, Max. *Enjoyment of Laughter.* New York: Simon & Schuster, 1936.

Elias, Robert. "James Thurber: The Primitive, the Innocent, and the Individual," *American Scholar*, XXVIII (Summer, 1968).

Fadiman, Clifton. "Reading I've Liked," *Holiday*, March, 1963.

Ford, Corey. *The Time of Laughter.* Boston: Little, Brown & Company, 1969.

"A Hamlet Who Sometimes Played the Fool," *Guardian*, November 2, 1961.

Holmes, Charles S. "James Thurber and the Art of Fantasy," *Yale Review*, LV (Autumn, 1965).

Jennings, Paul. "Thurber: Man Against Monsters," *Observer*, November 5, 1961.

MacLean, Kenneth. "The Imagination of James Thurber," *Canadian Forum*, XXXIII (December, 1953).

————. "James Thurber—A Portrait of the Dog Artist," *Acta Victorana*, LXVIII (Spring, 1944).

Mortimer, John. "Insomniac's Companion," *New Statesman*, January 10, 1964.

Stone, Edward. *The Battle and the Books*. Athens, Ohio: Ohio University Press, 1964.

Tobias, Richard C. *The Art of James Thurber*. Athens, Ohio: Ohio University Press, 1970.

Updike, John. "Indignations of a Senior Citizen," *New York Times Book Review*, November 25, 1962.

"Up with the Chuckle, Down with the Yuk," *Newsweek*, February 4, 1957.

Weales, Gerald. "The World in Thurber's Fables," *Commonweal*, LV (January 18, 1957).

White, E. B. "James Thurber," *The New Yorker*, XXXVII (November 11, 1961).

Wilson, Edmund. "Books," *The New Yorker*, XVI (October 27, 1945).

Yates, Norris W. *The American Humorist*. Ames, Iowa: Iowa State University Press, 1964.

A note on Robert Thurber's scrapbooks (RTS): the scrapbooks are a treasure-house of newspaper and magazine clippings recording the public career of James Thurber from 1929 to 1961. Sometimes the clippings are fully identified, sometimes not. Newspaper stories are sometimes pasted in without identifying headlines or precise dates. In such cases, I have simply noted that my source is an undated or incompletely identified clipping in the scrapbooks.

Index

348 (Index)

Johnson, Nunnally, 83, 314
Jolas, Eugene, 74
Joyce, James, 4, 67, 244, 259, 284
Judge, humor magazine, 92, 96–97, 120

Kaufman, George S., 25
Kaye, Danny, 248, 250
Kenyon College, 271, 278
Killiam, Bert, 55
Kinney, James R. and Ann Honey-
    cutt
    How to Raise a Dog, 145
Klee, Paul, 131
Kospoth, B. J., 78
Kruif, Paul de
    Microbe Hunters, 83
Krutch, Joseph Wood, 206
Ku Klux Klan, 56
Kuehner, Norman, 53–54, 56, 57, 74,
    267

Language
    decline of, 299–300, 306, 317
    oddities of speech, 301
Lantern (Ohio State University paper),
    32, 34, 78, 79
Lardner, Ring, 94, 176, 219, 244
Lavaillant, René, 78
Lawrence, D. H., 67, 287, 303
Leacock, Stephen, 124
Lenglen, Suzanne, 79–81
Leonard, Baird, 89
Lewisohn, Ludwig, 21
    Upstream, 62
Life magazine, 249, 291
Literary Digest, 24
Literary forms, James Thurber's
    anecdote of personal experience, 69,
        70–72
    Babbitt style of writing, 35
    comedy of manners, 246
    conversation piece, 255, 256–257,
        303–305
    paragraphing, 35, 38, 69, 107

Literary forms *(continued)*
    Ryder's influence, 23–24, 38
    parody, 54, 59, 69, 83, 125, 130, 175–
        176, 284
        of *Evening Post* pet department,
            126–128
        of *Fowler's Dictionary of Modern
            English Usage,* 126, 128–129
        of Hemingway, 102
        of Hero and Leander story, 85
        of Henry James, 247, 257–258
        of mystery stories, 69
        of news features (*Chicago Tribune,*
            Paris edition), 75–76
        of popular psychology, 114
        verse parody, 69
    quotations and literary allusions in
        Thurber's later works, 307
    words, word games, 11, 25, 177, 220,
        236, 238, 255–256, 259, 282,
        285–287, 288, 297–307
Lobrano, Gus, 269
Longfellow, Henry Wadsworth, 214
Loos, Anita
    Gentlemen Prefer Blondes, 83
Lord, Russell, 87
Luce, Henry
    New Yorker, profile of, 95

MacDonald, Dwight, 148
Mackay, Ellin, 82
Mackenzie, Sir Compton, 294
MacLean, Kenneth, 279
Maloney, Russell, 106
Markey, Morris, 90
Marlowe, Doc, 10
Marquis, Don, 63, 96, 277
Marriage
    fathers of the bride and, 288
    Mr. and Mrs. Monroe stories, 122–
        126
    as trap, 116
Marxism
    literary Marxism in America, 192–193